To Nelson and Mar...
with warm regards —

Dealing
Creatively
with

Life✿

Ernest Morgan

Youth

Middle Age

Old Age

ERNEST MORGAN

Dealing Creatively

with

Life

The
Life Adventure
of
Ernest Morgan

Ernest Morgan

Barclay House Publishers
New York

Dealing Creatively With Life

A Barclay Trade Paperback
Published by: Barclay House Publishers
A division of the:
Barclay Holdings Group, Inc. / New York

ISBN: 0-935016-61-9

Printed in the United States of America

Library of Congress Cataloging-in-Publication Data

Morgan, Ernest.
    Dealing creatively with life : the life adventure of Ernest Morgan / Ernest Morgan.
       p. cm.
    ISBN 0-935016-61-9 (alk. paper)
       1. Morgan, Ernest. 2. Businessmen--Ohio. 3. Antioch Bookplate Company.
       4. Ohio--Biography. 5. North Carolina--Biography. I. Title.

       CT275.M5985 A3 1999
       338.7'6176952'092--dc21
       [B]   99-049708

CONTENTS

PREFACE

Why, at age ninety-four am I investing the time and expense needed to tell the story of my life?

It is because I want to share the sense of adventure, the excitement, the ups and downs and particularly the feeling of commitment to humanity and to life which has been my engine. I am writing for my extended family, which I cherish, and for other kindred spirits with whom my story may strike a responsive chord.

In one of his early writings my father tells of a wild duck, winging its way with strong steady strokes toward a tiny speck of blue which it always sees on the horizon. It was, of course, himself that he was writing about and that speck of blue was before him to the end of his days. His goal was always Utopia, and always he got part way there.

I grew up on the outskirts of Utopia. My wings may not have been as powerful as his, but that speck of blue was right there, and grew brighter as the years passed, always calling forth fresh effort.

Looking back from a vantage of eighty years I'm astonished to see where that effort has led me: adventurous youth, family man, craftsman, entrepreneur, publisher, administrator of Arab Relief, author, political candidate, leader in social causes. And the effort has led me into seeming contradictions, as when I was the major employing printer in our county and simultaneously served as president of the printers' union, and when I ran a national business monopoly and simultaneously was Socialist candidate for Governor of Ohio.

Considering my family background it is not surprising that I married a young woman of unusual intelligence and energy. Elizabeth not only shared my concerns and adventures but frequently took the lead in them. Her death from cancer after forty years of happy and creative marriage did not check the momentum of her life, but it left me with an identity crisis which took several years to resolve.

In 1983, twelve years after Elizabeth's death, I married Christine, whom I had known in college almost sixty years before and who, like myself, had been widowed. She, too, was an adventurous type with strong social concerns. We happily shared a lively old age until her death in 1996.

Enough years have elapsed now so that I can tell my story without leaving out some of the more intriguing episodes. Some sections are based on earlier writings. *Ten Years in the Bookplate Business* I wrote in 1937. Daily letters that I wrote home from the Gaza Strip recounted one of the great adventures of my life. Intimate experiences with death, which profoundly influenced the quality of my life, are recounted in my book, *Dealing Creatively with Death*, which is about to appear in its fourteenth edition. My father figures prominently in my narrative, especially in the early chapters. Thus there is some overlap with my story of his life as recounted in *Arthur Morgan Remembered (1991)*.

My lifetime covers a turbulent period of history, in which I took an active part. Hence this book is more than a biography. It includes as well a good deal of social and political history and biographical fragments relating to a number of personalities who had important parts in that history. Outstanding among these is my father.

Please bear with me as my story leaps back and forth through time to better deal with episodes and personalities. It defies telling as a simple chronicle.

INTRODUCTION

What is it like to be the son of one of the truly great men of our age? Ernest Morgan has given an answer in this fascinating autobiography, written from the perspective of his 94th year. One thinks of the many such sons who have found it necessary to break with their fathers to achieve their own identities.

Not so with Ernest. It is a testament to his father's greatness that his son remained from first to last his admirer, disciple, companion, colleague, and, in the end, his biographer. Not that he followed him slavishly, for that is something his father would not have wished, and he surely had a mind and will of his own that took him in many directions his father had not explored. Rather, he found his father's presence and example so benevolently persuasive that there was no need for rebellion.

Arthur Morgan's life cast more illumination than shadow for young Ernest. Between them there was a bedrock of trust that gave them both growing room. Even when Ernest finished college without graduating, his college president father did not demur. After all, had he not become a world-famous engineer and innovative college president without a college degree? "Live and help live" was the philosophy of both father and son, and their mutual recognition of this gave them an invincible confidence in each other, and in their ability to deal with whatever challenges this multivaried Twentieth Century might present.

Ernest's story of his upbringing; how he managed his relationships with family; the early years of Antioch; the fabulous story of his company, the Antioch Bookplate Company, which became the majority-employee-owned Antioch Company, a multi- national corporation dominant in its field; his leadership in social causes; his adventures in wilderness exploration with his children, and taking his canoe through the conduit of one of his father's giant dams; his service on the Quaker/UN team that administered Arab Relief in the Gaza Strip; his pioneering with his wife, Elizabeth, who was always his equal partner, in the intentional community at Celo and the innovative Arthur Morgan School there; his education of his own children; and, after

Elizabeth's death, his marriage in his late seventies, to Christine Balacz Wise and their creative partnership; all make fascinating reading. Here is a lesson in life-long liberating creativity.

In this money-grubbing civilization of ours Ernest never wanted, or lacked for, money. His mind and heart were set on more important things—helping to improve the quality of life for everyone, wherever he might be, and ultimately for all living beings. He could easily earn all he had need of, and so spent most of his time living, trying to understand, and possibly help save his world. As he comments toward the end of his saga:

"While I am able to contemplate my own death with equanimity, I am deeply troubled by the state of the world . . . The syndrome of greed and perpetual growth which characterizes our society at the present time can ultimately lead only to disaster. I dream of a society motivated by genuine human concern and characterized by a spirit of sharing—a society in which our life style, technology and economic organization are geared to the well being of our planet and the creatures that live on it—especially humankind. . . . I cling to the dream that human civilization can be saved, and the earth with it."

Ernest Morgan has served that dream, and has had a grand time doing so. *Allons! Great Companion!*

> Rev. Dr. Donald Szantho Harrington
> Minister Emeritus of the Community Church of N.Y.

CHRONOLOGY

1905 I was born • My Mother, Urania, dies of typhoid fever • My father and I go to live with his parents and older sister, Jessie who becomes my foster mother

1911 My father marries again, Lucy Griscom. We move to Memphis.

1912 I live for a time with the Hutton family in Maryland • My brother Griscom is born

1913 The Great Flood comes and I witness it on the Mississippi

1914 My sister Frances is born. • Move to Dayton, where my father heads the flood control project

1915 Arthur and Lucy buy a couple of abandoned farms in the Berkshires (Jacob's Pillow) as the site for a future school and we spend summers there. • That fall I enroll at Marienfeld, a boys school in North Carolina

1916 I attend the Organic School at Fairhope, Alabama

1917 My father takes the initiative in organizing Moraine Park School in Dayton and I enroll there. • My second sister, Lucy, is born. Dies in infancy.

1918 I join a friend in launching "The Cooperative Messenger Service."

1919 Our family moves to Englewood, ten miles north of Dayton. • I get a summer job on a nearby dairy.

1920 I buy a cow, raise chickens, ducks and rabbits and have a big garden. • Lucy

suggests I add "Arthur" to my name and be Arthur Ernest Morgan, Jr. I try it for a while, then drift back to plain Ernest.

1921 Our family moves to Yellow Springs where my father heads Antioch College. • I enter the Antioch Academy and write the song which becomes the Antioch Alma Mater. • In the winter I run a furnace route, in the summer mow lawns and cultivate a series of gardens on shares. • Jessie dies of cancer, so I sell my gardens and leave for the summer to attend Camp Wanaki in Minnesota.

1923 In the summer I go to Colorado where I work as a mule driver and trail builder.• In the fall I enter Antioch as a freshman. • Planning to be an engineer, I take a co-op job with a crew building the O'Shaughnesy Dam, north of Columbus.

1924 At Lucy's suggestion I shift my field from engineering to business administration. For my co-op job I work as a printer's apprentice at the Printing House of Wm. Edwin Rudge, in Mt. Vernon, New York.

1925 I take part in editing and publishing *The Blaze*, a student magazine with which I continue off and on for nine years. • Switch my co-op job to the Antioch Press • Bought my first car, a 1920 Model T Ford

1926 I join Walter Kahoe in his fledgling bookplate business, and shortly take it over. Running this business becomes my co-op job. • I am engaged to Evelyn

Thoman and hitch-hike to Colorado to visit her family.

1927 Evelyn terminates our engagement.• I function as stage manager for Antioch Players. We put on "The Pirates of Penzance" and other shows.

1928 Reviewing graduation requirements, I switch my field to English, where I seem to have the most credits.

1929 After six years of college, I fail to graduate—credits too scattered. • I set up a plan whereby I and my two employees each live on $10 a week for the rest of the year in order to have money to get more dealers. In return, I will divide the profits at the end. This scheme works well and saves the company in the crash of 1929.

1931 I marry Elizabeth Morey. For our honeymoon we take a canoe trip in Northern Minnesota. We occupy the Morgan presidential mansion while Arthur and Lucy are in Europe.

1932 We move into an apartment above the Bookplate Shop. • A son, Art, is born. • I manage the Antioch Press for a year in addition to the Bookplate Company while Walter Kahoe takes leave of absence.

1933 We move to a comfortable house on Dayton Street (Rent: $17.50/month.) • We take the lead in organizing the Socialist Party in our county .• My father organizes the Yellow Springs Exchange and Midwest Exchange, barter organizations to combat the Depression. He buys the Bookplate building to use for a store, so we move the shop to a side street. I become manager of the Exchanges.

1934 My parents give us a tumbledown cottage and 16 acres of land at "The Vale," two miles south of town. With much barter and hard work we fix it up and start "homesteading," with garden, bees, goats and chickens. • Daughter, Jenifer, is born. • I am accepted into membership in the International Typographical Union of which I later become local President. • Elizabeth becomes "Proprietor" of the

Bookplate Company so the shop will have a non-proprietor journeyman, and thus qualify for a union contract. • The National Recovery Act threatens to outlaw barter and we close out the Midwest and Yellow Springs Exchanges, but carry on extensive "underground" barter activity based on the Bookplate Company. • We move the Bookplate shop back to its old location. • Two young Socialists live in the back of the Bookplate Shop, and help carry on Party activity. • I serve as Secretary of the Miami Valley Socialist League, a federation of Party branches, and am elected to the State Executive Committee.

1935 We sign a contract with the Typographical Union. With the union label we are able to do printing for a wide range of social causes—and we do, often below cost.• The Bookplate Company assumes an alter ego—the Miami Valley Socialist Press.• Elizabeth and I are accepted into membership in the Society of Friends. • With neighboring farmers we start construction of a two-mile power line from the village. • The Antioch Press needs a manager. I apply, but am turned down because I'm a Socialist. (The Bookplate Company is saved!)

1936 Daughter Benetta Lucy is born. • The power line is finished and current turned on. (Hooray!) We string telephone lines on the same poles. • I am keynote speaker at Ohio Socialist Convention and serve as a delegate to the National Convention. • My brother Griscom joins us in the Bookplate business and becomes a valuable colleague. Later he drops out through limitations of health. • I am threatened with violence for union organizing in Xenia. • Our shop becomes official printer for the Workers Alliance, a national organization of WPA workers and the unemployed. Credit from us helps get them started.

1937 Our close friend and associate Louis Moon collapses from overwork and dies suddenly. I speak at his funeral. • An article by me, "The Bankruptcy of

Bolshevism" appears in *The Christian Register.*

1938 My article "Ten Years in the Bookplate Business" comes to the attention of Christopher Morley who says, "that fellow has a book in him." • I run for State Representative on the Socialist ticket.

1939 We abandon rural homesteading and buy (with borrowed funds) a place in the village with a house and an acre of land. • I set up a plan whereby the Bookplate staff will receive 80 percent of their wages each week—and half the profits at the end of the year. When the war-time wage freeze comes on, this saves the company. • While Elizabeth is away, I pick apples and can 170 quarts of applesauce. • Our union contract expires.

1940 I suffer a case of mumps, so Elizabeth attends the Socialist National Convention in my stead. • After farming out our children to relatives and friends, Elizabeth, as Socialist candidate for Congressman-at-large, leads a campaign caravan all over southern Ohio. I stay home and keep the financial support coming.

1941 I am elected to School Board with the highest vote cast for any candidate for any office. (Four years later I am defeated for re-election.)

1942 We take over the *Yellow Springs News.* Elizabeth becomes editor after three days apprenticeship. We have help from family and friends in caring for the children. She later resigns. • Fierce controversy arises in the public school system; I find myself in the middle. • The *News* comes under attack for opposing the cultivation of hatred in wartime.

1943 Son, Lee, is born. • We start bringing in Japanese-Americans.

1944 The Rhoades Paper Box factory burns, taking 35,000 bookplate boxes with it. The firm then goes out of business, so we take it over and get it running again. Later we sell it to the people there. • The Bookplate Company has a disastrous fire. We cannot rebuild without War Production Board authorization, but the fact that we publish the *News* gets us by. • We sell our country place to Lynton and Valeska Appleberry. • We launch a summer series of outdoor concerts. These continue for several years.

1945 We buy, for $6,000, a rundown old brick mansion at 130 Glen Street because we need a place that could accommodate apartments. This houses our Japanese-Americans to whom no one else will rent. We sell our previous home. • Taking a leading part in the Civil Rights struggle, I am threatened with violence and we have rocks through our windows at home and in the shop. • I put forward a scheme for "socializing" the Bookplate Company, but it meets with staff opposition and I drop it.

1946 Having failed to socialize the business, I incorporate it with the proviso that two Board members be elected by and from the staff. Ownership spreads steadily through the staff. Wage and Operating committees are drawn from the staff. • I am a delegate to the Socialist Party National Convention. • The *News*, jointly with Community Council, rents the Orton swimming pool to open it to black people. • We take leadership in a struggle to integrate the restaurants. This meets violent opposition but succeeds.

1947 The Bookplate Company takes over Shadowcraft, a business of manufacturing shadow puppets. This doesn't prosper and we later sell it. • We host at our home a national conference of the Young People's Socialist League. We expect 25, but 40 come. We move into a tent and turn the house over to them.

1948 We take a family bike/camping trip of 1500 miles. • The firm with which we share a sales organization goes down the drain. Our company is again saved by its profit-and-loss sharing plan. • I am chosen state chairman of the Ohio Socialist Party and am its candidate for governor. • I lead a struggle for ballot reform in Ohio.

1949 With the Bookplate Company having hard times, we sell the *Yellow Springs News* to Keith Howard and Lee Bullen .• I am recruited to join the Quaker/UN team that administers Arab relief in the Gaza Strip.

1950 I serve in Gaza until May, first in charge of a UNICEF Milk Center and later as Camp Leader in charge of food and shelter for 25,000 refugees. One of my camps is devastated by a near-hurricane and I deal with the crisis. • Returning home, I assume a new set of business responsibilities: "President, in charge of Product Development and Sales."

1951 The family drives to Scattergood School in Iowa to attend Jenifer's graduation.

1952 I help my father and Jenifer put together a new book, *Industries for Small Communities, with Cases from Yellow Springs.*

1953 I take on the 10-14 year age group in Friends Sunday School, leading them in a variety of projects. I serve on the regional Executive Committee of the American Friends Service Committee.• I am appointed in place of my father, chairman of the Burial Committee of the Yellow Springs Friends Meeting. This triggers an important new facet of my career, resulting in leadership in the funeral reform movement.

1954 My parents give us their beautiful log cabin, high in the Black Mountains above Celo, North Carolina.

1955 Camp Celo, where Lee had benefitted greatly is about to close because its owners, Doug and Ruby Moody, leave Celo. Bob and Dot Barrus agree to take it up if we will join them as partners, which we do. I negotiate with the Moodys and then take responsibility for recruiting campers.

1956 We help with Camp Celo and start laying plans for our long-dreamed-of school. At the close of camp, Elizabeth moves into a nearby house on the site of the projected school. • I return to Yellow Springs, where I share the family apartment with Jenifer, then a junior at Antioch.

1957 In response to a crisis at Koinonia Farm, which is subjected to boycott and violence because of its interracial policies, Elizabeth goes there to manage the office. There she has some alarming adventures. • Lee, expelled from Scattergood School, joins Elizabeth at Koinonia and finishes the school year there.

1958 We resume family life in Yellow Springs.• We launch Celo Work Camp in the summer, in preparation for starting the school.

1959 We are joined in Yellow Springs, by Alphonce Okuku, younger brother of Tom Mboya, who lives with us and goes to high school with Lee. • Jenifer is married to Robert Hart.• Bennetta is married to Don Blain.

1960 Lee and Alphonce graduate from High School.• With our elder son and two daughters married, Lee on his trip around the world and Alphonce in College, Elizabeth and I focus on the work camp and future school, to be called the Arthur Morgan School and scheduled to open in 1962. • I am living in Yellow Springs, Elizabeth in Celo, and I shuttle back and forth.

1961 When not involved in business or in work camp leadership, I am writing a book, *A Manual of Simple Burial.* • Lee, having completed his trip around the world, enters Antioch and, for his first co-op job, travels as a rep for the Bookplate Company. Very successful. I book him, en route, for illustrated talks on his travels.

1962 The Arthur Morgan School is launched under Elizabeth's leadership with 16 students.

1963 On the strength of my book, I am

asked to give a keynote address at an international meeting of memorial societies. I am put on an organizing committee, help launch the Continental Association of Funeral & Memorial Societies, and am elected to its board. • I launch Celo Press as part of the school and to publish the *Manual*.

1964 Sadly, we sell the lovely cabin on the Black Mountains and use the money to buy a "holding" in Celo Community, of which Elizabeth is now a member. • Celo Press progresses. The *Manual* has appeared in its second edition. • The school is gaining momentum.

1965 Daughter Benetta is killed in a motor accident. • Jenifer and Bob are divorced.• Art is a skilled typographer and president of his local union. • Lee, after serving as Assistant Community Manager at Antioch and as Student Representative on the Administrative Council, goes to the Mitraniketan project in India for two years to get their printshop into operation, organize a credit union and help install an accounting system. • 14,000 copies of the *Manual* are sold and I am busy editing a 3rd Edition. • The school acquires "Silver Cove," a beautiful 45 acre tract with two buildings, adjacent to the school "holding".

1966 I am asked to fly to Houston to address a national meeting of the Catholic Art Association devoted to "The Liturgy of Death." I do this in exchange for some woodcut designs by Catholic artists, which we had long coveted for bookplates. The text of my talk is later published. • The Third Edition of the *Manual* appears. • The Bookplate Company pays a generous dividend—just in time to bail the Arthur Morgan School out of a financial crunch.

1967 Jenny marries Doug Schroeder and they spend considerable time with us at Celo. Doug helps with architectural and land use plans at the school. • I start reducing my Bookplate Company time to have more time at Celo.

1968 Lee marries Vicki Neff, an Antioch classmate. He comes into Bookplate Company administration, dividing his time between that and his final year in college. • Elizabeth and I, together with my sister Frances and father, Arthur, drive to the Dakotas to interview Indians there in connection with a book Arthur is writing. • I am hit by a car while on my bike. The injuries slow me down for a while, but are not permanent. • The Fourth Edition of the *Manual* appears.

1968 At the end of the year Elizabeth resigns as Director of the School. The Board refuses to accept her resignation.

1969 I take my father to the Cleveland Clinic for spinal surgery necessitated by a fall the previous year. • Similarly, Elizabeth underwent cancer surgery and I rush to Celo to take care of her. Jenifer comes to help.

1970 At age 65, I retire as CEO of the Bookplate Company, being succeeded by Lee. A gala party is held. Then I join Elizabeth at Celo. • I lead a school field trip to the Florida Everglades carrying five canoes on my Travelall. En route, we do a service project at Koinonia Farm and one in the Everglades. • I have been reluctant to mortgage the house in Yellow Springs to build one in Celo, but after Elizabeth's illness I "throw caution to the winds" and we build a nice house near the school.

1971 Elizabeth suffers a recurrence of the cancer and dies. I nurse her through the illness, again with the help of Jenifer. The Burial Committee of Celo Friends Meeting (patterned after the Yellow Springs Committee) handles all arrangements beautifully and at nominal cost. • By way of personal therapy, I embark as soon as possible on a sales trip, where I will be actively involved with people. • The Fifth revised Edition of the *Manual* appears.

1972 Facing a financial crisis, both in the family and the school, I travel as a rep for the Bookplate Company, living in my

Travelall to save expenses. Grandson Mike Morgan travels with me for two weeks. • I continue my travels for several years, pay off the mortgage and the debts, get some buildings up and an endowment started. • Lucy dies. My father and I are with her at the time. I and my daughter-in-law Vicki take her body to the medical school.

1973 I end ten years of service on the Board of the Continental Association of Funeral and Memorial Societies and Jenifer takes my place.

1974 I edit the Seventh Edition of the *Manual*, expanding the name to *A Manual of Death Education and Simple Burial*.

1975 My father dies at age 97. • I convey his body to the medical school. • The Bookplate Company moves into a fine new building on the edge of town.

1976 I speak at a conference in Asheville on "Survival After the Collapse." (The Arthur Morgan School receives $500 for this.)

1977 The Eighth Edition of the *Manual* comes off the press. • I act as chairman of the committee for building a solar house (Falcon House) in Silver Cove for the school.

1978 I lead a course in Death Education for health professionals. It is held at Mars Hill and Hendersonville under the auspices of Mars Hill College.

1979 I rejoice that under Lee's leadership, the company adopts an "Employee Stock Ownership Plan" (ESOP) through which the employees will gradually come into major ownership of the company.

1980 There is a gala celebration of my 75th birthday. • I survive a bad wreck unscathed. (The other driver's fault.)• The Antioch Bookplate Company becomes the Antioch Publishing Company.

1981 I collapse from pneumonia while on my sales travels, but after a day in the hospital am back on the road (napping after each call). • My major sales travels end, though I still keep a small and lucrative territory. • I revive the school letter-press printshop—almost a replica of the Antioch Bookplate Company of 1929.

1982 In connection with the Rural Southern Voice for Peace, I recruit a "Letters-to-the-Editor Network" of 40 people who write a letter to their local newspaper every two months. I furnish draft letters. • As a son of Arthur Morgan, I take part in the opening of the World's Fair at Knoxville, in dedicating the TVA's educational barge, the "Morgan."

1983 I marry Christine Wise. Gala receptions all over the place. • I retire from my remaining sales territory. A celebration is held and the company gives the school valuable printing equipment.

1984 Christine and I attend conferences: •Americans Against Nuclear War, New York•Harvest of History, Dayton (I speak)•Democracy in the Workplace, Yellow Springs•Folk School Assn. of America, near Knoxville•Fellowship of Intentional Communities, Barnesville•Synergetics, Hendersonville• Christine sells her house in Appleton and builds a beautiful home for us here. (Property of the Arthur Morgan School.)• The *Manual*, now a full-fledged book, appears in its Tenth Edition with a new title *Dealing Creatively with Death: A Manual of Death Education and Simple Burial.* • Christine takes a four weeks goodwill tour of Russia under the auspices of the American Friends Service Committee

1985 Family gathering at Celo to celebrate my 80th birthday. • Trip to China with Christine, Jenifer, and my sister Frances.

1986 I speak for memorial societies, the TVA and Community Service, and lead a "history walk" in Yellow Springs. • I introduce Myles Horton at a national meeting of the Fellowship of Reconciliation where Myles received the annual F.O.R. award for creative social change. • I undergo cataract surgery on my left eye.

1987 Christine had hip surgery, followed later by a dislocation which again hospitalized her. I move into her hospital room as a nurse. • I set up printing exhibits at three public schools, transporting a small printing press to the scene and putting an AMS student in charge.

1988 The Eleventh Edition of the *Manual* comes off the press. • I receive "The Horace Mann" award from the Antioch Alumni Association, in recognition of my book. • We get a second VCR machine and start a video library for the school and community. • I start working on my autobiography—a long job. • I fly to my birthplace, St. Cloud, Minnesota, for a meeting of the board of my company, which now has a subsidiary there. • We attend Friends General Conference at Boone and also the SAYMA Conference at Black Mountain, at each of which I lead a discussion on death.

1989 Encouraged by a generous grant from Bill Preis, I get for the school a Macintosh Computer and Laser Printer. A great boon to the School, and to me. • Antioch Publishing has emerged as a multinational corporation, "Antioch Worldwide", with sections in England and Canada. • On the occasion of the 50th anniversary of the founding of Community Service, I am asked to write a biography of my father. This was one of many projects in 1989.

1990 I become Secretary of Celo Community, Inc. (I had already been Corresponding Secretary for several years.) • I rejoice at seeing the younger generation of the Barrus family take over Camp Celo, giving it the promise of another thirty years of life. • The school and the Rural Southern Voice for Peace hold a celebration of my 85th birthday.

1991 My biography of my father, *Arthur Morgan Remembered*, comes from the press, published by Community Service, and is selling well. • Celo Press having been laid down (but not the letterpress shop) the Twelfth Edition of the *Manual* is

taken up by Barclay House Books, a firm in which AMS alumnus David Zinn is involved. • I assist Christine in editing the story of her years in Transylvania, "Alabaster Village". (Anne Welsh is the chief editor.)

1992 I continue busily writing letters and articles about the Middle East, putting forth a plan for "Giving History a New Turn" there. • Christine and I are in a collision (the other driver's fault) which narrowly escapes being a disaster. • The same day my "African son" Alphonce Okuku, is killed in a motor accident in Kenya. • My autobiography is in the final stages of editing with help from Irwin Abrams, Lynton Appleberry and Robin Dreyer.

1993 My brother Griscom dies. • I retire as Chairman of the Board of the Antioch Publishing Company, as I don't like to leave Christine once a month. • Shortly before her stroke Christine "remembers" a number of poems she has written. I make these into a booklet. • I give a talk on memorial societies at the annual meeting of the N.C. Association for Death Education and Counselling.

1994 Christine suffers a stroke in early March. After a week in the hospital she spends nine weeks in a nursing home. Then I take her home to care for her. • I become a great-great-grandfather. • The 13th edition of *Dealing Creatively with Death* appears.

1995 I speak on "The Dimensions of Community" at the annual meeting of the World Futures Society in Atlanta. • I speak at the Biennial Meeting of the Funeral and Memorial Societies of America, in Nashville. • The beautiful new building at the Arthur Morgan School is finished.

1996 Lydia Wexler and her young son move in to take care of Christine. • Christine dies. • Lydia stays on to keep house. (My health has sagged.) • I find a publisher for Christine's book, *Alabaster Village*, and a publisher also for Elizabeth's book, *Socialist and Labor Songs* of the 1930's, which she collected and edited nearly fifty years ago. • I make a trip to Ohio for a meeting honoring Lee, and an Antioch Reunion, followed by a trip to Minnesota to visit our company there. • I fly to Indiana to visit son Art's family, including my great-great-grandson.

1997 The two books finally appear! • I make a trip to Ohio to attend a special Stockholders Meeting of the Antioch Company and to be recorded at length on video for Yellow Springs history.

1998 Lydia Wexler leaves and my daughter Jenifer takes charge of my health and general wellbeing.

1999 My sister, Frances Bolling, age 84, comes to live with me. Jenny assumes major responsibility for us.

Arthur Morgan, Ernest's father. Linoleum cut by Dr. P. B. Wingfield, 1930.

1

MEMORIES AND LEGENDS

I was born in 1905 in St. Cloud, Minnesota. Even at ninety-four my childhood memories are clear. The tiger lilies in my grandmother's garden; the swing on the scrub oak tree beside the house; the lively German band that played on Friday nights in the summertime in Waite Park a few blocks away; and the deep, straight paths cut through the snow during the long winters.

I remember the creak of the windmill on Monday mornings, when my grandfather released the vane and the blades swung into the steady Minnesota wind with a pleasant whir, pumping water for washday. (We had no indoor plumbing.)

I remember Saturday nights, when I would sit in a washtub on the kitchen floor with warm water from the stove, while my Aunt Jessie would scrub me from head to toe.

I remember when my grandfather brought in a Christmas tree too tall for the living room and had to take it outside and saw off a piece. My grandfather chewed Star Plug tobacco and I collected the little metal stars that came with each plug.

I remember how, after I had wet my bed, Aunt Jessie would stand me up naked behind the house and slosh me down with a bucket of cold water. I remember, too, when I ran around the house barefoot and stepped on an upturned rake, and how tenderly Jessie nursed me through that painful injury.

I remember listening, on still nights, to the distant, steady roar of the Mississippi where it poured over the power dam a quarter of a mile or so from our house. Because of that dam our town, St. Cloud, was the farthest point upriver to which the Mississippi steamboats could come.

Most vividly I remember standing on the bridge above the dam just after the ice had gone out in the spring. The river was filled with logs floating down from the north woods, headed for the sawmill, the product of a winter's logging. Upstream from the dam two long floating platforms, or booms, extended downstream from either bank, coming together at the center of the dam to form a huge V, at the point of which a narrow passage let the logs go over the dam. To keep the logs from jamming in this giant funnel, two "boom runners" with spiked shoes darted about over the logs carrying pike poles with which they pushed and pulled the logs to get them straight in the funnel.

The logs would roll and sink beneath the runners' feet as they sprang lightly from one log to the next, this way and that. Now and then one of them would poise for a moment on two large logs to shove some recalcitrant log into position. An instant later he would be off again, darting gracefully about, using his pike as a balancing rod. In a lifetime of ballet-going I have never seen speed or grace to excel the unchoreographed performance of those boom runners.

I remember dog teams going through town on a sled race from Montreal to St. Paul. The mercury stood at twenty below as the huskies trotted briskly along, their drivers alternately trotting for a while, then hopping on the long sleds. One team stopped overnight in a livery stable, and we went down to see them. One dog, overheated in his heavy coat, slept flat on his back with his legs sticking straight up.

I remember the pond, Lake George it was called, where ice for the town was harvested. Men stood on the ice, working saws up and down through the thirty inches, the thermometer at 43 below. A channel through the ice was kept open by continuous use, and through this channel the big cakes were pushed to where a chain belt lifted them out of the water and up to the large storehouse where they were packed away in sawdust—enough to last all summer.

I remember counting with pride the five times I had ridden in an automobile.

I remember my grandfather's workshop, full of tools and useful junk with which he built and repaired all kinds of things. (Not so different from my own shop of today. But without electricity.) I loved the cyclone cellar, just big enough for the family to squeeze in, which he had hollowed out in the side of the basement and neatly lined with brick, including the rounded ceiling.

A legend dating back more than 150 years tells of a time when the Morgan family owned a slave named Cuffy. They were, however, a family of Welsh Quakers, living in Pennsylvania, and the idea of slavery went against their consciences to the point where they gave Cuffy his freedom. He was happy about this and left to make his way in the world. After a time, however, he came back and asked to be a member of the family again. They welcomed him as a free man and he spent the rest of his life with them.

My great-grandfather, Benjamin Morgan, was expelled from the Friends for marrying out of Meeting. Accordingly, he and his thirteen-year-old bride headed west, settling at Harrison, Indiana, by the Ohio River, just west of Cincinnati. They raised thirteen children, of whom John, the youngest, born in 1849, was my grandfather. Benjamin was a blacksmith and millwright by trade, an important calling on the frontier. It was from this background that John, my grandfather, got his start as an engineer.

The family was caught in the Civil War. Some of the brothers served in the Union Army and one was killed at the Battle of Memphis. John was too young for the draft but got briefly involved just the same. When Confederate General John Morgan and his Raiders came through Harrison, rounding up the horses and mules, they happened onto John, then seventeen, on a street corner, and took him prisoner. Learning his name, the men took him to see the General, who greeted him kindly.

"Would you care to join us, John?" he was asked. No, he wouldn't. Thereupon the General presented John with a Confederate belt and told his men to give the boy a mule and let him go. On his way back to Harrison, John was intercepted by Union troops in pursuit of the Raiders. He had the presence of mind to throw away the Confederate belt, but they took him for a spy and proposed to hang him. Back at Harrison, however, people vouched for him and he was released.

When I was a boy, I went with my father and grandfather to visit the old family haunts at Harrison. The only thing I remember from that visit was a horse-drawn street car on the main street. It was a summer car, with open sides, wooden slat seats, and a long running board on either side. It travelled at a good clip, stopping only for women. The male passengers simply hopped on as the car came by. The women, with their ankle-length skirts, couldn't do that.

John Morgan was a venturesome youth and a skilled swimmer. One of his stunts was to dive in above a dam when the flume was open at the bottom, and shoot through the dam in the flume.

For a time he attended Lebanon Academy, some 30 miles north of Cincinnati. He and his roommate once collected some wooden advertising signs to use for fuel. Hearing a knock on the door one day they realized that they were about to be apprehended for stealing the signs. The evidence was in plain sight in their woodbox. Accordingly they launched into a prayer meeting, long and loud, while stuffing the wood into the stove. When the incriminating evidence was finally gone, they ended their prayers with, "Aye, an adulterate generation shall ask for a sign, but no sign shall be given."

At one point, John found his way into the Pennsylvania oil fields, where he soon gained a reputation as a sharpener of drills for oil wells. In his father's shop he had learned how to temper steel. Carried away by his success he tempered the drills harder and harder until one of them broke off in use, and ruined a well. At that point he quickly left Pennsylvania.

John finally settled in St. Cloud, Minnesota, where in the course of time, he met and married a young school teacher from New England, Anna Wiley. Both were educated and of good character. Beyond that they had very little in common. John was an easygoing free thinker. Anna was a straight-laced, fundamentalist Baptist, albeit a warm and outgoing person. John was a devotee of Shakespeare and read extensively in modern science. Anna read the Bible. Mutual affection and respect they had—but no philosophical rapport. I enjoyed them both as grandparents. Together they raised three children: Jessie, Arthur, and Edith. (A fourth, Walter, died in childhood.)

Anna traced her ancestors to Puritan immigrants at Plymouth, in the year 1630. She attached little significance to this, but the profound ethical and utopian ideals of the Puritans were at the center of her value system.

Anna's father, Enos Wiley, was a shoemaker in Wakefield, Massachusetts. His wife died, leaving him with eight kids. He was desperate for a mother for these children, but who would want to marry a poor shoemaker with eight kids? There was in Wakefield a homely old maid whose chances for marriage were very poor and Enos was able to persuade her to take on his family. Happily, this woman proved to be as beautiful in character as she was homely in looks, and the children loved her dearly.

One day one of them gave her a big hug and said, "What makes you so nice?"

She laughed, "Anyone as homely as I am had better be nice."

That woman left the imprint of her ideals and character on those children and, through my grandmother, helped illuminate generations of the Morgan family.

Life was not easy for the Morgans in St. Cloud. In time my grandfather became the official Surveyor for Stearns County. In those days the surveyor travelled about the county by horse and buggy and was given overnight hospitality by his clients. He was "wined and dined" by them, especially "wined." Every Stearns County Surveyor for many years developed a drinking problem, and John was no exception. For a considerable period this caused suffering and humiliation for his family.

When my father was a boy, his mother would send him to search the saloons and bring his father home. There were some sixteen saloons in the little town of St. Cloud, and alcohol was a major social problem. The twelve City Councilmen were saloon-keepers. At one point nearly all of them bore the names of Apostles, and the chairman was named Chris. Anna held the Morgan family together, and in time John managed to overcome his drinking. His unhappy experience made teetotalers of the rest of us for several generations.

John Morgan's engineering practice had a quasi-legal character. Because of his reputation for honesty and competence he was often called upon to settle boundary disputes, the disputants agreeing in advance to accept his judgment. He was skillful not only in reaching fair conclusions but in explaining these conclusions.

My father's younger sister Edith was a gentle and sensitive person who became a librarian. I never knew her very well. She died in Washington, D.C., in the influenza epidemic of 1918.

Aunt Jessie was also involved in the 1918 influenza epidemic. She was living with her parents in St. Cloud. People were stricken by the thousands, the health professions were hopelessly swamped, and death stalked the streets almost unopposed. Jessie was a capable practical nurse. Each day she would make a tour of stricken families, feeding and nursing them. She had the physical and emotional strength to do this day after day until the epidemic ended, and with no thought of financial reward. Despite continuous exposure she never caught the disease.

That was the family in which my father grew up, and in which I spent the first six years of my life.

The sons of distinguished men sometimes feel overshadowed by their fathers. I didn't have that problem. Arthur Morgan was a man who always preached the importance of the little, intimate things in life, the small "molecular forces" in society which, he said, largely shape the quality of human life. He felt that the big things in life are the outgrowth of those forces.

His own life illustrated that. The small daily acts of his parents—and of that homely old step-grandmother—laid the foundation for both his character and his career. I was proud of my father's large, creative accomplishments, but I took to heart his admonition about the small things, and this helped give meaning and value to the small things that have mostly made up my own life.

His life was characterized by great energy, creativity, and social involvement. Few men in history have had creative impact in as many areas of human concern—and without a college education. He put himself forward vigorously, but never at the expense of others. He became a world famous engineer who directed giant projects for which there was no precedent. At the same time he was a strong conservationist who twice forestalled the destruction of the Florida Everglades, and who firmly sponsored natural parks.

He designed innovative legal and political structures which became prototypes for financing and executing complex engineering projects. He was one of the architects of the League of Nations and had an important role in selling the idea of international organization to the American people. He was called in as an advisor to governments in America, Europe, Asia, and Africa.

He was invited to come in on the ground floor of General Motors but instead turned his attention to education, becoming one of the great educational pioneers of the twentieth century and first president of the Progressive Education Association. He founded the Moraine Park School in Dayton, Ohio, he was president of Antioch College and created the Antioch Plan, and he instigated the establishment of a system of Rural Universities in India.

He was a lifelong apostle of the small community. On his engineering projects, the "camps" were actually model villages.

While president of Antioch College he took initiative in transforming the moribund town of Yellow Springs into a dynamic small community. He organized Community Service, Inc., to carry on his work in the field of community. He initiated Celo Community, one of the oldest and most successful intentional communities in the U.S., and was instrumental in establishing the Mitraniketan project in Southern India, transforming a stagnant rural village into a dynamic and progressive community. The influence of this village became a factor in what is known as "The Miracle of Kerala."

He exercised important leadership in the Unitarian denomination and later in the Society of Friends. He led Civil Rights marches and served as the first chairman of the Human Relations Commission in Yellow Springs. He championed the cause of the Seneca Indians in their struggle against the U.S. Army Corps of Engineers—and was made an honorary member of the Senecas. He was a skilled botanist, and classified some previously unknown species of plants. He was interested in paleontology and collected the world's largest trilobite, which now resides in the Smithsonian Institution. He did not have a college education, but wound up with five honorary doctoral degrees, each in a different field.

He wrote twenty books—on engineering, education, biography, philosophy, sociology and history. Similarly, five books about him have been published. The most recent of these is mine, *Arthur Morgan Remembered*. This is not a scholarly work but is probably the most lively of the five.

My mother, Urania Jones, was also an unusual personality. As a girl in Princeton, Illinois, she set an ambitious course for herself. She planned to qualify herself as a doctor of osteopathy, establish herself in that profession, and then add a medical degree (although this was a time when women rarely entered either of these professions). With these two disciplines at her command she would be in a position to provide health care of superior quality.

In pursuit of this career she entered the A.T. Still College of Osteopathy at Kirksville, Missouri and in due time received a D.O. degree. Following that she established a successful practice in St. Cloud. Her practice was characterized by close cooperation with the medical doctors although she had not received formal medical training. This was in striking contrast to the aloof and almost hostile attitude between the two disciplines which was prevalent at the time.

Her attitude toward marriage and a family was that she would interrupt her professional career if, and only if, a young man of exceptional personality and character showed up. Among Urania's patients and personal friends was Dad's sister, Jessie Morgan, herself a young woman of strong and independent spirit. Through Jessie, Urania met Arthur Morgan. He too had come to doubt that he would find a lifemate capable of sharing his hopes and dreams. It did not take long for them to discover in one another the personal qualities they valued.

They were married by the same minister who had married John and Anna, and set up housekeeping a block away from the original Morgan home. A year later I was born, amidst general rejoicing. One of my treasured possessions is a yellowed copy of the St. Cloud *Daily Times* for July 6, 1905, which carries an announcement of my birth on the front page. "A new engineer has arrived in town and is living at the home of Mr. and Mrs. Arthur Morgan. . . . He will not run any lines until he is stronger."

What I treasure about that paper is not the announcement of my birth but the world news it contains. A headline across the front page proclaims the abortive Russian Revolution of 1905. The crew of the Russian battleship *Potemkin* had mutinied and taken over the ship. The revolutionary leadership had come aboard, declaring Russia a republic, and sending messages to the major world capitals asking for recognition and assuring them that foreign shipping would be inviolate. The Russian people were called upon to rise and support this provisional government.

The Morgan family seemed happily safe in Minnesota, far away from the violent events in Russia. A few months later, however, Urania died of typhoid fever. Dad and I moved in with his parents and his sister Jessie, who became my foster mother.

When my father was born, Jessie had begged their parents to name him Ernest. There was a vogue for that name at the time, especially among the ladies, who thought it was just too sweet for anything. Oscar Wilde's play, *The Importance of Being Earnest,* was a spoof on this vogue. But my grandparents were firm, and the boy was named Arthur. Jessie was a determined little girl, however, and she kept telling her little brother that his middle name was Ernest—and she made it stick. In later life all his honorary degrees and other official documents carried the full name.

When I came along there was no escape. Urania and Jessie were close friends, and they lived only a block apart, so Ernest it was. Later, when I was in my teens, my stepmother suggested that I might like to pick up the "Arthur" and be Arthur Ernest, Jr. I liked the idea and tried it for a while, but never felt comfortable with it, so I gradually drifted back to plain Ernest.

I remember the gentleness of the family toward one another and especially toward me. My father once remarked, late in life, "When someone you love dies, your love doesn't die, it gets redistributed." His own life illustrated that. Much of the love and tenderness he had felt for my mother was transferred to me. I can't recall his ever punishing me—or even scolding me. He didn't need to. I was devoted to him and eager to do what he wanted.

Likewise, my aunt and grandparents gave me affectionate attention and care. In total, I enjoyed an almost idyllic childhood, surrounded by affectionate adults who not only loved me but respected me as a person. In a profound sense, my mother's death illuminated my life.

There was a touch of hypochondria in my father's makeup, and he was haunted by the fear that I would not have a chance to know him when I grew up (he lived to be 97). So from the time I was born until he married again on my sixth birthday, he wrote letters to me at frequent intervals, each marked with some future date on which it was to be opened. I did so, faithfully on the appointed dates, and read them eagerly. They were gentle, thoughtful letters, frequently expressing his grief and loneliness at the loss of Urania. In them he shared his ideals, and his hopes and dreams for the future in a way that would have been difficult to do in personal contact. I was much moved and influenced by them.

Ernest at age 6, with his Aunt Jessie, who was his foster mother for the first six years of his life.

2

A NEW FAMILY

My father's second marriage, to another remarkable young woman, brought about a major upheaval in my life. Lucy was sometimes difficult but was brilliant and enormously conscientious. I was somewhat difficult myself. But our relationship was a happy and creative one. The early years of our new family were a time of challenge and growth for all of us.

On my sixth birthday my father married again; this is how it happened:

As a young man, Dad dreamed of a new kind of education in which students and teachers would live and work together as a community: sharing, learning, philosophizing, and growing together. Through all his years of professional struggle this dream stuck with him and when at last he became a successful engineer with a comfortable middle-class income he took steps to found that school.

The first step was to find someone who might work with him—a person with knowledge and vision who would share his dream and help bring it to life. Various people were suggested to him. Among these was a woman, Lucy Griscom, of Woodbury, New Jersey, whose father, a Quaker farmer, had helped establish a small, pioneering private school in the Pestalozzi tradition. Pestalozzi was a Swiss educator of the Napoleonic era who conceived of education in terms of experience and community. Dad had never heard of him, but Lucy had, and knew about a lot of other people and movements too. She opened new windows on the world for Dad, and shared his educational dreams. Not surprisingly, they married.

Dad had been warned, before the wedding, about one of Lucy's cousins, Clement Biddle, who was a great practical joker. As the guests were arriving Clem was pointed out to Dad, who promptly walked over to him and, smiling, lifted him off the ground and laid him on his back. My father was a tall and powerful man. Clem looked up at him and remarked, "I guess we'll wait until the rest of the boys get here before we haze thee." He and Dad became good friends, and in later years he was a substantial contributor to Antioch College.

Lucy's family opened their homes and hearts to me in a fine way and I spent happy times with them. One evening, however, when I was weary and a bit homesick, I exclaimed, "Don't say 'thee' to me. I'm no Quaker. I'm a pure American." They took this in good spirit, and many years later I became an active Quaker myself.

During Dad and Lucy's honeymoon, Jessie and I stayed in a cottage on the beach at Avalon, New Jersey. I was entranced by the profusion of aquatic life and the inexhaustible supply of beautiful shells. It was a happy time for me. In later years, every time I got to an ocean beach I hoped to find the little sea creatures swarming in the water as they did at Avalon. Alas, those days are gone.

Dad chose Memphis, Tennessee as the location in which to set up the new Morgan Engineering Company, because that area offered many engineering opportunities. In Memphis, a new life began for me with a new home and a new mother. Lucy was an inspiration. She accepted me, not only as a child but as a person. She would talk with me about serious things, and in language I could understand. She was a biologist; I remember her cleaning a chicken and explaining the function of each organ as she removed it. She showed me the anatomy of flowers and how they reproduced. She explained what caused the rain to form. She had a master's degree in the chemistry of nutrition and was feeding our family in 1912 the kind of modern diet that did not become generally recognized until fifty years later. She had a good sense of humor and a quick wit.

Urania had a nephew, Merle Sutton, an attractive, intelligent boy, who needed a home. Dad and Urania had taken him in, and after Urania's death Dad had provided for his support. Lucy volunteered to take this boy into our home—an indication of her generous character—so Merle came to live with us at Memphis, as my elder brother.

Lucy had an unhappy side, too. She had severe emotional problems and sometimes was very unreasonable and difficult to live with. At her best she was understanding and flexible; at her worst she was irritable and intolerant.

On one occasion I objected to going to bed. She was firm about it. So I asked if I could get up early. She said yes. I said, "Six o'clock?"

"Yes."

"Five o'clock?"

"Yes."

"Four o'clock?"

"Yes."

"Three o'clock?"

"Yes."

"Two o'clock?"

"Yes."

"One o'clock?"

"Yes."

I couldn't think of anything earlier than that.

At one o'clock I woke up, got dressed, and came downstairs. Without a word of complaint Lucy came down and gave me breakfast. Then I went out, put my little dog on a leash and set forth around the block. On the street behind us lived a policeman, and when I went by his place he and another officer were just starting away from the house on horseback. At that moment I spoke to the dog, who was starting around the wrong side of a lamp post. The officers swung around.

"What are you doing here?"

"Just out for a little walk with the pup." I replied. The two men just looked at each other.

That afternoon I got very tired and remarked to Lucy, "Most days have two halves—but this one has three." I never pulled that early morning trick again.

In contrast to my warm relationship with my new step-mother, Jessie and Lucy hated each other. This was understandable. Lucy had taken away the child whom Jessie had come to regard as her own; also her brother, whose career she had so diligently promoted. Jessie was an educated person, a graduate of St. Cloud Normal School, but Lucy was a cultivated easterner, with a background of books and travel and innovative education behind her.

My father and I were caught in the middle. Each of the women told me how bad the other was. I was bewildered at first, but after a while I didn't believe either of them—and loved them both. Thus I could appreciate Jessie without feeling bound by her ideas. Likewise, I could appreciate Lucy without being overwhelmed with guilt when she berated me during one of her difficult spells. Six years was a good age to make the transfer. I was old enough not to be hurt by Lucy's limitations, yet young enough to respond to her fine qualities.

Keeping my cousin Merle proved untenable, so Dad arranged other care for him. As for me, I alternated between being at home and being away. The first separation came when I went to live for some months with the family of one of Dad's partners on a farm in Maryland. I was seven then, and there were children in the family about my age. I helped collect the eggs, and I learned how to swim, to milk the cows, and to set box traps for rabbits. In warm weather we went to school with a horse and buggy; in wintry weather, in a sleigh, with hot slabs of soapstone wrapped in a blanket under our feet. It was a good life.

One day Lucy told me that I was going to have a little brother or sister. I said, "Yes, I know."

"How did you know?" she asked.

"Because I've been praying for one."

My brother Griscom was a disappointment at first. He was so small and helpless.

"When is he going to be big enough to be good for something?" I asked.

Our younger sister, Frances, followed two years later. I can recall no sibling rivalry, at least as far as I was concerned. Of course, I was several years older. Our relationships were companionable and mutually supportive.

Lucy and I were always frank and open about the step relationship, but it never occurred to either of us to mention it to Griscom and Frances. One day Griscom, out of curiosity, looked up his father in *Who's Who in America*, and read with astonishment the passage, "Married in 1904 to Urania Jones. One son, Ernest."

He and Frances put their heads together, realizing that I was their half-brother and Frances remarked, "Maybe that's why Mother is so mean to Ernest." That incident may have to strained their relationship with their mother, but in general Lucy was harder on her natural children than on her step-child.

Lucy had two older sisters, Mary and Lydia. Their visits to our home were always a source of pleasure and excitement. Lydia was full of fun—jokes, stories, games. Mary was a doctor, which was unusual for a woman at that time. She had the intelligence and staying power to overcome the obstacles. What charmed me most was what she told us about her travels, and the fascinating objects she collected. She had practiced medicine in Persia (now Iran) and then for a much longer time in China.

I was much interested in China and asked if she knew of someone there who would correspond with me. She knew an American woman living in China who was willing to write to a youngster. Once I asked this woman what kind of government China had and she replied that it might be more accurate to inquire what kind of *misgovernment* China had. She was so right.

Aunt Mary told many stories about her life in China, but the one that stands out involved her asking a Chinese woman how many children she had. The woman replied that she had three, although five were in evidence.

"The other two," asked Aunt Mary, "are they the neighbor's children?"

"No, they're mine. But they haven't had smallpox yet."

Apparently people didn't count their children until they had survived smallpox.

I was reminded of that story sixty years later when I visited China. After the Revolution, plagues and famines were eliminated and the population exploded—a three hundred million increase in about twenty-five years, to over a billion. Yet they have only a small fraction of the arable land that we do. In desperation they now allow only one child per family. I wish Aunt Mary could see China today.

Mary died the day before she was to have entered a nursing home. Whether this was a coincidence or whether she ended her life with a drug or by "psychic suicide" I don't know. I find it hard to imagine a vigorous and independent person like her in a nursing home.

Lydia did enter a nursing home in Philadelphia, and I visited her there on my way to the Middle East in December, 1949. She was unable to speak but her face lit up and spoke for her, while I reported at length on all the family doings. She died before my return in May, l950.

After their deaths Lucy told me something I had never even suspected— these wonderful Quaker sisters were bitter enemies. That explained why they never visited us at the same time.

One idiosyncracy that my parents had to put up with was that I wouldn't accept an allowance. I wanted to earn my money. So they dreamed up things to pay me for, things that most kids simply do as members of their families. After a while I decided that I wanted to buy my own clothes. That raised another problem. I didn't much care how I looked, and wasted very little on clothes. To keep me from disgracing the family they gave me clothes for my birthdays and at Christmas. I still marvel at their patience and understanding.

It was at public school in Memphis that I learned a lifetime lesson about fighting. I started a fight at school from sheer exuberance and without the slightest animosity or ill will. It ended suddenly when I got a bloody nose. A crowd of boys had been cheering for me because I was smaller and the most aggressive so, when I lost, they beat up the other boy, even though he had not been unfriendly and had not started the fight. I felt badly about that, and never fought again.

I once played hooky for a couple of days. I had a little hide-out in the tall weeds in a vacant lot and at the appropriate time I would go home. I dreamed up some homework to report to Lucy. On my second day out my father came home early. I could see him from my hide-out in the weeds as he walked by. He looked tired. I wanted to rush out and greet him, but I was supposed to be in school. I was overcome with remorse and never played hooky again.

My father was a tall, lean man, physically and intellectually tough, but at the same time gentle and soft-hearted. Kate Bradford Stockton, a Tennessee farm wife who ran for governor on the Socialist ticket, remarked to me once, "Some people are soft-headed and hard-hearted; others are hard-headed and soft-hearted." Dad was the latter.

Once when I was a little boy he came home very dejected. He had done something that day which he hated to do; he had fired a man. In my childish imagination I pictured him, on the roof of the office building, commanding a firing squad. "So," I thought, "that's what happens when you don't make good on a job." I resolved then and there that when I grew up I would work

At Memphis. Ernest, age 7, with his grandmother and his father. This grandmother was a major source of Morgan family ideals and values.

hard and make sure I didn't get *fired*. (Now, when someone asks why I work so hard, I tell them that story and say that by the time I discovered my misunderstanding it was too late to change my habits.)

On one important occasion, however, Dad's soft-heartedness paid off. A young engineer in his employ was not suited to his work, and Dad had decided to let him go. Twice he visited the surveying camp in Arkansas, led by this man, but couldn't bring himself to break the news. Not long after, he visited again, for the third time, firmly resolved to deliver his unpleasant message.

Finally, when they were alone together, the man spoke up. "Arthur," he said, "I wouldn't leave you in the lurch for anything, but I've been offered the job of City Engineer at Dayton, Ohio. If you could possibly spare me, I'd be grateful." Dad encouraged him to take the job.

A year or so later came the great flood of 1913. Hardest hit was the city of Dayton, which was submerged beneath sixteen feet of rushing water. When the water went down and the city fathers gathered to consider how to prevent future floods, the City Engineer spoke up—the same man whom Dad had almost fired. "There's just one man in the country who can handle this job: Arthur Morgan." That is how our family came to Ohio. My father quipped to me once that he got the Dayton flood-control job through weakness of character.

3

THE DAYTON FLOOD

The Dayton Flood was perhaps the most important external event in the life of our family and one which impacted the lives of thousands of other families, and on the destiny of a great city. I pause here in my personal narrative to briefly recount the tremendous drama of that flood and of the personalities— including my father—who came forward to cope with it.

For centuries, people have built towns and cities on flood plains and then have wondered why the gods sent floods to plague them. Dayton was built squarely on the flood plain at the confluence of three active rivers. Every few decades during the nineteenth century it got flooded. There is a story that the Indians told them not to build there.

Historically, Dayton was a city of strong civic morale, and early in the century the citizens determined to put an end, once and for all, to the flood problem. A flood control plan was developed, contracts were let, and work was scheduled to begin in the spring of 1913.

The projected plan was designed to control floods up to 90,000 cubic feet of water per second. That is how river flow is measured—in cubic feet per second. 90,000 cubic feet per second is a lot of water. The work was about to start and equipment had been moved into place in March, 1913, when the Great Flood came. Not 90,000 cubic feet per second, but 250,000 cubic feet. Dayton was in a new ball game. That flood was a humdinger, and it wasn't confined to Dayton. The weather conditions were very unusual, with floods and tornados all over the place.

During the flood, my father took me with him for a steamboat ride on the Mississippi at Memphis. The rushing brown water stretched almost to the horizon; houses were overturned, the boat's paddles swished through the tops of the willow trees, the levees were piled high with sandbags. I was excited and inspired, and when we got home I hunted up some bags and patiently filled them with pebbles, hoping that a truck would come and take them to the levee.

It was Dayton, however, that was hardest hit by the most disastrous flood recorded in America up to that time. Flood waters from the Stillwater and the Great Miami filled the downtown channel and came pouring over the levees. Some of the people in downtown Dayton, fleeing from this deluge, were confronted by another great rush of flood water coming in through the eastern part of the city from the Mad River.

Thousands took refuge in hotels and office buildings. At first, few people took the flood seriously: a little water in the streets for a few hours and then it would go away. So they just retired to their homes and offices and waited. But the water kept rising, and by the time it started coming through the doors and up the hot air registers it was too late to escape, so they went upstairs. Still the waters rose and finally invaded the second floor, driving the people into the attics.

It rushed through downtown Dayton sixteen feet deep, carrying great masses of debris with it, and covering everything with deep mud. Then a new terror arose: fires broke out which would sweep unchecked for a whole block, burning all the buildings down to the water level. Then cold weather set in, adding to the misery of the thousands who were trapped without food, heat, or drinking water. When the flood reached its crest, people looking down onto the city from the surrounding hills estimated that at least 10,000 lives would be lost.

Dayton's response to the flood disaster was magnificent—a proud moment in the city's history. In the face of catastrophe, Dayton became a city of heros, and the outstanding hero of them all was John H. Patterson. He had developed the cash register and created a great new industry in a beautiful plant in a park-like setting on high ground at the south edge of Dayton. He quickly realized the magnitude of the approaching flood. A man of imagination and energy, accustomed to exercising authority, he quickly went into action. Even as the waters were rising, he assembled a small army of carpenters and began the mass production of a sturdy flat-bottomed boat. This team produced a big fleet of boats, consuming some 50,000 feet of lumber. When in full swing, they were completing one boat every five minutes.

As quickly as the boats were finished, they were hauled to the water's edge and manned by volunteers. This hastily constructed fleet swarmed over the city, rescuing thousands of people from rooftops and upper story windows. The fact that only about 400 people lost their lives in the flood in the entire valley was an enormous tribute to that rescue operation. Some of those who did lose their lives were rescue crews whose boats were trapped by masses of debris in the swirling current.

I remember those boats well. After the flood they were piled high in big rows, beneath a pavilion-type roof on the south edge of Dayton where I passed every day on my way to Moraine Park School. They were kept there as a safety measure until the flood-control project was completed.

The people rescued from the flood were taken to homes and institutions on high ground, where they were fed and housed. Chief among these places was the National Cash Register Company itself, whose buildings were converted into dormitories and whose grounds accommodated a tent city. Patterson brought in whole train loads of supplies to help feed and care for these people. Martial law was declared and the National Guard came in to help maintain order and safety as the flood waters receded. Governor Cox promptly appointed Patterson as relief director for the entire city.

There is an interesting sidelight on Patterson's career which can be told now. Some time prior to the Great Flood, Patterson had a sales manager by the name of Chalmers—later famous as the manufacturer of the Chalmers Automobile and the Allis-Chalmers tractor. Chalmers was an able man and Patterson valued him highly, paying him a salary reported to have been $50,000 a year. In those days that was astronomical, especially in the absence of any substantial income tax. Patterson kept worrying about Chalmers' health and inquiring into his personal habits. Once, I understand, he thought Chalmers should have a special vacation and sent him off to Europe. This attention seems to have annoyed Chalmers.

Finally, in his concern for Chalmers' health, Patterson asked if he were being moderate in his relations with his wife. This was one too many, and Chalmers proceeded to resign as sales manager for NCR. Before leaving, he took from the files of the company sufficient evidence to convict Patterson of the violation of certain laws regulating the conduct of business.

Chalmers turned this material over to the federal authorities, and Patterson was brought to trial in the Federal Court at Troy, Ohio. He hired the best lawyers he could find, but was losing every round. It was at this juncture that the flood occurred, and Patterson proved his mettle. The case was permanently dropped. Who on earth would want to convict a man like that? Patterson saved Dayton—and the flood saved Patterson!

When the water went down, Dayton had to dig itself out—literally. Thick slimy mud was everywhere. The high-water mark which appeared on every telephone pole and building in downtown Dayton was sixteen feet above street level (in the central part of the city). That mark stayed there for years, and as a boy I used to wonder if it would ever disappear.

Dayton tackled the problem of flood control with the same strong morale that it showed in coping with the flood itself. Whereas Patterson had taken the main leadership in flood relief, the problem of flood control brought a new man to center stage. Edward A. Deeds was vice president of the National Cash Register Company. He was a man of personal charm, great energy and strength of personality. He plunged into the work with the same determination that Patterson had shown in the relief operation.

A whirlwind financial campaign was conducted, under the slogan "Remember the promise you made in the attic." The sum of $2,130,000 (a lot of money in 1914) was raised from 23,000 contributors in the stricken city. That fund financed the entire engineering operation for the first four years until the necessary bonds were issued and construction begun. Probably unique in the annals of public funds, 83% of that money was returned to the contributors.

My father was confronted with one of the most formidable problems—or sets of problems—of his career. On the face of it, the job looked impossible. A channel large enough to carry all that water would require half of downtown Dayton. To build a channel through the hills around the city was beyond the realm of reason. To cut a huge channel to the Ohio River almost sixty miles away was also out of the question.

Dad had a policy which he dignified by the term "conclusive engineering analysis" which meant that before deciding on a plan he would explore every possibility—even the most unlikely. That is what he did at Dayton, and one of the least likely alternatives turned out to be the best: they would build five huge dams which would create great dry reservoirs in which flood waters could be stored.

Fierce opposition ensued, because there was no precedent. Furthermore, "conclusive studies" by the U.S. Army Corps of Engineers had determined that dams were not practical for flood control. I remember Dad coming home weary from defending his plan at extensive hearings. But he finally found a precedent. Some feudal lord, generations before, had built a castle too close to the Loire River in rural France, and this castle and its roadway had, quite by chance, formed a dam which protected the valley below from floods. An absurd precedent, but it held. Many years later, Dad and I went to visit that structure.

The opposition argued that dams weren't safe, and would endanger the city. Dad responded by assembling a whole typewritten book of dam failures in which he analyzed the cause of each failure.

Dad actively sought criticism and input from other engineers. When the Dayton flood control plans were essentially complete he recruited a panel of distinguished engineers, including two former chiefs-of-staff of the U.S. Army Corps of Engineers, to review them. After days of intensive study the panel approved the plans.

Another problem arose for which there was no satisfactory precedent. Just how big can a flood get? My father collected data from all over the world in an effort to answer this question. Finally he decided that the flood control system for Dayton should be capable of controlling floods up to 500,000 cubic feet per second—twice the size of the 1913 flood—and that's the way the dams were designed and built.

In the course of researching historic floods to find out how big a flood could possibly get, Dad discovered a remarkable thing. At the top of a cliff above the Danube River there stood a castle for several centuries. After each flood on the Danube, people from this castle chiseled on the face of the cliff the high-water mark of that flood, along with the date. This offered a priceless record, going back nearly a thousand years. Many high-water marks had been chiseled on the cliff, most of them within a few feet of one another. Almost 50% above this cluster was one solitary high-water mark dated 1066, (the year of the Battle of Hastings). My father wondered for years what had happened to precipitate such a giant flood.

Many years after the completion of the Dayton Flood Control project he learned that Chinese astronomers had recorded a large nova in the year 1065. He wondered whether it was possible that this nova for a time influenced atmospheric conditions on earth, and accordingly entered into correspondence with several astronomers. In each case he was assured that the flood was just a coincidence. Finally he came across an astrophysicist who told him that, until a few years earlier, they would have considered it just a coincidence, but now there was evidence to indicate that a nova of this sort might result in the ionization of the upper atmosphere and might have produced flood conditions.

Engineering the project was only half the battle. There were no financial resources available and no political body with the authority or the resources to tackle the job. So Dad conceived a new kind of political entity, which he called a "conservancy district," which would comprise the entire area affected by flooding or by the flood-control project. It would freely cross city and county lines, and would have authority to issue bonds, levy taxes, and carry on construction.

He drafted a bill to create such an entity and hired a lawyer to phrase it in legal language. The lawyer said this was not possible, so he got another lawyer. The bill was drafted, and in due time was enacted into law by the Ohio Legislature. It was not popular. One upriver editor characterized it as "the most pernicious piece of legislation ever contrived." But it worked well and became the model for other states with flood control problems.

The story of the Dayton flood and the flood control project is told at length in Arthur Morgan's book, *The Miami Conservancy District*. I have touched here on some intimate details not covered in that book, and have covered a few of the high spots, because the events of that time had such an important impact on the life of our family.

Suffice it to say that Dayton has been flood-free for eighty years and both the engineering plan and the legal structure have been widely copied.

Ernest, age 12, in Dayton.

4

A CHALLENGING BOYHOOD

This chapter recounts the adventuresome boyhood I experienced during those years in Dayton. It tells also the inside story of Moraine Park School, an innovative school initiated by my father, which I attended in my junior high years.

When we first arrived in Dayton I attended the public schools, but my parents felt these were not good for me. Accordingly, in 1915 when I was about ten, they sent me to a new and promising boarding school, Marienfeld, which was founded and directed by Hanford Henderson, an outstanding philosopher/educator. It was a boys' school, located in a wilderness area near Samarcand, in southeastern North Carolina, not far from Southern Pines. The atmosphere of the place was easygoing, and the boys normally dressed only in light shorts and shirts, or just in shorts. Sometimes they wore nothing at all.

My favorite pastime was collecting Indian relics. I would go into a corn-field and walk back and forth along the rows, covering the whole field in search of arrowheads. Likewise I loved to roam the woods, wearing only a pair of shorts, and soon got a tan. I was given the nickname of "Mowgli" (or "Mowg", for short), after the wild boy in Kipling's *Jungle Book,* who was raised by wolves.

The high spot of my year at Marienfeld was a canoe trip on the Lumber River. This trip had been planned for a group of older boys but at the last moment it turned out that one of them didn't know how to swim. I was a swimmer, and immediately put myself forward.

Of all the rivers I have canoed, from Northern Minnesota to the Everglades, I can think of none more beautiful than the Lumber, where it winds through forests of stately cypress trees standing in water and festooned with Spanish moss. It was like a vast, silent cathedral filled with wildlife.

The one feature that marred that school was the spirit among the boys—the tendency to putdowns and lack of wholesome fellowship. One boy who entered the school a few weeks late was promptly dubbed "New Guy" and was pestered and tormented for the rest of the year. He was my roommate, and I liked him and did what I could to ease his lot. He turned out to be a grandson of Alexander Graham Bell, with whom I had a chance to visit when he came to the school.

Over all, I enjoyed Marienfeld, and it was good for me. When the time came to go home I packed my Indian relics and geology specimens—the important things—in my suitcase. Minor incidentals, such as clothing, I shipped home in a carton. I wrapped up that season by taking a canoe trip with my Dad on the old Chesapeake & Ohio Canal, from Washington to Harpers Ferry. In those days the canal still had canal boats drawn by mules. The canal went through locks and over bridges. At one point we loaded our canoe onto one of the boats. Dad slept upstairs while I slept down under in the hay, near the mules. There were two teams; one rode while the other pulled. There was a tow path on only one side, so when two boats passed, the outside boat would stop its team and let the tow rope sink so the other boat and team could pass over it.

Back in Dayton, I had another whirl at public school, but that wasn't so good. Then I was enrolled at Marietta Johnson's Organic School, at Fairhope, Alabama. That was, and I think, still is, a famous school. What I most remember, however, is the woodworking shop, where I ran a jigsaw, and Mobile Bay, where I dove for shrimp.

World War I was going on at that time, and America was getting closer to it. I was feeling very patriotic, so I got a short piece of pipe and set it in the ground to serve as a socket for a little pole in front of the house where I was staying in Fairhope. I got an American flag and fastened it to a pole which I put up every morning and took down each evening.

While I was away at school a crisis arose at home. Actually, two crises—one in the family and the other in the flood-control program. Dad was taken seriously ill with blood poisoning in his foot. His doctor diagnosed it as appendicitis, and removed his appendix. With that stress added to the blood poisoning, he was at death's door. Lucy, who was knowledgeable in health matters, promptly fired the doctor and engaged Dr. Brower, a capable young man, who managed to pull him through, albeit with the loss of one toe.

At about the time he was able to sit up in bed, the Conservancy Board came to him with the shocking news that they had decided to abandon the project. They instructed Dad to dismiss the engineering staff and prepare to close things out. This would have ended the Miami Conservancy.

The Chairman of the Board, Edward Deeds, was off in the Caribbean at the time. His personality was the driving force behind the project. Dad's strategy was to stall for time until Deeds returned. Sure enough, when Deeds got back he quickly turned things around, and the flood control project again went full speed ahead. Seen in hindsight, Deeds and Morgan were the two men without whom no effective Dayton flood control system would have been carried out. They worked well together and enjoyed active mutual esteem.

Another outstanding Dayton man with whom Dad enjoyed strong rapport was a close colleague of Deeds, Charles F. Kettering, the inventor of the self-starter for automobiles. At one point Deeds and Kettering told Dad that they were planning to launch a new company, to be called General Motors. They asked him if he would like to get in on the ground floor. He thanked them but said that his main focus in the future was to be on education, which he regarded as a key instrument in building a good society.

Even while preoccupied with the Dayton flood control process, he and Lucy were busily laying plans for the future school which was to express the educational philosophy that had brought them together. After an extensive search they located and bought two abandoned farms in the Berkshires, which were to provide the site for their school. These farms were located near Lee, Massachusetts, on a highway known as the Jacob's Ladder Road. Noting the profusion of boulders everywhere, Lucy remarked, "Jacob would certainly have no trouble finding a pillow here," referring to the time when Jacob "cradled his head on a stone." Thus the place got its name, Jacob's Pillow.

We spent our summers there, getting Jacob's Pillow ready to become a school. Lucy named things after Jacob's family. Our cow was Rachel, the pig was Reuben, the hydraulic ram (which pumped our water) was Levi, our Model T Ford was Gad. I was ten years old that first summer, and it was my job to milk Rachel and take care of her, which I did with considerable satisfaction. I also had fun exploring the woods and building dams, with little water wheels, in the creek.

I loved to pick berries and roamed the woods and fields in search of them, picking each kind in season: strawberries, raspberries, thimbleberries, blueberries, and blackberries. It was at that time that friends of ours were in the process of domesticating blueberries—the first time that had been done. I carried in my pocket a little card with a hole in it. If I found any blueberries too large to go through that hole, I was to mark the bush and report it at once.

Dad was away most of the time, so I was the man of the place. I would bring in ice from the ice house, chase the woodchucks out of the garden, and pick up on odd chores.

Lucy and I hit it off well in that environment, though we did have a clash now and then. One of these occurred in connection with the cranberries which grew in our bog. It bothered me that they ripened late in the season, after we had left. Then one day I noticed that some of the cranberries had turned red. I picked them eagerly and took them to Lucy, to make cranberry sauce. She examined them carefully and explained to me that they had turned red prematurely because they had spoiled. She said it would be a waste of sugar to cook them because they were bad.

I was sure they were good and stubbornly insisted that she cook them. I promised to eat them. She warned me again, then went ahead and cooked them. They were terrible, and I refused to eat them. She said I'd have to eat them before I had anything else to eat, so I didn't eat anything for two days. Then Lucy decided that this couldn't go on, and relented. Feeling that I had won a moral victory I proclaimed that now I would eat the spoiled cranberries, but Lucy thought this might be dangerous on an empty stomach and threw them out.

On another occasion I pulled some of my father's grouseberry seedlings. (This was a shrub he was experimenting with, sometimes called highbush cranberry.) Lucy said I must write him a letter and tell him what I'd done. She sat me down with a pencil and paper. Returning later she saw some writing on the paper and picked it up before I could stop her. Instead of a letter to my father, it was a poem about how mean she was. She managed to restrain her mirth until she got out of the room.

One time a cousin of Lucy's, visiting us at Jacob's Pillow, remonstrated with Lucy for letting me eat so much. "That child will hurt himself," she exclaimed. Meeting her in the garden shortly after, I remarked to her, "Cousin Bessie, I rarely get enough to eat. I have to go out in the garden and eat carrots." Bessie promptly reported this to Lucy for her amusement. A good sense of humor is an essential requirement for raising children; at least it was for raising me.

The school at Jacob's Pillow was still years away and Dad couldn't wait. For one thing, he had a son who needed a good school right away, and shipping him off to boarding schools was too disruptive to the family. So Dad got Dayton's leaders together and proposed that they start an experimental school in which active experience and initiative would be key elements, along with democratic community life and responsibility. He was gifted, not only in having ideas and dreams, but in imparting these to others, and they bought the idea. This may have been helped by the fact that a number of Dayton's leading families, including the Wrights, Ketterings, Pattersons, and Deeds, also had boys of junior high school or high school age.

Dad searched the country for an imaginative educator to head this school. In this search he was as contagious and convincing as he had been with the business leaders. A fine educator, Frank D. Slutz, resigned his job as Superintendent of Schools in Pueblo, Colorado to assume leadership of this small, nebulous private school.

"Prof" as we called him, was a fine educator and an inspiration to us.

Associated with him was Arthur Hauck, a little younger, affectionately known as "Dad Hauck." Because of his German background he felt it his duty to enlist in the American Army. When he announced this in assembly we all cried. Hauck later became president of the University of Maine.

With the war going on it was hard to find a building for the school, so C. F. Kettering offered the use of a 300 foot greenhouse that he owned at Moraine Park, some five miles south of Dayton. Hence the project was known as Moraine Park School. I was one of the original group of sixteen boys who came together at the beginning—"the immortal sixteen" we called ourselves. Our first job, which we enjoyed, was to haul dirt out of that greenhouse in wheelbarrows to lower the ground level enough to make room for a floor.

Moraine Park was a school for children of the elite, but neither Dad nor Slutz would settle for that alone. It also served less advantaged families, albeit not many, by adjusting tuition based on ability to pay.

The assembly hall of the school was a large room at the end of the greenhouse, with little offices marked off by low partitions, opening on narrow aisles. They were equipped with chairs and tables and occasionally with book shelves and other amenities. For study purposes and at assembly times, each boy would sit in his own office. The offices were large enough so that, as the school grew, each one could accommodate two boys (and later, girls as well).

There were many interesting features of life at Moraine Park. All sorts of guests visited the school, and were commonly asked to speak. I particularly remember Wilfred Grenfell, the Arctic explorer, after whom we named one of our literary clubs. We made periodic visits to various industries and always enjoyed watching the people and the machines and finding out what was happening there. Misdemeanors were punishable by window washing. (A greenhouse has a lot of windows.) If you didn't get the windows washed by the appointed time, the penalty was doubled. I once washed a hundred windows.

Each boy had one or more "projects." Some of these could be described as service projects, others were moneymaking businesses. I had the Moraine Furniture Repair Company. It was my responsibility to mend the folding chairs which seemed to get broken all the time. With a drill, a screwdriver, and a good supply of screws and mending plates I put them back together. This process might have shocked a cabinet maker, but it kept the chairs in service.

I was also student curator of the school museum which had long glass-fronted shelves filled with fossils, Indian relics and geology specimens. One day Dad called me up and said, "I have something for your museum." On one of his routine visits to the Huffman Dam site, where excavation was going on, a foreman had remarked, "One of our workmen found a fossil turtle this morning." Dad asked to see the fossil and at once recognized it as a giant trilobite, an ancient crustacean which was once the most highly evolved form of life on earth. He immediately thought of me and the school museum.

I never got my hands on that trilobite. Dad showed it to Dr. August Foerste, who was the leading authority on paleontology and geology in our area. Dr. Foerste latched onto that fossil, carefully cleaned it up and coated it with a preservative to prevent its deterioration from exposure to the air. I think he took it to bed with him.

That wonderful crustacean, fourteen inches long and ten inches wide, was by far the largest specimen ever found, so it went to the Smithsonian Institution. Two paleontologists came all the way from Washington to receive it. Dad took them and me out to dinner, where we talked trilobites. I told them I'd seen lots of small trilobites and this big one, but I wondered if there were medium size trilobites. When they went back to Washington they generously sent me some specimens for the school museum.

That big trilobite still occupies a place of honor in the Smithsonian, and likewise has for years been the emblem of the Dayton Museum. I still have a miniature bronze replica of it which I use as a paperweight on my desk. In 1985, through the efforts of Doris Swab, an energetic school teacher, it became, by an Act of the Ohio Legislature, the official state fossil. There were only two dissenting votes, from representatives who felt that ex-Governor James Rhodes should have had that honor.

Some of the Moraine Park School projects were of a business nature. The lunch room and the school bank, for example. Some were stock companies; there was even a stock exchange. It was a microcosm of the capitalist world. There was also a school court, in which students could sue each other.

One highly functional project was the janitorial work. The school didn't have a janitor, so the students organized to do the work, and the money saved financed a summer camp for the whole school. We rented Camp Kern, on the Little Miami River near Fort Ancient, an extensive prehistoric earthworks.

Upriver from the camp were the ruins of an old village, probably abandoned due to flooding. It was said to be haunted, so one night another boy and I decided to sleep there. We chose a spot within four ruined masonry walls of what had once been a small house. In the middle of the night something awakened us. In the doorway we could dimly make out a white figure, some seven feet tall, swaying slightly. We didn't believe in ghosts, but that apparition was very convincing. We lay very, very still. Then suddenly the intruder gave a snort and galloped away.

Another concern of Moraine Park School was the topic of *Mate Seeking*. It was felt that this should be a matter for serious thought on the part of young teenagers not yet faced with the actual problem. I can't recall the content of our discussions on the topic, but it was taken seriously. (It should be taken even more seriously today, with the divorce rate reaching catastrophic proportions.)

I do remember, when I was about fourteen, driving home with Dad one evening and asking him, "How can you tell who you should marry?" He deliberated for a time before replying. "The kind of person you marry," he said, "will largely depend on the kind of person you yourself are. If you develop sound health and habits and ideals, you will likely marry that kind of person." Then he went on to add, "When you meet a really fine person whom you would like to marry, the question will be: have you become a fine enough person so she'll want to marry you?" Lucy also made a cogent comment once, "Before you let yourself get seriously interested in a girl, take a good look at her mother."

I started driving at age fourteen. There were no driver's licenses in those days, and the speed limit posted in our village was eight miles per hour. Normal cruising speed on the highways was twenty-five miles-per-hour.

The Dayton Flood of 1913. One of the worst floods in American history.

These pictures show two of the five huge flood-control dams in the early stages of construction. They were the first of their kind ever built and have worked perfectly for seventy years.

5

TEENAGE ADVENTURES AND ENTERPRISES

This chapter takes me into my middle teens, my first contact with the "wireless telephone," how I coped with hostile boys, how I got around the child labor laws that wouldn't let me work, and about my "farm" project and my adventures in animal husbandry. It also recounts additional dramatic episodes in the Dayton Flood-Control Project.

I had my first contact with radio while I was at Moraine Park. One of my schoolmates, Harry Eldridge, was an amateur radio operator—hams, they called themselves—and belonged to the Amateur Radio Relay League. These amateurs were licensed only after they were able to show technical competence and a working mastery of Morse code.

One day Harry was whistling a new tune, and I asked him where he heard that. He said, "Over the wireless telephone."

"Wireless telephone?" I responded. "What do you mean 'wireless telephone'?" It sounded fishy to me. I could imagine sounds being transmitted through the air for a mile or so and then being picked up and amplified. But not from any substantial distance.

"Come out to my house," Harry said, "and listen in." He had a radio room set up in a large linen closet with both a receiver and transmitter. He tuned in a station in Detroit, and I put on the earphones and listened. I was fascinated and listened without stopping to the news reports, the weather reports, the stock market reports. Then Harry switched to other wave lengths, tuning in code stations in France, Germany, and Japan. It was a whole new world.

His code transmitter used an old-fashioned rotary spark gap that made a roaring noise and had a limited range. Harry had previously shifted to *continuous wave*, a more modern and efficient form of transmitter, but had then gone back to spark transmission. His father didn't understand this, but I did. The rotary spark gap produced a lot of ozone, and in that small enclosed space it pepped Harry up. Normally a mild-mannered person, he became bold and aggressive with a little ozone in him.

Radio receivers were not yet available in the stores, and within a year I was building receivers which tuned in stations within a six-hundred mile radius, though my knowledge and skill did not remotely approach Harry's. Teen-age boys were the radio pioneers in America.

Coming into my teens in Dayton I enjoyed Moraine Park, but there were problems in others areas of life. When our family moved to a new location the boys in the neighborhood would come and want to fight with me. I didn't want to fight and I didn't want to run away, so I would offer to wrestle. I liked to wrestle and was good at it. The other boys would insist on a fight, and say things to make me angry. My response was, "Maybe you're too weak to wrestle, or don't know how . . ." That did it. We would wrestle all over the yard and wind up as friends.

That experience in nonviolence was valuable, and stood me in good stead in the years to come. I learned the power of goodwill, of self-understanding, and also of understanding the other fellow. We are all, to some extent, automatons programmed to respond to stimuli in certain ways. Given a fair degree of self-understanding we can reprogram ourselves to respond differently. (This goes for nations as well as individuals.) I didn't have to respond with anger or fear. I determined that nobody was going to pull my strings and make me dance like a toy monkey on a stick. Understanding both myself and the other boy I could generally get more desirable behavior from him if I tried.

Another teenage problem that plagued me was my inability to get a job during the summer because I wasn't willing to lie about my age. Together with a friend I canvassed the city in vain for work. So we gave up and went into business for ourselves. We started the Cooperative Messenger Service. The Morgan Engineering Company had an unused office, complete with telephone, right in the middle of town. We borrowed that office, got our name in the phone book, and distributed our cards throughout the business district.

One of us would answer the phone and say, "Yes, we'll send a boy right around." Then he'd hop on his bike and off he'd go. At the end of summer, when school resumed, we managed to keep it going. There was a law firm next door to our office and the secretary there kindly answered the phone for us (there weren't a great many calls) and gave us the messages when we came in after school.

My partner, Melvin Brown, was a bright, alert boy. After our Moraine

Park School days we lost touch, except for exchanging one or two letters. Melvin joined the Marines and in time became a colonel.

Many years later, when I was in middle age and the Korean War was going on, my eye was caught by the picture of a soldier in a war bond ad. There was something strikingly familiar about the eager young face. The caption read, "Pfc. Melvin Brown, Jr., U.S. Marine Corps, missing in action in Korea. When last seen had run out of ammunition and was using his gun as a club." Obviously, this was the son of my old friend, and his resemblance to his father had caught my attention. I too had a son in Korea, but he came home—all in one piece.

In Dayton, my second sister was born, named Lucy, after her mother. We were all very happy about this event. A few weeks later she died suddenly, for no apparent cause. Before we took the body to the cemetery, Dad and Lucy and I stood with our arms around each other, and looked at the baby. That was a precious moment. We took the baby to the cemetery in the car with us, while the hearse drove on in front, empty.

Ever since that time I've felt that *viewing* of a dead person by the immediate family promptly after death should be encouraged, although cosmetic preparation of a corpse, followed by public display, has never impressed me as desirable.

Lucy's life was not easy. Dad was enormously preoccupied with his work and other concerns, and tended to be rather sober and undemonstrative. Lucy would have had him be more jolly, but he just wasn't. He did have a sense of humor, however, and would tell funny stories or quote amusing limericks and rhymes, especially to punctuate an idea. But often he was very tired, and at the table was characteristically quiet.

Worst of all were Lucy's inner problems, which plagued her from time to time. Despite her idealism and brilliance, Lucy was readily upset and could be very unreasonable. She was sometimes difficult to live with. At one point she took Griscom and Frances and went back to New Jersey. Dad immediately went there himself and persuaded her to return.

Dad was forging ahead with the flood-control project. The conservancy law had been passed, bonds issued, plans drawn up and construction begun. Instead of the usual construction camps, he built five model villages for the workmen to live in: one at each dam. They even had experimental schools for the children.

Lucy was a brilliant house planner and designed four different houses, attractive and functional, each using standard lengths of lumber. Sites were chosen in wooded areas, water and sewer systems were installed, and streets curved among the trees. The four house designs were mixed on each street. They were painted different colors and set at different angles. This made an attractive community. For single men there was a comfortable bunk house.

The quality and efficiency of the work force was high and turnover was small. Costs were actually reduced.

Not only that, but the accident rate was phenomenally low. In those days there was a rule-of-thumb that one man was killed for every million dollars spent. On the Miami Conservancy project they reduced that death rate by nearly 90%.

As if he didn't have enough to do, Dad was a charter member and first secretary of the League to Enforce Peace, which developed the League of Nations idea and presented it to Woodrow Wilson.

Then it became his responsibility to *sell* the League of Nations idea to James Cox, a popular governor of Ohio and publisher of several newspapers. He and Cox knew each other well through the Dayton flood-control project, and Cox had sent his son to Moraine Park School. Cox liked the idea of an international organization to preserve peace, but did not consider it an *issue*.

Later, when Cox became the Democratic candidate for president (with Franklin Roosevelt as his running mate) and the League of Nations *had* become an issue, he supported the idea vigorously. Alas, it was a Republican year and the party nominated another Ohioan, Warren G. Harding, who was an isolationist. He was cool toward the League of Nations, and the party took its line from him. He won, and the U.S. stayed out. Happily, years later, Franklin Roosevelt exercised leadership in taking the idea off the shelf and launching the United Nations.

As the Conservancy work got under way, our family moved out of Dayton and we made our home near Englewood, ten miles to the north, in a comfortable house located in the future reservoir a mile above the Englewood dam. From there I commuted 15 miles each way to Moraine Park School. Sometimes I got a ride with Dad, but mostly I went by trolley.

Street cars! What an important part they played in my life during those years in Dayton. With a population of 150,000, Dayton had six separate street railway companies, each with a franchise to cover a certain part of the city. They converged downtown and there were often several cars coming down the street at the same time. The six companies had cars of different designs and colors, so you could tell them apart at a distance.

There were few spots in the city more than a few minutes away from a street car line. The cars came along frequently in the daytime and less often at night and picked up passengers at any street intersection. The companies exchanged free transfers, so you could go anywhere in the city for a nickel. There was no lack of passengers.

There were also interurban cars connected with the city cars. They were larger and faster, speeding smoothly between cities at 50 miles an hour, while automobiles were bumping along at 25.

I rode an interurban from Englewood to the center of Dayton, where it connected with an interurban for Moraine Park. The two cars were scheduled to arrive at the same moment, one coming in from the North on Main Street, the other coming in from the South on Third Street. As we approached from the North I would stand on the bottom step watching for the other car. If it was in sight I would leap from the step and dash down the middle of the street. Sometimes the car would have already left and would be half a block or so away. I chased it anyhow, hoping that a train would block it at the crossing three blocks south or that a kindly motorist might help me overtake it. Sometimes I missed it altogether, and had to wait for an hour.

That first summer at Englewood, Lucy encouraged me to seek a job with Charles Ewing, a nearby dairyman. Charles had come to Dayton as a member of the National Guard during the flood. One day a comrade jokingly pointed a gun at him and said, "Charley, we die before morning," and pulled the trigger. He didn't know it was loaded. The bullet passed close to Charles' heart, but he recovered, married his nurse, settled in the area and took up dairy farming.

I applied for a job, and Charles took me on. I was to get my board and keep, and 15 cents an hour for four hours work each day: $3.60 per week. The pay was important, not for the money but because it made me an official part of the action. I helped with the milking and helped bottle the milk, wash the bottles, and herd the cows. Most important of all was the milk route. Charles' wife would drive their Model T roadster (which sold new, in those days, for $380) pulling a trailer loaded with cases of milk. I ran back and forth from the trailer to the houses, delivering the milk and picking up the empty bottles.

They put me on a horse to herd the cows, but the horse soon discovered that it had an inexperienced rider. When I pulled on a rein it would turn its head but not change its direction, so I herded on foot. Well, not entirely on foot. Often I hopped onto one of the cows and rode. That didn't please the cow, but she got used to it. My four hours a day were more like ten, but that was fine with me. It was a good summer.

Back at Moraine Park in the fall, I made the Grenfell Club debating team. We never lost a debate. I thought I was a pretty smart kid, but Dad took a dim view of it. Debating, he said, was a dishonest activity in which both sides try to twist the truth to their own advantage. He said it would be better to see which side could make the best presentation of the case. Years later I came to agree with him and ever since have started debates with an effort to seek maximum common ground with my opponent. This makes the whole process more constructive.

The fall of 1919, when I was fourteen, Lucy suggested that I buy a cow and loaned me the money. She helped take care of the milk, and paid me ten cents a quart for it. We had a barn and an ample pasture nearby. I would yodel for the cow at milking time, and she would come hurrying. After a while, when my voice started changing, I found it difficult to yodel, so I blew on a big conch shell. I named the cow Katy, after a popular song which I liked:

K-K-K-Katy, beautiful Katy,
You're the only g-g-g-girl that I adore.
When the m-moon shines
Over the c-cow shed,
I'll be waiting by the k-k-k-kitchen door.

I had a rain gauge and every day measured the precipitation and recorded it on a chart. I wondered if there might be a connection between rainfall and milk production so I shifted from a chart to a graph, with one line plotted for rainfall and another for milk production. Sure enough, production dropped during a prolonged rain, but gradually rose as the vegetation freshened up.

Not content with just a cow, I added chickens, then ducks, and finally, rabbits. The following spring I planted an enormous garden, and when summer came I fashioned a vegetable cart from an old baby buggy and peddled vegetables door to door in the Conservancy village. I was riding high.

My farming career came to an end the following year, near the close of our stay at Englewood. I developed a serious eye infection, for which I was hospitalized for some time. With my agreement the cow was sold.

Dad and Lucy were patient with my vagaries. Once, when the rest of the family was away, I had a bright idea—or so I thought. To rid the house of flies I burned a pan of sulphur on the kitchen stove. It killed the flies all right, but it also killed all of Lucy's house plants. She was unhappy about that, but scolding would have been anticlimactic, and she refrained.

At about that time, Dad and Lucy played a trick on me. One Christmas morning when Griscom and Frances and I came down to the living room to get our stockings full of goodies, mine was filled with pieces of wood and coal—a sign that Santa thought I had been a bad boy. Had I been an insecure youngster, with tender feelings, this might have been cruel. But I was merely astonished. Then, having had their little joke, my folks produced the real stocking, full of good things.

I think it was that Christmas that my folks gave me a set of the Harvard Classics. I revelled in those books and especially recall Benjamin Franklin's autobiography, in which he tells how, as a boy, he kept a chart listing all the faults he could think of. Every evening he would put a mark on the chart for each fault he had demonstrated during the day. Each week he would concentrate on correcting some particular fault. Having my full share of faults I decided to try Franklin's system, and did for quite a while.

During that time I learned that the Conservancy needed young elm trees to plant above the dams to prevent driftwood coming into the conduits. I knew of a large patch of elm seedlings along the river, so I offered to supply a quantity of these at $5 per thousand. They took me up on this.

Accordingly, I put the word out among the kids at the Conservancy village that if they would bring shovels to a certain place along the river on Saturday morning I would hire them. I had friendly relations with these kids, unlike the Englewood boys.

That Saturday twelve or fifteen boys and girls showed up at the river. They dug seedlings all day while I bundled them and kept records. At the end of the operation they assembled on the long porch at my house. I sat at a table at one end, with the records and a box of money while the kids stood patiently in line, being paid off. On Monday I delivered the seedlings, nine thousand of them.

The Miami Conservancy was going ahead full speed. The giant dragline a quarter of a mile from our house was roaring night and day, stopping only at meal times. Sometimes the sudden silence at midnight would wake me up.

There was bitter opposition to the project in the towns above Dayton. It was said to be just a racket for a few crooks to enrich themselves at public expense. In one up-river town they even threatened to shoot Arthur Morgan if he ever came there.

Englewood was hostile. Sometimes, when I got off the traction car on my way home from Moraine Park and started down the road, a gang of boys would lie in wait and block my path, shouting threats and taunts. After all, wasn't I the son of the chief crook? I would put on a bold front and challenge any one of them to tangle with me if the others would agree to stay out of it. I must have been protected by an aura of evil; no champion ever came forward.

I lived in fear that they might all jump me at once, so I bought a book on jujitsu, a Japanese martial art which was popular at that time. I studied this carefully hoping it might give me some magic by which I could vanquish a whole crowd. Fortunately I was never put to the test.

In one area I did outwit the Englewood boys. I had a big garden and wanted to raise watermelons, which were my favorite food, but I knew they would steal the crop. So I planted "baby watermelons," a variety that ripens at about the size of a cantaloupe. Then, to divert attention, I planted a couple of hills of regular size watermelons next to the road. Sure enough, every one of the big melons was stolen before it was ripe but the small ones which constituted my real crop were untouched.

As the construction work on the flood control project neared completion and the dams began to function, the hostility in the upriver towns subsided. A banquet was held in Dad's honor in the very town where they had previously threatened to shoot him.

The Conservancy Board prepared to sell off the wooded river valleys which had been bought in the course of carrying out the construction. Dad urged that choice areas, close to the dams, be preserved as natural parks. The Board replied that their business was flood control, not parks.

Dad drafted a letter to the newspapers, which stressed the need for more park land in this heavily settled area and said that it would be a betrayal of posterity to lose this chance to acquire it. He read this draft to the Board and told them he would publish the letter if they didn't arrange for the parks. Confronted by this blackmail and being unwilling to fire Dad, they acquiesced. Today those parks provide recreation for thousands.

He also urged the Board to preserve the construction villages which had been built at each dam site. The board thought differently, and removed all but the village at Englewood Dam. That village, now known as Morgan Place, is still happily occupied and enjoys high community morale. This is particularly appropriate in the light of Dad's lifelong interest in the values of the small community.

The Conservancy had developed a wonderful team of people, skilled, disciplined, well-integrated, with strong morale, who could have tackled any engineering job on earth and done it well, but when the job was done this team quietly dissolved.

When the dams were finished and Dayton was at last safe, a celebration seemed to be in order. But Deeds said they wouldn't celebrate until the bonds were paid off. Many years later, Deeds and Morgan, by that time old men, appeared on the platform at the celebration and recounted the great adventure which had finally made Dayton safe from floods.

Looking back now, after three-quarters of a century, I can see the Dayton Flood Control Project in clearer perspective. In it Dad introduced a revolutionary new concept in engineering, pioneered in construction methods and in social organization and, last but not least, introduced a creative new concept of legal and political organization—*Regionalism*, he called it. Happily, he lived to see the Miami Conservancy District declared a National Historic Engineering Monument.

6

WE MOVE TO YELLOW SPRINGS

This chapter tells of the third major shift of our family in my lifetime, when Dad suddenly transferred from engineering to education as his central occupation. A moribund Antioch sprang back to life. Soon we were living in a village and suddenly I was old enough to dig ditches and swing a hammer. I raised turtles, built radios, ran a furnace route, operated a string of gardens, and wrote a song. Jessie died—and I dropped everything and went off to Minnesota.

Our family's move to Yellow Springs happened logically enough but no one in his right mind could have guessed the sequence of events which led to it.

Meeting Dad on the street one day in 1921, a friend remarked, "I see by the paper you've been made a trustee of Antioch."

"Antioch?" said Dad. "What's that?"

"It's a college, at Yellow Springs."

Dad told me later how his appointment came about. It seems that back in the mid-nineteenth century, when the college was starting, the Unitarian Church made a major contribution. In turn, the Unitarians were entitled to appoint a member of the Board. There was also a proviso that if the college were ever to be laid down, the denomination would have a claim on part of the residual assets. Furthermore, the Unitarians were concerned that Antioch not develop into a sectarian institution.

When word reached Unitarian headquarters that Antioch College was about to close, they thought it important to appoint someone to the board to protect their interests. They immediately thought of Dad, who was prominent in Unitarian circles, and appointed him. But they forgot to tell him and he learned of it through the grapevine.

He and Lucy drove to Yellow Springs to look the place over. The college was indeed about done for. The enrollment had dropped to fifteen students, all local. The faculty had left except for a few who owned homes there. The buildings were in disrepair, and the two dormitories had outdoor plumbing.

The institution had a noble tradition. It had, for example, been the first college in America to admit women and blacks on equal terms with white men. What had more immediate appeal to Dad and Lucy, however, was the Glen, the beautiful wild park in which the Yellow Spring is located. This comprised several hundred acres, and flanked the campus on the east.

Dad and Lucy had planned to start a school at Jacob's Pillow as soon as the Dayton job was finished, but starting out at the college level had a certain amount of appeal. For one thing, Dad wasn't sure how Lucy's nervous system would stand up under the impact of a boarding school. Furthermore, he and Lucy had come into their forties, and were "no longer young." So they reflected on what might be done with Antioch. After visiting the place Dad remarked to Lucy, "I think it's dead enough so that we could do what we want to with it."

Accordingly, he met with the trustees and proposed reorganizing the college along new and revolutionary lines. The idea was to pursue symmetry in education—to develop the whole person. Part of this would be a plan whereby students would alternate between periods of work and study. At that point the board was ready to settle for anything. They would accept his plan if he could raise the money for it. And they offered to supply him with as many resignations from the board as he might need.

Dad raised the money and set abou to launch the revitalized institution.

Lacking a college education, he tried to find someone else to serve as president and carry out his plans. He had no luck, so he took the presidency himself and brought Antioch into national prominence. The only college president without a degree.

A few years later we had a family meeting and decided to sell Jacob's Pillow. It was bought by Ted Shawn and became a famous school of dance— but it was still called Jacob's Pillow.

Yellow Springs was a new experience for all of us. It was a pleasant village of shady streets and friendly people, with a population of 1300, including many retired farmers and about one-third black people. It had two small industries (a sawmill and canning factory) both dying. It owned its own electric system but had no water or sewer system.

However, it was rich in history. It had been the site of a communal Owenite colony and other social experiments. It had been a stagecoach stop on the historic Bullskin Trail from Cincinnati to Lake Erie. The big iron-bearing spring from which it got its name had attracted visitors for generations, even back in Indian times. The water was said to be healthful and slightly laxative. At any event, people who rested and drank lots of water seemed to benefit. Yellow Springs is reported to have been a station on the underground railroad, harboring escaped slaves as they made their way north.

A leading citizen, back in the mid-nineteenth century, was Judge William Mills, who settled in Yellow Springs and built himself a mansion in the middle of town. Through his influence the railroad came through Yellow Springs instead of through nearby Clifton, and it was his gift of twenty acres and $20,000 that brought Antioch College to Yellow Springs.

When we came to Yellow Springs I left behind my livestock, the hostile boys, the Moraine Park projects, and the long trolley rides.

I was just turning sixteen so I was old enough to take a regular job. There was an immense amount of work to be done at Antioch College. The two dorms were still using privies. The men's privy was a separate brick building a few yards from the west end of the men's dormitory. The women's privy was a four story hexagonal brick structure attached to the women's dorm. One side of this structure contained a door on each floor through which it could be entered directly from the corresponding floor of the dorm. Another side contained windows for the three upper floors, and an outside door for the ground floor. The other four sides had rows of seats—a different side for each floor, with a direct drop to the basement. We tore down that structure and also the men's privy, and installed modern bathrooms. We chipped the mortar off the old bricks and reused them elsewhere.

The wiring was completely obsolete: one light bulb in each room. One of my jobs was to drill holes through the incredibly thick brick walls to bring in a new electrical service. I would notch the end of an iron pipe with a hacksaw until it formed a sharp-pointed crown. Then I'd hold the jagged end against the wall and tap the other end with a hammer, turning the pipe a little after each blow. It was slow, but it worked, and made a nice round hole. I dug ditches, too. Dad had given firm orders to cut no tree roots over two inches in diameter—he was always strong on trees—so we dug under them instead.

Aunt Jessie was recovering from an operation for cancer, and she and my grandmother joined us in Yellow Springs shortly after we moved there, living in their own comfortable apartment a block or so away. I spent a good deal of time with them.

When fall came and college opened, the boys' dorm was ready, and I moved there. The house my folks were building wasn't complete yet, and their temporary residence was too small. I was still in high school, but I enjoyed fraternizing with the college students.

Living in the boys' dorm did have its drawbacks. A lot of the fellows smoked, and they knew I didn't like it. One evening, just for fun, a bunch of them came into my room with cigarettes and puffed furiously until the room was densely filled with smoke. Later in the evening I dropped by my folks' place and Lucy smelled me from all the way upstairs.

The next time they tried this I was ready for them. I had a tiny stink bomb in my desk which I quietly dropped into my metal wastebasket without anyone noticing. A stink bomb doesn't do violence, it's just plain nasty. I was expecting it, so I didn't mind, but my would-be tormentors fled precipitously and soon there were shouts of outrage from the nearby rooms as well. My tactic was a great success.

On one occasion a group of us young fellows rented my folks' car and made a trip to New Straightsville, in the Hocking Valley, where a mine fire had been burning for some forty years. It was an impressive scene—smoke and steam coming up out of the ground over a whole valley. The ground had caved in here and there, sometimes with houses on it.

That night we hunted up the sheriff and asked for accommodations at the jail. He opened it up for us and let us sleep there. We chatted with him while a crowd gathered outside. Some of them came in, and they weren't too friendly. That was back in prohibition days, and there were a lot of moonshiners in that county. They took us for revenuers, and we were told later that every still in the county was dismantled and hidden away in honor of our visit.

The next day we hiked about and saw the sights, and that night we camped in the shelter of a rocky overhang where an outcropping of coal provided fuel for our camp fire. There were strange noises about: trampling in the bushes and an occasional low whistle. This went on most of the night, so we took turns sitting by the fire until morning. When daylight came we investigated and found that we had camped near the entrance of an abandoned mine in which a still had been operating. There was corn mash on the floor and other remnants of the operation. The moonshiners had dismantled and moved their equipment during the night. I found a carbide miner's lamp on the floor which I took home and used for years.

In collaboration with an architect, Louis Granjent, Lucy had planned and supervised the building of the presidential home in Yellow Springs. It had to be big to accommodate numerous guests and presidential functions, but Lucy kept it simple. It was both functional and attractive. The floors of the kitchen and the dining/living room were made of a polished, somewhat resilient, red composition, marked off in squares. In lieu of a baseboard, the floor itself curved upward at the edge to meet the wall. No sharp corners to catch dirt. The dining room table, in natural walnut, tipped up to form a settee. Lucy didn't miss a bet. I was the first person to live in that house, occupying a room on the third floor while it was still being built.

As first lady of the town, Lucy set a pattern of Quaker simplicity. Good taste took the place of elegance. She went shopping on a bike and avoided ostentation. Her example was, I think, a force for democracy in the community. It encouraged economic development too. Young people starting businesses on a shoestring enjoyed equal social status with their more affluent neighbors. Mansions, fancy clothes and big cars carried no prestige.

In true Quaker style her simplicity and forthrightness were blended with sharp wit and strong concern for social justice. Once, during a period of severe unemployment, there was a heavy snowstorm and someone remarked what a blessing this was for the unemployed because it would give the men work shoveling snow. Lucy shot back that this reminded her of the rich man who made himself sick drinking cream so there would be enough skim milk for the poor people.

Yellow Springs, of course, meant another school for me; about the ninth, as close as I can remember. The Antioch Academy, like the College, was rooted in history. When the College prepared to open in 1853, the administration found they had a lot of promising applicants, very few of whom were ready for college. Antioch didn't want to turn these young people away, nor did they want to lower their academic standards. The Antioch Academy was established to get these applicants ready for college. Dad revived the Academy, along with the College, and installed a forward-looking educator to run it. That's where I finished high school.

I thrived in the challenging, freewheeling atmosphere of this little school. It was conducted in the old Mills mansion, which had been taken over by Antioch. I remember with pleasure the School Glee Club. The director, Matilda Swinnerton, prized my participation, not because I was a good singer—which I wasn't— but for another reason. I was a big, rough and ready kid, who liked to wrestle and climb trees. My being in the Club made it "respectable" for the other boys to join.

One day Matilda suggested that we have a contest to see who could write the best Antioch song. She suggested two or three tunes that we might use. One evening not long after that I was sick in bed with a temperature of 103, just the right condition for writing a song. So I wrote one to the tune of "Tannenbaum." I showed it to Dad. He read it over, and suggested changing three words. It was amazing; those three words changed it from doggerel to poetry.

I turned in the song anonymously. To cover my tracks I wrote another song, to the tune of "Juanita" which I turned in over my signature. Matilda was impressed with the anonymous one, and declared it the winner. She took it to the College and soon it was adopted as the Antioch Alma Mater.

Here is the text of the song. (Blue and gold were the college colors.)

ANTIOCH ALMA MATER

Thy towers are goodly to behold,
Antioch our Antioch;
Against the twilight blue and gold,
Antioch our Antioch.

In office, field and factory great
We labor on and dedicate
The glory of what we create
To our dear old Antioch.

Thou art not living in the past,
Antioch our Antioch;
Thy high ideals must always last,
Antioch, our Antioch
We love to linger in thy halls,
Thy spirit yet each heart enthralls,
And e'en the ivy on the walls
Speaks to us of Antioch.

It was handy being in the Antioch Academy. I was able to take a couple of college courses while still in high school. Perhaps in honor of my graduation, Dad gave the Academy commencement talk that year. He commented that graduation classes were getting larger. There were eight of us whereas his own graduating class had only seven.

It is shocking that within five years, three of the eight members of our class died of tuberculosis, a great killer of youth in those days.

About this time a new crisis arose for Antioch. The Glen, the wild park which figured so prominently in Dad's decision to come to Antioch, was sold to a group of businessmen who planned to build an amusement park there—ferris wheels, roller coasters, and the like. The prospect of the Glen being ruined and a commercial amusement park being built at the edge of the campus was appalling.

Dad's solution to the problem was to form a Water Supply District in which the Yellow Spring was preempted by legal action as a source of water for the village. The surrounding watershed was preempted along with it to protect the spring. The entire property was condemned for this purpose and bonds were issued to buy the land.

This saved the Glen, but not the plumbing. Water from the huge spring was piped into the village and stained all the fixtures bright orange. Later the Glen was purchased for the college by Hugh Taylor Birch and named Glen Helen, after Birch's daughter. Then Yellow Springs village found a source of nice, non-yellowing water.

As I said before, I was bitten by the radio bug, and wanted to build myself a radio. You couldn't buy radios then, and the Dayton paper ran a radio column, telling how to build a radio in easy stages. Jessie clipped this column and pasted the clippings in a scrapbook for me. That was my bible. I took a galena crystal out of my rock collection to use as a detector, wound a coil of old bell wire on an empty oatmeal box and fashioned alligator clips from bits of tin and rubber bands. For an antenna I salvaged some old telephone wire and for insulators used porcelain cleats of the kind used by electricians in "knob and tube" wiring, salvaged from the old wiring at the college. The only parts I actually bought were headphones, a variable condenser, and a couple of little fixed condensers.

I stretched an antenna 100 feet long, high above the housetop, between two tall oak trees, and brought a lead in from one end, down through the window, to my room on the third floor. It worked! With no electrical connection and no tubes or batteries, it brought in Atlanta, Kansas City, Chicago, Detroit, Pittsburgh, Schenectady and lots of closer stations. A friend of mine, with a similar set, tuned in Ft. Worth. The signals were clear but generally faint. I would listen late at night when everything was still. My hearing became sharp. My usual aim was to tune in new stations—the further away the better. Sometimes, just as the announcer gave the call letters, a car would honk in the distance or a dog would bark, and I'd lose it.

There were only a few radio broadcasting stations in those days, and most of their listeners were radio amateurs who had built their own sets. But the manufacture of receivers was starting and was clearly destined to become an industry. Some time later, commercial sets appeared which could actually be listened to without head phones. These sets even had knobs marked VOLUME. What a silly idea, I thought. How could any set possibly have enough volume?

After using my crystal set for a time, I built another set using a small vacuum tube which ran off a couple of dry cells. This made the reception a little stronger. I installed this one in Jessie's apartment and did my listening there, where she and my grandmother could share it. The high point with that set came when I tuned in a performance of *The Pirates of Penzance*. I had never heard of Gilbert & Sullivan, and was entranced by *The Pirates*.

Exploring for interesting activities, remunerative or otherwise, I conceived the notion of a wintertime furnace route. For people who liked their furnaces tended early in the morning, I would come before daylight, take out the ashes and clinkers and stoke the fires. Coal was king in those days. I tended hot air, hot water, and steam furnaces. It was a good professional activity.

As spring came on, my thoughts turned to gardening, but now I had no land. So I hunted up elderly widows and others with garden plots they couldn't manage, and made deals with them to work their gardens, they to have the privilege of gathering what they might need for their own use. I lined up six gardens, had them plowed and harrowed, and then planted them. At the appropriate time I developed a regular route, peddling the produce from door to door.

Early that summer my Aunt Jessie died, and Dad and Lucy thought it would be good for me to get away for a time. It happened that Frank Slutz, of Moraine Park School, and two other men whom we knew well, were starting a summer camp for boys, Camp Wanaki, on the shore of Cass Lake in northern Minnesota. They offered me a special rate to attend the opening session. They said my being there would help establish the kind of atmosphere they wanted. I willingly agreed to go.

But what about my responsibility for those six gardens? I hunted around and found an Antioch freshman who was in town for the summer, and recruited him to take over the gardens. I charged him $20 for the project; a reasonable figure—if he knew how to garden. Without thinking I assumed that everybody knew how to garden. But this poor fellow didn't, and Lucy told me afterward that he had a hard time.

I headed for Camp Wanaki clad in white duck trousers. Those were the days of steam locomotives, and I arrived in gray ducks. Camp was fun; we hiked, canoed, and did all the usual things. I threw a rope over the limb of a giant pine tree and hauled myself up to install an antenna for the crystal radio receiver which I had brought along.

My most striking experience there occurred one day when three of us were out on Cass Lake in a canoe. A static condition developed in the air, and our hair all stood on end. (I had lots of hair then.) We scooped water out of the lake and plastered our hair down, but in a few moments, hair by hair, it would pull loose and stand on end again.

At the close of camp I was picked up by my cousin Grace Morgan Lawson and her husband, who were on a camping trip. They took me with them to visit other cousins. It was a pleasant trip, but there was one incident that particularly sticks in my mind. I caught a large snapping turtle—a real big one. I just reached down in the water and grabbed him by the shell with both hands.

Now, I thought, we'll have turtle steak and turtle soup. So I chopped off his head. Imagine my astonishment when he started calmly walking away. Then I took my big scout knife and started to dig him out of his shell, but no—he reached up with one foot and pushed the knife away. All this was happening with no head. He finally died, and we cooked him. Surprisingly, the front end tasted like chicken, the back end like fish.

As the summer drew to a close and the camping episode ended, my cousins dropped me in St. Cloud, where I was to take the train for Ohio. There they left me with Stewart Graves and his family, where I would encounter snapping turtles once again.

The Graves family have been friends of our family for a century or more. Stewart's father and my maternal grandfather had a business in St. Cloud, around the turn of the century, constructing farm sleds.

Stewart had volunteered during World War I and had seen action in France. A French war orphan, Charles, had been taken in as mascot by

Stewart's outfit. At the end of the war Stewart Graves brought him home and adopted him. I had just turned seventeen when I visited them, and Charles was about twelve.

Charles and I went for a hike along the Mississippi. Years before, following Urania's death, my father had sat on a bluff overlooking the river near St. Cloud and written me a long and thoughtful letter, to be opened when I was older. I located that very bluff and sat there for a time, thinking of my father and meditating on life, while Charles waited patiently.

Then we resumed our hike along the river and presently came onto a deposit of snapping turtle eggs, just starting to hatch. The eggs were round, slightly smaller than ping pong balls, and with leathery shells. There was a huge cache of them buried in the sand. As they hatched, the babies would dig their way out of the sand and head downhill for the river.

Because the eggs were round, the baby snappers were all humped up when they emerged, and their stomach plates were separated in the middle, with their intestines and other innards bulging out in a clump which they dragged along as they walked. This was distinctly gruesome. As I learned later, these organs retract into the turtle in two or three days, as the little creatures straighten out. Then their stomach plates close and they look like proper turtles.

Charles and I dug up the turtle eggs and divided them between us. I took mine in a basket when I got on the train for Ohio. As usual I had an upper berth. It was a warm night, and the eggs started to hatch. The little turtles, with their sharp claws, climbed out of the basket, dragging their intestines with them, crawled round my berth and dropped down to entertain my neighbor in the berth below. A new variety of bedbug? Some found their way to the floor. The Pulman Porter picked them up all over the car and brought them back to me.

Home at last in Yellow Springs, I put my turtles in an appropriate tank which provided both land and water. Every now and then one or two would manage to climb out. One crawled over the edge of the stairwell (my room was on the third floor) and bounced all the way down into the front hall, just as guests were arriving. On one or two occasions one of them found its way to Lucy's lily pond, much to her distress. She was sure it would eat her goldfish. So I released them in the Yellow Springs brook.

Ernest at age 16, with brother Griscom and sister Frances—and dog Stikeen.

7

RITES OF PASSAGE

It is a custom, among Australian aborigines, for a boy in his teens to leave home for a few months on a Walkabout, during which he lives off the land and makes his way in the world. Then, no longer a child, he returns home and relates to his family as a young adult. In my own family, for at least five generations, we have followed a similar practice. In this chapter I record the experiences of these generations, with major attention given to my own.

Once, in the mid-nineteenth century, when my grandfather John Morgan and his older brother Squire were in their teens, they were in the woods in southern Indiana not far from Cincinnati, splitting rails. Squire was restless.

"John," he said, "let's go to Minnesota." Minnesota was the popular frontier at the time.

"All right," said John. "We'll leave next week."

"That's too long to wait," said Squire.

"Very well. We'll leave tomorrow."

"Why not right now?"

"All right. Wait till I knock out this wedge."

"Oh, leave the old wedge there."

So the boys went back to the house, collected a few things, and set off for Minnesota where they wound up in St. Cloud. The story of their adventures has no place here except to suggest that their urge to go—and their act of going—were normal and constructive functions of growing up.

My father followed the same pattern. At age nineteen he improvised a log raft which he navigated down the Mississippi to Minneapolis. There he left the river and headed for Colorado. Enroute, and while in Colorado, he worked as a farm hand, coal miner (narrowly escaping death in a mine cave-in), typesetter, beekeeper, lumberjack, vegetable gardener, and would-be bookseller. He attended the University of Colorado for six weeks but dropped out because of eye problems—and lack of money. That six-week period was his only college education. Returning home as a young adult he went to work with his father, rapidly mastering the skills of a surveyor.

My own experience, while parallel, was very different, probably because my father knew and understood the need. He asked, as I was graduating from high school, if I would like to work with the U.S. Forest Service in Colorado for the summer.

That suited me fine. We recruited two other boys, Harry and Seth, and set off by train along with Dad, who was scheduled to receive an honorary degree from the University of Colorado at Boulder. Since he had attended the university briefly as a boy, they now saw fit to honor him with a doctorate.

I had never seen the Rockies before, and my first glimpse of them was early in the morning, from my Pulman window. For an instant I thought they must be clouds, those jagged, snow-covered, peaks in the sky.

We arrived in the midst of a flood and the track up ahead was washed out. A passing motorist saw this and observed the headlight of the approaching train. Quickly he took off his shirt, dipped it in his gas tank, lit it, and flagged down the train. So the train backed up, switched to a different line, and wound up in Cheyenne, Wyoming. It was evening, Dad had to be in Boulder the next morning, and the rail lines to Boulder were washed out.

After some inquiry we found a man with a Packard automobile who agreed to drive us through, and off we went through the downpour. Presently we came to a bridge completely under water. The swift black current not only covered the bridge, but the approaches to it. Only the railings of the bridge were showing. On a bit of high ground near the bridge stood a man in boots and slicker holding a lantern, stationed there to keep an eye on the bridge and warn motorists in case it washed out. We paused to ask if it were safe. He said it was. Then he cut loose with a stream of profanity directed at the weather. In the midst of this he checked himself: "I hope there are no ladies present." From the depths of the back seat Dad spoke up, in a high falsetto. "Just one." We pulled into Boulder at three in the morning and a few hours later watched Dad receive his degree.

The flood had not come to Boulder. Driving through the city with Dad the next day, I noticed where the river, flowing out of the mountains, passed through the town in a narrow, walled-in channel.

"Aren't they going to have a flood here?" I asked Dad.

"Yes, they are."

"Shouldn't you tell them?"

"No. They would just resent me as a trouble maker. After they've had the flood they'll send for me."

Years later I asked Dad, "Has Boulder had its flood yet?"

"No," he said, "and they aren't going to. They are now protected by Boulder Dam."

Harry, Seth and I went to work high in the mountains, stripping bug timber. A patch of timber was infected by an insect whose larvae burrowed into the bark and killed the trees. Loggers felled the trees and our job was to sit on the trunks with draw knives and strip off the bark.

The terrain was interesting, especially the beaver dams, of which there were several. These were remarkable creations, skillfully engineered. But we never saw the beavers; apparently they worked at night.

The social structure of the camp was surprising. The men were mostly floaters. Every night they had a big poker game. My impression was that the Rangers were the best players and managed to keep the workmen broke so they had to stay on the job.

Meanwhile, the Morgan Engineering Company was engineering a flood control project for the city of Pueblo, Colorado, having rewritten the Colorado engineering laws in the process. Dad's partner, Carl Bock, was on the job full time as chief engineer and took us three boys under his wing. When the bug timber job wound up he drove us to a construction site.

A dam was being built in the desert to catch the runoff from the mountain snow and hold it for irrigation. We went to the construction office and hired in as mule drivers. Then we went to the bunk house where we found three unoccupied bunks and left our duffles.

Outside the door sat a man on a nail keg beside a big cactus, smoking a pipe. We asked him where the toilet was. Very deliberately he took the pipe from his mouth. "Oh, out there," he said, indicating the whole horizon in a slow, sweeping gesture with his pipe.

Then we went to the mess hall. Such food! Two or three kinds of meat, vegetables, different fruit juices to choose from, several kinds of pie. Wow! I learned that the men who commonly frequent outdoor type construction jobs—at least in those days—had three major interests in life: women, booze and food—but most especially food. Give them fancy food and they won't quibble about such trifles as dust and filth and alkali water, not to mention a total absence of music, reading matter, and intellectual fellowship.

A favorite activity of western farm-hands in those days was doing rope tricks. A group of these men, during a moment of leisure, were trying the only rope trick I knew—throwing a half-hitch over a post, and they were doing it wrong. So I demonstrated it, sending the loop flying down the rope and around the post. That was a proud moment.

At dusk we returned to the bunk house. Reaching into the bunk where my duffle was, my hand came against the bottom of the bunk above. It was covered with flies. That was no place to sleep, so we decided to move out into the desert. Then we remembered where the "toilet" was. Accordingly we walked a good long distance from camp before spreading our beds on the sand. Aside from stepping on a cactus with my bare foot, all went well.

In the morning we packed up our duffles, hid them in the sagebrush and reported for work. Each of us was given a dump wagon drawn by three mules. Throwing a half hitch is easy, but harnessing three mules in a span— that's complicated business. I was lost and so were my two companions. Finally, with the help of the foreman, we hitched up and joined the great circle of wagons at the dam.

I'll never forget that sight. There was a giant team of forty or fifty horses and mules drawing a big machine. Scattered evenly over this team, on the backs of some of the animals, were drivers, each driver responsible for one section of the team. In the center of the machine was a huge plow and scoop device which lifted sand and dirt from the ground and pushed it onto a moving belt which carried it sideways, pouring it out in a steady stream. Each dump wagon, in turn, would swing under this brown Niagara of dirt to get a load, then swing out and join the procession headed up the dam.

If this wasn't done just right the dirt would miss the wagon—or land on the driver. Or the team's harness would get tangled with one of the harnesses of the big team. After we got a load we joined the wagon procession up and across the dam, where a man would give the signal to dump. Then, as the wagon started down the dam, at the far end a man would stick a "sprag" in the left rear wheel. This was a block of wood hanging on a chain from the side of the wagon, which stopped the wheel from turning and braked the descent. At the bottom the team stopped and backed up a few steps to let the sprag drop out, then the whole process started over again. Actually, the driver didn't have to remember this, as the mules knew, and backed up routinely to release the sprag. To make life even more interesting, the alkali water caused us a slight diarrhea. Taken all together the job was a real challenge.

After supper that evening I got together with Seth, but we couldn't find Harry. Finally we went to our duffles in the sagebrush. Harry's duffle was gone and we found a note. "This is too much. I'm off for home."

Seth and I reported for work the next morning and were given our teams. In my anxiety I had apparently been pushing my mules too hard, for this time I was given a span of four. Now it was even harder to swing under that stream of dirt without getting the harness tangled.

When we reported back for work after lunch, the foreman said, "Go to the Commissary, and ask for George." We went, and asked for George.

"You've come for your money?" he asked. Yes, we guessed we had.

We were ashamed to be seen leaving, so after collecting our duffles, we sneaked down into an arroyo—a desert gully with vertical walls, in this case ten or twelve feet high. Thus concealed, we left the camp.

After walking in the arroyo for a suitable distance, we found a lateral gully and climbed out. All around was desert. In the distance we saw smoke. Assuming there were people there, we started hiking. It was a hot afternoon and our progress toward the smoke was slow. After awhile our canteens were empty, and we got thirsty. Then we found a clear little brook flowing—out there in the desert. We scooped up some water—then spit it out. Alkali!

At about dusk we reached the smoke—almost. It was on the other side of a big river, the Arkansas, across which was a railway trestle. On our side was a stone quarry with a narrow gauge railway track in it. Beside the track was an open pipe, with clear water gushing out. I cupped my hands to catch some and got a sharp electric shock. Looking down the track a ways I saw where a trolley line had fallen on the pipe.

We camped there overnight, and in the morning crossed over on the trestle to the town on the other side, and went to a store. The store wouldn't cash our paychecks, and we had only some small change which we used to buy flour. Back at our camping place we scrubbed out an old can, mixed flour and water, and cooked it over an open fire. Then we ate the paste, joking about it all the while. Later we managed to cash our checks.

We knew that another Forest Service job was due to open up soon, so I dropped a line to Dad, who was in Pueblo at the time, to let us know when to come. In the meantime I got a job in a cement mill near where we were camped. Being almost 18, I was able to pass for 21, but Seth, a little younger, couldn't get by. He had to cool his heels in our camping place while I worked, which was pretty hard on him.

That cement mill was a formidable place. The noise level—a steady roar —was so loud that to speak to someone you had to get close to his ear and shout. The total impact was one of dense silence. The air was filled with dust, like a heavy fog. I was offered a dust mask (possibly as required by law) which I accepted and wore, though no one else was wearing one. Breathing was work, and every now and then I would rinse the cement dust out of the sponge in my mask. My job was to sweep and shovel up the dust that constantly fell to the floor. The whole thing was a good experience—as a short interlude.

Each day I hurried to the post office, hoping for word from Dad. Days passed, and none came. Then, to my astonishment, I met him on the street. I had flubbed: there were two cement mill towns not far apart, one was named Cement, the other, Concrete. I had thought we were in Cement, and wrote Dad to address me there. Actually, we were in Concrete so his reply didn't reach us. He got worried when I failed to respond, and came to Cement, finding my mail there unclaimed. On an off chance he went to Concrete, just looking around, and saw me on the street.

I quit at the cement mill and Dad took us to our next assignment, which was to start in a few days. A crew of four was to build a horseback trail up to and above timberline in the Sangre de Cristo Mountains. Seth and I set up camp in the mountains not far from a small resort hotel run by an English family.

The folks that ran that hotel knew Dad who had been up there occasionally. They had read an article by him in the *Atlantic Monthly* in which he projected a future in which human wisdom and well-being would prevail.

"So," they said, "Arthur Morgan is going to raise a race of angels, is he?" Then, when I showed up, they added, "And here's the first sample." Accordingly, for the rest of the summer I was known as "Angel." Of all the nicknames I have worn, that was perhaps the least appropriate.

Waiting for the trail-building project to start, Seth and I fraternized with the young people at the hotel. One evening Dad dropped in for a visit. I was dancing with a daughter of the owner of the resort. During a pause in the dancing he said, "Are you particularly interested in that girl?"

"No," I said. "Why do you ask?"

"Because," he replied, "I think she's starting to get ideas."

That jolted me, and with my eyes opened I could observe for myself. Dancing and chatting, sure. But romance? No way. I'd never been in that spot before. I didn't want to hurt the girl's feelings, but I sure didn't want any misunderstandings either. My defense, I'm sorry to say, was a bit juvenile; I took to being mildly rude.

Happily, our expedition headed out within another day or so. Two men, two boys, and two horses loaded down with equipment and supplies. I led a horse, carrying among other things, fifty pounds of explosives which bumped occasionally against the trees along the narrow trail.

Hours passed as we got higher and higher, and the air got thinner and thinner. Seth and I were breathing hard and started to get lightheaded. Everything began to strike us as uproariously funny, and we went up the trail panting and laughing hysterically in the afternoon rain. After awhile this wore off, and we made camp at about ten thousand feet, not far below timberline.

We soon adapted to the thin air and were working with picks and shovels, rolling rocks out of the way, blasting trees out of the ground, shattering big boulders with explosive charges of TNT, and building switchbacks. It was satisfying work.

The four of us took turns cooking. I realized that I needed more knowledge in this, so I sent a letter to Dad, asking him to send me a cookbook. In time it came; Fanny Farmer's Boston Cookbook.

If you ever plan to cook in a workcamp at ten thousand feet, don't get Fanny Farmer's Boston Cookbook. It assumes that you have a regular kitchen at your disposal with all the appropriate supplies and equipment. Worst of all, it assumes that water boils at 212 degrees Fahrenheit. At ten thousand feet water boils when it's a little more than warm and won't cook anything. You have to bake or fry everything. After one or two tries, I put Fanny Farmer in my duffle bag. (Later it gave my family good service for fifty years.)

I loved the high camp. Marmots would whistle at us from under the rock slides. We saw deer. On still nights we would sometimes hear big rocks crashing down those slides, dislodged by the geological movement of a rising mountain range. On weekends we hiked, and climbed the snow banks. We caught trout in the mountain lake. We made beds of evergreen boughs, on which we slept soundly. I loved the mountains, the work, the adventure.

Back in Yellow Springs after the strenuous summer, I had a few days to spare before the fall season opened at Antioch. Dad was helping with my college expenses, but I needed a little more money, so I took a contract to dig a ditch for a waterline at twenty-five cents a foot.

To help me with this I drafted a friend of mine, a boy who owed me some money. Together we tackled the hard, dry clay. But his grandmother objected. He might hurt himself doing that hard work. She told him to quit. He said he couldn't, and she asked why not.

"Because I owe money to Ernie Morgan."

So she paid off the debt and pulled him out of the ditch.

I have mentioned briefly my grandfather's and my father's Rites of Passage and have recounted my own at length. My children also followed the pattern, which I tell about in a later chapter.

Climbing a glacier in the Rockies.

Building horseback trail.

8

MY COLLEGE YEARS

Looking back, my six years at Antioch brought a tumultuous mix of ideas, ideals, community action, and challenging work. Besides a strong academic life, there was college journalism, student insurgency, a broken romance, international outreach, exciting job involvement and a shift of careers. It is hard for me to believe how much was packed into those six years; this is a long chapter.

In 1923, with high school and my summer of work in Colorado behind me, I plunged happily into college life. What a change that was.

My freshman classes opened windows onto a new world, calling for intense concentration and study. Campus life, too, brought challenges—not all of them positive. Understandably, some students and faculty members brought with them customs and habits from other colleges. Much of the enthusiasm in those early years found expression in old, conventional ways: athletics, rah-rah, hazing.

This tendency was encouraged by the fact that, during its first couple of years, the new Antioch did enjoy some athletic glory. My friend Russ Stewart was a brilliant tennis player and had for a teammate Walter Rutnam (the handsome, dark-skinned tennis champion of Ceylon), who had enrolled at Antioch. They gave a good account of themselves at intercollegiate matches.

More spectacular was the basketball team. Two pairs of brothers, the Dawsons and the Northups, who had played together through their years at the Antioch Academy, entered the college together. They were tall, athletic boys with teamwork so incredibly swift and accurate that one would think they practiced mental telepathy. When blocked by a five-man defense, Clyde

Dawson would stand calmly in the center of the floor, take careful aim, and shoot a basket without touching the rim. Then, of course, the stands went wild. I don't think they ever lost a game.

Obnoxious to me was the practice of hazing, which had been imported from other colleges. The freshmen were compelled to wear green caps and were paddled and subjected to a variety of indignities and humiliations. Most freshmen lived for the day when they would themselves be sophomores and could pass along the abuse.

As a freshman myself I went to the president of the sophomore class and protested the green cap rule. He made an eloquent case for it, explaining that it helped the freshmen to know each other. I agreed with him and said I would support the rule if it were submitted to the freshmen for a vote. However, unless the freshmen themselves voted for it, I wouldn't be caught dead wearing a green cap. The issue was never submitted to the freshmen and remained strictly a rule imposed by the sophomores. I never wore a green cap.

Dad took a sensible position on hazing. He said that hazing was OK if it was fun for both sides. True to form, in an assembly talk he recited a limerick:

> *There was a young lady from Siam*
> *Who said to her lover named Priam*
> *To kiss me, of course*
> *You will have to use force*
> *But the Lord knows you're stronger than I am.*

Hazing was *not* fun for both sides. It was later abolished by the joint efforts of the students and the college administration. One of my friends, Harris Peckham, got himself appointed editor of the *A Book* (the Antioch Student Handbook), for the specific purpose of ending hazing. In the *A Book* he proclaimed that hazing was out at Antioch.

The Administration took a parallel course. They substituted three freshman/sophomore athletic contests which channelled sophomore aggressiveness in a more acceptable direction. As a sophomore I took part in all three. One was a football game. More unusual was a sack rush, in which a lot of bags of sawdust were piled in the middle of the football field, opposing teams lined up at opposite ends of the field and ran for the sacks when a pistol was fired. The sophomores devised a winning strategy. Our biggest, fastest men dashed ahead past the sacks and rolled at the feet of the approaching "frosh," who landed in a big pile while the smaller sophomore men lugged away most of the sacks.

The third event was the most fun of all. We stretched a big rope across the canal above Grinnell's Mill, with ten men on either side. On a given signal we all began furiously digging in, preparing footholds. Then we all lay down on the rope, with our left feet anchored in the footholds and the rope passing under our right arms. At the next shot we began to heave. Each team had a cox'n, a man who chanted the signals—"catch, catch, heave; catch, catch, heave"—waving his arms in time with his calls, so that the team would all pull together.

Here again we had a strategy which gave us victory. By prearrangement we pretended to be pulling while our cox'n was exhorting us to greater efforts. Actually we were just lying on the rope. Then the freshmen took a turn at pulling while we held firm. Then we pretended again. Finally, when the freshmen were tired, we really started to pull and dragged them through the canal.

Athletic contests successfully replaced hazing and were more in line with Dad's ideas. In a few years even the inter-class contests were abandoned.

My first five weeks on campus were soon past and I went to my first co-op job. In those days the alternating periods of work and study at Antioch were five weeks long—not three months, as they are today.

At that stage of my life I was planning to be a civil engineer like my father and grandfather before me. So the college placed me on a construction job. It turned out to be the construction of the O'Shaughnesy Dam, on the Scioto River, north of Columbus. Ten young Antioch men went to that job together.

Before we left, Lucy expressed to me her satisfaction that my character was sufficiently formed that I could go into a rough environment like that without being harmed. I soon found out what she meant. The construction camp was an assemblage of tarpaper shacks. The recreation center was a pool hall lined with slot machines. The main interests of the men outside of working hours seemed to be drinking, gambling, fighting, and sex. Interestingly, the young Antioch men seemed neither shocked nor influenced by this environment.

I was struck by the contrast between this camp and the model villages I had known on my father's construction jobs. A dramatic illustration of this contrast was the accident rate. During the five weeks I was on the O'Shaughnessy job there were two fatal accidents, in a work force of seventy men. In Dad's flood control project at Dayton, employing thousands of men for six years, there were half a dozen fatal accidents altogether.

At the O'Shaughnessy I was probably in the top physical condition of my life. Eighteen years old, six feet tall, and tough as nails from a summer of strenuous work, I was ready for anything. One evening I had a wrestling match with one of my Antioch colleagues, an athletic fellow considerably bigger than me. By strength and skill, spiced with a little jujitsu, I easily threw him three times in a row. Another, and somewhat disreputable contest was to decide who could eat the most at one sitting. My rival and I weighed in before supper and weighed out after. He took on three and a half pounds, I four and three quarters. He was ill and couldn't go to work in the morning. I merely skipped breakfast and carried on as usual.

One tough guy, not an Antiochian, was bragging while we worked, about the men he could lick. Without thinking I paused for a moment, regarding him as I leaned on my shovel. Suddenly his eye caught me. "Oh! Not you!" he exclaimed.

The foremen put me on the heaviest jobs. There was a tower housing two giant concrete mixers which dumped their loads into big buckets that were carried out over the dam by a system of cables. Bags of cement were carried up this tower in an elevator, one ton at a time. It was my job to unload this elevator. On one busy day I did that 62 times. (My memory says 162, but I don't believe that.) One night a special crew was assembled to handle a giant hose to flush loose rock and dirt from the base of a new section of the dam. I was chosen to guide the nozzle.

The young men from Antioch were well appreciated on that job. Toward the end of the work period a foreman asked me, "You're going back to college next week?"

"That's right."

"Will another bunch be coming out?"

"Very likely. I don't know."

"Tell them I'll take five."

I think that the co-op jobs of most Antioch students—especially during the early part of their college careers—were also Rites of Passage, serving a vital function in the emergence of their adult personalities. This gave them a tremendous advantage in life over students whose education had been largely confined to the academic sphere.

Back on campus once more, I could hardly believe it. Suddenly, no more roaring machinery, shouting men, and violent exertions. With the shady campus, neat buildings, and orderly classrooms, the rough and ready construction job faded into a dream.

The educational philosophy of the new Antioch called for the development of the whole person. Whether we were majoring in Engineering or Business or Education, we all studied English and Math and Science, including Earth Science. We learned how to work, how to keep a personal budget, and how to take care of our health. We were taught History, Psychology, and an appreciation of aesthetic values. Sociology, Ethics, and Life Aims came under review. The world of ideas opened up.

Gradually a new movement developed at Antioch—of students and staff who had been attracted by Arthur Morgan's challenge and were trying to give it expression. They were actively seeking to develop new value patterns and new ways of doing things, but it was a slow process. For a considerable period Dad and Lucy had open house Thursday evenings for students who wanted to sit around the fireplace and visit with them. I remember these meetings well. The students who showed up each week seemed to be ones who were challenged by Dad's ideas but hadn't yet found the creativity they had hoped for.

One of these, a close friend of mine, was Horace Champney, a son of Anarchist parents, who frequently found himself in conflict with the prevalent habits and mores of the college community. The college administration wanted to get rid of him, but Dad objected, saying the college needed such people.

In 1925 Horace became editor of the college weekly newspaper, the *Antiochian*. In it he published an attack on intercollegiate football at Antioch. This sport was a disaster there because the five week shifts wrought havoc with the training schedule. We lost virtually every game, and our men, being half-trained, were commonly carried from the field on stretchers. Horace's attack was scathing, but he leaned over backwards, printing it as a letter to the editor.

When that letter appeared, a copy of it was nailed to a tree in front of the Main Building with a message scrawled above it, "Are we going to stand for this sort of thing at Antioch?" Horace was paddled, ducked in a horse trough, and forced to resign as editor of the paper.

His response was to get his friends together and start an unofficial college magazine, the *Blaze*. The little group which had initially met at the Morgans' on Thursdays had migrated to the living room of the Chatterjee family next door. We called ourselves "The League of Youth," which we borrowed from the book, *Courage*, by J. M. Barrie, of *Peter Pan* fame, in which he calls upon youth to help create a new world. Some others on the Antioch campus had a different name for our group: "The Dying Intellectuals." It was this group that launched the *Blaze* as a guerrilla journal. Dad contributed money and occasional articles.

The *Blaze* printed poetry and prose; it indulged in satire; it debated education, philosophy, religion, morals, ethics, and politics. It carried out Dad's dictum, "Ask questions. Ask *all* questions." In a sense the *Blaze* and the movement it represented became a sort of nether millstone, with Dad functioning as the upper millstone, grinding away at Antioch to make it a more creative institution. Our magazine survived through thirty issues over a period of seven years.

I was active in the *Blaze* almost from its inception. One of the concerns which I repeatedly ventilated was the status of women. The women I had known in my childhood were strong, well-educated, and outspoken. They related to men as equals. When I was a boy, Lucy joked that she and I were having a race, to see who would get to vote first (happily, she won). As I grew older I took a dim view of the conventional male ego, which I regarded as stuffy. I was also displeased by the way women commonly found it necessary to adapt to this and how they encouraged and exploited it with "feminine wiles." I wrote articles arguing that women should have equal social initiative with men—and should pay their share of the expenses on dates.

Sometimes the *Blaze* got us into hot water. On one occasion a black student, inquiring about admission, was told that in view of his qualifications he would almost certainly be accepted if he applied. According to reports, however, he was told also that the college would appreciate it if he didn't apply, as they were having a hard struggle to survive and this would add another issue. So he didn't apply.

We got wind of this, and one of us wrote an article, "Ideals When They Hurt," leading off with a quotation from Antioch's first president, Horace Mann: "Antioch College shall stand, always, a place where neither sex, color, nor creed shall ever bar young people from an education."

Dad was away when all this was going on, and Lucy urged that we hold up publication until his return. She said I would be stabbing him in the back. Our family went through whole meals in strained silence. The college administration tried to stop us too, but we were stubborn; I don't know why we were in such a hurry. We gave Lucy some space for response, but that wasn't much help. The *Nation* picked up our story and gave it national circulation, and it did cost the college at least one substantial gift. But Dad never complained, and, ultimately, Antioch accepted black students on an equal basis with whites.

On another occasion we published a lead article in which a Chinese student reported on his co-op experience. It made the co-op employer look bad. To embarrass the college with one of its co-op employers could be awkward, so we were called before the Publications Committee and charged with being irresponsible. We turned the tables on the Committee by asking if any of them (all were students) had seen anything wrong with the article when it appeared. None had.

In the *Blaze,* Horace Champney criticized Antioch's Student Government. He argued that it meant very little. He proposed that it be abolished and replaced with a Community Government which would involve students, faculty, and administrative personnel. Such a government would exercise substantial responsibility in the life of the college. He urged furthermore that ordinary voting be replaced with proportional representation, using the Hare System.

After a year or so of agitation and discussion, Community Government took the place of Student Government, and proportional representation was adopted. A full time Community Manager (a student) was employed and a broad area of campus life came under Community Government management. This innovation proved a great success and has continued ever since.

In time the *Blaze* organization broadened its scope. One committee ran the magazine, another kept a special bulletin board posted with clippings of important current events, another organized informal social affairs (folk dances, steak roasts, etc.), another conducted forums. A political committee recruited candidates to run for Community Council, not neccesarily "*Blaze* people" but any community members who seemed solid and responsible. They usually got elected.

Eventually, Horace Champney himself was chosen as Community Manager. The revolution had apparently prevailed. The *Blaze* people quietly took over the campus and the student newspaper. The *Blaze* itself was no longer needed so, also quietly, it came to an end.

The new Antioch seemed to be coming of age. Along with the quiet social revolution which had already taken place on the campus, the Great Depression had set in. This had a strong influence on the students that came to Antioch. No longer did they come with the rah-rah, Joe College mentality. They tended to be more serious young people, concerned with social and educational issues.

The *Blaze* was not the only guerrilla journal which appeared at Antioch. There was also the *Turret*, the *Blasé* (a takeoff on the *Blaze*), and the *Nonsensor,* started by Walter Kahoe.

Dad had remarked to Walter once that humor could be a powerful instrument for change and Walter, being a person of lively humor himself, decided to give it a whirl. He conceived the name of the magazine as a three-way pun: nonsense, noncensored, and nonsensory. It was devoted to humor, satire, and poetry. Carried on mainly by student printers, the magazine went through a number of issues.

It was during this period that a friend of ours, George Adshead, committed suicide. George drowned himself in the Little Miami River, about a mile from Yellow Springs. His body was discovered some weeks later. Dad was away from the house at the time, so I was called to help identify the body. A number of people had gathered at the river. The body, partly decomposed, was barely identifiable. An officious young man in a business suit was excitedly asking questions and making notes.

I took this young man for a newspaper reporter looking for clues for a murder story and refused to cooperate. He threatened to arrest me, and I realized that he was the coroner and gave him what information I could, though I did not like his attitude at all.

It happened that at this very time we were bringing out an issue of the *Nonsensor.* By way of variety, it was to be in tabloid form, and done on pink newsprint. In my resentment against the coroner I wrote a scathing story about him which I put on the front page under a big scare headline, "MURDER VERDICT NOT FOUND." Luckily a friend, somewhat older and wiser than I, came into the shop just as we were starting to print. He convinced me of my folly and bad taste, and we stopped the press. I quickly wrote another story to fill the space.

An aspect of those early years at Antioch which I remember happily was participation in college dramatics. Early in the new Antioch, a play-reading group began meeting at the Morgan home. The meetings became regular and in time blossomed into performances under the leadership of Imogene Putnam, a talented faculty wife.

They called themselves The Antioch Players and got the use of the Yellow Springs Opera House, owned by Miami Township, in which the village is located. That Opera House was a priceless resource. The auditorium seated 350 people and the acoustics were wonderful. The stage was deep, had wide wings and was surmounted by a lofty grid equipped with a network of ropes and pulleys. It was a stage manager's dream. I appeared now and then in minor parts, but it was in stage managing that I found the greatest excitement and challenge.

I once built a set which called for brown tree trunks beneath a leafy green drop. To make these, I spread long strips of white muslin on newspapers, and stained them brown. To my dismay the muslin stuck to the newspaper, and proceeded to wrinkle and curl. But it worked out wonderfully. The curl was just right to give the effect of tree trunks, and the wrinkles made a convincing representation of bark. I turned them over, trimmed them to tree like profiles, stained the backs and suspended them from the grid. They were the best stage trees I ever saw. If I had done all this on purpose it would have been brilliant.

An even greater challenge came later. The Players, in conjunction with the Music Department, decided to put on a Gilbert & Sullivan opera. "If you put on *The Pirates,* I'll stage it," I told them. Actors were plentiful, but stage managers were in short supply, so *The Pirates of Penzance* it was.

I spent about 150 hours on that show. My greatest triumph was the opening set, on "The Rocky Coast of Cornwall." In front of the stage, across the top and down both sides, I built a huge black frame with irregular edges, made of heavy wrapping paper stuck together with gummed tape. When the curtain went up the audience found itself in a huge dark cave, looking out on the sunny, rocky beach where the action takes place, an effect almost as dramatic as the action itself.

With fine mechanical resources to work with my stage crew could change sets so rapidly that the curtain was ready to go up on the next scene almost before the applause subsided. The entire show was a huge success.

About that wonderful Opera House. The neighbors didn't like it because of the parking congestion which occurred on show nights—so they arranged to have it torn down. The greatest regret of my career was my failure to come forward and organize the community to save that priceless resource.

It was during this time, around 1927, that an unusual crisis developed behind the scenes at Antioch. Some new buildings had been built and the cost of heating the buildings had become considerable. Dad got the idea that a small steam power plant could generate electricity, and the exhaust steam could be used to heat the college buildings. Since the village owned its own electric distribution system, it would be possible for it to buy current from Antioch.

When this plan became known, it alarmed the president of the Dayton Power and Light Company, the private utility company that supplied power for the area. He said to Dad, "If you go through with that plan I'll destroy Antioch."

Dad was not easily intimidated, and he went right ahead and built the power plant, locating it in an old stone quarry at the edge of the campus. It had its own railway siding where coal could be unloaded by gravity. The village, activated by self-interest and also by loyalty to the college, terminated its contract with the power company and contracted with the college for power. As it worked out, the savings to the village were roughly comparable to the total local taxes paid by the community.

But the president of the power company wasn't kidding. He set about to destroy Antioch. He proceeded to clip from the *Yellow Springs News* some of my articles which were critical of American industry. These he mailed to friends of C. F. Kettering, who was Antioch's chief benefactor, urging them to pressure Kettering to stop his support of the college. The theme was, "What sort of man is Arthur Morgan, who lets his son bite the hand that feeds the college?"

After a while Kettering told Dad that he was getting so much flack about Antioch that he would have to discontinue his support. When Dad told him where the flack was coming from, however, he *increased* his support. Kettering at that time was Vice-President and Chief Engineer of General Motors. Like Dad, he was a man with a ranging imagination and creativity and not one to be easily pushed around. As in previous cases when my activities had embarrassed the college, Dad respected my independence and never once suggested that I take it easy. Only later did I learn the details of the power plant story.

In 1923, in the course of his travels for Antioch, Dad had met William Edwin Rudge, a famous printer whose shop was in Mt. Vernon, New York. At that time the Printing House of Rudge was winning more awards for beautiful books than any other shop in the world. To be a Rudge apprentice was considered a great privilege. Rudge sold Dad on fine printing, and Dad sold Rudge on Antioch. The result was that Rudge opened up a job in his printshop for a pair of Antioch co-op students.

Dad asked me if I was interested, and Lucy urged me to give it a try. I was still planning a career in engineering, and she pointed out that an engineer's family leads a dog's life because it has to move so often. It was good, she said, to live in one community and put down roots there. My boyhood experiences added weight to her argument. At that point I wasn't contemplating marriage but I felt that by the time I did, it would probably be difficult, if not too late, to change occupations. The time for a decision was now. So I took the co-op job with Rudge.

The student with whom I alternated on that job was Walter Kahoe, founder of the *Nonsensor*, who later became my business partner and life-long friend. Walter's parents, long-time residents of Yellow Springs, were of modest circumstances and education but of fine character and intelligence. His father, Lyle Kahoe, was conductor on the Xenia-Springfield Street Railway, which ran a car through Yellow Springs. Lyle was the last conductor the line had before it went out of business. He was Irish and had a sharp wit and a roguish sense of humor—both of which Walter inherited in generous measure.

The Kahoes' nearest neighbor, seventy-odd years ago, was a highly educated maiden lady, Nellie Lewis, of retiring personality and substantial literary skill. As a child, Walter made her acquaintance. Recognizing the boy's quick mind, Nellie introduced him to the world of ideas and books.

Walter's parents were Catholics. They apparently hoped that he might become a priest, and he served for a time as altar boy in the local church. But Nellie Lewis changed that picture. Walter delved deeply into philosophy, poetry, and history and read books that good Catholics weren't supposed to read. Then he entered Antioch, came into close association with Dad and, in time, married Dad's secretary. He ultimately became a Quaker.

Walter and I alternated at the Printing House of W. E. Rudge for two years, and it changed our lives. For me the change was profound. Gone was the world of rivers and floods, steel and concrete. In its place was a world of art and craftsmanship, books and ideas. Bruce Rogers—possibly the greatest book designer of all time—was at Rudge's. I saw him at work and got to know him well. One Saturday I happened to be in the shop when he came in to set a few lines of type for a book he was working on. In the course of his work he asked me where to find the exclamation point. It didn't seem to bother him at all—the world's greatest designer of printing and a designer of beautiful type as well—to ask a lowly apprentice where to find the exclamation point.

Emboldened by this contact I looked over his shoulder at his work and asked, "What rule do you follow in a case like that?"

He gave an impatient gesture. "Forget the rules. The question is, 'how does it look?' "

Almost as talented as Rogers, though less famous, was James Hendrickson, who became my special friend and mentor. Jim was a wonderful fellow, tall and well-built with a strong, kind face and large, slightly protruding eyes. He had a clear, deep voice. During the winter months he toured with a

Shakespearean troupe lead by the famous actor, Mantell. The rest of the year he worked at Rudge's with Bruce Rogers, designing beautiful books. He told me once that his stage experience made him a better book designer and vice versa.

My friendship with Jim continued until his death, many years after I left Rudge's. Once, while I was still in college, Mantell's Shakespeare troupe came to Columbus. Jim wired me the time and date and the name of the theater. I was on hand for the matinee performance of The Merchant of Venice. I was with Jim in his dressing-room afterwards when the troupe manager stuck his head in the door and said, "Jim, Mantell is ill. Can you do Brutus tonight?" Jim nodded.

Then we went to Jim's hotel room, and his wife read the cue lines to him in a rapid monotone. He in turn recited the appropriate lines, also in a rapid monotone. There was no chance to rehearse. That evening, when the curtain went up on Julius Caesar, Jim was Brutus. As for me, I was dressed as a Roman soldier, carrying a spear. I walked on and off stage as required and helped carry the murdered Caesar.

There came the scene before Phillipi, when Brutus and Cassius are in a bitter argument—almost on the verge of blows. At that instant, Jim forgot his lines. I saw the whole business from the wings, just a few feet away. Cassius leaned toward Brutus in a menacing manner—and whispered the lines to him.

In time the Mantell troupe stopped—but not Jim. He and his wife, Claire Bruce, started their own troupe—performing Shakespeare for schools and colleges with a backdrop and half a dozen actors. I printed their contract forms and recall a clause which specified that ". . . the auditorium shall be lighted and heated." It was a rugged life, but Shakespeare was in Jim's heart. "No matter how badly we play it," he remarked to me once, "you'll have to admit the lines are wonderful."

The Rudge plant was at the edge of Mt. Vernon, just out of New York City. It was in a large, handsome stone building, with its own railway siding. Well-equipped and employing fine craftsmen, it was patronized by the elite. Rudge himself was an impressive personality who promoted beautiful printing almost with a sense of mission. Both his sons became outstanding printers.

Whatever skills I may have acquired or work performed over a long lifetime, the consciousness of being a printer yields me the strongest sense of identity and competence. This, despite the fact that my particular printing skills are now largely obsolete.

My work at Rudge's was mainly concerned with type and proofs—except when I was moving furniture or unloading freight cars. Much of my time there was spent "holding copy" for the proofreader. This consisted of reading aloud from the original copy while the proofreader read the proof for errors. I would read at full speed, pronouncing clearly and including punctuation, paragraphs, italics, and any special capitalization. Imagine being paid for reading all sorts of interesting books and documents. I was reminded of the Irish laborer who said he had the best job of his life; tearing down a Protestant church and getting paid for it.

I followed the adventures of Rockwell Kent in the Antarctic through his words and drawings, and gained insight into the coal industry through the *Coal Trade Journal,* both of which Rudge published; his devotion to fine printing did not prevent him from turning an honest dollar with such ordinary printing or publishing as might come his way.

An incident which occurred in the printshop became a turning point in my learning experience there. Taking advantage of a brief lull in my work, I had set the type for a small job of my own, and had pulled a proof of it. It was poorly done and I had marked it up heavily when the superintendent happened by. Glancing at the proof, he proceeded to scold me for doing such a lousy job.

That was a golden opportunity. "Look, Mr. Duenewald," I said, "I came here to learn printing but because I've got a strong back you've had me moving furniture and unloading freight cars. I'm glad to do that work, but I also want more solid printing experience. How about letting me handle the typesetting on that greeting card project?" There was a moment of thoughtful silence—then he gave me the work I wanted. This greatly helped develop my skill as a printer.

The editor of the *Coal Trade Journal* had left, and one of the Rudge salesmen was keeping it going temporarily. He was hard pressed for copy, so I wrote a story about the burning coal fields in the Hocking Valley and contributed a few items such as editorials, letters to the editor and a review of the book, *The Human Story of Coal.* The author wrote Rudge that he had never read a finer or more perceptive review. Rudge congratulated the salesman who promptly said, "Morgan wrote it." Rudge was surprised, and for the first time took note of the Antioch freshman. That incident was the beginning of an emergent relationship between Rudge and myself, similar in some ways to a father and son relationship, characterized by warm mutual regard and some lively differences of opinion.

One of my tasks was to stuff envelopes for a promotional mailing to a list of Rudge's select customers and prospects. I was skeptical about the effectiveness of the mailing piece, which was quaint, but totally irrelevant. To satisfy my curiosity I wrote to half a dozen of the recipients, asking their opinion. All the responses were enthusiastic except Dad's. The strongest praise came from Bruce Barton, a popular author and advertising executive. He sent my letter, along with a copy of his reply, to Rudge, who came to me in the shop, waving the letters. "*Now* do you believe it?" he exclaimed.

Another exchange with Mr. Rudge occurred in connection with a piece of political printing. The veterans of World War I, of whom there were several million, demanded—and got—a bonus. This involved a large appropriation. Only a few Senators and Congressmen had the temerity to vote against it. Rudge was asked to design and print an "Honor Roll" of those who had voted no.

The job of designing was handed to one of the compositors, John Fass, who did a strikingly beautiful job of it. The customer was delighted and Rudge was told that if enough copies of that document could have been distributed it might have changed the election. Rudge happily passed this information along to me.

Seeing John Fass a little later I remarked, "John, you must be very proud of that Honor Roll job."

"No," he said. "Why?"

"Didn't the boss tell you about all the praise he's been getting?"

"No. He didn't say anything to me."

The next time I saw Rudge I remonstrated, "You never told John Fass what people are saying about the Honor Roll job. Surely a man has some moral equity in his work and deserves to share the psychic rewards."

Rudge took time then and there to "educate" me. It was he as entrepreneur, he said, who made it possible for the craftsmen to do their work. Whatever they created was solely his property. Most of them, he said, had tried to run shops of their own and had failed. These were some of the facts of life I needed to recognize.

That exchange did as much as anything I can remember to make a socialist of me, and I lived to see the day when John Fass was doing fine work in a printshop of his own.

Rudge had a customer with an epileptic son about my age whom he put to work in the plant. He asked me to be the boy's companion, and I did so, arranging for him to have a room where I stayed.

His seizures were violent and fairly frequent. He would suddenly freeze, then fall to the ground (unless I was close enough to catch him). Then his eyes would roll back and he would go into convulsions, gasping and frothing at the mouth. In a little while they would subside, and he would regain consciousness and become normal again. I soon became acclimated to these performances, but the horror expressed by strangers, when he had seizures in public, was most eloquent. The chief hardship that he and I experienced was that our tastes and interests were totally different. He wanted to go to the movies, and I wanted to read.

Once Rudge put me on the spot in quite another way. One of his friends had bought a large, complicated radio set and it didn't work. Rudge told him about a young fellow at the plant, a regular whiz, who had built his own set which was able to tune in Cincinnati. I must go and fix that big radio. I protested in vain that my set was small and simple and that I didn't know the first thing about superheterodynes. They dragged me to the house. I dutifully looked at the set and found that they had connected the battery cables backwards. With that simple detail corrected the set worked perfectly, and my false reputation was preserved.

At Rudge's I met a chap about my own age who was not a regular Rudge employee but who came in from time to time at odd hours to work on a special project. We enjoyed each other's company and one Saturday afternoon when we were alone in the plant we got into a limerick contest. He started it off:

> *My friend Ernest Morgan is young*
> *Which accounts for the length of his tongue*
> *It makes him rejoice*
> *To hear his own voice*
> *And his brain's not a brain, it's a lung.*

I came right back at him:

> *There is a young fellow whose rhymes*
> *Grow rather obnoxious at times.*
> *Till the other chap said*
> *That he ought to be dead*
> *And sizzling in the warmest of climes.*

My friend promptly responded:

> *So the Rhymist descended to Hell*
> *And there he made out very well*
> *The Devil just said*
> *With your verse go ahead*
> *Your rhymes all my torments excel.*

Then it was my turn:

> *Then the Devil, in order to wreak*
> *His vengeance upon this mad freak*
> *Said, "Make me a rhyme*
> *Using 'crinoid' and 'mime'*
> *And your torment no longer I'll seek."*

My opponent came right back:

> *O what is a mime and a crinoid I cry*
> *And opening mine ears I hear the reply:*
> *In the merry springtime*
> *A mime is a mime*
> *And a crinoid is a noid that will cry.*

My turn again:

> *Said old Nick in a voice hoarse and gruff*
> *"Of this rhymster I've had quite enough*

And him I'll expel
From the domains of Hell
For the scoundrel is stealing my stuff."

Then my friend wrapped it up:

So the rhymist in unsettled state
Ascended to Heaven's fair gate,
But St. Peter got sore
And slammed shut the door
And cried, "You've a Hell of a wait!"

The afternoon passed quickly.

While at Rudge's, I had a room with a nice family by the name of Gilroy. The man was a theater organist, an important job in the days of silent films. Now and then he would take me into the theater (for free), and I would sit just behind his bench at the console. What a marvel that organ was—a tremendous instrument with lots of extra sound effects—bells, an automobile horn, and so on. In the basement my friend had a library of organ music. With each film would come a "cue sheet" indicating what kind of music was called for with each part of the film. When a parade came down the street he kept pace with a march tune; in scenes of traffic he would honk the horn now and then. Whatever the action, whether romantic, violent, or nostalgic, he could match the mood on that wonderful organ. Sometimes I miss the "silent" films.

The Gilroys were friendly people but they barely knew the names of the three other families in the apartment house. Their neighbors were strangers. Coming as I did from a small community where we all knew and reached out to each other, this isolation seemed tragic. I learned later that this tends to be typical of cities. People crowded together build invisible walls around themselves to shut each other out.

Mt. Vernon was, indeed, very different from Yellow Springs. On my way home late one night after visiting friends in New York, I left the subway and headed for my room half a dozen blocks away. It was a winter night, but I hadn't bothered with an overcoat, preferring to run to keep warm. I had hardly run a block before a policeman stopped me. Where was I going in such a hurry? I told him about Antioch and the Co-op Plan and my job at Rudge's. So he let me go, albeit somewhat chilled from standing.

One or two more blocks and another cop stopped me. Again the Antioch story and all that. The officer was friendly and walked with me all the way to my house while we chatted. One of my student successors at Rudge's was less fortunate. Perhaps he was less gifted with gab. The police locked him up for the night, removing his necktie and belt so he couldn't hang himself in his cell.

Having ended my employment with Rudge in 1925, my activities were centered on Yellow Springs. That was when I got my first automobile, a 1920 Ford (the famous Model T).

Now and then, at slow speed, the front wheels of that car would shimmy violently from side to side, and I'd have to stop the car for a moment. Hence I named it "Oscillatoria" after a species of algae that oscillates (at a much slower rate) But I loved it. It had two forward speeds, you shifted gears with your feet, and worked the accelerator with the middle finger of your right hand. It had a self-starter, so I didn't have to crank it. Furthermore, I didn't carry a jack. In case of a flat, I leaned a wooden block against the axle, then stood with my back to the wheel, bent my knees, grasped the wheel between its wooden spokes, and straightened up. The block dropped in place under the axle. I didn't change tires; I just took the tire off the rim and patched the tube right there, then went on. One day I patched a tire eight times. (I bought a new tube the next day.) The entire car could be taken apart and put together again with a monkey wrench, screwdriver, and pair of pliers. If I bashed a fender I didn't go to a body shop; I just bought a new fender for a few dollars and bolted it in place. Those were the days.

About 1926, midway through my college career, I became engaged to a classmate, Evelyn Thoman, the daughter of a Colorado rancher, a tall, beautiful girl, energetic and capable. We hiked and canoed together and worked together in the *Blaze* organization. One summer I took time off to hitchhike out to the western edge of Colorado to visit her and her folks.

I printed myself a sign on white cloth, in big block letters:

SURE I'LL RIDE
OHIO
TO
UTAH
ANTIOCH STUDENT

With this sign on my back, a scoutmaster's hat on my head, a blanket roll around my shoulder, and $10 in my pocket, I set off for the West.

The first afternoon out I was picked up by a moving van. The driver had been at the wheel for 20 hours, so I took over while he slept. Darkness fell. Presently the highway veered diagonally across some railway tracks. My companion, suddenly half awake, glimpsed the tracks and, mistaking them for the road, thought we were going into the ditch. He shouted, leaped across the cab, flung himself on the wheel, and tried to swing the truck onto the tracks. For a moment we wrestled for the wheel, but I had the inside grip and the truck stayed on the road. In a few seconds he was wide awake. He gave a long, gasping sigh and thanked me for hanging on. I slept, that night, in the back of the van.

The next night I slept in a police station. Instead of locking me up, the sergeant let me sleep on his desk. The following evening, just before dark, I was followed by two rough looking characters. To see if they were really following me, I stepped away from the road for a minute, then returned. Sure enough, they were waiting for me and started following again. Just before dark a family came along and picked me up, squeezing the kids over to make room.

The next day I was picked up by a couple of drunks. They were friendly and took me some distance beyond their destination—to help me on my way. Later I was picked up by two women and a little girl, and chauffeured them all the way to Estes Park in Colorado.

At Estes Park I still had the mountains to cross. On the map I found a road which went directly over—the Gore Mountain Pass it was called. I took it, and walked for almost an entire day. During that time seven cars came by and six of them picked me up. The last one was driven by a young couple from Denver who, like me, had seen the road on the map but didn't know anything about it. They had come out for a weekend drive. We soon found out why the traffic was so light. The road became very narrow, and incredibly steep. On one side we looked down a thousand feet or so; on the other side we looked up. The road became too steep for the car, so the wife drove while the husband and I pushed from behind with all our might. Backing down would have been virtually impossible. Had we met another car there would have been a crisis, but there was little danger of that. By evening we made it across.

The next day I arrived at my fiancee's home. It was good to be with her again, and I liked her folks. They ran a fruit ranch up on a mesa. For the first and only time in my life I saw a farm on which weeds were not allowed. Some weed seeds did come in with the irrigation water, and sprouted up along the little canals, but they were rooted out before they had a chance to bloom.

Later my engagement ended. I was so heavily absorbed with trying to carry a college course and my other work that I neglected the girl. As gently as possible she called it off. It was painful, but I couldn't blame her.

I was in the class of '29, and had attended college for six years. That was the length of time it took to complete the Antioch course in those days, in light of the work-study program which took the students off the campus half-time. But I didn't graduate. I had started out as an Engineering major and then shifted to Business Administration. A year from graduating time, I paused to take inventory of my credits, and found that I didn't have enough credits in Business Administration to come even close.

What had interested me most was English, and that's where my credits were concentrated: journalism, creative writing, and similar subjects. But to graduate in English required a foreign language, which I didn't have. My faculty advisor had assumed that surely Arthur Morgan's son would know what he was doing and hadn't paid much attention. I took a crash course in

French that last year and flunked it. When commencement time came I didn't have the heart to go and see my classmates graduate. Years later my son Lee flunked French under the same instructor. In his case, he was distracted by his role in the Yellow Springs civil rights struggle.

I've gone through life without a degree but I haven't missed it. I've always been my own boss. It is interesting that most of the women in our family have had college degrees—some of them Master's degrees—but the men have almost uniformly fallen short of them. It was not until 1965, when my younger son, Lee, graduated from Antioch, that the spell was broken. At that time the *Antiochian* ran a front page picture of him receiving his diploma with the caption, "The First Morgan Man to Earn a Diploma."

I must admit that my college career was cramped a bit by the launching of a business, a story which begins in the next chapter.

Snapshot in 1926. Antioch classmates Don and Jean Berkey in foreground. Ernest and fiancée Evelyn Thoman in the background. With them is Ernest's Model T Ford coupe, which had two forward speeds, low and high. You shifted gears with your feet.

9

AN UNLIKELY BEGINNING

No one would have dreamed, seventy-three years ago, that the little student project, started on a shoestring to find a use for scrap paper, would someday grow into a multinational corporation. But it did—and here's the story of how it started.

When Dad became president of Antioch College in 1921, he envisioned, among other things, college industries developing in the village, operated by students, faculty members, friends of the college, or by the college itself. With his usual contagious spirit he spread this idea.

Within the first five expansive years there appeared The Antioch Press, Antioch Art Foundry, Antioch Specialties Company, Antioch Picture Shop, Antioch Landscaping Company, Antioch Shoe Project, Antioch Dairy, Kahoe & Spieth, Antioch Bookplate Company, a contracting firm, and numerous student enterprises serving the student body. Of all these firms, however, only the Bookplate Company (now Antioch Company) survived.

While at Rudge's shop, Walter Kahoe and I had developed a lasting interest in fine printing. Eventually we both transferred our co-op work to the Antioch Press. Though on a more modest level of craftsmanship, this broadened our skills.

Working at the Press in 1925 and 1926, Walter noticed narrow strips of good paper, trimmed from large sheets, being thrown away. This happens in all printshops. Walter came from a thrifty home and wondered what use could be made of those strips.

The only thing he could think of was bookplates. So in odd moments he rummaged in the cut files and type cases and found a few cuts and type ornaments which he was able to adapt to bookplate use. Then he salvaged some of the waste strips, cut them to bookplate size, and printed a few hundred bookplates. Another Antioch co-op worker, Ruth Sinkes, was to handle the sale of them. Ruth didn't sell any, so Walter gave her two dollars for her interest in the project and took me in as a partner.

There was method in my madness in joining up with Walter in the bookplate project. I liked printing—especially beautiful printing—but I was turned off by job printing as a business. At Rudge's it was always feast or famine—overtime or idleness. Then too, it seemed to me that if you bid high enough to make money, you lost the order, and if you bid low enough to get the order you lost money. Far better to design a beautiful product, put a reasonable price on it, and merchandise it. Bookplates seemed to offer possibilities in that direction.

By way of raising some capital, I had a bookplate sale on the Antioch campus and disposed of sixty dollars worth. With this money we bought some more type ornaments, a few cuts, and some supplies to use in getting out sample sets.

That was in the spring of 1926. At the end of the school year there was not enough work at the Antioch Press to keep me full time so I quit and went to Cleveland in search of a job while Walter, still employed at the Press, printed up the first sales albums. With the permission of the College we called our business the Antioch Bookplate Company.

As soon as the albums were done I set out to get dealers via the thumb route. Six-foot men have a hard time getting rides, and my progress was hopelessly slow. No one picked me up so, at the end of the first morning, I bought a yard of white muslin and dropped in at a country print shop where they let me print myself a cloth sign, which read, in huge block letters:

SURE I'LL RIDE
***
ANTIOCH STUDENT

Then rides came easily. In five-and-a-half days with this sign I covered a route that included Cleveland, Sandusky, Toledo, Ann Arbor, Battle Creek, Michigan City, South Bend, Ft. Wayne, and Lima, interviewed about twenty- five dealers (mostly bookstores), and made sales arrangements with the twenty most desirable ones. I got my food in grocery stores and spent fifty cents per night for lodging in tourist homes. The trip cost about ten dollars.

Then I went back to Yellow Springs to take hold of the home end of the business. Walter had gotten involved in a book publishing project and was glad to turn the bookplate responsibility over to me. Not long after that, the manager of the Antioch Press died suddenly and Walt was drafted, at the age of twenty and still a student, to take charge of the plant. Under these circumstances he was willing to sell me his interest in the Bookplate Company for two hundred dollars.

Instead of dividing my time between five-week shifts of work and study, I ran the business at night and went to school in the daytime. Lots of energy, not much sense.

At first I used the equipment at the Antioch Press in exchange for doing their janitor work. After awhile I rented a little building next door for ten dollars a month, and set up my own shop. I painted the building a deep blue with orange trim; it created a bit of a sensation. The paint I made from old printers ink which had been discarded by a publisher in a nearby city.

The going was hard. Sales were slow and collections were even slower. To complicate life the dealers demanded gummed paper. I was determined to use rough-finish paper, but there was no such gummed stock available. I had a roll of stock specially gummed with animal glue at considerable expense. The paper curled up like cigarettes as soon as the air hit it. I put weights on the stacks of bookplates, but the curling lifted them off, and the bookplates fell on the floor. In desperation I had made a supply of heavy kraft-covered boxes with metal clips to hold the lids on. Before taking bookplates out of a box for imprinting I would sprinkle water on the heater to make the air humid. This kept the bookplates from curling so badly. Eventually we developed a rough finish gummed paper that did not curl.

That was a mighty tough winter, but it was just the beginning. By the end of the year the total sales had reached $400, and I had accumulated a debt.

It was then I bought my first printing press, for twenty dollars. It was a small 1888-model Golding Press—an obsolete make. I was so proud of that press. I had a man help me, and we took it all apart and cleaned and oiled it. Parts suitable for painting I painted, of all colors, white.

Then we tried to put it together again. We tried and tried—in vain. Finally supper time came and I went home in despair. "I can't get the Golding back together again," I lamented. "I don't know what I'm going to do." In the morning I walked into the shop, not knowing how I was going to cope with the situation. Wonder of wonders. There stood the press, fully assembled. Griscom, my sixteen-year-old kid brother, had come in after supper, figured it out, and reassembled it.

How was this possible? When Griscom came into his teens Lucy had arranged a job for him as a helper for Ed Hackett, the Yellow Springs blacksmith. Ed was a good man and a good mechanic, and his skill was apparently contagious. Gris became a clever mechanic.

Griscom was not the only sibling who rescued me in those early years. Once I was in bed with the flu, and there was no one to take care of orders at the shop. My sister Frances, who was then about 14, brought my mail to me each day. Then an order came for bookplates to be printed with a name. I was always a stickler for getting orders out quickly, but I had no printer to fall back on.

So I explained to my sister in great detail what type to use, how to set the type, justify it, lock it in a chase, put it on the press, position it on the paper, adjust the impression and print the bookplates. She recruited her friend, Mary Doris Folck, and the two girls worked all afternoon, using up an extra box of bookplates in getting it just right. They turned the press flywheel by hand, printing the bookplates slowly, one at time. Then they brought the finished product to me for approval. The job was fine, and I told Frances to wrap it up and mail it. I've trained dozens of printers since then, but I never had an experience to beat that.

In 1927 I got myself a new partner, Jesse Emerson Rice Shelton, a spirited, happy-go-lucky youth, part Cherokee, five-feet-four-inches-tall, handsome and irresponsible. I never knew for sure whether he flunked out of Antioch or just ran out of money. But it didn't matter, he entered into the project with good spirit.

We needed more equipment so we invested (with borrowed money and time payments) in a good rebuilt job press, a fair layout of type and miscellaneous supplementary equipment. Jesse acted as scout, hitch-hiking all over southwestern Ohio in search of second-hand equipment. After a few days he had a notebook filled with descriptions and prices of used printing equipment available in a number of cities and villages. Chartering a truck, we set out on a tour, buying the things we needed. At the end of two days we had a complete print shop, which we installed in the tiny back room of the little building I had rented. We first poured concrete under the shaky floor in the place where our presses were to stand.

That shop was a marvel of compactness. The paper cabinet was hung from the ceiling above the paper cutter, and we sawed off the ends of the press drive-shafts to get the presses closer together. There was mighty little cubic space, not to mention floor space, wasted in that shop. The longest stretch of clear floor space, in the middle of the shop, could not have been over six feet.

Patiently and by every possible means, we got in touch with bookstores and gradually extended our dealer list. We sent Jesse on a long tour, again via the thumb route. A short, nice-looking young man, he got rides easily. We projected this tour because the handsome scamp had gotten himself engaged and there was nothing for it but to get him out of town until he cooled off a bit. He would never write a letter and any separation of more than a week or so was enough to end one of his engagements.

I too got engaged, but was so busy between college and business that I neglected the girl, and she terminated the engagement.

Despite poverty and vicissitudes, we enjoyed ourselves. I was still in college, but doing a rather sorry job of it. We served now and then as deputy marshals for the local constable, getting into various interesting situations. One afternoon, as a result of some of my "detective" work, a gentleman with a reputation for expert pistol shooting stepped into the bookplate shop "to clear up a little misunderstanding." Jess secretly covered him from the back room with a .38 automatic, "just in case." It was somewhat to Jess's disappointment that an understanding was reached, with good will on both sides.

It was his romantic fondness for that .38 that finally ended our partnership. An obnoxious advertising billboard had been erected near the Antioch campus. Students had twice taken down this sign and the third time my partner attempted the job single-handed. He took his .38 along "to scare away possible intruders." But the town marshal came upon him and not only refused to be scared, but started blazing away himself. Jess believed his identity had not been discovered, but was indiscreet enough to brag about his adventure to a girlfriend; the next day the law was after him.

The constable and his deputy held down full-time jobs and had to do their hunting after 4:30. For a couple of days it was nip and tuck. This couldn't go on, so we mapped out a sales trip and worked all night getting my old Model T Ford in shape for travelling. He took off at dawn. That ended both the partnership and the Model T. I took over my partner's local debts in exchange for his equity in the business.

It was in one of those years that Antioch's Dean Philip Nash offered me some urgent advice. "Ernest," he said. "Make up your mind and set a deadline. If the bookplate business hasn't started to pay by—say—next January, drop it, and take a job." When January rolled around, it hadn't but I didn't. Years later Nash dropped in and praised me for having stuck it out.

It was around that time also that Dean David Hanchett, of the Antioch Personnel Department, called me in. His department was the one responsible for placing students on their co-op jobs. He told me that McGraw-Hill was scouting for editorial and executive talent. He asked if I would like to be recommended. I said I didn't think my academic record would suggest such a recommendation. He said no, but my other activities would. I was pleased, and said I'd think about it and let him know. Then I asked Dad's advice.

Dad didn't tell me what to do, but he helped clarify the issues. "McGraw-Hill," he said, "is a substantial firm, with integrity. If you join them and do a good job, your future is secure. They are fairly conservative, however, and you might not feel free to do some of the things you are interested in. You need to decide how much freedom you want, and how much security."

I thanked Hanchett and told him I had decided to sweat it out in the bookplate business. Then he called in another student, Ed Booher, and made him the offer. Ed was student manager of the college bookstore, a strong and capable youth of good personality and social ideals. He accepted the offer and, in the course of years, became president of McGraw-Hill and exercised progressive influence in that organization. I think both Ed and I made the right decisions.

Early in my printing career I had a rare experience which I have cherished ever since. With two friends I drove to Chillicothe to visit Dard Hunter. He was unique in the world of graphic arts in more ways than one. Most important, he was the world's authority on primitive paper making. (There is a museum of paper making named after him.) Beyond that he was a supreme example of "do it yourself" in the printing craft. He designed and cast his own type, made his own paper and ink and did his own printing. If you wanted a Dard Hunter book you ordered it and paid (a lot!) for it before it was printed and without having seen what was in it.

Hunter was friendly. He talked with us and showed us around. On his printer's stone slab I noticed a piece of board with nails driven part way in, forming a circle. Obviously, he was going to print a circle of dots.

"Can you print from *nails*?" I exclaimed stupidly.

"Of course," he replied. "You can print from anything."

You can print from anything. What an idea. Why of course. I toyed with the idea and elaborated on it: "You can print with anything and you can print on anything; but you can't print on anything with anything." That became one of my mottos.

Many years later I had a nice visit from W.E. Rudge, Jr., and subscribed to his magazine, *Print,* from which I learned how to print directly from natural objects such as grasses, leaves and ferns. Remembering Dard Hunter, I took this up enthusiastically, and it has been a prolific source of beautiful art work for me ever since.

Actually it is a simple technique. You use a flat nature object such as a leaf or a fern (not a blossom or a twig). You press it in a book or under a weight until it is almost dry but not yet brittle. Then you lay it on a flat surface covered with fresh printer's ink. To get this ink coverage you use a printer's hand roller, called a brayer.

Then you lay a sheet of clean paper on top of it and squeeze the leaf against the inky surface. A proof press is fine for this—or a clothes wringer. Or a squeeze press can be used—or you can lay a sheet of cardboard over it and walk on it.

Then you remove the covering paper and lift the leaf carefully with tweezers and place it on a piece of clean paper. Then you repeat the squeeze operation.

But return to my career:

Financially I was almost unsinkable. I learned to feed myself on two dollars a week. Oatmeal in the top of the double boiler and beans in the bottom. Gradually I got more dealers. Sales for 1927 rose to $700. Not a munificent figure, but encouraging.

By way of community service I became a scoutmaster, and the little printshop functioned as Boy Scout headquarters, the boys often giving a hand with odd jobs.

Another thing I squeezed into that shop was a book selling project. For $100 I bought a library of a thousand volumes that had belonged to a young man killed in the war. I augmented this with an arrangement whereby students brought me their used textbooks and I resold them on a commission basis. Books, bookplates and Boy Scouts made a good mix. In 1928 sales increased to $1,300, so I quit book selling and moved the bookplate business into less crowded quarters.

The business continued growing in 1929, and I had two fellows working for me, youths in their late teens whom I was training as printers. I had big plans for expanding the business that year, but lacked the working capital to carry them out. So I made a proposition to my young colleagues, that we each draw only ten dollars a week pay for the last months of the year. Then we'd have money to launch a big promotion. If sales went well, we'd divide the profits among us at the end of the year. Morale was strong, and they agreed. We did the promotion, and the orders began rolling in. Things looked great.

Then came the stock market crash, just at the beginning of the Christmas season when we usually did half the year's business. The country seemed to fall apart. Investors jumped from tenth-story windows. Bookplate orders slowed to a bare trickle. Sales for the year had grown but were far less than we had projected on the basis of our promotion. There were no profits—only debts. But my helpers kept their jobs, and there was no complaint. Without that promotion, though, I doubt the business would have survived.

As the business grew I often hired Antioch students under the co-op plan of work and study, as did the Antioch Press next door. The mixture of idealistic students and printing equipment was a major factor in the upsurge of *guerrilla journalism*—the blossoming of unofficial student publications—which took place at that time. Most of the thirty issues of the *Blaze* were printed by volunteers, two pages at a time, on Bookplate Company presses.

Unexpectedly, my role as student/printer thrust me into close association with a distinguished man who influenced my thinking and broadened my horizons. This association continued for some time after I finished college.

An Austrian by birth, Rudolf Broda was an outstanding scholar in history and economics and was inspired by strong social idealism. Prior to World War I he had inherited a substantial fortune from his father, and had devoted his energy and resources to the cause of peace and social justice. The clouds of war were already on the horizon as he set in motion his organization, modestly titled the League for the Organization of Progress. Among his associates were scholars and statesmen from all over Europe. Together they published, in three languages, an international journal, *Records of Progress*, financed by Rudolf Broda's inheritance.

Broda himself wisely transferred his citizenship to Switzerland to provide a neutral base from which to carry on his activities. His organization gained many influential adherents and undoubtedly had strong impact for the cause of peace and international organization. It was a noble try, but, as we all know, World War I came anyhow. Dr. Broda's organization collapsed, his magazine ceased, and his fortune was gone.

A few years later he arrived in America with no resources or connections. Antioch College hired his wife, Erna, to teach German. To get her they had to find a place for him. They didn't realize what a bargain they were getting. His knowledge was encyclopedic.

Though his organization was shattered and his fortune gone, Dr. Broda's spirit was undimmed, and he set about to revive the organization and to renew the magazine. A group of students—especially student printers like myself—rallied to his aid. We got *Records of Progress* going once more, and a news bulletin, *Political Letters*. We gave a lot of time to this project, and learned a great deal.

Under Dr. Broda's tutelage I started giving lectures for an organization in Springfield called The International Friendship Club. They could name any topic relating to history, politics, or geography, and I would run with it. All I needed was an hour's session in advance with Dr. Broda. Being one of his faithful aides, I felt free to call upon him. I quickly acquired a great reputation.

Dr. Broda's brilliance was matched by an amusing naiveté, as when he is reported to have rushed into the cafeteria saying, "Quick. Fix me a three-minute egg. I only have two minutes." On one occasion he dropped by when my wife, Elizabeth, and I were loading our canoe on top of our car and asked what we were doing. I explained that when we came to a river we just turned the whole thing over, with the car on top. Completely taken in, he replied, "But isn't it dangerous to do that in the dark?"

Alas, Dr. Broda died suddenly of peritonitis in his middle fifties. Briefly I considered rallying our friends and trying to carry on "The League for the Organization of Progress" and its publications. But that was clearly beyond our knowledge and ability at that stage so I reluctantly gave up the idea. His widow, Erna, brought out a final memorial issue of the magazine, and the project was laid to rest.

I was through college at last, and full-time with the Bookplate Company when Walter Kahoe took a leave of absence from the Antioch Press to do postgraduate work at Harvard. A temporary manager was needed to take his place. The Press and Bookplate were next door to each other, and I was asked to manage the Press for a year, along with my own business.

Dad was president of the Press and Walt was my friend. I couldn't refuse, so I ran both companies for a year. Things went along on an even keel, with nothing very exciting happening, until suddenly we got a windfall. An Antiochian, working for the J. Walter Thompson Advertising Agency, told the agency about a family budget system that our accounting professor, D. A. Magruder, had developed. They conceived the idea of using a budget book as an advertising device for one of their clients, the Piggly Wiggly grocery chain. The agency contacted me at the Press, and I got together with Magruder. With his accounting knowledge and my training in printing layout we developed a splendid family budget book. The advertising agency was delighted and so was Piggly Wiggly. They bought 225,000 copies.

In preparing a bid on the job I made a mistake. In figuring the cost I included the cost of the paper twice, making the price $3,000 higher than I intended. I discovered my mistake too late, but they accepted the job at the price quoted. For the first time the Antioch Press actually made money. Thanks to that bungle my year at the Press was a success.

When that project ended I turned my thoughts to other ideas which I might sell to Piggly Wiggly. Happily I had access to an expert as talented as Magruder: Lucy Morgan. She came forward with an idea for a concise book on food preparation. Not a conventional cookbook, but more of a manual. It would have tables showing all kinds of food and all the ways of preparing them. Some of these tables were to be broken down into different levels of cost, for budgeting purposes.

This would make a concise book, no bigger than the budget book, invaluable for ready reference in the kitchen or in shopping. It would be supplemented by a monthly bulletin containing a group of budgeted menus, sorted by cost, but also targeted at families with varying levels of activity.

Lucy prepared some preliminary tables, and I submitted them, along with the total idea, to the J. Walter Thompson Advertising Agency. They in turn took the idea to Piggly Wiggly. The response was enthusiastic. Alas, Piggly Wiggly was taken over about then by Kroger, who dropped the J. Walter Thompson firm and placed the advertising job with their own agency. It didn't occur to me to tackle the Kroger empire, so the project came to an end.

Once, in the early years, I was tempted to lay down the Bookplate Company. I had a young family and business was very slow. Walter Kahoe had been transferred from the management of the Antioch Press to a job in the Antioch Personnel Department, where his talents were more urgently needed. So they needed a new manager for the Press.

The Depression was at its worst just then, and we were living in the country, surviving by producing our own fruit and vegetables, milk, meat, eggs and honey and cutting our own firewood—a very strenuous life. It made sense to lay down the bookplate business and take on the Antioch Press.

So, after some deliberation I applied for the job. I had managed the Press successfully for a year when Walter was away—and I was the only qualified candidate they had. It looked like a pushover. But I was already active in the Socialist Party, and Lester Sontag, the College doctor and a member of the Administrative Council, objected to hiring a socialist, so I was turned down, and kept on with the Bookplate Company. I've been grateful to Lester ever since.

I was able to help fill the vacancy, however. Freeman Champney had worked for me off-and-on for some years and had become an able printer. He was the younger brother of Horace Champney, who initiated Antioch's Community Government. Like Horace, he had the capacity for occasional strong utterances. This led to a bitter altercation with Algo Henderson, who had succeeded Dad as president of Antioch. Shortly after that, Freeman left Yellow Springs and took a job in Washington, D.C. When I was turned down for the Press job, I suggested to Henderson that young Champney might be a good prospect. Despite their strained relations, those two got together, Freeman was hired, and managed the Press with distinction for 25 years. A tribute to the characters of both men.

Once, when I needed a secretary, I offered the job to an Antioch co-op student whom I knew to be competent. She consulted her faculty advisor as to whether she should take the job. He happened to be William Leiserson, well known as an economist and labor arbitrator. His response was brief and to the point, "You can work for Ernie Morgan under one condition, *that you don't think you're learning business.*"

Uncle Billy, as we called him, was right. I was not a businessman. I had flubbed my business education and emerged from college with a paradigm very different from that of the conventional business world. Apart from making a modest living, I wasn't interested in money. Business was to serve human needs. I underpriced everything. I made friends of my competitors. I regarded my employees as colleagues rather than hired help. They shared in the risks and earnings of the business and in decision-making as well. Like me, they were underpaid. I almost never fired anyone or laid anyone off.

Some of my foibles did have survival value: morale was strong, and my practice of sharing risks and earnings brought the business through repeated crises. I may have been a lousy businessman, but I was a good team man and cherished colleagues who chose to differ with me. Thanks in large measure to such colleagues (plus a generous measure of good luck) the business survived and prospered.

10

EARLY YEARS OF MARRIAGE

What a marriage that was. During our forty years together, we raised a family, homesteaded, organized concerts, ran political campaigns, hiked forests, climbed mountains, canoed wild rivers, published a newspaper, founded a school, and carried on many other activities—always as equal partners. This chapter touches on the first few years.

After the breakup of my first engagement, I had no other serious relationship for several years. I did, however, date interesting young women as opportunity offered. We would attend dances, go hiking or canoeing, work on projects together, and discuss philosophy and social issues. This was an enjoyable activity whereby I got acquainted with a number of fine girls. By deliberately spreading my dates around I was able to retain a fair amount of objectivity and also avoid generating unwarranted expectations on their part. Marriage is, at best, a lottery, and the more objective judgment one is able to exercise the better the chances of success.

In the fall of 1930 I met Elizabeth Morey. Five years my junior, she had come to Antioch as an advanced student. Her educational background was unusual. Her parents had kept her home from school on grounds of "delicate health." They tutored her lightly and the family did a lot of reading together. She played around her home, made music, and helped her mother. She was reading at the age of five and was playing both violin and piano by the age of ten.

When Elizabeth was the right age for eighth grade, her parents sent her to school. Never having experienced school before, she found it exciting and raced through high school in three and a half years as an honor student. Then she embarked on a career of music. While still in her teens, however, she was profoundly affected by the death of her older sister, and this led to a reassessment of her values and activities. She was repelled by the fiercely competitive nature of professional music and by the synthetic way in which reputations were built. To the dismay of her music instructors, who had pinned their hopes on her winning the prize in an upcoming competition, she turned her back on professional music and directed her talents toward a business career. She became highly competent as a secretary and after a couple of years had saved enough money to enter Antioch.

The qualities of charm and vigor, an active, searching mind, wide-ranging interests and strong social idealism made an irresistible combination as far as I was concerned. Other men were interested in her too, but I had the edge in several respects. She liked strenuous outdoor activities, we had closely similar values and interests and, very important, I treated her as an equal. (She liked to stand on her own feet.)

We were married the following year, at Elizabeth's home in Illinois. The words for our ceremony we wrote ourselves, based on a ceremony designed by our good friend, Bishop Paul Jones, who was college pastor at Antioch. "I, Ernest, take you, Elizabeth, to be my wife, to love, to work with, to share with and to grow with." Then she repeated the same words to me. The minister had no lines; he just stood there and beamed, and signed the necessary papers. We lost our marriage license somewhere on our honeymoon, but that didn't bother us.

For our honeymoon we took my old Studebaker Erskine with my eighteen-foot Sponson canoe mounted on top and headed for northern Minnesota. Our car was comfortable for sleeping but was not mosquito-proof. We had neglected to bring insect repellent, and our first night in the Minnesota lake country the mosquitoes ate us up. Elizabeth was fairly beside herself trying to swat the mosquitoes. As for me, I became hysterical and started to laugh. Poor Elizabeth. She wondered what sort of monster she had married. I think she would have walked home that night if she could have. On subsequent nights, when we pitched our tent, we had ample mosquito protection.

At length we came to Cass Lake, where I had camped as a boy. A high wind was blowing, so we rigged a crude sail from a tarpaulin and raced across the whole width of the lake in the canoe. Then we headed north into the crystal waters of the upper Mississippi. It was a glorious trip.

On our way home we paused in St. Cloud to visit Mrs. Capple, a wonderful Irish woman who had been a close friend of the family for nearly fifty years. Mrs. Capple regarded Elizabeth thoughtfully—the wavy windblown hair, the peeling nose. "Well, Ernest," she said approvingly, "I see you didn't marry a flapper."

Our first months in Yellow Springs were not easy for Elizabeth. A cozy apartment would have been nice—or a modest cottage. But instead she found herself presiding over the Presidential Mansion. Dad and Lucy were taking a leave of absence and had gone to Europe, leaving their house in our care—housekeeper, flow of guests, four-year old adopted daughter and all— a tough assignment for a young bride. Elizabeth rose to the occasion but it certainly wouldn't have been her choice.

Hilda, my adopted sister, came into our family while Lucy was serving on the Board of the Greene County Home. Among the children in this home was a bright, charming three-year-old girl who seemed to be having a hard time with the matron. Lucy's heart went out to the child, and several times she took her home for a visit. Finally she adopted her. She was a charming young sprite whom I remember fondly.

Alas, the assimilation of this child was not easy. Lucy would cuddle her and try to call forth an affectionate response. The little girl would respond with appreciation for "the nice things" that Lucy was giving her, but without any visible affection. Furthermore, Lucy was no longer young and, despite her keen intelligence and fine character, did have limitations of temperament which rendered her a dubious mother for an injured child.

Lucy was aware of her own limitations and asked whether Elizabeth and I might take Hilda. Just setting forth on our own marriage, we were reluctant to do that. A year or so later, Dad became Chairman of the Tennessee Valley Authority and the family moved to Norris, Tennessee. The situation there proved even less suitable for the child than it had been in Yellow Springs.

At this time a beautiful thing happened. I have already mentioned my cousin Merle Sutton, Urania's abandoned nephew for whom Urania and Dad provided a home until Urania's death in 1905. After Lucy married Dad in 1911, she took the boy into their home for a time. Along about 1934 Merle and his wife, Maybelle dropped by Norris to visit Dad and Lucy. Quickly observing that Lucy and Hilda were having a difficult time, this fine couple, having no children of their own, invited Hilda to come and live with them. She must have been around six or seven years old at the time. Thus did Merle and his wife repay Lucy's earlier kindness and give Hilda a good home.

When Dad and Lucy finished their leave of absence, we gladly returned to them the Mansion and moved into a pleasant apartment that we fixed up over the Bookplate Shop. We kept a downstairs room in addition, as the stairs were too narrow to get Elizabeth's piano up them. It was while we were living in this apartment that our son Arthur was born.

I'll never forget the first time I saw him and the overwhelming sense of awe and joy I felt. My friends may not believe this, but for once in my life I was speechless.

We innocently believed everything we were told by the people who sold baby clothing. We dressed the child night and day in layers of unnecessary garments, all of which were removed at the first sign of dampness. Every night we accumulated a small mountain of damp baby clothes. These I washed laboriously in a bucket of sudsy water, using a plunger which resembled a large inverted funnel on a broomstick. After several rinses these garments had to be boiled on the stove for twenty minutes. By the time our other children were born we knew better.

It wasn't only in the matter of clothing and laundry that we were young and green. Everything had to be done just right, by the book. We couldn't simply relax and love the child, we had to be scientific about everything. This made for a difficult childhood and adolescence for the boy, but he survived. He was the pioneer who prepared the way for the wiser and more relaxed upbringing of his two sisters and brother.

The Bookplate Company apartment in which we lived was cozy, but it was no place for the long haul. The front door, at the foot of the stairs, opened directly onto the sidewalk of the busy main street, in the center of the business section. There was no yard or front porch. A beer joint across the street had a loudspeaker above their door which blared raucous music far into the night. One night I dashed across the street in my bathrobe, and pulled the switch on their record player.

Then there was the Fourth of July after Art was born. There we were, in the center of town, with fireworks going off all around. Every time a firecracker exploded in the neighborhood the poor baby would jerk. We quickly pitched a tent in the country and moved out for a few days.

Happily, our occupation of the Bookplate apartment ended sooner than expected. The Great Depression was on, in all its dismal fury, and Dad had ideas for coping with it. He initiated two unique barter organizations, one local and one regional. The Yellow Springs Exchange, as we called it, needed a downtown location, so we moved the Bookplate Company, machinery and all, to a side street and turned our building over to the Exchange.

Elizabeth and I moved to a modest corner house on Dayton Street, only about a block from the new Bookplate location and just across from the Methodist Church. The young minister there was a friend of ours whose views we respected, and who was the son of the couple who managed the local Exchange. To help him get established in the church, Elizabeth agreed to serve as choir director, a post she filled with her usual energy and skill.

Our proximity to the church led to an embarrassing incident. Art was a toddler then, and we commonly turned him loose in the back yard, which was surrounded by a picket fence. One sunny spring day we put him out there with nothing on. Apparently the side gate, which was opposite the church, was unlatched, for the baby got out. A wedding party emerged from the church just in time to see this naked cherub roll into the gutter. I don't think the bride ever forgave us for that.

Another incident from our Dayton Street stay I remember well—almost too well. I was keeping bees, as I did off and on for fifty years. A swarm had collected high up in a tree in our front yard, and I wanted them. Accordingly I put on veil and gloves, got out my tools, and went up after them.

Bees freshly swarmed are usually gentle, but this swarm had apparently been out for some time, because they weren't. I was wearing a cylindrical veil, with a bandana handkerchief on top of my head. The bees started stinging through that handkerchief. Alas, the hair that formerly held the handkerchief away from my scalp had gotten thinner than I realized.

I would have come down and added a little more protection but a crowd had gathered in the street below to watch me. Pride goeth before a lot of stings, as you might say, so I stayed with it. Every time I jostled that swarm some of the bees would fall on my head—like red hot sand. But I got the swarm, and I didn't disappoint my audience.

Once, in our Dayton Street home, we had an unusual visitor. A teenage Socialist from Cleveland, John Lazarowski, had hitchhiked to Chicago for a conference. It was winter time, and on his way home he got cold and hungry. Though normally an intelligent boy, he became confused and started taking rides in any direction, winding up at Springfield, Ohio, just north of Yellow Springs, and 180 miles south of Cleveland. There the police took pity on him, locked him up, and contacted his father.

The father, a modest Polish shoemaker, didn't know what to do, so he consulted the State Secretary of the Socialist Party, who lived in Cleveland. Referring to a map, the secretary noted that Springfield was close to Yellow Springs. He knew I was driving to Cleveland in a couple of days for a meeting, so he wrote, asking me to bring John with me. The father sent the money to the police for bus fare from Springfield to Yellow Springs and asked them to put the boy on the bus with instructions to come to me.

About midmorning a cheerful young man walked into the shop. "Good morning, Comrade Lazarowski," I said. But it wasn't Comrade Lazarowski. It was a carbon paper salesman named Paul Serene.

I met the bus on its next trip through town, and spoke with the driver. Yes, the police had put a young fellow on the bus the previous trip, and he had let him off in Yellow Springs. The driver had seen Walter Kahoe and asked him to direct the boy to my place. I tracked Walter to the barber shop. Yes, he had directed the boy. There the trail ended. The boy, I was told, seemed to be confused.

Recruiting some help, I set out in search. We notified the local police, and cruised slowly to Springfield and back. No trace. That evening, as it happened, we were having a Socialist meeting in our living room when the police came to the door. "Is this the boy you're looking for?" they asked. The poor chap had wandered to the edge of town and sat down in the cemetery. He had been there all day without shelter, food, or water. Finally a neighbor had seen him and phoned the police. We got some hot soup into him and put him to bed. He was cheered by a picture of Norman Thomas on the wall. Soon he was back to normal.

In the morning I prepared to drive to Cleveland, and asked if he was ready to go. He said, no, he'd rather stay. So we made him at home at our house, and I headed for Cleveland alone.

Quiet, intelligent and friendly, John stayed with us into the summer. He helped around the shop, served as babysitter and cheerfully picked up on any chores that needed doing. He also helped us move to our next home.

My folks had made us a gift of a pleasant tract of land a couple of miles from town. It had a tumbledown cottage on it, a wooded area and a large garden space. Now we had a place of our own. One of John's tasks was to lead our goat all the way out there. The animal insisted on eating along the way, so it took him hours.

One evening shortly after that, one of my Bookplate Company people, passing the shop, saw a young girl sitting on the step, crying. He spoke to her and she inquired for Ernest Morgan. So he brought her out to our house in the country. She turned out to be John's younger sister, Helen. John had written about our family and she had decided to join us. She arrived unannounced, found the shop closed, and didn't know what to do. Industrious and well-behaved, she made a nice addition to our family.

A little later John asked if his younger'brother Matthew might join us also. We said no, better not, we're pretty full already. So, of course, Matthew promptly came. We assimilated him as well, and he was with us for some time. Ultimately they all returned to Cleveland, but John remained a long-time friend.

The unexpected influx of these young people into our home offers a commentary on Elizabeth's personality. The fact that the boy wanted to stay in the first place and brought his sister and brother to join him indicated the warmth and acceptance which he felt. That Elizabeth cheerfully took it all in stride reflected her resilience. Just the same, she could be tough if she observed someone being phony or exploitive.

Our new rural situation did have its drawbacks. Once Art, while still a toddler, walked up to the beehive and started playing with the bees. They went for him. I grabbed him under my arm and made a dash for the house. We pulled about twenty stingers out of him, and he was a pretty sick child for a while.

Our water supply consisted of a "two-bucket pump." You could pump two buckets of water—then you'd have to wait half an hour before there was any more.

With a second child on the way the water situation became serious, so I dug a cistern, calculated to hold 4,000 gallons of rainwater. Despite the considerable effort of building this tank, when I took Elizabeth to the hospital, we still had no water. There had been no rain, and the cistern stood empty.

Jenifer arrived safely, and my Dad made a special trip from the TVA to visit Elizabeth and the baby in the hospital. "You don't know how much this means," he said. He was so right.

When I took Elizabeth and Jenifer home there still had been no rain, so I hauled water in my car from our nearest neighbor, a quarter of a mile away. Finally, to my great relief, it rained, and we had plenty of water.

Benetta was born a couple of years later, in 1936. Our timing had not been good. The Bookplate business was highly seasonal, with the personalized orders arriving in a great rush just before Christmas. The activity peaked on the third Monday before Christmas, which we dubbed Mad Monday. While the rush was on, I was buoyed up by the excitement and could work at top speed "26 hours a day." During that time I seemed indestructible, but early in the new year I invariably became ill. That year it was appendicitis, and I went to Florida to recuperate with my parents. This left Elizabeth, eight months pregnant, two miles from town, alone with two small children. After a week or so the doctor said, "Tell Ernest to get home right away!"

Benetta was the only one of our children whose birth I attended. I sat beside Elizabeth, held her hand and relayed the doctor's instructions to her. Fathers are little help at a time like that, but I was able to give her some comfort and moral support. It meant a lot to me to share in the birthing, if only vicariously.

We lived in the country for six years, but when Art reached school age Elizabeth felt that it would be too much for him to walk the considerable distance to the highway and wait for the school bus in all kinds of weather. So we borrowed money and bought a house in town.

I think she was right about that, but there was another dimension to her thinking: every six or seven years Elizabeth needed a change. However, she was sensitive and highly intelligent and could always think of valid, rational reasons for making a change. Knowing this, I sometimes wondered how long I might last as her husband. I needn't have worried about that. While our marriage may have been difficult once in awhile, it was never in doubt.

Canoeing wild rivers was just one of Ernest and Elizabeth's adventures.

Elizabeth Morey Morgan. Charming, brilliant, and creative, she played seven instruments, typed 125 words a minute, raised a family, ran for Congress, founded a school, and did much more.

11

ADVENTURES IN BUSINESS

Strange things happen when an eager young idealist tries to run a business. Curiously, in this case, the idealism seemed to have survival value. The business outlived some twenty competitors and is now well into its second half-century. This chapter gives an overview of that story, and is followed by two chapters detailing the human and artistic sides of the business.

While I was in college I had turned away from engineering in the interest of a stable living situation. I had also turned down a promising career opportunity to remain in my tiny struggling enterprise. I had begun to develop active social concerns and wanted to be a free man, to pursue my ideals and convictions wherever they might lead. The American syndrome of bigger, better, and more had begun to pale on me. To fight my way endlessly up the ladder of SUCCESS in a career made about as much sense to me as a fur-lined bathtub. I wanted a life with more meaningful content than that, and I was prepared to accept a simple lifestyle in order to pursue it.

I may have carried that impulse a bit far in the beginning. During the first couple of years in the bookplate business my monthly sales were in two figures and it was many years before the total annual sales reached the $14,000 mark. But looking back, my little business was quite an adventure.

Mostly the folks I hired in the early years were young people, whom I trained myself. I paid them meager wages, but no one complained. They could see me and my family living on the same economic level that they did. They had a share in the decision-making and in the sense of adventure. I tried systematically to make our group a community. When I hired a new person I took him or her on a tour of the office and plant, to be introduced to all the workers. Each person was given a key to the plant and permission to use the equipment for personal or nonprofit printing.

A strong sense of community developed and racial differences ceased to matter. Our folks often declined offers of higher pay from other firms.

A major problem in the early years was that I trained all the workers, and I was rather green myself. Working in this situation I developed a firm conviction that, no matter how I might be doing something, there *must* be a better way. As a result, experimentation became a way of life.

Happily, Elizabeth shared my taste for a simple lifestyle and had little concern for luxuries or social status. (She was so talented that she didn't have to worry about status anyhow.) She also shared my interest in social experiments. Together we developed the idea of establishing a rural cooperative. It would be a farm with a printshop. We met an interesting young couple who had recently graduated from Purdue, he in Agriculture and she in Home Economics. They were interested in coming in with us. Antioch College owned a farm which we could rent on reasonable terms. It had a building on it suitable for a printshop.

But there was a hitch. Al and Mary, our two employees, didn't like the idea. They had grown up on farms. "There ain't nothing in farming," Al said. It was against our habits to try to force anyone, so we gave up the idea. That was lucky for us. As green young idealists, we had no concept of the social dynamics involved in such a project and would certainly have flubbed it.

In the late 1930s the business suddenly took a great leap forward, not through good management but through good luck. Dick Steinbeck, a friend of ours and an Antioch alumnus, dropped into the office one day. He had been laid off from his job and had decided to try selling. He wanted to travel for us.

"Look, Dick," I said, "you can't make a living selling bookplates."

"But would you mind letting me try? I can live in my car."

"Not at all; but I would be deceiving you if I gave you any encouragement."

So we fixed up a set of samples, gave him our dealer list and turned him loose. To my astonishment the business doubled in a year, and the climb continued. I think Dick was almost as pleased at proving me wrong as he was in making a living.

But the travelling was hard on Dick's family life. We talked it over and I suggested that in his travels he try to find another small firm with a comparable line—then travel with both lines in a smaller territory.

Out in Denver Dick contacted Richardson Rome, a distinguished artist who manufactured stationery ornamented with his etchings. Beautiful merchandise, beautifully packaged, it enjoyed a good market. Rome himself was a man of charm and many talents. We hit it off well. The Rome sales organization took on our line and assimilated Dick Steinbeck, who then could travel in a small territory. This was a lucky move for us: not long after that Dick was drafted in World War II, but with our Rome connection our sales continued to climb.

We were prospering as never before, and the staff had grown, but our wages were still low. The staff talked it over and asked me for a 20% wage increase across the board. After studying the matter I agreed that we could readily afford a 20 percent increase and that they certainly deserved it. However, I made them an alternative offer: let wages stay where they were, and at the end of the year I would split the profits with them 50/50. From every indication this would yield them closer to 40 percent instead of 20 percent.

I had several reasons for making this offer. First, I'd been through several ups and downs and didn't really trust our new prosperity. Second, I liked the idea of sharing—whether I was sharing chicken or sharing feathers.

Morale was good and the staff accepted the offer. Sure enough, their share of the profits gave them nearly a 40 percent increase. So we formalized the arrangement and continued it. We developed terminology to go with the scheme. The weekly wages were "base pay," which was considered to be "80% of theoretical pay." The share of profits to be received at the end of the year we called the "contingent pay."

This arrangement would have been a brilliant stroke of management—if I had known what I was doing. Not long after that there was a wartime wage freeze. It became illegal to raise wages without authorization from the War Production Board. Unless your product or service was necessary to the war effort, or to the local community, you couldn't get permission, and bookplates were hardly essential. But our contingent wage plan was in place and so was legal. The contingent pay rose every year, finally reaching 80% of base pay. This arrangement kept our staff from having to find other jobs and undoubtedly saved the business.

After the war our sales collapsed, and so did the profits. We automatically dropped back to base pay. Again the business was saved by the contingent wage plan.

Dick Rome was less fortunate. His sales collapsed too, and his business went down the drain. His situation was complicated by the fact that he was enormously talented and insisted on making all the important decisions himself. I, being less talented, generally shared decision-making, and this gave my business a strong advantage.

About 1945, when sales were going well, I proposed that the company be turned over to the employees. We would incorporate and form a "Staff Association" which would hold the stock. I was busily working out the details. As we got close to the time of carrying it out, the morale of the staff dropped, and little power cliques began to form. They trusted me but didn't trust each other. Finally my two senior colleagues, Dave Sallume and Marie Treuer, took me into the back room and said, "Ernest, you simply can't go through with this thing. You'll wreck the business." So I backed off, and everyone relaxed.

Looking back, I think that was a wise decision. Industrial cooperatives can be highly successful, (for example, the famous Mondragon development in Spain) but sound principles are needed. It's also helpful to have a homogeneous group or a unifying social philosophy. We had none of those things.

Having been turned back from my plans for employee ownership, I set up a corporation for profit, but with special features. The employees would nominate two board members who would then be elected by the stockholders. This procedure was followed faithfully for many years and acquired the force of what might be called "tribal law." But it was later superceded by another plan.

Each year, at the time of the annual profit share distribution, staff members were invited to lend all or part of their contingent pay to the company at interest, callable at any time. Soon the employees became the major creditors of the company, with a double stake in the business—their jobs and their savings.

In later years, with the company more stable, the plan was changed so the employees received their full pay each week, plus a profit share at the end of the year.

Another step in the development of internal democracy was the formation of an Operating Committee with a representative from each department. Participation in this committee was flexible, depending on what matters were under consideration. Anyone in the organization who might have special knowledge or experience in a matter under discussion was likely to be called on.

Dave Sallume ordinarily convened the meetings and he took pains always to include persons who he though might disagree with him on the question at hand. Meetings varied in size from as few as three people to as many as six or eight, depending on the nature and importance of the matter under consideration. I repeatedly found myself overruled by the committee on important matters. It nearly always turned out in such cases that the committee was right.

Another democratic innovation was the Wage Committee, consisting of two people representing management and two elected by the staff. In January of each year this committee conducted a complete wage review, and at midyear it reviewed special cases. Sitting in on meetings of this committee, a stranger could hardly have known which persons were management representatives and which were staff-elected members.

Once we had a young man on the staff who was highly intelligent, a good worker and well regarded by his colleagues, but somewhat eccentric. He was elected to serve on the Wage Committee but it turned out that he didn't approve of raises for women. Nearly all our women, he said, had working husbands and didn't need raises. Understandably, the women voted him off the committee on the next round.

In time he had a change of heart. He felt that the bindery women, who did the lower-skilled handwork, were underpaid. He was right about that, though our bindery women were paid a little more than the going rate for that category. The young man protested vigorously, but didn't get much attention. Then, at eleven o'clock one night, I got an agitated phone call from him. If something weren't done about the bindery wages right now, there would be a picket line at the shop in the morning. I rolled over and went back to sleep.

Sure enough, when I arrived at the shop in the morning three or four of our men were walking with signs, though none of them had a personal stake in the matter. I took a sign from one of them and walked with them for a few minutes to indicate my sympathy with their concern. At just that moment a friend of mine came along, who happened to be local correspondent for the Associated Press. He almost fell over backward. I made the national news wires that day: "President pickets own firm."

When I went inside I found the Bindery women all hard at work and angry at the pickets. We still had to satisfy the protestors, but the total cost to the company of the final wage adjustment was only about fifty cents an hour. By midafternoon everyone was back at work. Just another day at the Antioch Bookplate Company.

In the early years I often hired Antioch co-op students and trained them as printers. As the technology advanced, however, this became less practical. Later, I hired them as travelling representatives. They made a good impression, but more important, they were teachable. Training a rep with previous experience was almost a waste of time. They already knew all about selling and generally weren't interested in new ideas. All they wanted from me was information about the product and about company policies. I trained the student reps myself, travelling with them for a day or so and helping them identify with the dealers they were servicing. They did an excellent job.

The most exciting and meaningful student participation, however, occurred in the late 1960s, at the management level. Bill Finlay was head of the Department of Business Education at Antioch and we recruited him to serve on the Bookplate Company board. At one point he and another professor were conducting a Senior Seminar in Business Administration. This group asked if they might study the Bookplate Company. Our response was that they could study our company if they would include our executives in their seminar. They agreed—and then the fun began.

These young people were self-possessed. They had studied business administration at Antioch and had been seasoned by their co-op jobs. The group broke into teams and studied our accounting, distribution, and production. Each week the group would meet, including our executives. They had no inhibitions about asking questions and making suggestions. Having no professional reputations to worry about, they could swing freely. The seminar meetings turned into administrative planning sessions. They were dynamite. Improvements were made in our accounting and distribution procedures and important new equipment was installed. This was Antioch education at its best.

At the end of the course the students produced a report on what they had learned and what they had done. Each was given a copy of it and at least one got a job after graduation on the strength of it. One professor remarked later that it had been the best class he had ever taken part in, either as student or as instructor. Our company was lucky to be the guinea pig.

When I reached sixty-five, after managing the company for forty-four years, I retired from active leadership to join Elizabeth at Celo, where she was running the Arthur Morgan School, and my younger son, Lee, took the helm. He was well trained in business administration and was experienced through the Antioch work-study plan. Further, he had a printing background. Thus he had a good foundation for running a small, complicated printing and publishing enterprise.

Most of our outside stockholders, however, quietly panicked. In their view my departure signified the beginning of the end. They urged us to give favorable consideration to a merger offer we had received from a larger firm. Failing in that, they quietly unloaded their stock for whatever they could get.

They were almost right. At that very moment the company was making the difficult transition from old-fashioned letterpress printing to modern off-set. Various things went wrong. Financial problems were compounded when Lee raised wages to respectable levels. There was talk of closing out the business.

At this point Lee quietly set aside the Operating Committee and reduced the staff by about a third—without loss of productivity. This was a drastic move, but it probably avoided bankruptcy. It would seem that my management had left a good deal to be desired. Slowly the business righted itself and began to move ahead. Lee had brought with him additional talent in the person of a capable classmate, Mike Gardner. Another important factor in the turnaround was that the Arthur Morgan School, which Elizabeth and I had founded, was bankrupt and I took to the road as a salesman for the Bookplate Company, baled out the school and boosted the company. That remarkable stoty is told in another chapter. I take pride also in the fact that a new product line which I had conceived and projected was important in turning the tide.

The climb was rapid: new products, expanding markets, new machinery, foreign subsidiaries, a new building, and new employees. The decimal point of the operation was moved. Employee representation on the board was continued and a new practice was adopted: an Employee Stock Ownership Plan which distributes a substantial portion of the company's profits to the staff in the form of stock. As I write this, the employees own a majority of the company's stock.

In 1980, celebrating the tenth anniversary of Lee's assumption of leadership, Beulah Champney, an old friend who was Lee's secretary for a time, wrote a parody on the song of "Sir Joseph Porter, KCB" from Gilbert & Sullivan's *HMS Pinafore*, which lightheartedly celebrates Lee's first ten years of management. It was performed at a company banquet.

WHEN LEE WAS A LAD
by Beulah Champney — December 1980
With some help from Gilbert & Sullivan

When Lee was a lad he served a term
As copy-setter for the Bookplate firm.
He set the copy for the imprint press,
And he sometimes landed in an awful mess.
(He sometimes landed in an awful mess)
But he handled that mess so carefully
That now he is the Boss of the Company.
(He handled that mess so carefully
That now he is the Boss of the Company.)

It's ten years now since Ernest retired,
And told us all that Lee was hired
To run the Company as best he could.
And we all began knocking on the nearest wood
(We all began knocking on the nearest wood.)
We knocked on that wood so handily
That Lee is still the Boss of the Company.
(We knocked on that wood so handily
That Lee is still the Boss of the Company.)

The first few years that Lee was Boss
We suffered a gigantic loss.
We lost money here and we lost money there.
It's a wonder that Lee didn't lose his hair.
(It's a wonder that Lee didn't lost his hair.)
But he handled those losses so well that he
Still remained the Boss of the Company.
(He handled those losses so well that he
Still remained the Boss of the Company.)

And then we made money, and we made a lot,
And soon we were buying a building plot.
We built a building and we bought a press,

As Lee (and Mike) pulled us out of that mess.
(As Lee and Mike pulled us out of that mess.)
They handled that mess so expertly
That Lee is still the Boss of the Company.
(They handled that mess so expertly
That Lee is still the Boss of the Company.)

Now workers all, whoever you may be,
You can't all climb to the top of the tree.
For if, of a Plant, you'd be President
You have to pick the right Parent.
(You have to pick the right Parent.)
Lee picked his Father so carefully
That now he is the Boss of the Company.
(Lee picked his Father so carefully
That now he is the Boss of the Company.)

It was seventy-three years ago that Walter Kahoe and I started the Antioch Bookplate Company (now the Antioch Company). Looking back, I can see a whole spectrum of meanings which the enterprise had.

First of all, it gave me a strong sense of identity because it involved a full range of printing skills, and printers are, as everyone knows, the noblest work of God. Other professional identities which I can claim, such as administrator, author, or salesman, pale in satisfaction alongside that of printer.

The second meaning was the freedom it gave me to pursue my ideals and values. I had the feeling of being a free man, able to look the world in the eye and do what I thought was right.

This freedom was something which I tried to share with my co-workers. What actually happened along this line was different from what I expected: instead of young idealists joining me in seeking freedom, I found myself attracting people with problems—folks with personality difficulties, unmarried mothers, ethnic minorities, conscientious objectors. In our little business they found a social and economic base for coping successfully with life. Worthwhile, certainly, but not what I had planned. This aspect of the business is detailed in the next chapter.

The third value of my business life was that it supported my family. This support was at a modest level, to be sure, but we were happy and healthy and felt no envy of our more affluent friends. And, of course, the business supported other families too, on the same modest level as my own.

Fourth, we made beautiful products which gave people pleasure.

Fifth, the business gave me social, political, and economic leverage, and the challenge to exercise this leverage in creative ways in the community and the world.

Lastly, and enormously complex and challenging, it involved me in a network of social and economic relationships with a growing number of co-workers: how to divide the income, how to share the work and responsibility and decision-making, how to share the excitement and sense of adventure of the business. Also, how to relate to one another in a happy spirit of community.

It is hard to measure an intangible quality like community, but there were indicators of some degree of success in our company. One was a stable work force. Our people tended to stay with us for many years. Several, having taken jobs elsewhere at higher wages, quit and returned.

Shortly after WWII we were visited by three people experienced in the field of community, and they brought perspective and inspiration.

The first was Godrick Bader, the son of Ernest Bader of the Scott-Bader Commonwealth in England. This is a successful industry which was turned over to its employees and has prospered for many years. Godrick Bader said that our company was the closest thing to it that he had found in America and urged us to continue in that direction.

The second was Claire Huchet Bishop, the French author of *All Things Common*. She had studied the French "Communities of Work" that emerged following the war, and gave us an inspiring account of these ventures.

Last was Henrik Infield, who headed an organization devoted to community. He was much interested in our company and urged us to strengthen the quality of community in the organization by reaching out into other areas of life for common activity.

After considerable reflection I found myself differing with Infield. Each of us, I reasoned, belongs to a number of different communities. There is the family, the neighborhood, the church, perhaps a bowling league or a stamp collectors club. The workplace, too, should be a community, but it should not try to compete with the other communities. The problem is, how to make it a happy and vigorous community in its own right. Along this line, I wrote in 1951 a short article for the Staff Bulletin of the company. Aside from slight differences of formulation, I would say the same thing today. Here it is:

WHY NOT LIVE WHILE WORKING?

In choosing a mate, economic considerations are very important. Will the man be able to provide at least a modest level of security and support? Will the woman be able to manage the home economically and skillfully? Everyone knows that failure in either of these things may wreck a marriage, yet economic considerations are rarely the determining factor in choosing a mate. Nearly always the prime question is "Will we be happy together?"

In choosing a job, on the other hand, the average person

does not ask himself first, "Will I be happy in it?" but rather, "How much does it pay?" Yet the best of his waking hours, the very cream of his time and energy, are devoted to his job, all through the most vigorous years of his life. What greater failure could happen to a man than to have "sold" himself for eight hours a day, year after year, to some occupation which yielded him nothing but his paycheck? Yet this is exactly what happens to the majority of industrial workers, who, to judge by Dr. Gallup's "Happiness Poll," are the UNhappiest section of the American people.

It takes a lot of effort to achieve a really successful marriage. Patient years of thoughtful growth and understanding are required, even with the best-chosen mates. And most of us make, at best, just a medium job of it. But at least we do try.

Likewise, it takes patient effort to achieve success on a job, in terms of real living. But we rarely think of our jobs in these terms, despite the fact that we devote more time to our jobs than to our marriages.

In a marriage there are two central personalities between and around which relationships and values gradually develop. On the job there is a whole group of diverse personalities, who actually spend more waking hours together than do most husbands and wives. A small working group has wonderful possibilities for developing a sense of belonging and of sharing. Even tiresome routine work can be changed from drudgery to pleasant activity by the feeling that one is taking part in a group effort for the common good.

I'm interested in this development, not through any desire to "do good" for the "workers," but because it is something that I myself want to take part in. When I leave my family and go from town to town selling bookplates and bookmarks in driblets, sleeping in shabby hotels, getting my food in groceries and cheap restaurants, and struggling hard twelve hours a day, six days a week to just make enough commissions to cover my salary and expenses, I sometimes wonder about it. At age 46, after 25 years in business, have I finally come to this, a small-time peddler in a sort of periodic exile and punishment? Phooey. Better to sell out the business and hunt for a worthwhile job.

Oddly enough, I don't feel that way about it. The business has meant a lot in my life, and it has meant and does mean a lot in the lives of a number of other people, and to the community in which we live. I have a dream of it growing into a group venture, possibly a "community of work," in which we all share and which will challenge our energy and enthusiasm and give us a new sense of freedom and belonging. Just thinking about this, and knowing that my colleagues are interested too, has made a big difference to me. It changes my work from dismal drudgery to real living.

Can a group effort thrive economically in a capitalist society characterized by selfish individualism? Group solidarity can be a great source of strength. A handful of poorly armed Jews from the cooperative farms of Palestine, united in strong social morale, routed the whole Egyptian Army. Arab individualism was no match for Jewish solidarity.

Any group effort is bound to be involved in complications, frustrations, and difficulties. That's part of the game. It takes a long time and is risky. That's part of the game too. As for me, I'd rather take part in this risky and difficult game than be the owner of a snug and profitable private business or hold a comfortable high-salaried job. But one or two people can't do it alone.

Who wants to come along?

The Bookplate Company team, 1928. Left to right: Tom Carter, Ernest Morgan, Freeman Champney, Russel Mills. Tom died from smoking. Ernest is now 94. Freeman later ran the Antioch Press. Russel died in a motor accident. The little building was rented by the Bookplate Company for ten dollars a month.

This drawing by Balfour Ker is of Ernest feeding a printing press.

12

THE HUMAN SIDE OF BUSINESS

One of the most challenging, creative and rewarding aspects of my career was the unfolding of relationships with people I worked with in my business. And what a collection they were. Blacks, Jewish refugees, Japanese-Americans, Native Americans, people with personality problems—and just garden variety folks. This chapter tells about some of them.

My first regular employee was Tom Carter, a local boy who came to work with me when he was eighteen. He was an intelligent, sensitive youth, six-feet-four-inches tall, and quick to learn. The business was small, and I hadn't been thinking of hiring anyone, but he just hung around, made himself useful, and before long I was paying him. Hardly the approved procedure for selecting employees, but he became my right-hand man.

He soon turned into a skillful worker but he had some bad habits. He was not dependable and, worse still, he dipped into the till now and then. Friends had warned me about this when he first came to work for me, and for a long time I puzzled what to do about it. But I lacked firm proof and was hesitant to confront him, hoping he would just grow out of it.

After a while he married a local girl, an attractive, intelligent person. As far as she could see he was a responsible, rising, young printer. In time they had a little girl. His habits hadn't improved. Sometimes he would lose his pay in gambling. Then he would steal some more. His wife left him, and for a time Elizabeth and I kept the little girl until Tom's sister, who lived in Buffalo, provided a home for the wife and child.

Finally Tom started stealing money from our mail, money paid by prospective customers to have catalogs sent to them. Now I had evidence. I went to his house and sat down in the living room with him.

"Tom," I said. "You've been taking money from our mail." He said nothing.

"You know," I continued, "taking money from the mail could earn you a long vacation with free room and board." No response.

"Furthermore, you've been dipping into the till for a long time, and taking money from other people too." Following that we had a still longer period of silence.

Then I suggested a plan for restoring the stolen money over a period of time, through a system of payroll deduction. Together we estimated the amount involved. Sure enough, he quit stealing and worked off the debt. That done, he went to Buffalo and got a printing job there, visiting his family regularly and contributing to their support. Before long they were reunited in a home of their own. Tom became manager of a printshop, and put two daughters through college. I was proud of him.

Unfortunately, one bad habit he didn't break was smoking. Once, in our early years together, I said to him, "Tom, you're likely to shorten your life that way."

"I'll take that chance," he replied. "I'm not all that hung up on life anyway."

When, in middle age, he was stricken with lung cancer, he couldn't face it. His wife told me after his death that he went into shock and simply withdrew. He had not been defying death; he had been denying it.

Another young man who came to work with me some years later was Clayton Cook, an intelligent, personable youth, who became a good printer. He was sincerely patriotic and, when our country entered World War II, he tried to enlist in the Air Force. He was turned down because, previously unknown to him, he had a hernia. So he got the hernia repaired, and tried again.

This time he was accepted, and after a period of training was stationed in England and served as a gunner on a medium bomber. The Air Force had a rule that any man who survived fifty missions over Germany would be relieved of active duty. This policy improved morale because it gave the crew members some hope of survival.

Clayton survived fifty missions unscathed. On one of those missions his plane was badly shot up. The pilot was killed, the copilot was wounded and unconscious, and the crippled plane was wandering aimlessly over Germany. Clayton was not a pilot but he had watched a lot of pilots. He came down from his gun turret, dragged the pilot's body out of the seat and managed to fly the plane back. He found the English Channel, missed England, and landed the plane safely in Scotland. For this achievement he was heavily decorated.

The war over, he returned to Yellow Springs and resumed work as a printer. Perhaps he found it a bit dull; anyhow, he got a motorcycle. He was not as lucky then as he had been in combat. He suffered a bad wreck. With several broken bones and a concussion of the brain he hovered between life and death, unconscious for almost a week. However, he pulled through and made a complete recovery. No more motorcycles after that.

The irony of Clayton's story is that, after surviving terrible dangers, he was finally killed by smoking and, like Tom, died in middle age.

A remarkable circumstance of my business career was a relationship of creative tension, which existed for a period of thirty years, between me and one of my principal colleagues.

It was about 1932, and the Depression was at its worst. Elizabeth was alone in the cottage one day when a strange man came to the door. He was a rough-looking fellow and huge: six feet tall and weighing over 300 pounds. Elizabeth was uneasy at first, until she noticed a little Socialist Party pin on his jacket. Then she relaxed. Our prominence in the Socialist movement made it natural for a visiting Socialist to look us up.

His name was Dave Sallume, and he had come to Yellow Springs to visit his older sister, Xarifa Bean. She and her husband, both Antioch graduates, were developing Morris Bean and Company, which was destined to become the town's leading industry.

How the Sallume family had come to America was interesting. Dave and Xarifa's uncle Najib Sallume was a Syrian—an Arab scholar who Dave claimed could speak ten languages including Sanskrit. He was also an officer in the Turkish Army and had associated himself with the "Young Turks," who were seeking to humanize and modernize the country. In time he was invited to have tea with the Sultan. He knew what that meant—death—so he swam out to an American warship anchored in the harbor, and made his way to America where he established himself as a doctor.

His younger brother followed and likewise established himself as a physician. In America, the brother married a woman of Dutch background. The cultural dichotomy proved too great and the marriage broke up, leaving Dave somewhat short on family training.

Dave's major interest when he came to Yellow Springs was in Socialist work, so his activities tended to center around the Bookplate Shop, where he collaborated with me in doing Socialist printing and secretarial work. I set up a cot for him in the back room of the shop and squeezed out $7 a week for him to subsist on.

As with Tom Carter, I never did actually hire him. In the course of time he just started helping with some of the Bookplate Company printing as need arose, and I started paying him. Dave was a brilliant fellow, well educated and with a remarkable memory. He was a connoisseur of poetry, which he could recite by the ream in his deep voice. "The elephant never forgets," he quipped, referring to his large size.

But he had shortcomings too. He smoked a lot, didn't bathe very often, and was gruff and rude. In our Socialist work he frequently antagonized people and was almost as much a liability as an asset. One evening, driving home together from a meeting in Toledo, I explained his shortcomings to him. I did it as gently as I could but it was still painful, like doing surgery without an anesthetic.

His response was little short of heroic. He said nothing, but he stopped smoking and started bathing regularly and having his laundry done oftener. He reduced his weight by 120 pounds. He even tried to be less abrasive in his personality and, although this was much more difficult, he made considerable progress. In short, he became more livable and, not long after, married an attractive and intelligent Antioch graduate.

Alas, the time came, at the end of the Christmas rush, when I didn't have enough work to keep him. I had another young printer, Al Morgan (no relation), who had more experience and seniority than Dave, and was a lot more productive. I couldn't afford to keep them both. Dave was a difficult fellow to find a job for, so I went to see his brother-in-law, Morris Bean. Morris was friendly and concerned, but he had a firm policy against nepotism.

I pointed out to him that Dave's wife was pregnant. All he could do was offer to give me all his printing.

Then I went to the manager of the Antioch Press and asked if they had a job for Dave

"No," said the manager, "but we'll take Al."

"Damn," I thought. But there was no way out. I let them have Al.

I had one other employee at that time, a young woman named Mary. Capable but withdrawn, she handled the shipping, billing and other office work. She despised Dave, and kept making digs at him. Finally, when I remonstrated with her, she said, "If you want to get rid of me, why do you have to hide behind Dave?"

Eventually she quit picking on him and stopped speaking to him altogether. Shortly after that I became ill with appendicitis and took time off to recuperate with my parents in Florida. That left Dave and Mary, not speaking, to run the shop. Mary would open the mail, get out the orders and put them on the table. Dave would pick them up, print them, and put the finished work back on the table. Then Mary would mail the orders out. If Dave needed to communicate with Mary he would phone Elizabeth, and she would call back to Mary and give her the message.

Such irony. Here was I, who preached fellowship, good will, and sharing; who held that the time we spend together at work should be a happy social experience. Here was I, with only two employees—and they couldn't even speak to each other.

But time brought changes. The business grew. More people joined the staff. Mary left to get married. Gradually Dave began taking supervisory responsibility and as the years passed, he emerged as superintendent and vice-president, with responsibility for estimating and setting prices.

Dave's role as superintendent of production came to a sudden end in 1951. This is how it happened:

We were installing a sprinkler system and building an addition to the plant. It was supposed to be finished by August, but the contractor's foreman quit and construction slowed almost to a halt. The fall season found us with the new construction barely begun and the old part of the plant still disrupted. Orders poured in and didn't get filled. I was away on a sales trip. Dave struggled desperately and suffered a heart attack. I rushed home and rallied the troops and we made the best of a bad situation.

When the crisis was over, the Board decided to get Dave off the hot seat before he had another attack, so we brought in a new superintendent. This was Bernie Gross, an excellent man who had been with us before and who liked our organization because of its social policies.

For Dave we devised a new job to which we applied the title "Comptroller." At first he sharply resisted the change, but later he appreciated it. In his new role it was his responsibility, in addition to setting prices, to project sales and control the inventory. He was to keep the inventory small, but never run out of anything. He did this with such skill that it freed up enough capital for us to get the most expensive machine we had ever bought without borrowing a dime.

Dad remarked one time that the business could hardly have survived without Dave. I was the one who dreamed up new products, supervised the art work and organized sales. However, I always tried to price things too low; Dave would insist on adequate pricing. Sometimes I could change the design to bring the cost down. Otherwise, I accepted his pricing or dropped the product. Whatever the issue, I could always depend on him to stand up to me.

I recall one time when he swung slowly around on his swivel chair and pointed his finger at me.

"Please go away," he said. "I've had all of you I can stand for today."

Although he might argue fiercely on some matter of policy or procedure, he was always open to reason. Now and then I convinced him he was wrong. On such occasions he would concede cheerfully and help carry out the decision. He remarked to me one time, "Things always go better when you're away, but it would be bad for the company if you stayed away too long."

I got a certain sense of security from Dave. I could let my imagination run free, knowing he would haul me up short before I did anything really foolish. After he retired from the business I felt a touch of anxiety. Who was going to protect the company from my follies now?

On one occasion Dave led a minority stockholders' revolt, seeking to change the composition of the Board. It had been my policy, after the company was incorporated, to have the employees elect two of the directors. Dave wanted to replace these with two businessmen who would certainly contribute more experience and business savvy. But I was the majority stockholder, and steam-rollered the election to keep the staff representatives.

Not long before his death in the late 1960s, Dave summed up our relationship nicely. "We always fought but we never quarreled." Especially in our later years together he was a great strength to me.

Whereas Dad chose most of his colleagues with care, mine seemed to just happen, but they worked out pretty well.

My role as a business man and employer allowed me, from time to time, to express my philosophy through hiring members of various ethnic minorities. The first were European Jews.

As the Nazis took over Germany and the situation of the Jewish people there became desperate, I was much concerned; so I took an active part in bringing refugees to America and helping them find places to settle. One couple I took into my home and business. Fritz and Marie Treuer, with their young teenage son, were the only survivors among all their relatives. Fritz was a native of Vienna, Marie was a Czech.

Marie came first. A smallish, vigorous woman, she spoke fluent English interspersed with occasional idiomatic fumbles which her listeners enjoyed. Later in her stay she was in demand as a speaker for women's clubs. "They like to hear me because I talk funny," she said. She was an excellent music teacher and soon had a number of pupils. She also baked tasty Viennese cookies which were very popular.

In time the Bookplate Company needed a new person in the office. Dave Sallume suggested that we hire Marie. She was businesslike and thorough, and after a while she pointed out that we needed better bookkeeping. I agreed, but said that I didn't know how to do it. "Well, let's find out," she said, and soon had an effective system in place.

Her husband, Fritz, had been living in a refugee hostel in Iowa, and when we had an opening for a man in the shop we arranged for him to come. We kept this from Marie, in order to surprise her.

Fritz was vigorous and intelligent, and had a lively sense of humor. We all liked him, but he had no rapport with machinery. I had planned to train him to run the paper cutter but gave up on that within a day. So we used him temporarily on low-skilled handwork, and later, when opportunity offered, put him in charge of shipping. He was energetic but erratic. We lived with him as a shipping clerk for many years, though not always comfortably.

One day Fritz locked himself in the washroom and couldn't get out. The locking doorknob was a simple mechanism, but Fritz just couldn't work it. After a time he gave up, and started banging on the door. We came and tried to tell him what to do, but he couldn't understand. Fritz had a hearing problem, a language problem, and a mechanical aptitude of minus ten, and he was stuck. When we finally got him out he exclaimed, "Some day you're going to find my skeleton in there."

Not surprisingly Marie soon became a key person in the organization, and, along with Dave, comprised my main executive support. With a full-time job she had to cut down on her music teaching so she kept only those pupils (mostly black) who could *not* pay. The others, she said, could find new teachers.

As soon as Marie and Fritz became settled in Yellow Springs, their teen-age son, Bob, joined them. An attractive, intelligent boy, he had been living in Ireland, and spoke English with an Irish brogue. He quickly did well in school.

Once Fritz pulled our chestnuts out of the fire in a remarkable way. At the end of the war we got a business associate in the Philippines. He called him-self "The Antioch Bookplate Company of the Philippines" and sold some of our products there quite successfully. After a while he owed us a tidy sum. Then his office manager went south with his funds, and he couldn't pay.

Fritz, a veteran stamp collector, said that if this man could send us Philip-pine stamps, we could turn them into cash. Sure enough, the man got a lot of stamps (I don't know how) and sent them to us, and Fritz was able to sell them for enough to cover the debt.

As time went on, Marie was drawn into civic activity and then, when she and Fritz finally got their citizenship papers, she was asked to run for Village Clerk. She protested that it was unseemly for her, an immigrant and a new-comer, to run against a long-established incumbent who was a member of a substantial local family. She was told, however, that as a citizen of America and of Yellow Springs, it was now her "duty." So she ran and won.

In the course of years Marie was offered a job as a financial officer in a larger firm, at a much higher salary than we were paying her. She asked what I thought and, much as I hated to lose her, I said she should take it. Years later she reproached me for this. "I was happy in the Bookplate Company," she said, "and if you had asked me to stay, I would have stayed. But you put money ahead, for me."

When Fritz reached retirement age we promptly retired him, but he missed the fellowship of the shop, so we arranged a regular part-time job which gave him a continued sense of belonging and which he performed quite well until his death.

After her retirement, Marie served as a volunteer, helping small busi-nesses with their accounting problems. Their son Bob married and, perhaps through an urge to restore the losses his family had suffered under the Nazis, had seven children. Austria's loss was America's gain.

Not all my efforts to help Jewish refugees worked out so well. I learned of a young Jewish farmer in Germany who needed to get out while there was still time. But he needed assurance of some way to make a living. There was a farm operated in connection with the Friends Home at Waynesville, Ohio, and they were in need of a new manager. I told them about the young man and they agreed to take him.

I immediately wrote to the American consul near where the man was located, saying that we had a job for him, and he could come now. What I didn't know was that it was illegal to bring in an immigrant to fill a pre-arranged job. I should have said nothing about the job and simply guaranteed the man's support. My ignorance sent him to the gas chambers. Good intentions are not enough. You need to know what you're doing.

A second group of "refugees" were brought into the business in response to domestic, rather than foreign, oppression. Immediately following the entry of the United States into World War II, all persons of Japanese ancestry on the West Coast were summarily evacuated and placed in concentration camps—"Relocation Centers," they were called. I considered this grossly unfair. Our country didn't behave that way toward persons of German or Italian ancestry. So I decided to arrange employment for some of them when I could. (In later years that injustice was recognized by our government and the surviving evacuees were indemnified.)

By that time the Bookplate Company was publishing the *Yellow Springs News*. When the job of linotype operator opened up I thought immediately of the Japanese Americans and got in touch with one of the Relocation Centers. We found a young man, Frank Kakoi, who had the necessary skills and a nice personality. He agreed to come.

At about that time his father died, so he brought his mother and two sisters with him. A new problem arose when no one would rent to them. So Elizabeth and I fixed up a comfortable apartment for them in our home. We had, not long before, bought an old, run-down, brick mansion and were slowly fixing it up. It had lots of space—great for apartments.

Frank's sisters were in school, so we gave his mother, Eda, a job in our bindery. There she joined two other women, one black and the other Caucasian. All three women bore the scars of earlier suffering, and found congenial fellowship in our group. This tri-ethnic team worked together happily for years.

Eda was a faithful worker but not very productive, so, when she finally reached sixty-five, we retired her. This was no financial hardship, as she made her home with her son and elder daughter, both of whom had good jobs. But she wasn't happy. Frank came to my office one day. "Mother is terribly lonely," he said, "and keeps wishing she were dead. Do you have something she could do?"

So we put her back in the bindery for one day a week. Every Wednesday she was with her old friends, and once more was part of the Bookplate Company community. She was happy again, and this arrangement continued for years.

The story of Frank's career, and our adventure in village journalism is told in detail in the chapter on the *Yellow Springs News.*

Our next Japanese-American was Jerry Noda. The company was growing, and Marie needed help in the Accounting Department. So Jerry and his mother came. Again the housing problem, so Elizabeth and I arranged another apartment.

Jerry and Marie worked on the opposite sides of a large desk. (East meets West.) He had an electric adding machine at his left hand which he used with great speed. Beside it he had an abacus, an ancient Asian device with beads which are pushed back and forth to do adding and subtracting. On some work Jerry resorted to the abacus for greater speed.

Jerry and his mother were nice neighbors. They wanted to invite us to a meal, but they didn't have room in their apartment. So they just took over our kitchen and entertained us in our own home. Mrs. Noda had marvelous skill as a flower arranger. She could collect a handful of greenery from the yard and produce a work of art.

Soon we brought in more Japanese-Americans to work in both the shop and the office with happy results. Some other employers followed us, but others held back. Once I visited the Ford garage and, observing that they were desperate for help, commented that I knew where they could find a skilled Japanese-American mechanic. The owner seemed shocked. " Oh no," he said, "I've got a big investment here."

After the war, most of the Japanese Americans returned to California but a number stayed permanently and have contributed substantially to the community.

Native Americans also contributed to our community. A Quaker woman in Cincinnati, Virgie Hortenstine, was doing systematic work to assist minority ethnic groups in meeting their problems, and through her I employed a young Navajo to work in the Bookplate Company.

Richard Mitchell was a tall, friendly youth, without printing experience. He arrived in Yellow Springs with no money, so I took him in as a guest for two weeks until he had drawn some pay and had time to make permanent living arrangements.

He proved to be a quick learner, a good worker, and a pleasant person to have around. For me it was a privilege to associate closely with a person from a very different culture—one who appreciated an audience and was willing to talk freely. His Navajo stories were fascinating. They included men who could control lightning and warriors who could change themselves into wolves. He told of men who could strike down a distant opponent with a sliver of bone, and of a giant, cattle-eating spider which lived on a ten-mile-high mesa.

Richard had a problem; he didn't know how to handle money. If he saw something he wanted, he bought it. He was paid every Friday, and by Monday his money was gone. This created an impossible situation. Finally we started holding back part of his pay, and spreading it over the week. He tried various tricks for getting his money sooner. Once he asked the woman in charge of payroll to let him have some money, and she asked him what he wanted it for. He said he needed some medicine. She asked him what medicine he needed. The only medicine he could think of was aspirin. She replied that she had some in her purse which she would give him. He just walked away. In time, Richard returned to the reservation and we never heard from him again.

We had a very different experience with a Cherokee by the name of Powell, an older man whom we hired to travel for us as a representative. He knew how to manage and was a good rep.

I was sales manager then, and when I sent out a new rep it was my practice to mail an announcement to the dealers just ahead of the salesman. I knew his schedule and when he would get to each city. I always made a point of telling the dealer anything especially interesting or unusual about the rep and this nearly always got him (or her) some extra welcome. To send out a Cherokee gave me something to write about.

I didn't know that among our dealers was a woman who had an irrational terror of Indians. When she learned that a real, live Indian was coming to see her she was petrified. When he finally walked in, the only thing she could think of to say was, "I always root for your side in the movies."

In the beginning of our company we made no special issue of hiring blacks, but did so when they happened to show up at the right time. When the Morgan family moved to Yellow Springs in 1921, the population of the town was about a third black, and the only equal opportunity employer was the Village Utilities Department, headed by our friend, Herb Ellis.

So we had no lack of black candidates and in time they were active in all departments, and at various levels of skill and responsibility. This situation was so matter-of-fact and taken for granted that we largely forgot who was "black" and who wasn't. When a visitor once asked how many black people we had in the organization, I had to stop and visualize the individual people before I could answer.

One of the most remarkable reps we had during that period was a black man named Wally Nelson. Short, stocky, and dark complexioned, with close-cropped hair and a strong accent, he was certainly not a glamorous type. He was, however, educated, intelligent, and infused with intense social idealism which had no boundaries of color or nationality.

He lived in Philadelphia and it happened that our important eastern territory, which included Philadelphia and New York, had just opened up. I was favorably impressed with him and took him on. At an appointed time I went East to train him.

We made a few calls together and, much to my surprise, given the times, Wally was more cordially received by the buyers than I was. He quickly became a successful rep: energetic, conscientious, and well liked by the dealers.

But there was trouble ahead. One fall he was driving home from Washington, D.C. to Philadelphia to start his autumn sales travels. With him were his wife, Juanita, and two other women, one white and one black. At Elkton, Maryland, they stopped for supper at a restaurant, but were refused service.

Wally asked to see the manager. Instead the sheriff was called and came with his deputies to arrest the four travellers for trespassing. Wally and his friends went limp and were carried off to jail. The white woman bailed herself out, and sounded the alarm. The three blacks went on a hunger strike, and the sheriff hauled them to a mental hospital. The hospital authorities refused to go along with this and returned them.

I found out about it early in the game and phoned Wally in the jail. Then I wrote him a letter. It was addressed to Wally but actually was beamed at the sheriff who, of course, would open and read it. In it I said that he should not hold his incarceration against the sheriff who was, by his functions, a man of action. It was the judge who would have to make the decision of right or wrong in the case. Then I went on to discuss the trouble that would soon befall Elkton: pickets, demonstrations, bad publicity. My remarks were couched as a reproach to Wally but were intended for the benefit of the authorities.

Then I wrote all the dealers in Wally's territory. "Our salesman is in jail," I said, and told them the reason why. There was an immediate cry of outrage from the dealers that their nice Mr. Nelson was being treated this way.

After seventeen days of fasting, the three companions were carried into court and given a full dress trial—with which they refused to cooperate. They were promptly found guilty, fined, and the fines suspended. Then they were released.

I wrote the dealers again, saying that Wally was out after what looked to us like a moral victory, and that as soon as he got a little meat on his bones he would be around to see them.

When he took to the road a few days later, he was unprepared for the welcome he got. The dealers bought enthusiastically, some offered him hospitality, all expressed their approval, first of his actions and second of our company for standing behind him. The prize remark of approval along this line was, "It was certainly white of them."

When I saw Wally again I said, tongue-in-cheek, "That Elkton act was a great success. How'd you like to repeat the performance on the West Coast?"

"No," said Wally, "You had better think of something else."

Many years later, an Antioch girl, after taking part in an anti-war demonstration, was in jail in Cincinnati, on a hunger strike. Wally, an active war-protester, came to Ohio to help and was arrested on the street for distributing leaflets. Again he went limp. I was told he was dragged up the courthouse steps by the feet while Juanita ran along behind him, cradling his head in her hands so it wouldn't bump on the stone steps.

In jail once more, Wally again went on a hunger strike. I immediately wrote the judge—a woman—testifying to Wally's character and to the fact that he was a valued business colleague who represented our company in dealing with business executives in the East.

Lee and I attended the trial. Wally's brother, a preacher, made an impassioned plea to the court. Then Wally was brought in to face the judge. As was his custom, he had gone limp and refused to cooperate. To avoid having him held in contempt of court, two sturdy officers carried him in upright, with his toes dragging on the floor behind him.

Again, he was found guilty. This time he was sentenced to serve time in jail—for the exact number of days he had already been confined.

Later on, in his testimony against militarism, Wally refused to pay his Federal Income Tax. By way of collecting this tax the Internal Revenue Service moved to garnishee his commissions from our company. We got around that by paying his commissions in advance, and then crediting him as he made sales. Thus he always owed us.

For a time this baffled the IRS. Then they served a "levy" on our company, forbidding us to remit funds to him at all. We consulted our lawyer, and he didn't know either, short of a court battle. Our board of directors agreed to support Wally in any way that would not endanger the company. Lee, who by that time was in charge, asked if Wally would pay half the court costs. Wally said no, he wasn't going to play the game on their terms. So, alas, our business association ended.

Lew Adams was a black man of quiet courage, with whom I was associated in Civil Rights and other civic activities. I mention him here because he had five daughters, four of whom worked with me in the Bookplate Company. The fifth and eldest I knew in Civil Rights activities.

The youngest, Evelyn, was with us for only a short while.

Another, Naomi, we trained as a press operator. She was with us for some years. She married a young man who later became Chief of Police and who recently retired from that post with great honor, after 36 years. Naomi herself, after leaving us, became Personnel Director of the Yellow Springs Instrument Company, which employs some 400 people.

Another sister, Charlotte, came with us in 1961 as an office worker. As the company grew, her responsibilities increased. A quiet, gentle person, she was put in charge of "Customer Service." She and her assistants had the job of answering phone calls from our dealers and reps, handling inquiries, orders and complaints. This she did with skill and grace, which earned respect and appreciation from customers and colleagues alike.

On one occasion, Charlotte was talking with a new Florida rep who had never seen her. At the close of the call he remarked. "You should come to Florida and bask on our beaches. You'd soon be brown as a berry." Charlotte reported this incident with amusement. She didn't need to go to Florida for that! Charlotte was with us until she retired in 1986.

The remaining sister, Isabel, was in total contrast to Charlotte. Tough and wiry, she was sharp of tongue and quick on the trigger. She came with us at seventeen, directly out of high school. That was in 1943 when we were publishing the *Yellow Springs News.* We needed a linotype operator, so we shipped this girl off to Brooklyn to be trained at the Mergenthaler Linotype School. She completed the course and took over our linotype work. I was annoyed with the Mergenthaler people; because she was a woman they trained her only in keyboard operation and skipped the important maintenance part.

During those war years there was a shortage of farm workers and men were brought from Jamaica to help on the farms. A camp for these men was established near Yellow Springs, and Elizabeth had the idea of arranging periodic social gatherings to which these men would be invited. She asked Isabel to be co-hostess with her, which she did. Later, after the camp was discontinued, Isabel married a young man she had met at these gatherings. They raised two daughters, but that didn't seriously interrupt Isabel's career with the company.

After being a linotype operator for a time, she took over the operation of an automatic press, and continued with that for quite a while. She noticed that the adjacent Bindery Department was not well managed. Never one afflicted with reticence, Isabel spoke about this to the superintendent, Bernie Gross. Bernie promptly gave her the job and she ran with it. For over forty years she managed the entire Bindery and Order Fulfillment area of the plant—a large and highly complex operation with a large staff and a lot of sophisticated equipment. And she was always brisk and spontaneous. Lew Adams certainly had remarkable daughters.

Our willingness to employ and promote blacks on an equal basis sometimes enabled us to get excellent people we might not have been able to attract otherwise. One such occasion occurred when Marie Treuer left and we needed a new accountant. I wrote a professor of accounting at Ohio State University and asked if he had graduated any capable black accountants lately. He said that the outstanding student in his latest class had been black. Furthermore, this young man was the only member of the class who had not yet found an accounting job; he was working as a janitor.

We hired him, and he proved to be a good accountant and valuable in the councils of the company. After a year or so he moved on to an accounting job in a larger firm. Again we approached the accounting professor and got another black accountant, who was also good. He also moved on after a year or two.

Late in the Civil Rights struggle our Superintendent, Bernie Gross, commented that there might be young black activists in the South who wanted to settle down, but who would have difficulty finding a job. He suggested that we inquire about this, and possibly open up a job for one of them.

We did, and a young man, Willie McCray, came to see us. He was nice looking and intelligent, but very nervous, as one might expect. We offered him a job, but he wasn't ready to decide yet and returned south. Later we heard from him again, and he came and joined us. He now had a wife, and she was pregnant. I rented them an apartment in my house, and he went to work.

He was a good worker, but he was nervous and seemed hostile towards white people. However, the black people in the organization helped him overcome that.

During his early months in Yellow Springs, he got into serious trouble. He and his wife were sitting at a table in a little eating place run by a black couple. A white customer was standing at the counter, chatting with the woman in charge. This man made some remark about women tenants being a problem because they tried to flush kotex down the toilets and loused up the plumbing.

Willie was insulted at such talk going on in the presence of his wife, and demanded an apology. The man apologized, though he wasn't sure what he was apologizing for. A few evenings later the two men met again in the eating place. Still puzzled as to what he had "apologized" for, the man asked Willie to step outside to talk with him.

"Step outside!" To Willie that meant just one thing—a challenge to fight. So as soon as they got outside he whipped out his pocket knife and started slashing. Badly cut, the other man fled down the street.

Arrest followed promptly. Bernie Gross went to the court to stand up with the prisoner, who was released on bond, pending trial. The Yellow Springs Police Chief, who happened to be black, protested our having brought a difficult person to town.

A considerable period elapsed before the trial, and Willie simmered down, relaxed, and became more human. Then the trial came, and with it new complications. It seems that Willie had been part of a group arrested in an earlier civil-rights action, and released on bail. Not realizing that he was supposed to appear at a certain time, he had unknowingly jumped bail, which compounded his trouble.

I wrote the judge, saying that while I did not for a moment question the seriousness of the offense in Yellow Springs, I felt that the young man had, in the intervening period, shown marked improvement in attitude and behavior and that some form of parole or other leniency would be in order. I commented, furthermore, that he had a sensible and responsible wife. This was true enough, but in her distress she had written an angry letter to the judge, which didn't help.

Willie was tried, sentenced to serve one to twenty years, and sent to Mansfield Penitentiary. He proved a model prisoner. He told me later how some of the prisoners were terrorized and robbed by prison gangs. He himself suffered a broken jaw in a prison football game, which he liked to think was an accident. After a few months he was transferred to the "correctional facility" at Lebanon, a more humane institution, and in time was paroled and returned to work at the Bookplate Company.

The entire situation came to a happy climax some time later when he was notified that his parole had been lifted, and, on the same day, he was elected to the Company's Board of Directors.

Some time later on the day after the assassination of Martin Luther King, Jr., a group of black Antioch students staged a march in Yellow Springs, carrying a sign which read, IS LOVE ENOUGH? I passed this procession on the street as I was heading for North Carolina. For the most part these students had taken a negative attitude toward King as an "Uncle Tom." I think King's assassination made them feel guilty and this heightened their reaction.

The procession marched to the center of town, where they proceeded to circle beneath the stop light, blocking all traffic. The police chief and the mayor, both black, were in a quandary. The demonstrators wouldn't listen to them. Whatever the officials did at that point was sure to be misinterpreted. At that moment the president of the Yellow Springs Instrument Company arrived on the scene. "Just route the traffic around," he said. With moral support from a prominent white community leader, the officials did exactly that, and the problem was solved—for the moment.

Then the crowd marched up the street to the Funeral Home and blocked a procession that was about to leave for the cemetery. Again the black officials tried in vain to talk with them. Then the Police Chief noticed, among the spectators, Willie McRay, the young man who had been such a problem to him before. "Do you know these fellows?" he asked.

"Yes."

"Could you talk with them?"

"I'll try."

After a brief conversation, the students stepped aside and let the procession pass. The next morning the Mayor and Police Chief were in the Bookplate Company office, singing Willie's praises.

Willie became one of our long-time stalwarts and a skilled craftsman. In later years he developed an alcohol problem which threatened to break up his family, and put his working future in doubt. However, he agreed to go away for treatment, which the company paid for and came out in fine shape. Later, when the company made a substantial contribution to the county program for the treatment of alcoholism, Willie attended the official banquet as our representative and made the presentation, receiving a hearty round of applause.

Looking back over the years it would seem that the most valuable product of our company has not been bookplates and bookmarks and calendars, but human lives. Of course, in almost every case, what we have done for people has been more than matched by what they have done for us. Samson's strength was in his hair. My strength seems to have been in the unusual people who came to work with me. (It certainly hasn't been in my hair.)

I once took part in a series of seminars conducted by the Society for the Advancement of Management. After a session dealing with non-work problems of employees, several executives got to reminiscing about problems their employees had experienced, and how they were able to help them. Finally, one member of the group, with a rather dour expression on his face, spoke up. "Wait a minute," he said. "Before we go any further let's get one thing clear. What is the purpose of a business?" ("To make money" was the expected answer.)

I grabbed the ball. "The purpose of a business," I said, "is to serve human needs. Its balance sheet is just a measure of its health." I looked around. The young executives were nodding in agreement.

Suddenly I realized that, at age 46, I was the oldest man in the group, next to the leader. No longer an obstreperous youth, I was now a dignified, middle-aged businessman, to be listened to with respect. What a good feeling.

Not long after that, Dad was scheduled to speak at the Harvard School of Business Administration, and he asked me what he should tell them.

"That the purpose of a business is to serve human needs," I replied.

"Good," he said. "That's what I'll tell them."

In 1970, at age 65, I retired as president of the Company to join Elizabeth at the Arthur Morgan School, which she headed in Celo Community in North Carolina. I was succeeded as president by my son Lee.

Lee proceeded to raise wages, and soon the company was threatened with bankruptcy. So . . . he laid off a third of the staff—*without loss of productivity.* (This says something about my management.)

Soon the business was in good shape again and Lee changed its name from Antioch Bookplate to Antioch Publishing, and built an excellent new plant at the edge of town.

Lee combined a high level of social idealism with an equally high level of organizational skill. As I remarked before, he adopted an Employee Stock Ownership Plan (ESOP) whereby a portion of the profits each year is distributed to the employees in the form of common stock. (Today the employees own most of the company stock.)

Next the company took a great leap forward. There was a firm in St. Cloud, Minnesota (the town where I was born) that manufactured photo albums. It had been started in 1926 (the same year I started our company).

This firm throve under the first generation of leadership—but went bankrupt under the second. Lee bought the bankrupt firm and added it to our company, which he re-named The Antioch Company.

With the aid of skillful colleagues, a system of "network merchandising" was developed whereby the company now has 34,000 people selling albums. Sales in 1998 were a hundred and sixty-four million dollars. (The Company sales were $300,000 when Lee took over.) The Antioch Company now has over 600 employees, is worker-owned and democratically run. It has plants in Ohio, Minnesota and Nevada. What the future holds remains to be seen.

Jerry Noda, a Japanese-American evacuated from the West Coast, and Marie Treuer, a Jewish refugee from Europe, managed the accounting department very skillfully.

Ernest with Isabel Adams Newman. Isabel came with the firm at age 17 to set type for the *Yellow Springs News.* Later she ran an automatic press and still later took charge of shipping, which she handled well. In the course of time she was elected to the Board of Directors. She was with the company for more than forty years.

13

IN PURSUIT OF ART

For almost half a century, in connection with the bookplate business, I pursued art and artists, and dreamed up ideas myself for bookplates and bookmarks. In this chapter I share some of the charm, whimsy, and astonishing circumstances of that pursuit, and some of the competition I encountered.

Since the bookplate business began as a student enterprise, it was not surprising that I drew heavily on the work of student artists. My favorite victim among my schoolmates was Gus Uhlmann. Charming and talented, he was strong on promises but dilatory on delivery. Once, when he had kept me waiting for a long time, I went to his room in the morning, dragged him out of bed and stood over him while he swiftly drew an excellent design.

Now and then, when Gus was short of money, he'd say "Ernie, if you'll let me have five dollars I'll bring you a new design tomorrow." I would give him the five dollars and then hound him for a couple of weeks to get the design. Once he asked for money when I already had a design of his which I hadn't yet paid for. So, actually I already owed him five dollars.

I didn't mention this, but gave him the five dollars and proceeded to hound him as usual. We repeated this little charade from time to time until he finished college. Then, when he left Antioch, I gave him the five dollars I had been owing him all along. His reaction was a choice blend of indignation and pleasure.

A fertile source of art work was our competition. Hardly a month passed, it seemed, without some new competitor appearing on the market. These ranged from big greeting card companies to small printers with a little press in the basement.

No one in his right mind—if he knew what he was doing—would go into the bookplate business for the money. I could have earned a lot more, with a lot less effort, if I had wanted to work for some respectable company.

It didn't take long for the competitors to find out how little money there was in the business, and then they would quit. I had, by personal inclination, always been friendly toward my bookplate competitors, with the result that they almost invariably sold out to me for a song. Noting that one big greeting card house, the Rustcraft Company, of Boston, had given up bookplates, I offered them fifty dollars for their plates. They ignored my offer and shipped me all their bookplate material at no charge. One time, in the 1950s, I counted the designs of fifteen former competitors in our catalog.

One of my more substantial competitors was Dolphin Bookplates, an eastern firm with an attractive line which they were selling nationally with some success. They weren't doing as well as they had hoped and negotiated to sell their line to me for a fairly stiff price. Shortly before the deal was to be completed I learned from an artist friend, Dan Burne Jones, that the Dolphin line had been largely plagiarized from the work of Rockwell Kent. Jones was a disciple of Kent, and knew his work well.

So instead of buying their line, I decided to put them out of business. My strategy was simple. We both advertised in many of the same periodicals. All my ads were keyed, so I could tell exactly where our inquiries were coming from. When we got a catalog request from an ad running in a magazine which also carried their ad, we gave it special treatment. Instead of the usual printed catalog, we shipped a handsome dealer album containing actual samples. It was packed in a reversible wrapper with postage for its return. This cost us some money, but it quickly wiped out Dolphin.

I had personal reasons for wanting to protect Rockwell Kent. I had admired his work ever since I helped proofread one of his books, *Voyaging South from the Cape,* when I was an apprentice at Rudge's. I considered him one of America's great artists and dreamed of the day when our company could afford to seek artwork from him. At last, I felt, the time had come to try. So I wrote him.

I received a blistering reply. He was astonished, Kent said, to think we would suggest *buying* work from him, after all we had stolen! This was a real shocker, and I had to think it over. Perhaps he was angry because we had bought work from Dan Jones, whose style was inspired by him. Or perhaps he was confusing us with Dolphin Bookplates whose line had indeed been plagiarized from him. If the latter were the case, then he would be interested to know that we had been on the verge of buying the Dolphin line but, instead, had put the firm out of business.

I wrote all this in a letter to him, and his response was almost affectionate. He had, indeed, confused us with Dolphin. As to Dan Jones, he remarked, "What do you do when someone imitates your work and then lays it lovingly at your feet?" He also said he'd be delighted to do some work for us.

So I took the train to Ausable Forks, in upstate New York, where Kent met me and took me home. I found him and his wife, Sally, charming and intelligent people, motivated by fine social ideals. My weekend with them was a pleasure, in addition to being productive.

He did a good series of bookplate designs for us, and these were printed in two colors, black and a shade of gray. When they were done, I had a letter from him remonstrating with me for making the color separations without consulting him. He commented that they had been done in good taste, but that we should never do a color separation without consulting the artist. I responded that I was pleased that he found the separations in good taste—he had chosen the colors himself.

We had one case of bookplate piracy which required no action at all. A firm issued, for $3, a substantial collection of bookplate designs in matrix form. That is, any printer with stereotype casting equipment (which most printers had in those days) could, with these matrixes, cast printing plates of all these bookplates at almost no cost. The sales pitch was "Go into the Bookplate Business for $3."

What especially interested me was that several of these designs had been stolen from us. I took comfort, however, from the fact that they had stolen our poorer selling designs. Their project died a natural death without any help from me.

Competition impacted on our business in surprising and creative ways. We had a competitor in Chicago, Louis Silver, who published a small line with some nice designs in it. Observing that he wasn't very active with the line, I offered to pay him for the privilege of using some of his designs.

He responded with a counter-proposal. He was making some plastic bookmarks. If I would merchandise these bookmarks to the stores, he would give me the use of any bookplate designs I wanted. He would provide me with the bookmark sales material, which I would enclose with my mailings to the trade. I wasn't enthusiastic, but I agreed.

For a year I included his promotion piece in all our mailings. At the end the sales had totalled about $70. Then I wrote him, suggesting that the promotion piece be redesigned and the bookmarks packaged differently. He wrote back and said, "Why don't you just take it over and change it to suit yourself?"

We paid him $60 for his cutting die and his stock of bookmarks, then we revamped the advertising and the packaging. The next year the bookmark sales went up to $1400.

Then we were approached by Clarence Dittmer, the sales manager of a church supply firm, asking if we could print Bible texts on these plastic bookmarks. If so, he would distribute them for us. He chose the texts and we printed the bookmarks—but the ink rubbed off! We couldn't buy any ink that would bond to the polished plastic. Finally I located a chemical which, added to the ink, would make it bond to the plastic. (Dave Sallume christened it "the Morgan ink.") Then we brought out a series of religious bookmarks and our bookmark sales rose to $30,000.

We weren't the only firm that Mr. Dittmer helped. An outfit in Philadelphia had a line of woven bookmarks which they sold mounted on cards. Attractive but flimsy. Said Mr. Dittmer, "Laminate these between layers of transparent plastic, punch a hole in the end and attach a tassel." They did this, and their sales took off far beyond ours. I countered with beautiful bookmarks of soft imitation leather, hot stamped with colored foil. Very nice, but too expensive. Finally, I came up with a colored, hot-stamped, tasseled bookmark made from a flexible fiber.

That was about 1970, when my son Lee was taking over. He asked me to outline the production method I had in mind. I had envisioned richly illuminated designs with classical motifs and wise sayings. In due time the line emerged. The production was as I planned it, but the art—that was something else. Lee's colleague and classmate, Mike Gardner, took charge of that. Instead of "richly illuminated designs" there were clever pictures and wisecracks like "May you be in Heaven half-an-hour before the Devil knows you're dead." That sort of thing.

I had hoped this new line might gain a foothold in the market. It not only gained a foothold—it moved out in front. Mike knew what he was doing. That line of bookmarks provided the central dynamic that sparked the remarkable growth of the company.

At the very beginning of our bookmark career I ran onto another pirate. We had just come out with the plastic bookmarks with Bible texts and were having good sales with them when another firm pirated the whole line.

I was in a store, checking the stock of our bookmarks and suddenly was puzzled. The plastic seemed a bit thin, the die-cutting lopsided, the type style not quite right. It took me a little while to realize that our line had been stolen —and the imitation was distinctly inferior.

Then I started getting complaints from dealers that we had cheapened our merchandise. Obviously the pirate line was being mistaken for ours. I phoned the offending firm and asked if they knew that their merchandise had been copied from ours, including the very quotations and the pattern of the bookmarks. They replied that the Bible quotes were in the public domain and the design carried no patent.

So I took a different tack. First, I collected from the dealers a stock of the pirate merchandise (which I took in exchange for ours). Then I drafted a letter which I proposed to send to all the Christian bookstores in the country. It said, in brief, that we had been getting complaints that the quality of our bookmarks had been cheapened. The inferior bookmarks in question were not ours but had been pirated from us by this other company. Then I went on to say that I was enclosing a sample of theirs and of ours, and invited them to compare the two. I sent a copy of this draft to the competitor, telling him that this would go to all the Christian bookstores if he persisted. This blackmail worked.

We weren't always that nasty. We had developed, as a sideline, a plastic convention badge which we patented and put on the market. Another manufacturer picked it up. Our patent lawyer wrote them a letter and they withdrew the product. Their work was good and we didn't want them to lose money on it, so we bought their inventory for what it would have cost us to produce it.

My search for bookplate art was sometimes random. On one occasion I went to the Antioch College Library and glanced through the various art books as they came to hand. In the course of this exploration I came onto a reproduction of *The Great Wave,* by Hokusai, a wonderful design for a bookplate.

On my next trip to Chicago I hunted up a Japanese art shop and ordered a print sent from Japan. That art shop, it turned out, was a rather special place, being run by none other than Tokyo Rose, a Japanese woman who had broadcast to the American troops in World War II to undermine their morale. When I dealt with her she was once more in good standing and running a nice store.

The Hokusai Wave is one of the world's art treasures, and it served our company well for years. Once, when Hokusai was ninety, he remarked to his daughter, "If I could have ten more years—or even five—I think I could be a great artist."

I had a letter once, in the early years, from Elisha Brown Bird, who was president of the American Society of Bookplate Designers and Collectors. He took me to task for producing stock bookplate designs. Bookplates, he said, should be strictly personal.

My own idea was that a bookplate, ideally, should give some concept of the personality of the owner and his/her feelings about literature and life. The important thing was not whether it was a steel engraving or a linoleum block, or a stock design or private one—the important question was, did it fit? Obviously, Mr. Bird and I had different ideas.

Perhaps I was behaving like a snake in the grass, but after Mr. Bird's death I bought from his widow one of his bookplate designs—a very nice one I thought—to use as a stock design. No doubt he turned over in his grave. However, Mr. Bird had the last laugh—his design didn't sell.

Perhaps the most inspired collaboration I experienced in my quest for art was my association with Lynd Ward. Lynd may well rank as the greatest woodcut artist of all time, at least for his style of work with its delicate detail and fine strokes.

Together we conceived a series of designs presenting depth in time as well as space. In the foreground of each design was a figure in a dark color; in the background, in a lighter shade of the same color, was a montage, delicately portrayed, from other cultures and periods of history. I considered these designs the finest art our company ever produced. Alas, they did not survive through the years in competition with other types of art.

Lynd Ward's woodcuts were not the only ones I pursued. I had long admired the woodcuts of Ade Bethune, a Catholic artist whose work somehow expressed, in simple terms, a depth of religious feeling. While her subject matter might not be religious, the work conveyed the feeling of being done "for the glory of God".I had repeatedly tried to obtain work from her, but she and her artist colleagues were always too busy. They didn't seem to care about money.

But at last my chance came. Ade had become president of the Catholic Art Association. The organization was projecting a national meeting devoted to the liturgy of death. She had read my book, *A Manual of Death Education and Simple Burial* and wrote to ask if I would address the meeting of the Association in Houston. They hoped to use the text of my talk as a chapter in a book they were planning.

I replied that I'd be glad to speak at Houston and that my company would pay all my expenses—if she would let us use some of her woodcuts. It was a deal. I prepared a talk and flew to Houston.

Ade Bethune was as good as her word and, shortly after my return, I received a sheaf of proofs from her. The next step was to break the designs for color and arrange them for bookplate use. For this task I chose a friend of mine, Read Viemeister, a talented industrial designer.

I had a special reason for choosing Read for this task. He had once offered to go over our bookplate line and criticize it. He took home one of our sample albums and looked at the contents, design by design. With unerring accuracy he recommended dropping all the best-selling numbers. I was impressed. Here was a man who thought differently. His work might be like a breath of fresh air.

He did a beautiful job with the Bethune woodcuts. They sold well for a time but, like the Rockwell Kent and Lynd Ward art, faded out of popularity in a few years. After all my years in the bookplate business, I'm still not sure how to please the public, but I've had a lot of fun trying.

Although I spent decades pursuing art, I never created any myself—with the exception of designs composed from type materials. My one significant personal contribution to the bookplate line was a text which I wrote in 1926. It took me about three hours to write it, and it sold millions. Even after all these years it continues to be one of our good-selling numbers. It was incorporated into a design—which is visually tantamount to setting it to music—by Owen Wise. The text is a very simple one:

"I enjoy sharing my books as I do my friends, asking only that you treat them well and see them safely home."

That has been my major literary creation.

I enjoy sharing my books as I do my friends, asking only that you treat them well and see them safely home

Ernest Morgan

Ernest wrote this bookplate text in 1926, and it has sold hundreds of thousands, mostly in color.

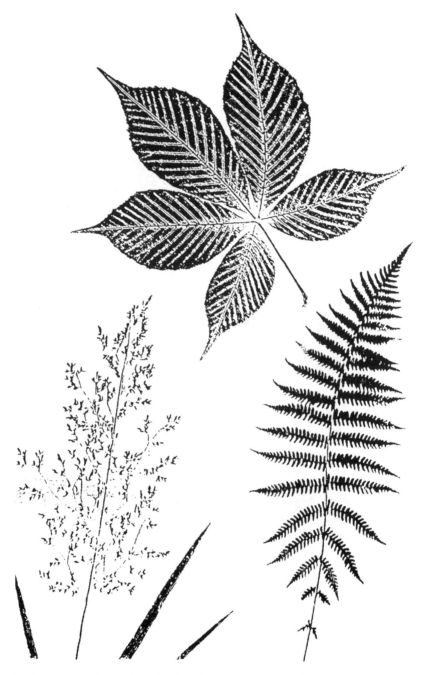

Early on, Ernest learned to print from leaves, grasses, and ferns. A valuable source of art.

14

ANIMALS I HAVE KNOWN

We humans are arrogant about other forms of life, as if we were, indeed, the only species with "genuine intelligence." We place our own kind at the top of all evolutionary charts. For me, animals are people. All my life I have observed and related to our fellow creatures, and in this narrative I share a few memories of them—some juvenile and some adult—some entertaining and some thought-provoking.

GLORIOUS HORSES

Many years ago, when I was a boy in Memphis, I attended Sunday School at the Unitarian Church. The thing I liked best about that Sunday School was the Fire Department next door, with its big white horses and its glorious engine and hook and ladder wagon. When the fire alarm sounded, our Sunday School class was instantly suspended and we would dash out to watch the scene. The horses, released from their stalls, rushed to their appointed places, quivering with excitement. The harness dropped on them from above and was quickly snapped into place. The firemen came sliding down the pole from upstairs, quickly put on their boots, hats, and slickers, jumped on the engine and off they went, bells clanging and the horses at full gallop. We always hoped for a fire on Sundays!

THE ADVENTURES OF WIGGLETAIL MORGAN

In 1947 our family acquired a puppy whom our four-year-old Lee promptly christened Wiggletail Morgan. He grew into a handsome Border Collie of medium size, with a bushy tail which he carried over his back like a plume, making him recognizable from far off.

When Wiggy, as we called him, was about a year old, we took him with us on a bicycle camping trip. Heading north for Canada, we stayed clear of the main highways, traveling well-paved rural roads that ran parallel to the main thoroughfares. In our planning we had not taken into account the farm dogs along the way, who frequently ran out and threatened Wiggy as we passed.

Happily, we found a solution to this problem. There were five of us in the party, my wife, Elizabeth, myself, and our daughters Jenifer and Benetta, with five-year-old Lee traveling as a passenger on my bike. When threatened by a hostile dog, we would move into a tight formation with Wiggy in the middle. The would-be attacker would dash frantically back and forth, and then around the bicycle formation trying to get through. We would soon ride out of range, and again drop back into single file.

A more serious problem was the exhaustion of the dog. We should have known that no dog, short of a greyhound or a whippet, could keep pace with bicycles for more than a day or so. The first afternoon, Wiggy was fine. The second day he managed to keep up with us pretty well, but needed to stop and cool himself whenever the road crossed a brook. The third day, as we left our camping place, Wiggy ran stiffly to the road and did his best. Elizabeth remarked, "This is the day that will tell the tale whether he can make it or not."

Our caravan slowed down a bit for him, and he was able to keep going until noon. After lunch, when we started out again he managed to go for a couple of hundred yards, and then sat down in the road, exhausted. We removed the luggage from Jenny's bike, distributing it among the other three bikes. Then we gently eased Wiggy, tail first, into a mesh onion sack and loaded him onto the back of Jenny's bike. He accepted this indignity without protest, and we continued on our journey.

Presently we came to the town of Mansfield, Ohio, where we learned that there would be a train heading south at about six o'clock. If Wiggy were put on that train he would arrive in Yellow Springs the next day. We went to the local lumber yard and asked if they could build a dog crate for us? Yes, they could, but not for about a week.

So I asked if they would supply us with some scrap lumber and let me use a bench saw? They loaned me a hammer and supplied a quantity of nails, and showed me to a bench saw and a pile of old crates from which I could extract the necessary lumber. Thus supplied, I fell to and soon had a presentable dog crate which we balanced on a bike and trundled to the railway station. There we put Wiggy in the crate along with appropriate food and water and nailed it shut. When the train came, we said goodbye and left him. He cried—and so did we.

He arrived home the next morning and Elizabeth's dad let him out of the crate. Wearily he dragged himself under the porch and lay down. From that time on he was much less prone to roaming than he had been before.

Equally memorable was his presence at my printshop. Wiggy was a sociable fellow who liked to come into the shop and lie down in the center of the largest concentration of people. Thus he would frequently block a work aisle. Finally the foreman remarked, "Ernest, we simply can't have Wiggy in the shop. He gets in the way."

So, the next time Wiggy came to the door, I let him in and led him through the shop to the side door and out that door. Again, not long after, he came to the front door, and again I let him in and led him through the shop and out the side door.

A third time he came to the door and again I let him in, but this time he didn't follow me to the side door but went directly upstairs to my office and lay down, out of the way in a far corner of the room. He understood exactly what the problem was—and how to solve it. After that he frequently came to the shop and lay in my office. Sometimes I would leave for awhile to tend to matters in the shop, and he would wait patiently for me to return.

On one such occasion, late in the afternoon, I was in the shop for some time and, forgetting that Wiggy was in the office, left for home at the end of the workday, shutting him in.

An hour or two later the janitor arrived and let Wiggy out. He immediately came home and found me. He walked up to me and proceeded to scold me severely. He didn't bark, or growl, or whine—he vocalized. What he had to say was very clear.

In his late years, Wiggy went with us to North Carolina. I recall an occasion when Elizabeth and I and two boys took a long and strenuous hike from Mt. Mitchell back to Celo. We didn't realize that Wiggy, approaching the age of 14, would have difficulty negotiating the rugged mountain trails for this distance. Suddenly he seemed to become disoriented, running off into the brush and complaining. Then his hind legs apparently failed him, and one of us had to hold up his rear end and trundle him like a wheelbarrow. Eventually, we had to carry him.

In our preoccupation with the dog we took a wrong turn and started down the mountain through almost impassable terrain. Just at dusk, we came out on a logging road. One of the boys stayed behind with Wiggy and me, and Elizabeth and the other boy went on ahead for help.

Using our jackets and poles which I cut with my jackknife, my companion and I fashioned a stretcher on which we were able to carry Wiggy. The dog was rather heavy, and my companion was pretty small, so we could only go a little distance at a time. We did manage to cover some ground and finally, when darkness set in, we stopped and built a fire and waited until Elizabeth finally came to our rescue with the Jeep.

Wiggy recovered from that episode, but his days were numbered.

Reproduced below is the obituary which I printed in the *Yellow Springs News.*

> *Wiggy is gone. Elizabeth phoned me about it from North Carolina this morning. He had suffered a couple of strokes, and the veterinarian said he was unlikely to recover. She held him in her arms while the doctor gave him a little shot and he went quietly to sleep. A humane procedure reserved for dogs.*
>
> *Wiggy (christened Wiggletail Morgan) had reached the ripe age of 14 in good condition. A handsome dog, intelligent and devoted, and unencumbered by pedigree, his jaunty plume was a familiar sight in Yellow Springs, and at Celo, North Carolina.*
>
> *His passing was timely. The children who loved and mauled him for so many years are young adults now. (Jenny took him along on her honeymoon.) Lee, our youngest and only unmarried child, is 12,000 miles from home.*
>
> *For Elizabeth and me, Wiggy's death signals the end of one era and the beginning of another whose horizons and challenges are already taking form.*
>
> *We have no plans for getting another dog.*

A FOX DEMONSTRATES ITS SKILL

In the woods near the house where we lived out in the country, early in our family life, there was a deep ravine on the side of which was a fox's den. I was passing by that way one day when my brother's dog, an energetic chow, came running along. He was getting perilously close to that den when one of the parent foxes showed itself at the top of the bank on the other side of the ravine. The fox ran back and forth, trying to attract the dog's attention, but in vain. Then it stopped and barked at the dog. This got results, and the dog started scrambling frantically up the side of the ravine after the fox. The fox waited calmly until the dog was close enough to make it interesting for him, then casually started loping away down the ravine with the dog in hot pursuit. Then, when they were far enough from the den to satisfy the fox, it darted out of sight through a fence and disappeared, leaving the dog frantically trying to get through. The whole maneuver was staged calmly and skillfully. The reputation held by foxes is well earned.

UNICORNS WERE REAL

 One of the most remarkable episodes of my career was my discovery that unicorns were real. This came about through a unique combination of activities.

I was, no doubt, the only person in the world who raised goats and at the same time made a living printing bookplates. I raised Saanen goats—a big white Swiss breed.

Bookplate printing frequently involves coats-of-arms, and coats-of-arms call for mythical beasts like the pegasus, the hippogriff, and the unicorn. To help me in this work I had a small heraldic library, including a book of old-time drawings of mythical beasts. Imagine my surprise when I discovered that the unicorns in the old pictures were Saanen goats. There wasn't a horse in the lot.

Then, I heard from my father about an Iowa farm boy who went away to college, where he studied Latin, and came across an old Latin document from Roman days, on "how to make a unicorn." According to this document the procedure consisted of selecting a baby horned animal at birth when the horns are merely little buds attached to the skin. To make a unicorn, these buds were removed surgically, split in two, and the two halves grafted to the center of the animals forehead, where they presently attached themselves to the skull. Returning home, the farm boy tried this on a bull calf and produced a bovine unicorn with a powerful central horn, who ruled the pasture.

But why, I wondered, would anyone—especially in olden times—want a unicorn goat? The answer was not far to seek. In those days it was a frequent practice to include a billy goat with a herd of sheep. The sheep would follow the goat and, in time of danger, would gather around it. When threatened by wolves or stray dogs, the billy goat would come forward and do battle.

A goat has three ways of fighting. One is to swing its horns from side to side like a club. Another is to stand on its hind legs, point its forehead downward and ram its enemy. A third way is to put its head down and run at its enemy. In any one of these three methods of fighting, a unicorn goat would be a very devil. I could readily understand why old-time sheep growers would value unicorn goats.

How did the unicorn get to be a horse? That is simply a perversion, no doubt based on the notion that horses are more "noble." No horse ever had a horn and for courage, intelligence, and agility, I'll put my money on the goat any day.

AN INTELLIGENT INSECT

 Mammals aren't the only creatures with intelligence. Here in the Black Mountains we have a large fly known to the natives as "the news bee." This creature earned its local title by its curious habit of hovering motionless in the air a few inches in front of a person's face as though it were delivering a message.

I was in my wife's office one day when one of these flies came in. It proceeded to hover briefly in front of the various people in the office, then hovered in front of the various items of furniture about the room.

Having satisfied its curiosity it started to leave and banged its head against the south window. Backing off, it hovered there for a moment, then headed for the west window where it banged its head again. Again it hovered and then proceeded to slowly cruise back and forth in front of all the windows. In two bumps, apparently, it had discovered the existence and properties of glass, and didn't bang its head again. It cruised about patiently in front of the windows until someone opened the door, whereupon it darted out. That contrasts sharply with the behavior of most other insects—and many humans as well.

A BRAVE, INTELLIGENT RAT

One day our cat dragged a young rat into our living room. The rat did not appear to be seriously injured, and the cat was having fun mauling it.

I watched as, between maulings, the rat looked carefully all about the room, sizing up the place and looking for a potential spot in which to escape. Finally its eye lit on the piano and it continued looking there. Between maulings it patiently edged its way toward the piano. The cat would drag it back each time but, being unaware of its strategy, didn't pull it all the way back. Patiently and doggedly the rat kept at it, gradually getting closer and closer to the piano. Finally, when it was only a few inches away, it darted beneath the piano and the cat couldn't reach it.

Ordinarily I destroy rats, but this youngster had shown such courage, intelligence and stamina that I felt it had earned the right to live. Accordingly, I caught it and turned it loose outdoors.

A TRAVELING COMPANION

Some years after Wiggy's death we did acquire another dog—a stray—with long hair, short legs, and large, expressive eyes. Chips, we named her, and she was devoted to Elizabeth.

I enjoyed second place in her hierarchy of humans. I recall the time when I returned from a trip and she was so glad to see me that she jumped up and down, then lay on the floor and rolled over and over.

After Elizabeth's death she attached herself to me. When I went off on a trip, Chips became totally forlorn. My sales travels at that time were carried on to finance the Arthur Morgan School, which Elizabeth had founded. I was able to save about a thousand dollars a month by living in my big International Travelall. In it I had a bunk, a table, a chair, and a wide variety of personal and business equipment. On top was a large carrier with commercial displays and supplies. On the end of the bunk, just behind the driver's seat, I put a small rug for Chips to lie on.

She was a good traveling companion, and waited patiently while I made my business calls. In the course of our travels I was once invited to fly to Boston, all expenses paid, to talk there on a matter of great concern to me. But this would have meant putting Chips in a boarding kennel—something I wasn't willing to do, so I passed it up.

After a time the little dog got an itch to follow me on my calls and jumped out of the car. I found her waiting at the entrance to a big shopping mall. This wouldn't do, so I tied a string to her collar and fastened it to the window post. I did this just once, and she got the point and never again jumped out to follow me.

Once, though, in Knoxville, I was in a garage having a tire changed. The electric lug wrench made such a terrible snarling noise that Chips jumped out in terror and ran out into the busy traffic, dodging under the vehicles. Luckily she survived that unscathed.

Alas, her life came to a sudden end in Florida, at the foot of Tampa Bay. I had finished my calls in St. Petersburg late in the afternoon and hurried to reach the great arched bridge to Tampa, so that I might cross it while the sun was setting. The sight was magnificent and at the far end I turned off from the causeway onto the beach.

I had failed to notice that there were gullies on that beach, and my car struck one of them with great force, sending my top carrier crashing to the ground in wreckage. There was a stiff wind blowing off the ocean and with the help of a passing motorist I collected fragments of the broken carrier and piled them on the loose papers and other contents to prevent their blowing away. There was no choice but to camp right there so I settled down comfortably to read a beautiful new edition of *Pinocchio* which I had recently gotten.

In the course of the night Chips asked to go out. When morning came I expected to find her waiting beside the door; no luck. I called; no response. Then, glancing along the expressway, I saw a little gray bunch of fur. Instead of the usual truck stop or filling station we had camped beside a busy expressway.

I fetched a shovel from my luggage and set off to bury Chips. As I reached her I was joined by a Highway truck with two men with shovels, bent on the same errand. I stood by while they carried out the burial. She had a good life and died suddenly.

I camped for two days, there beside the expressway, while I rebuilt my top carrier. Then I went on—alone.

MY PARTNERS, THE BEES

For more than fifty years, off and on, I have been a beekeeper. The obvious reason was that I and my family like honey, and this was one way to get it: lots of it! There were some intangible reasons, too. One reason, I suspect, was the unconscious attraction of danger. You're always likely to get stung when you work with bees, and this adds a touch of excitement that spices up the activity.

A more important factor and one which I recognized beyond all doubt was my interest in getting acquainted with another civilization. We speculate about alien civilizations from other worlds and here's one in our own backyard just waiting for us to make contact with it.

I developed a profound respect and admiration for bees and their civilization. Consider what a bee can do. It can tell directions accurately by the angle of the movement of the earth. Its eyes are constructed so that it can tell the direction of the sun even when the sun is behind a cloud. Returning from a honey find it can communicate accurately to the other bees the distance and direction of the find, even if it had to fly a roundabout course to get home— an instantaneous feat that would require a team of surveyors with sophisticated instruments several hours to perform. Simultaneously it can communicate its appraisal of the value of the find. The other bees will quickly locate the find, regardless of the route they have to follow.

The social organization of the bee is impressive. When a swarm sets forth in search of a new home, it sends scouts in all directions. These scouts report back on their findings, giving the exact location and direction of the prospective homes, and their appraisals of them. Immediately committees go to each of the sites and return with a report. There is much weighing of testimony in the swarm until finally consensus is reached and the colony moves off to its new home.

Water released from dehydrating nectar would quickly waterlog the hive, so the bees arrange themselves in formation to set up air currents to carry off the moisture.

Much of our knowledge of bee civilization originated with a clever German beekeeper who cracked the bees' code and learned to read their signals with a high degree of accuracy.

It is fashionable to say that creatures such as bees work only by instinct, whereas we humans employ intelligence. I would modify that statement to say that there are different kinds of intelligence, and bees have developed one of them to a high level.

Comparing their intelligence with ours, I call to mind a radio preacher shouting and gasping about heaven and hell and being "washed in the blood." I reflect on humankind spending $1.8 billion per minute on militarism—useful only for destroying its own kind. I call to mind our magnificent technology with which we are rapidly exhausting the earth and destroying the environment. I shudder at the population explosion which adds a quarter of a million humans to the earth's population every day. Where do we draw the line between intelligence and instinct? We can afford to show a little greater modesty with regard to our own kind, and a little greater respect with regard to our fellow creatures.

I regard myself as a partner of the bees, providing housing and equipment which is their sorest need and assisting with some elements of hive management. I take from them only as much honey as they can comfortably spare.

I NEVER DID LIKE WEASELS

 When I was ten years old, hiking through the woods in the Berkshires, I came upon an Oven Bird's nest. It was a cozy little structure built on the ground and shaped like an oven, with a roof and walls, gently rounded, and an opening on one side. It had baby birds in it. I admired it from all angles and at a respectful distance.

The next day I came back to look at it again. Alas, the baby birds lay dead, scattered about near the nest, their necks bitten. Only later did I learn that weasels commonly follow people in the woods. Apparently I had led a weasel to this nest, and he had killed the young and sucked their blood.

Four years later, in Ohio, I was gardening professionally and had rabbits, a cow and chickens. One day, in the woods where we lived, I encountered a weasel. Instantly I went for him. The weasel fled but I was gaining on him. In desperation he climbed a tree. I shinnied up after him.

We went higher and higher, and the branches got smaller. The weasel became agitated. He would come down and look at me, then go up and look at the little branches. Finally he gave a great leap and dropped to the ground, where he bounced up on the leaves and ran away. The chase was over.

What would I have done if I'd caught him? I'd have crushed him in my hand, probably getting a bite or two in the process.

Years later, in Yellow Springs, my friend Walter Kahoe and I were having fun out on his father's farm, building a dam across the creek there. Suddenly we heard a commotion on the bank. A weasel had caught a chipmunk. We rushed to the aid of the stricken creature, and the weasel fled. The chipmunk did not seem injured but was in a state of shock. As I held him in my hand he would roll over with a twisting motion, first his front end would turn, and then the rest of him. So we laid him gently in the grass to recover, and went back to our digging.

Imagine our surprise a few minutes later, when we spied the weasel, who had returned, looking for the chipmunk. Again we rushed after the weasel with our shovels but again he was too quick for us. The chipmunk was still in shock, and we couldn't leave him there at the mercy of the weasel, so we took him home in one of our jacket pockets, and put him in a carton. In the morning he was fully revived and frisking about, so we took him back by our dam, and turned him loose. We hoped he would survive.

SNAPPING BABIES

When I was sixteen, I was camping in northern Minnesota with a friend. We were walking along the bank of the Mississippi when we discovered a large deposit of snapping turtle eggs just starting to hatch. The eggs were round, slightly smaller than ping pong balls, and with leathery shells. There was a huge cache of them buried in the sand. As they hatched, the babies would dig their way out of the sand and head downhill for the river.

The baby snappers were all humped up when they emerged, and their stomach plates were separated in the middle, with their intestines and other innards bulging out in a clump which they dragged along as they walked. This was distinctly gruesome. As I learned later, these organs retract into the turtle in two or three days, as the little creatures straighten out. Then their stomach plates close and they look like proper turtles.

My friend and I dug up the turtle eggs and divided them between us. I took mine in a basket when I got on the train for Ohio. As usual I had an upper berth. It was a warm night, and the eggs started to hatch. The little turtles, with their sharp claws, climbed out of the basket, dragging their intestines with them, crawled round my berth and dropped down to entertain my neighbor in the berth below. A new variety of bedbug? Some found their way to the floor. The Pullman porter picked them up all over the car and brought them back to me.

When I got home, I put my turtles in an appropriate tank which provided both land and water. Every now and then one or two would manage to climb out. One crawled over the edge of the stairwell (my room was on the third floor) and bounced all the way down into the front hall, just as guests were arriving.

My stepmother had a lily pond with fish and ornamental plants. Somehow my turtles managed, now and then, to get to the pond and she was afraid they would eat her fish. So I elected to return them to the wild, but a long ways from their original habitat. Perhaps I should have left them by the Mississippi.

I CONTEMPLATE SKUNK FARMING

One day, when I was about fourteen, I was walking toward Dayton from my school when I spied a skunk foraging in a field. Walking over toward the creature I stood there, observing it from a safe distance. While I was standing there a farmer came along the road in a wagon and, seeing me, stopped his horse and came over to join me.

"Why don't you catch him?" he asked.

"Why don't *you*?" I replied.

We watched the skunk for a while and then I said, "You know, if we had an old blanket of some kind maybe we could run with it on both sides of him, and drop it on him."

The farmer went to his wagon and fetched a big horse blanket. We each took one end of it and tried to run on either side of the skunk. It was no use. The skunk ran and dodged, spraying as he went.

Finally the farmer grabbed the blanket and rushed the skunk directly, pinning him down and gripping him through the blanket. Then we walked back to the wagon. Very gingerly we worked the skunk into a burlap bag, which we then tied shut, and put in the back of the wagon.

Then I climbed up on the seat beside the farmer and we headed north for Dayton. Finally, at the edge of town, we came to the place where the man was to turn off. I gave him fifty cents for his equity in the skunk and, taking the bag dripping with skunk perfume, headed north on Main Street.

It was a long walk, through the heart of downtown Dayton, and windows closed as I went by. I was to hear of that episode for years to come. Finally I reached Monument Avenue, where my father's office was. Locating his car, I fastened the bag to the rear bumper. Then I went inside and past the receptionist. The reaction from every direction was dramatic—except for Dad. He never batted an eye.

Shortly we got into the car together and drove the ten miles north to Englewood where we lived. Mother met us at the door.

"Wait here," she said, "I'll bring you some clean clothes and you can change in the barn."

Up to this point I had been entertaining fantasies about starting a skunk farm. This animal was to be my first entry. I soon realized however that this was not practical, so I killed the unfortunate skunk, skinned it, and sold the pelt for three dollars.

Years later, when I was in college, and selling printing in Dayton for the Antioch Press, people still remembered that episode, and spoke of it when I called on them.

LIVING WITH A RACCOON

Antioch College had a rule that no pets were allowed in the dormitories. In Antioch's plan of alternating work and study, students would sometimes acquire pets during their work periods. Returning to the campus they would deposit these pets with—guess who—the Morgan family. This was particularly true when we had children of our own at Antioch.

Entering the kitchen-dining room one noon I heard an odd noise. There, on the window ledge, was a large round bird cage holding, of all things, an almost full-grown raccoon. That evening, when I came home, the creature was running loose in the house.

Elizabeth was away at the time, and Lee—who was in Antioch—was batching with me at home. One of his fellow students during his work period had rescued this baby female raccoon after its mother had been killed. Raising it with great care he had brought it back to the campus with him and it wound up at our house.

This animal had known only humans and apparently thought of itself as a person. It seemed happy only in the presence of humans. Confronted by a mirror, it was terrified. At the same time, it was absolutely undomesticated. Living with it was an interesting and sometimes entertaining experience.

Not surprisingly, her care and feeding fell to me. She wouldn't touch cat food. However, she liked my pancakes. I had a special batter of my own, "Morgan's Marvelous Mix," containing oatmeal, cornmeal, whole wheat and brewers yeast. Very wholesome. Each morning I made two pan-sized flapjacks, one for me and one for her. I ate a whole one; she got a half one for breakfast and the other half for supper. I had to feed her before I sat down to eat, or she would grab me on the ankles with her sharp claws. What she liked best of all, though, was graham crackers. She would lose all her manners over them.

Once, when Lee took a nap after lunch, she got into his room and climbed on the bed. She poked her little hands into his pockets and into his ears, so he set her out on the porch roof, whereupon she shinnied headfirst down the metal drain pipe, using her four hands. I saw her disappear over the edge of the gutter and went down to retrieve her.

She was already in the front yard where she was confronted by a dog and a cat. The cat she ignored—it was no bigger than she. But the dog was another matter. Facing the dog, with her chin held close to the ground, she advanced ominously toward him, slowly, one step at a time. The dog, step by step, began walking slowly backward. I picked her up and took her inside.

One evening she did us a good turn. My sister had visited us for supper and accidentally dropped her pearl ring on the floor in front of the refrigerator. It disappeared and she couldn't find it. Later, our raccoon reached a tiny hand into the refrigerator mechanism and found the ring where it had bounced through the ventilating hole.

How to release our little friend into the wild was a problem. We accomplished this by setting up a house for her beside the Trailside Museum, at the edge of Antioch's Glen Helen, a beautiful nature preserve. There she was fed daily and was free to come and go. By slow degrees she became independent, returning to the house less often until she finally made the transition back to nature.

WILD PIGS IN THE OKEFENOKEE

Driving through the Okefenokee Swamp on one of my sales trips I saw wild pigs: big black animals, tall and lean with huge ears. When one of them strolled across the road, the traffic stopped.

Seeing three of them foraging along the road I stopped to watch them. They looked at me for a moment, then—very deliberately—walked away. They are protected by law. They eat anything, from roots to rattlesnakes, and are afraid of nothing.

If I were to be an animal—other than a human—and had my choice, I would be a wild pig in the Okefenokee.

MORSE CODE OWL.

In recounting memories of animals, let me not forget the birds.

For many years our family lived on Glen Street, in Yellow Springs, a hundred yards or so from the edge of Antioch's Glen Helen. Sometimes we could hear the owls calling.

There was one owl that hooted with a peculiar rhythm: *whoo who whoo who, whoo whoo who whoo.* That rhythm had a familiar swing, which haunted me. Where had I heard it before?

Suddenly it came to me from memories of my boyhood. That call was Morse code for CQ, the signal that amateur radio operators ("hams," we called them) pounded out on their transmitters inviting someone—anyone—to answer. *Dash dot dash dot, dash dash dot dash.* I might not be able to read Morse Code, but I had heard that call many, many times.

I told Russ Stewart about this. Russ, then president of the local bank, was an old friend and classmate of mine, who had been a licensed ham radio operator in his youth.

"The next time you hear that owl, call me up," he said. Russ lived only a block away, also on the edge of the Glen.

It was a long time before the owl called again, but one morning, just before dawn, I heard him: *CQ, CQ.* I phoned Russ's house and his wife answered. She wasn't pleased at being called at five in the morning. I gave her the message for Russ, and went back to bed, waiting for the owl to repeat. For a long time there was silence, then the owl gave one long *whoooo*—and quit for the day. I could have wrung that bird's neck.

The next time I met my friend on the street he regarded me uneasily. I protested that the owl had let me down. He seemed unconvinced. Clearly, any reputation I might have had for sanity was under a cloud.

Some time later, however, Russ was hunting trilobites in the Little Miami Valley, along with some friends, and they were roasting wieners over a campfire. Then, in the dusk, they heard a CQ owl. My reputation was saved.

A PROBLEM DUCKLING

 Another bird experience happened when I was canoeing down the Little Miami River with my son Art.

Once, as we rounded a bend, we came onto a brood of wild baby ducks with their mother. The mother gave a signal and the babies dove out of sight while the mother staged the "broken wing" act, crying piteously and beating her way slowly down the river to lead us away from the babies. One baby, however, got his signals mixed and went dashing after the mother who, instead of taking off shortly as she would normally have done, kept beating her way down the river. We humans aren't the only ones with problem children!

Art started singing a song to the tune of "The Stars and Stripes Forever."

Be kind to your webfooted friend;
That duck may be somebody's moth—er.
She lives in a spot in the swamp,
Where the weather's cold and damp.

SEEING HUMANS AS PART OF NATURE

The Judeo-Christian tradition, both in its orthodox and liberal manifestations, places man at the center of the universe. In the Old Testament, God creates Adam and Eve, puts them in the Garden of Eden, and gives them dominion over all the other creatures. In my career as a Humanist, I refrained from signing the "Humanist Manifesto" because I felt that it was overly homocentric. At the same time, as Chairman of the Resolutions Committee of the American Humanist Association, I received acceptance from the members when I formulated resolutions in terms of humankind as part of nature.

Too often, in our culture, we have accepted the notion of man as the measure of all things and have used that concept as a mandate to exploit or destroy nature at will.

In this technological age such an idea is no longer tenable. The time has come to see ourselves as part of nature, as some other cultures have done, and to relate wisely to the earth. Failure to do this may spell our doom.

15

COPING WITH THE GREAT DEPRESSION

The Depression posed an enormous challenge, especially to a young couple launching a family at the very depths of it. Our response took three forms: sophisticated barter, rugged homesteading, and the organizing of the unemployed. It took all the energy and ingenuity we could muster.

The root cause of the Great Depression was clear: the maldistribution of ownership and income in our society produced a situation in which the total wages, salaries and commissions received by ordinary people were not sufficient to buy back what they produced.

This discrepancy had been compensated for by military spending and the rapid expansion of debt, both public and private. Then Herbert Hoover cut back on the military and tried to balance the budget. Sales started to slip, and then, like a bolt out of the blue, came the stock market crash, with general collapse.

Sales almost stopped, factories closed, and unemployment skyrocketed. Soon food was rotting in the fields while people went hungry, and factories stood idle while their products were urgently needed. Financiers and industrialists were jumping from tenth-story windows. Eddie Cantor, a radio comedian of that period, had a grim joke: A man comes into a hotel to rent a room. The clerk says, "Do you want it for sleeping or for jumping?"

I have already told how in 1929 the Bookplate Company was saved by my two workers agreeing, a few months before the collapse, to accept wages of ten dollars a week for several months so that we could expand our distribution. The profits which were to have been shared with them never materialized, but the arrangement saved the company.

Then a new and exciting project emerged in which Elizabeth and I had an active part. Always the innovator, Dad put forward a barter plan, which he promoted with his usual contagious enthusiasm. There were to be two levels of barter: local and regional. The local organization was to be the Yellow Springs Exchange. It would handle transactions through the use of a local currency, or scrip. The regional organization would be the Midwest Exchange, which would handle transactions by entries in a central set of books.

The local exchange needed a central retail outlet, so Dad bought our building and we moved the Bookplate Company from Xenia Avenue to Dayton Street. A store manager was hired, and I designed and printed scrip in denominations from ten cents to five dollars. Later, when making change in U.S. currency became a problem, I added nickels and pennies. I was proud of that scrip. It was durable, attractive and very difficult to counterfeit. In due time the store opened and the scrip went into circulation, visibly stimulating the local economy. People brought in all manner of merchandise and produce, some of which was bought outright for scrip and some taken on consignment.

From time to time we printed up a bulletin which listed the items on hand in the Exchange store and from the Midwest Exchange members, and also the services available. A quick glance at this impressive list was generally sufficient to persuade anyone to accept the scrip.

The launching of the exchanges had been financed by my father, from family savings. One might ask how Lucy, a thrifty person and the one who kept the family solvent, accepted this. A remark she made to me was characteristic. "Considering all the money he doesn't waste on alcohol and tobacco, I don't mind his using some of it for a good cause."

A small staff was assembled to launch the regional exchange and an excellent list of members was generated. These consisted of firms who were willing to accept orders from other members and take payment in credit with the organization. But the regional project lagged. The members were ready enough to accept exchange orders but slow in placing orders. The problem, as I saw it, was that production and consumption were separated. The employees of a firm might have a great variety of needs—especially if they had been laid off. But the firm itself might have very few needs, apart from the staple supplies and raw materials which it used and which commonly came through well established channels.

Elizabeth and I had ideas about this, and Dad finally said, "Why don't you take it over?" So we did. By that time we were fixing up the cottage in the country, so our first move was to prime the pump by ordering things we ourselves needed. The credit limit of each member was based on the relative demand for its product. Our product, printing, was in general demand, so we had a relatively high credit limit.

As we had hoped, there was a domino effect. A firm which filled an order on Exchange credit was immediately under the necessity of finding something to buy through the Exchange, in order to collect payment. The local

Exchange was tied in with the regional, and it too helped prime the pump. Our company included some scrip in the weekly payroll, and this was well accepted since Exchange orders for printing were helping to maintain full employment. It looked as if we had things going.

Then two developments occurred which cast a shadow over the operation. First was the National Recovery Act, under which each trade association had authority to legislate trade practices for its industry. Uniform credit procedures were commonly legislated. To sell on a barter basis to one customer and not to another could be considered as discrimination in credit terms and thus illegal. We got a warning of this when one of our Midwest Exchange members sent us a check in payment of what he owed, rather than waiting for another member to place an order with him I could see the handwriting on the wall. (Later The National Recovery Act was declared unconstitutional. We needn't have closed the Exchange.)

The other development was that Dad had gone to head the Tennessee Valley Authority and had told us that he would turn the Exchange project over to us debt-free if we wished, but then we'd be on our own. He would not be in a position to give active attention or support. So we decided to liquidate. Happily, a considerable amount of our local scrip had found its way into the hands of collectors, so didn't have to be redeemed.

Once, during that time, a Dayton business man came to my office with a plan for ending the Depression. "I will tell you the plan," he said, "and you can tell your father. He is close to the President and can pass it along to him." This was it: the government would place orders with all manufacturing firms sufficient for them to hire back all their laid-off workers and run at capacity. Then the government would take all these goods—clothing, food, radios, automobiles, everything—and dump them in the ocean. To put it on the market or otherwise distribute it to the people would only have made the Depression worse.

In fact, this man's suggestions were not very different from what actually happened. The Depression was never solved, but was merely postponed through inflation and through massive borrowing, fueled largely by military expenditures. This is a form of medicine which must be taken in ever-increasing doses—until it kills the patient.

Be that as it may, the two Exchanges went out of business and we moved the Bookplate Company back to its old location. The barter experience had not been wasted on me, however. I quietly resumed barter activity as a form of outreach for my own business and continued this for years. (I called it The Commonwealth Exchange.) In some cases we bartered printing directly for what we needed. In other cases that wouldn't work, as when we needed printing equipment. In such cases we bartered printing for paint, and then bartered paint credit for printing machinery. I don't know how we could have pulled through the Depression without barter.

Our most picturesque barter deal occurred in connection with plumbing.

We needed a complete plumbing job for our new home but had no money for it. So I wrote all the plumbers in the three neighboring cities, offering to swap printing for plumbing—anything from a single fixture to a complete job. I picked up a few minor fixtures in this way.

Then one day we got a postcard from a plumber in Dayton, and Elizabeth and I drove over to see him. There we found a black plumber and his wife in a small shop. We introduced ourselves and, after a little chat, asked what printing they needed. There was no response, so I asked if they needed letterheads. No, they had plenty of letterheads.

Did they need envelopes? No, they had plenty. Advertising, perhaps? No. "But you did write us, didn't you?"

With a shy glance at her husband, the wife reached into the desk and produced a sheaf of poetry, *Echoes of Heartthrobs and Whispers of Love.* They wanted this made into a book, and the husband was willing to do a whole plumbing job to get it printed.

So we put up a tent in our yard and the plumber and his helper came and lived with us while they installed all the plumbing. I purchased a bargain lot of paper, got the type set at the *Yellow Springs News,* and worked nights and Sundays printing the poems two pages at a time, on a hand-fed press. It was a big job—and so was the plumbing. Finally both were finished, everybody was happy and we had acquired some good friends.

Important though it was, barter was not the only survival procedure we resorted to during the Depression.

I've already spoken of "the tumbledown cottage" which my folks had given us. With our printing business at low ebb, that cottage and the few acres that came with it were essential to the survival and well-being of our family. Our experience there proved to be quite an adventure. The cottage had a leaky roof, was infested with bedbugs, and had a "two-bucket pump" as the only water supply. (it only produced two buckets of water at a time). The barn leaked too, and its sills had rotted away. There was no electricity.

We bartered for some good roofing, drove out the bedbugs with sulphur fumes and paint, jacked up the barn and poured a foundation under it using gravel which we dug from our own gravel pit. We installed an old Delco light plant.

The pump was replaced with my hand-dug cistern and the bartered plumbing. To irrigate the garden I installed a hydraulic ram in the nearby creek, which pumped water into an old 500-gallon pressure tank that I bought for five dollars.

I recall a disaster from that period—when I mistook maple syrup for machine oil—and had to replace the motor in our car.

Within a year we were producing our own milk, meat, eggs, honey, fruit, vegetables, and firewood. However, if you think "simple living" is simple, you're wrong. It was a complicated and strenuous life, though happy and healthy.

When Elizabeth's father came to see us, he was appalled and couldn't see how we could survive there. Actually, the strenuous life agreed with Elizabeth, and she was quite happy. Her father had visited us before, when she was presiding over the Antioch Presidential Mansion, where we provided him with a room and private bath. He had been impressed and pleased to see his daughter in such a good situation. Ironically, what he didn't see was that Elizabeth *wasn't* happy in that menage.

The way we got electricity was even more unusual than the way we got plumbing. Our old Delco light plant gave us 32-volt DC current, useless with most appliances. It ran on kerosene, and I had to dismantle the engine and grind the valves once a week. When a bulb was turned on we had to wait while the engine came up to speed before light was produced. We wanted regular 110/220 AC, but there was no power line in our neighborhood.

The private power company would probably have built a line into our area if we and our neighbors had asked for it, but the rates would have been high. Furthermore, that was the company that tried to destroy Antioch, using my writings for the purpose. So we wanted to buy our power from the Village of Yellow Springs.

The catch to that plan was that we were two miles from the village boundary, and the village could not legally build power lines beyond its boundaries. However, the village could accept lines turned over to it by others, and could maintain those lines and service the customers. So . . . the logical thing was to build our line.

There were six families in our neighborhood that needed power. These included four neighboring farmers, Elizabeth and myself, and my parents, who had a cottage about a quarter of a mile beyond us. I called a meeting of the farmers, and we talked it over.

We would have liked to hire a company to build the line, but we didn't have that kind of money, so we decided to tackle it ourselves. My parents put up some of the money to buy wire and other materials. The street car line, which had just gone out of business, sold us all the poles needed for twenty dollars. We borrowed a huge jack to pull the poles out of the ground. We had oak crossarms sawed at a nearby sawmill, and we coated them with yellow paint made from discarded printers' ink. One of the farmers, Faye Funderburg, had an old, homemade tractor on which he mounted a mast, with rope and pulleys, for raising the poles.

Funderburg belonged to a now vanished breed of American farmers who grew up during the emergence of twentieth-century technology. He was not only a farmer, but also a carpenter, plumber, electrician, and mechanic. His skills were invaluable in building our power line. I well remember driving Funderburg's improvised tractor, with a telephone pole waving precariously over my head, as I guided the rig to the hole where the pole was to be planted.

We started building at the far end of the line, and it took us about a year.

At one point we ran out of money, so I bartered printing for more electrical equipment, and the work went ahead.

The climax came in the final stretch of line as we approached the village boundary. Two brothers named Spillan owned the last section of property between us and the village, and they weren't going to let us past. They claimed they owned the land to the middle of the public road, from either side. We held that the right-of-way was public and that utility poles could be erected along the road. We wrote them a polite letter, which we all signed. They reiterated their stand.

We weren't about to be stopped a couple of hundred yards from our goal, so one Saturday morning we took the bull by the horns and started digging holes along the right-of-way in front of their place. They rushed out and protested. I talked with them, while my friends gritted their teeth and kept on digging. Soon the Spillans went back to their house and a short while later their car dashed out of their driveway and headed downtown. In another half hour we received a special delivery letter from them. It said:

> *This morning, I noticed some men digging holes and putting up poles on our property. Those poles must be removed and the holes filled up at once.*
>
> *Signed,*
Wilbur Spillan
> *P.S. You are liable for writing a unanimous letter.*

The "unanimous" letter referred to was, of course, the one we had all signed. Clearly, they had confused "unanimous" with "anonymous." Anyhow, that did it. Stimulated by that letter, our farmer-crew postponed their home chores and went on putting up poles.

By late afternoon all the poles, with crossarms attached, were up, and the wires had been draped over them, ready to be pulled tight. Then the Spillans played their last card. They went across the highway at the far side of the field, parallel to the road along which we were working. Going to the farm there, they borrowed a team of horses and a hay ladder, a wagon with tall uprights at either end, made for hauling hay.

They drove this team onto the far side of the field, tossed a few ears of corn into the wagon, by way of an excuse for the trip, and headed for the gate on our side. Then we saw their game. The gate was halfway between two of our poles, and the wires were sagging down over it. The hay ladder would snag the wires and either pull them down or break the ladder. We ran to the ends of the wires and grabbed them with gloves and pliers—whatever we had. No time to use the block and tackle we had brought for the purpose. We pulled with all our might. Slowly the wires came up as the team approached, just clearing the uprights. The battle was over and we had won.

Soon we transferred our line to the village, they connected it and turned on the juice. One of the first things they did was to hang a transformer on one of our poles across from the Spillans' house, connect them to our line, and take down their old line. We loved that. As a bonus, I strung telephone wires below the electric wires, and the Telephone Company then agreed to install service for us. Today, after fifty years, that line serves a large residential area.

I learned, after the line was finished, that Lyle Kahoe, one of my farmer friends who was helping with the line, had tweaked the Spillans a bit, in his mischievous Irish way. Passing by their place one day, early in the power line construction, he asked, "How much are they paying to pass *your* property?" As if *he* were being paid!

At one point the line crossed the railroad tracks, where the road right-of-way passed over the tracks on a bridge. After the line was built a man came from the railroad company to inspect this crossing. Our poles were supposed to be on the road right-of-way, which was thirty-six-feet wide. The location of the pole near the bridge was in question. The railroad man started pacing from the center of the road. When he reached the edge of the right-of-way he was still several yards from the pole. Clearly, and quite inadvertently we had put it on railroad property. The man paused a moment, then he said, "Well, it's hard to tell just where the middle of the road is." Quite a contrast to the Spillans. We were home free.

The only casualty of the project was little Arthur. We had a stack of poles at our place, and beside them a can of creosote which I was using to treat the poles. Once, when no one was around, he took a hand in that, getting creosote all over himself as well as the poles. We quickly washed him in alcohol, but the stuff burned him painfully.

With the leftover poles I built a grape arbor, a solid structure which my brother-in-law characterized as a mine tipple. Maybe so, but it sure held up the grapevines.

The kindly way in which the railroad official winked at our wrongly placed telephone pole was not consistent with the rail company's history. Early in the century, when Yellow Springs first built its power system, it brought a line in from a plant in Cedarville, seven miles away. When the line reached the railroad at the edge of the village the railroad company would not let it cross. Every time the electrical crew put the wires up, the railroad would send a steam shovel on a flat car and pull them down. Finally the power men got everything ready, strung the wires and turned on the current. When the locomotive arrived to pull them down the men yelled, *"Six thousand volts."* The locomotive skidded to a halt and the battle was over.

In the country we had more room for goats, so we got some companions for our solitary animal. We were fortunate to get Saanens, a Swiss breed: large, pure white, and intelligent. They were nice to work with. I built a milking stand in the barn and each goat knew its turn to jump on the stand to be milked (and get a cup of feed).

The goats gave fine, rich milk which spoiled us for drinking cow's milk. There was, however, one complication; the milk was *too* rich—6% butterfat. As a small child, Art couldn't handle that much fat, despite being a robust youngster. We couldn't skim the cream off, because goat's milk is naturally homogenized. So I got a table model cream separator and that did the trick. The faster you turned the crank, the richer the cream. I borrowed Elizabeth's metronome to time the cranking. We generally preferred adagio cream, though allegro cream was best for making butter.

The baby goats were wonderful. A few minutes after they were born they would be on their legs, wobbling around. In a day or two they were running and jumping. Once we had three does giving birth simultaneously and I had to rush from one to the next, assisting them. I lost one of our most promising baby does in that situation by not getting there quickly enough.

At one time we had ten baby goats roaming the place in a little herd. When Elizabeth's brother came to see us, this herd swarmed up over his car and stood on their hind legs on the roof to get at the tree leaves. They left little hoof prints on the car. After that, when he came to see us, he parked down the road a ways.

Sometimes, if a car parked near the woodshed, they would swarm onto the car, then onto the shed, then onto the barn roof. Then they would come down to the eaves and look down at us impishly. Sometimes, when Elizabeth left the kitchen door open, they would cautiously steal in, then scamper out when she took a broom to them.

The pasture we had was full of brush and brambles, from long disuse. We turned the goats in there and they cleaned it up in a hurry. Within a year it was clear, and covered with grass. The worst problem we had with the goats was that they were diabolically clever at getting through fences. They loved to squeeze through and get into Funderburg's corn.

We ate the surplus goats. This posed a dilemma for me, as I was strongly averse to hurting or killing anything. So I had Funderburg do the butchering on shares. This bothered me. Was I willing to feed the meat to my family and eat it myself, but too squeamish to do the butchering? When the time came to butcher another goat I borrowed a rifle and shot the animal myself, neatly through the forehead. Instantly every muscle relaxed, all four legs folded and the goat dropped without so much as a quiver. A moment before, the animal had been standing there, completely unconcerned. A split second later, poof!, it was dead. It is a rare human who has the privilege of dying so easily. There was another good thing about doing it myself—we got all the meat.

Rugged homesteading and barter not only helped us survive the Depression—they were a great adventure. Our third response to the Great Depression was to help organize the unemployed. The story of this effort is told in the next chapter.

16

ORGANIZING TRADE UNIONS AND THE UNEMPLOYED

This chapter tells the inside story, almost overlooked in history, of the mass organization of the unemployed during the Depression—critical to their survival—an organizational effort in which I had an active part. It also recounts my somewhat eccentric career as a trade unionist.

Almost unknown today, is the epic story of the organizing of the unemployed during the Depression. I took active part in that movement, knew the rival left-wing organizations that led it, and can animate the story with personal incidents. Writing this account sixty-five years later, I hope that other veterans of that struggle will check my memories for major errors or omissions.

Prior to the Depression, most relief was based on private charity. The sudden onset of the Depression, with its mass unemployment, found the country woefully unprepared. Unemployment insurance had not yet been invented and there were few public agencies prepared to cope with the need. Without vigorous organized action by the unemployed themselves, thousands would have faced starvation. Meetings, marches and demonstrations were held and, above all, "grievance committees" were formed, whose function it was to visit the relief offices to call their attention to special hardship cases—an unemployed family without fuel in midwinter, a sick child needing medical attention, a family without food or shelter. These committees were generally made up of the biggest, toughest and most articulate members of the organization, and it was their job to haunt the relief offices. They were instrumental in the survival of many stricken families.

Marches and demonstrations had an important role too. Once the Socialists, to get relief going in Chicago, collected ten thousand hungry men and marched them down State Street. Whereas "the establishment" was willing to let the unemployed starve—as long as they did it quietly—the outpouring in Chicago got action, and public relief began to flow more adequately.

Almost as important as the material relief was the lift which the organizations of the unemployed gave to the morale of their members, and to their will to struggle and survive. "It is not your fault that you are out of work," their leaders would tell them. "It is the faulty organization of society which creates want in the midst of plenty. Stand up, look the world in the eye and join with your fellow sufferers in the struggle for survival and a better world."

In every case that I recall, the organizations of the unemployed were inspired and formed under left-wing leadership. The left-wing organizations and the intrigues which shaped the organizations of the unemployed during the Depression constitute an obscure and fascinating fragment of modern American history. I'll give a thumbnail sketch of it here.

First in the field were the Communist-led Unemployment Councils. Next came the Unemployed Leagues, led at first largely by Socialists. The two groups became rivals. Then another left-wing organization entered the scene, the Conference for Progressive Labor Action (CPLA). This was a small, highly select group of cadres under the leadership of A.J. Muste, later distinguished as a leader of the peace movement.

The CPLA became active with the Leagues and gradually moved into the dominant position of leadership among them. I was myself a delegate to the state convention of the Unemployed Leagues in Ohio, held at Columbus.

I had never seen anything quite like it. There being no funds for housing, the convention remained in session continuously, day and night. Each delegation presented a speaker who described the conditions and activities in his or her community. This went on for hours and hours. By the second day, when the time came to conduct business, the delegates were so groggy they hardly knew what they were doing.

Inevitably the Communist-led Unemployment Councils applied for admission, but the CPLA didn't want the Councils in. So the matter was shrewdly brought to the floor at the very moment that lunch was being served. The meal was already late and as the waiters started down the aisles with trays of baloney and buns, a motion was made to exclude the Councils. It was quickly passed by voice vote of the hungry delegates, and without discussion.

In time the Unemployed Leagues formed a national organization, under CPLA leadership. Soon their strategy became clear; the Leagues were to provide a mass base for launching a new left-wing party to compete with the Socialist and Communist parties.

The Socialists weren't happy about this. Having worked hard to build the Leagues, they felt let down. At this point I tangled with Muste, bringing out a pamphlet citing chapter and verse on the whole strategy. But they went right ahead and launched the American Workers Party.

Not long after that, the followers of Leon Trotsky quietly joined the new party. Trotsky, betrayed by Stalin, had fled Russia to save his life and formed the Fourth International, composed mainly of anti-Stalin Communists. Lacking a mass base, they had decided, secretly, to join the various democratic socialist parties of the world with a view to either capturing them, or wrecking them and then taking out of them such elements as might share the Trotskyite position. The American Workers Party, although it was not the Socialist Party, offered a first step. The Trotskyites quietly moved in and took it over. At about that time, A.J. Muste shifted his attention to the Peace Movement.

This left the Communists running the Unemployment Councils, and the Trotskyites, with their CPLA colleagues, running the Unemployed Leagues. The Socialists, out in the cold, proceeded to launch a new organization, the Workers' Alliance, which was geared to the needs of the Works Progress Administration (WPA) workers as well as the unemployed. This made it more timely than the other two organizations and it quickly surpassed them in membership and activity.

This organization was launched on a shoestring. The Bookplate Company did the initial printing on credit—membership cards, stationery, and handbills. Before long the Workers Alliance had 400,000 members and was a power to be reckoned with. Then the other two organizations merged with the Workers Alliance.

Soon the Trotskyite-CPLA group came into the Socialist Party, but they managed neither to capture nor to wreck it. They did take out a few of our people, however. My Bookplate Company colleague, Dave Sallume, was one of these. It became my unhappy duty to expel him from the Socialist Party, but I could never get a quorum of the local party together for the purpose. Finally he got impatient and obliged by just quitting. Interestingly, this never seemed to interfere with our personal or business relationships.

In the Workers Alliance nationwide, the Communists gradually took control. This was partly because of larger membership and also because of tighter discipline, more concentrated effort, and skillful tactics. At the same time they tried, for reasons of public relations, to keep Socialists in the titular roles.

The Communist Party was monolithic (one stone). What its members throughout the world did (and thought) was largely dictated from Moscow, and the international party became an instrument of Soviet foreign policy.

When Hitler came to power in Germany, threatening Europe and the world, Russia desperately needed friends and allies. Word came from Moscow: be patriotic; support Roosevelt; don't do anything that might embarrass the New Deal. Suddenly the American Communists became very patriotic —and pulled the teeth out of the Workers Alliance, which shortly died.

I recall an incident which dramatically illustrated the role of the Communist Party in the Workers Alliance at that point. Eugene Triquet, the secretary of the Socialist Party in Springfield, Ohio, came to see me. The Alliance, he said, was planning a relief demonstration. A local man, an unaffiliated radical, was talking violence. He was a strong talker, and they didn't know how to handle him. Triquet asked if I would come up for the next public meeting and help keep the situation under control.

It was a big meeting. Almost at the beginning this man got up and gave a harangue, calling for the smashing of windows and other violence. I took the floor immediately, praising him for his militancy. Then I went on to add that we must be very careful to avoid violence, as that would destroy any good effect we might have. I then suggested ways in which the demonstration could be made dramatic without being violent.

To my pleasure the man swung in behind me and supported this position. He happened to be a sign painter and agreed to make signs for the demonstration. Slogans were chosen and we were off to the races. A Communist member of the group offered to transport the signs.

The time for the demonstration came and the crowd gathered, but the signs didn't come. The crowd waited and waited and finally dispersed. Then our Communist friend arrived with the signs. A coincidence? Knowing the Communist Party line and tactics, I doubt it.

The death of the Alliance ended the organization of the unemployed in America.

Were all those years of organizing efforts by the Alliance and other unemployed organizations wasted? Certainly not. They contributed significantly to the survival and relative wellbeing of the unemployed during a period of economic collapse. Had they not been organized, many thousands of unemployed, and their families, would almost certainly have starved to death. At the time the Workers Alliance went down the drain, the economy was moving upward again. Partly this was taking place through the efforts of the New Deal, but more it was a result of the rising tide of military preparation for World War II. The role of the unemployed organization was no longer crucial.

Having told, in outline, the story of the organizing of the unemployed, let me flash back to personal anecdotes and comments.

The Unemployed League in Yellow Springs once resisted the eviction of a black family. The eviction papers had been served and Al Pultz, the local constable, was setting the tenant's furniture out in the yard. At that point an Unemployed League delegation arrived, headed by Dave Sallume and myself. Al was nonplussed and sent for the County Sheriff, while we started moving the furniture up onto the front porch. The sheriff arrived shortly, with a group of deputies.

My relationship with that sheriff was rather odd. He had been involved in shady activities which I had exposed in my newspaper column. In fact, that particular column had been featured by the editor as the lead story in that week's issue. Furthermore, the sheriff happened to be a printer—and a union brother of mine—who had opposed my election as president of the printers' union in the county. Our relationship was hardly a cordial one.

When he appeared on the scene, I approached him with the eviction notice in my hand. "George," I said, "take a look at this eviction notice. It's a carbon copy, and was put in the typewriter wrong, so the typing appears on the wrong lines. This poor guy is confused. You can't put him out on this basis." The Sheriff looked at the paper, handed the man a $10 bill, and left. Then we finished putting the furniture back on the front porch. There must be a moral to that story but I can't think of it.

Elizabeth worked actively with the unemployed organization in Dayton, and discovered some interesting sidelights. One was that unemployment frequently broke up families. There were even cases where a couple would get together again when one of them had a job, only to break up once more when both were unemployed.

One remarkable experience of our lives occurred in connection with the Workers Alliance. David Sarvis, a young Socialist friend of ours, was a talented artist. He painted a clever antiwar sign which four young Socialists carried in a parade in the town of Piqua, Ohio, being held in honor of the Spanish-American War veterans there.

At the end of the march a group of National Guardsmen, who had taken part in the march, discovered the young Socialists with their sign and beat them up. Then they had them arrested for "inciting an officer to commit a breach of the peace."

We read about this in the Dayton paper and Elizabeth drove immediately to Piqua to arrange for their defense. She had no experience along this line but was energetic and resourceful. Needing bail money, she phoned Russell Stewart, president of the bank at Yellow Springs. Russ was an old schoolmate of mine and had helped finance my company. Without waiting for a signature he wired the money to Elizabeth, "from the Miami Valley Socialist League, Russell Stewart, agent."

For legal defense, Elizabeth recruited Joseph Sharts, of Dayton, one of the attorneys who had defended Eugene Debs during World War I. Joe was State Chairman of the Socialist Party at that time and repeatedly served as its candidate for governor. He was himself a veteran of the Spanish-American War and tended to be critical of the young pacifists in the party. But he took the case without hesitation—and also without pay. From all reports, he made a monkey of the Prosecutor.

In Piqua no one dared speak to Elizabeth on the street, though one old Socialist beckoned her into an alley and gave her some money to help with the defense. The local Presbyterian minister, Harry Parrot, provided hospitality for her and as a result lost his pulpit.

Three of the young Socialists who had taken part in the march became more subdued in their activities, but the fourth, Louis Moon, found himself challenged to greater activity. He came to Dayton, not long after, to assume leadership in the Workers Alliance there.

The organization was large, but in bad shape, with conflicts and rivalries and backbiting. Louis' situation there was almost impossible and he became exhausted.

Then something amazing happened. I never quite understood it. Louis quietly approached each of the troublesome individuals and factions and opened his heart to them. "I'm going to trust you and I want you to trust me." Something about the way he did it seemed to ring a bell. As if by magic the opposition rallied to him, the factions dissolved, and he was leading a strong, unified organization.

Louis himself was astonished by this wonderful discovery. Now, he thought, he had the key to creative change and social justice. He must share this with the world. He sent a message to me to come to Dayton at once. Likewise he sent telegrams to Norman Thomas and A.J. Muste to come to Dayton immediately for a vital message.

I wasn't free to get away just then, so my brother Griscom went in my stead. Gris reported that Louis was very, very tired and that he was going to his parents' farm near Piqua for a few days rest.

The next development, a couple of days later, was shocking and totally unexpected. Louis's brother, Harold, came to Yellow Springs to see me and Dave Sallume. Louis, he said, was delirious and frequently mentioned our names. Perhaps we might help to quiet him.

We went at once to see him. Louis was on his bed, naked, tossing about and raving. When we came into the room he raised himself on one elbow. Looking at me wildly he exclaimed, "I know who you are. You're *Trotsky.*"

We sat beside the bed and tried to talk with him. No luck. Then Dave started reciting poetry in his deep rich voice. Louis relaxed, while Dave recited on and on.

After varied consultations it was decided to take him to the Dayton State Hospital where there was an outstanding specialist who might help. A few days later he died there.

Clearly, there had been an organic problem and this may have been related in some way to the burst of messianic power which he had shown. This led me to wonder whether there might be people who could summon that power without having the organic problem. My Dad had touches of that power, when he could infuse others with his ideals and dreams. With him this power seemed to come on and off. After these experiences I could understand how messianic power could be a vital phenomenon in human life.

Louis Moon's funeral was held in a church near his parents' home at Fletcher, Ohio. My heart went out to the parents as they entered the church. They seemed forlorn and utterly crushed.

The Rev. Harry Parrot spoke, and Paul Jones and myself. Elizabeth sang a beautiful song, for which she had composed the music. When it came my turn to speak I remembered the thoughts I had when my Aunt Jessie died, some twelve years before, and how I had taken inspiration from the idea that I could carry on her life. So I spoke of Louis's life and his courage and his devotion to his ideals. I said that it was for us, the living, to carry forward his life by devoting ourselves to those ideals.

In the audience were many young people who had known Louis and worked with him. I could see the response in their faces, and most of all in the faces of his parents. Now all these young people were, in a sense, their children. As we left the church the parents were almost radiant, and his mother exclaimed, "Wasn't it fine?"

The music for the following song was written by Elizabeth Morgan, and the song was first sung by her at Louis's funeral. The words were adapted from the Foreword of The Rebel Song Book, by Samuel H. Friedman.

FOR AN AMERICAN REVOLUTIONARY

Flesh of our flesh, bone of our bone,
No worker anywhere struggles alone.
No worker anywhere suffers in vain,
For everywhere workers are stirred by his pain.
No worker anywhere lays down his life,
But workers around him are roused to the strife
Flesh of our flesh, bone of our bone,
No worker anywhere struggles alone.

The Workers Alliance was not my only experience in organizing workers. I inadvertently had a somewhat checkered career as a trade unionist, as well.

When I applied for membership in the International Typographical Union, I had only three years of half-time apprenticeship, plus experience in my own shop. You were supposed to have six years full-time apprenticeship under experienced journeymen. But the union brothers were friendly and voted me in anyhow.

Soon I wanted a union contract so I might use the union label on the printing I was doing for social causes. In lieu of the label I had been using the phrase "Printed by Volunteer Socialist Labor." Better than nothing, but not good.

To have a union contract, however, you had to employ at least one journeyman printer in addition to the proprietor. Very well; Elizabeth became the proprietor, I was the journeyman, and Dave Sallume was my apprentice. Thus we got the label and were able to supply printing for all manner of progressive causes.

To carry on this printing, I gave the Bookplate Company an alter ego: The Miami Valley Socialist Press. We did printing at cost (or less) for struggling causes that needed the union label on their work. Among these were the Workers Alliance, The Southern Tenant Farmers Union (headed by H. L. Mitchell), the Fellowship of Southern Churchmen (headed by Buck Kester), the War Resisters League and, of course, the Socialist organizations. We issued a little price list of Union Label Printing. One item was handbills at $1 per thousand.

But printing wasn't the only thing we supplied. One day two men walked into the shop and said, "We understand you're interested in labor problems."

"Labor problems?" I said. "From what standpoint are you speaking, management or labor?"

"Labor," they said. They were from the Krippendorf-Dittman company, a shoe factory in nearby Xenia. There had been a series of wage reductions there, and the workers were going to walk out. They wanted me to come down and give them a talk.

When I arrived, there was an auditorium full of people, and I gave them a good rabble-rousing labor talk, ending with the admonition that they form a union and deal with their employer collectively and in a mutually responsible way. A union was formed, the strike was promptly settled, and the people went back to work.

Not long after that the factory moved to Cincinnati, for reasons which had no connection with the union. I checked this out from several sources. But in Xenia I got the blame for driving out the town's chief industry. There were mutterings about lynching "outside agitators." I approached the president of the Retail Merchants Association and said there were some things I thought he ought to know. He replied coldly that he knew all he wanted to know.

I then proposed to my fellow Socialists that we print a leaflet giving the facts about why the factory moved. They said no, better just keep quiet. So for years I enjoyed the status of Public Devil in the city of Xenia.

Once, Elizabeth invited the Xenia Women's Music Club to perform at one of the outdoor concerts that she organized. Just to be ornery she arranged for me to be master of ceremonies that evening. Greeting the women, I apologized for the poor weather we had provided, to which their leader replied, "Well, that's one thing we can't hold you responsible for."

In time my reputation as a union organizer reached Lebanon, some thirty miles away, and a man came to ask if I would help organize the shoe workers there. I agreed and went to the appointed place at the appointed time, along with a Socialist friend, Walter Townsend.

The meeting was in a large hall, with a big stage. We didn't know a soul, and no one greeted us when we came in or even took notice of us. We sat in the auditorium until people stopped coming. Then we walked up onto the stage and started talking; first me and then Walter. We talked in a general way about the values of organizing. Then we asked if they wanted a union. (Stupid question.) Yes, they did.

"The first thing to do," I said, "is to get a president." Who would you like for president?" A man was named.

"Are there other nominations?" There were none.

"All in favor of this man for president, say aye."

"Aye."

"Opposed?" Silence.

"All right," I said to the man. "You come up here and take charge." Then I sat down. He came up and stood there, looking at the people with half a smile on his face, saying nothing.

After a while I whispered to him, "Get a secretary."

"Who do you want for secretary?" A name was called.

"All in favor say aye."

"Aye." They had a secretary.

Again he stood there for a long time. Then I whispered, "Get a treasurer."

"Who do you want for treasurer?" Same performance.

After that the meeting seemed to come to life. Committees were formed, representatives from various departments were chosen. They seemed to know what they wanted to do and how to do it.

Mission accomplished. We left. We hadn't known anyone, and no one had spoken to us.

Another time, some men came from the cement mill in nearby Fairborn. They were on strike and had heard that there were labor sympathizers in Yellow Springs who might help. So two of us went over. I was posted in front of a driveway, handed a club, and told not to let anyone through. So there I was, an apostle of nonviolence, standing guard with a club. I quickly thought of a solution: if someone came, I'd grasp the club at both ends and hold it up like a bar. But no one did. I guess the sight of a six-foot man with a club was sufficient.

Another incident, both bizarre and amusing, occurred in connection with the organizing of agricultural workers. Conditions for the onion workers in northwestern Ohio were bad, and Socialists from Toledo were helping them to organize. At that time I had two young Socialists living in the back room of the Bookplate Shop while doing organizing work in our area. Learning of the problems of the onion workers and their need for help, one of the young men arranged to offer his assistance and, with my blessing, went north to Hardin County.

Soon I had a letter from him; the situation there had become tense, he said. He asked me to send the rest of his expense money for the month and said also that he needed another shirt.

I wrote him immediately. "I'm enclosing the expense money," I said, "and am sending the only shirt I can spare." After a couple of paragraphs of local news I wound up the letter with the wisecrack, "Don't throw any bombs." It was of the same genre as "don't take any wooden nickels." He and I had joshed each other a bit, I leaning toward the pacifist line and he being not so sure about that.

When that letter arrived he was in jail following a spell of local turbulence. The sheriff opened the letter. What's this? A message from the Executive Secretary of the Miami Valley Socialist League, instructing his agent to not throw any bombs. Wow! The sheriff is said to have remarked that he had a special cell for me in the basement of the jail if I ever came to town.

I learned a lesson from that experience—be careful of your wisecracks.

My membership in the International Typographical Union continued and years passed. At length my shop became the largest employing printer in the county. At the same time, ironically, I was elected president of the local union. What was it Emerson said about consistency?

But that wasn't my only inconsistency. My firm was enjoying a virtual monopoly in its field at the very time I was running for governor of Ohio on the Socialist Ticket. In politics, as in life, it helps to have a sense of humor.

17

RAISING A FAMILY

Four wonderful kids, lively, unpredictable, and all very differ-
ent! We learned from them, and they from us, as we shared life
in many dimensions. That experience could take a whole
book. In this chapter I touch on a few interesting incidents and
episodes.

When Art came of school age, Elizabeth decided that we should leave
our homestead and move to town. We got a very nice place: a comfortable
eight-room house, a two-story barn, an acre of ground with fruit trees and a
big garden space. The neighbors were nice.

We got it cheap, too—$1900. It was in a black neighborhood and,
furthermore, it was haunted. The previous owner had hung himself in the
barn. When we moved in, a friend of ours, Anna Riedel, an old and blind
German woman who had never seen the house, wrote a poem about it which
she sent to us at Christmas time.

THE HAUNTED HOUSE

Gnarled branches overhang a gabled roof,
White, dirty walls, and shutters old and brown
The termites steadily gnawing the foundation . . .
All is so still . . . so still . . .
The shades are closely drawn on dingy rooms
Where spirits dream the reverent dreams of yore.
The house is haunted, so the people say,
There is no doubt . . . no doubt . . .
As if with trumpets sound new life is rushing in.
Enthusiasm sings and happy Socialism calls the day.

The sleepy little house is rubbing weary eyes
When tiny rooms are widening into space
And plumbers and the sewerage diggers roam.
When soapsuds, whitewash, paint and varnish splash
The ghosts go out! the ghosts go out!
Free laughter of the little children rings.
Here is our home!
HERE IS OUR HOME!

When it came time for little Arthur to start school, he ran a fever. Elizabeth's mother protested, "I wouldn't think of sending a sick child to school!" But Elizabeth disagreed. She figured it was a matter of anxiety, and sent him to school anyhow. In two or three days his temperature was normal and he was in good shape.

A more difficult problem arose when two black youngsters in our neighborhood started terrorizing Art, threatening to beat him up. This made his life miserable, and he had to sneak back and forth from school by the alleys.

I didn't know what to do about this, but Elizabeth did. She visited the boys' mother, not to complain, but to invite the two brothers to supper. They came, all scrubbed and dressed up, as stiff as a couple of wooden soldiers. Art, on the other hand, was nervous and excited; it was a funny meal. After supper we played some games. The scheme worked, and the three boys became good friends.

While still very young, Art took on an evening paper route. This was an exciting new adventure, and he wanted to take a morning route in addition. His mother and I persuaded him to hold off on that. Good thing, because after a while he got tired of carrying papers and wanted to quit. But he hadn't learned yet how to handle money properly. He had spent more than his share of the collections, so was in debt. I wouldn't let him quit until he had worked off the debt. One of his problems was that he didn't collect very well, so I went with him to encourage him, and he collected nearly all his accounts.

"See," I said, "people pay up if you just ask them."

"Yes," he replied, "but they could see you standing out there by the gate."

In town we were able to continue producing much of our own food. For a time we kept a billy goat in the barn. Art, then ten or eleven years old, liked to go out to the barn and wrestle the goat, which the billy seemed to enjoy. He would back the boy against the wall and push against his chest until the youngster was red in the face. He was bigger and stronger than Art but was careful not to hurt him. Billy goats stink, and Art would come in the house fairly reeking.

Lee was born in 1943, and we spent that summer in our old place in the country, which we had been renting out but which happened to come vacant at that time. Art was eleven then and a bit restless, so he decided to run away.

He told his sisters that he planned to stay away long enough that when he returned he would be "the long-lost lamb."

He took with him his ration book (it was wartime), a butcher knife, a bedspread, what money he had, and a few personal effects. Elizabeth was worried. I said to not let it bother her too much. If he were fourteen he might make it stick. At eleven he would come back in three or four days—which he did. He had taken a bus to Cincinnati and, apart from a boat trip up the river and spending a night with a family there, he had lived mostly in the bus station. Finally his bag had been stolen, containing his money and his ration book. Who paid his way home we never found out. We didn't punish him, though we did consider it wise for him to have typhoid shots—that was punishment enough!

It was that summer, too, that Benetta fell from a swing and broke her right arm. We had put that swing up some years before and it had not been used or taken care of for a long time. The ropes were rotten. One of them broke when Beni was doing some juvenile gymnastics. Her arm was broken at the elbow and took a long time to heal. When she entered school that fall she learned to write with her left hand, a habit she continued all her life. I think this led to a trace of confused dominance which persisted for some years. She often had a struggle making up her mind about simple things. Did she want a drink of water—or didn't she!

As Art got older he began having responsibilities at the Bookplate Shop. The first of these was the job of Printer's Devil, which consisted mostly of sweeping and carrying out the trash. On the Fourth of July 1944, this led to trouble. At that time, the company was manufacturing celluloid products and was putting the flammable celluloid scrap in a steel barrel in the back room, which was kept locked for safety. One of Art's jobs was to put scrap in this barrel, so he had a key. On the Fourth of July, he went back there to get some material to make fireworks. Testing a piece of the material, he accidentally dropped it in the barrel, touching off a volcano.

He could have ducked out and played ignorant, but to his everlasting credit he rushed into the shop and told Frank Kakoi, our linotype operator, who was setting type for the *Yellow Springs News*. Frank quickly turned in the alarm.

I was at home shaving when the siren went off. I was sensitive to fire alarms, and looked out the window. Smoke was rising from downtown. I dried my face, jumped on my bike, and headed for the shop. The closer I got the more ominous it looked and when I finally came down the alley behind the shop there it was, an inferno in the back part of the Bookplate Shop. Moments later the volunteer Fire Department got there and went into action.

It was a hard battle. The back end of the shop was destroyed and the front part scorched and covered with a thick, sticky deposit. In the midst of the struggle Dave Sallume arrived on the scene. Sizing up the situation he remarked that we had piles of sheets of six-color bookplates in there beside the press, waiting for their final color. He wondered if we might duck in through the smoke and carry out a couple of stacks. We held our breaths and tried it. He made it to the door with his stack, but I had to abandon mine.

The linotype was gummed up and its insulation was charred, but we managed to get it running and set the rest of that week's paper. Our pile of newsprint was in the midst of the flames, but the fire had not penetrated it. The *Yellow Springs News* came out with brown edges that week. There was no need to punish Art. The problem was to cheer him up!

In the end the fire proved a blessing—albeit well disguised. The masonry front portion of our building was saved. The frame rear sections, beyond repair, were replaced with a good, new industrial building. It was wartime and you couldn't get permission to build unless your product was essential. Bookplates were not, but the *Yellow Springs News* was, and that saved us.

Jenifer, our second child, was a perky little redhead, and a good deal more feisty than Art. Once, through an open window, I heard her playing in the yard with a group of neighbor children. There came a lull in the playing and Jenny said, "Let's have a meeting and decide what to play next." Her friends grumbled. They didn't want to have a meeting. That being the case, Jenny promptly made the decision herself!

By second grade Jenny was riding high. She had read all the third-grade books and was boasting that she was the smartest kid in the class. We urged the school to move her ahead a grade, so she would have to work. They wouldn't, so we transferred her to the Antioch School, where she could go at her own pace.

When she finally transferred back to the Public School we asked the Superintendent to move her into the seventh grade instead of the sixth. He finally agreed, provided she got at least two B's and nothing less than a C. He expressed concern also that, being younger than the others, she might not contribute her share of leadership.

He needn't have worried. She got two B's all right, but the rest were A's. As for leadership, she gave almost too much. She was elected an officer of her class and took it upon herself to write a letter to one of the teachers pointing out that he was being unduly severe with one of the girls who was a bit unstable emotionally. She went on to criticize the way he taught his classes. She showed me the letter and I helped her smooth down some of the rough spots. She typed it up, had the whole class sign it, then walked to the front of the room and presented it to the teacher.

The teacher agreed about the unstable girl, but said that if they didn't like his teaching style they could talk with the principal. So Jenny led a delegation to talk with the principal.

Jenny always tried to protect that girl. Once when one of the boys was teasing the girl and getting her worked up, Jenny tried in vain to stop him.

Finally she grabbed his school books away from him. He recruited the help of a big boy, and Jenny dashed out of the school and up the street with both boys in hot pursuit. She ran into my office, followed a moment later by the two boys, who grabbed at her. Naturally I tossed the boys out. Then Jenny left the books with me and I phoned the boy that he could come and get them.

One evening we were in the living room and Jenny was studying. Presently she got up, walked slowly across the room and confronted me accusingly. "You . . . never . . . told . . . me," she said severely, "about currency and credit."

Once, when Jenny was fifteen or sixteen, she sat in on a conference of young college people in the auditorium at Antioch. When they called for a volunteer to take minutes she raised her hand. After the meeting she came down to my office and asked me to help her write up the meeting.

"OK," I said, "where are your notes?"

"Notes?" she said. "What notes?"

Fortunately she had paid close attention and was able to remember the details of the meeting. And she certainly learned about taking notes!

Our younger girl, Benetta, was a sensitive youngster, less perky and adventurous than Jenny. As the girls came into their teens, however, the situation changed. Beni grew to be a little taller and more rugged than Jenny —and more assertive, too.

Beni had a close friend, a girl of her own age. This girl's mother told me that her daughter refused to wear any clothing that Beni didn't expressly approve of. The same woman once led Beni's Girl Scout troop on a camping trip. She told me afterwards that she lived in terror lest Beni might disagree with her about something. That, she said, would have made her situation impossible. But Beni didn't, and commented to me privately that the troop had difficulty finding a woman to go with them and that she, Beni, felt responsible for shielding the woman from difficulties.

That Girl Scout troop had been organized by Elizabeth, and was mixed black and white, like our neighborhood. For a long time the black girls were too shy to come to our house for meetings, so each week our two girls would tour the neighborhood, collecting the black girls and bringing them to our house. The county Girl Scout organization took a dim view of our integrated troop—but the national organization actively approved.

Both girls went to high school at the Scattergood School, a Quaker boarding school in Iowa. The school had very strict discipline at that time. Jenny accepted this with good grace, but Beni resented it. Both did well and graduated.

I realize that Benetta gets less attention in this narrative than do our other children. She was an attractive child, quiet and gentle. We loved her as much as we did them, but she was less adventurous when she was little and didn't get into devilment the way her sister and brothers did. There was little to suggest the strong young adult of fine character that she would grow to be.

We would have sharply denied any favoritism, but Elizabeth enjoyed an easier rapport with Beni, while I seemed to mesh more readily with Jenny and Lee. Art, the pioneer, found both his parents a bit difficult.

Years later, when Benetta was in her late twenties, she came to Chicago to visit Jenny and her family. I happened to be visiting at the time and the two of us took the opportunity to spend some time together, visiting museums, walking on the beach and observing the city lights from a high tower. During that brief time we came into closer fellowship than ever before. A few weeks later Beni was killed in a motor accident in Detroit, caused by a drinking driver. I was thankful to have had that visit with her in Chicago.

After seven years in our "haunted house," Elizabeth was ready to move again. Again she found a compelling reason. Her parents needed to be near us, and our house was not suitable for dividing into apartments or having an addition built. So we found a big, rundown brick mansion which was available for $6,000, and which could readily be remodelled to provide the desired apartment. So we moved into this house and had an apartment added to it for Elizabeth's parents.

We were in a new home then, a three-generation family with the older kids coming into their teens. Lee, eleven years younger than Art, was about four. Life was full of excitement and challenge.

The house had eleven-foot ceilings, which meant a long staircase to the second floor. The kids routinely slid down the railing. We could tell by the sound which one was sliding down. Art always slid down fast, with a light swishing sound, hitting the newel post with a thud. Jenny gripped the rail with her hands, which produced a steady squeak all the way down. Beni reached for the rungs under the railing and came down with a rapid bumping noise.

Lee was constantly getting into things. On one occasion Elizabeth and I came into the kitchen and found him, aged four or five at the time, with a big bowl into which he was putting all manner of food. "I'm making some very good stuff," he exclaimed. Elizabeth showed neither surprise nor disapproval. Looking carefully at the contents of the bowl, she added a few essential ingredients, put it in the oven and produced a tasty casserole. Lee was very proud.

Another problem we had was that Lee attached himself admiringly to a predelinquent neighbor boy, somewhat older than himself. Again Elizabeth found a creative solution to the problem. She gave the neighbor boy music lessons—he was quite musical—and gently regulated the association of the two boys. Later, when this boy was in serious trouble, his association with our family was an active factor in his successful rehabilitation.

Our two girls, however, were less tolerant of this boy. Once, when he had been pestering them, they seized him by the hands and feet and swung him back and forth over the edge of a deep trash pit, threatening to let him go.

Once upon a time, so the story goes, there was a little boy whose dog was run over and killed while the boy was at school. His mother broke the sad news. "I'm sorry to tell you, dear, that Paddy was run over and killed by a car." To her relief the boy took it casually. "That's too bad," he said, and went on cheerfully about his play.

A little later he came into the house. "Where's Paddy?" he asked. "I told you, dear, Paddy was killed by a car."

"Oh," said the boy in distress, "I thought you said Daddy!"

As Art came into his teens I realized that I had not been relating to him in the easy, relaxed way a father should. So, at that late date, I sought ways to change this. For starters I invited him to go canoeing with me on the Little Miami, which flows past Yellow Springs. He liked the idea of canoeing—but not with his old man. Accordingly, he and a couple of his friends borrowed a rubber raft and went down the river. Wrong boat, no river experience, and three smart-alecky kids.

Art found it a bore and told his mother. She suggested he try his Dad, who was a good river man. So he did, and we had a great time. We shot the rips, paddled through the quiet shady stretches, and enjoyed the abundant wildlife.

At one point we wanted to portage around a dam, but the bank on both sides was densely lined with brush for a long way. At the center of the dam was a low spot about four-feet wide over which the water poured. We decided to shoot it. We aimed for the gap and, paddling furiously, shot over the dam. The canoe dived into the water, but bobbed up quickly and darted across to the bank which faced the dam. There we beached the canoe, dumped out the water, and continued our voyage.

We were shocked to discover that a town downriver a ways was dumping raw sewage into the stream. Paddling in this open sewer we took pains not to splash any of the dirty water into the boat. The frequent rapids, however, apparently aerated the water, which soon cleared up. In an hour or so we found people swimming in that river.

Art and I canoed repeatedly after that and it helped establish a closer friendship between us. Once we took the canoe up to Indian Lake, near St. Mary's, Ohio, where we had excellent paddling. Here and there we found big patches of water plants just below the surface. On one of these we saw a large fish, apparently grazing over the plants, with his back sticking out of the water. I said, "Let's catch that fish and take him over to the island and cook him."

We sneaked up on the fish and I slapped him with my paddle and scooped him aboard before he could collect himself. There he lay, flopping in the bottom of the boat. Art looked at the fish. "That fish was minding his own business," Art said. "He wasn't doing anybody any harm. Then we came and hit him with a paddle. I couldn't eat that fish!" So we let the fish go and he happily dashed away. Art was a rugged youngster but always gentle.

I went canoeing with Jenny also. Our most memorable trip was down Mad River. We entered the river southwest of Springfield and headed downstream for Fairborn and Dayton. The river was in freshet, nearly filling its banks, which made for swift, exciting canoeing. Once we came to a triple bend. We positioned ourselves easily for the first turn, then paddled furiously for the second, barely making it. On the third we had no chance and were swept against a mass of trees and dead brush. The canoe overturned.

We were both good swimmers and I called to Jenny to capture the paddles and then cling to the bushes along the river. Then I grappled with the canoe and managed to get it into shallow water near the bank where I could dump the water out and right it. Then I shoved off and drifted down, and Jenny swam out with the paddles and climbed aboard.

We had forgotten drinking water, so we beached on an island near a road, swam ashore, and walked to the nearest farm house. Resuming our journey we came suddenly around a bend and into the midst of a baptizing party. They didn't seem disturbed as we floated quietly by.

Getting close to Dayton, we came to Huffman Dam, one of the giant flood control dams my father had built. To portage over or around it would be a formidable job. The river passed through the dam in two narrow tubes which were nearly filled. We walked over the dam and looked at where the tubes came out. The water shot out at the bottom in powerful streams where heavy concrete barriers were erected to break the force of the current. The river, running full, leaped and frothed at the end of those tubes. I decided that the canoe could safely handle this turbulence, so we launched again and headed for the conduits. There was barely headroom in the tunnel at first, but as the water gained speed the headroom increased. The little circle of light at the end of the tunnel grew rapidly larger and we came out like a bullet, the boat racing through the turbulence, swerving this way and that, then straightening out in the even flow of the river once more.

I canoed with Beni and Lee as well. We canoed the Little Miami, the Great Miami, Mad River and the Stillwater. Sometimes, taking a day-and-a-half, we would be picked up at Fort Ancient. With two-and-a-half days we would come out onto the Ohio River, and be picked up in Cincinnati. It was strenuous, fun, and always exciting. The little rivers were wild and beautiful and the Little Miami was the best of all. I had fantasies about starting an organization to remove trash and fallen trees. Later, after I moved to North Carolina, an organization was formed,—Little Miami, Incorporated—which has cleaned up the river and now protects it.

In our new home we were less than a hundred yards from the railroad, and trains passed twice a day. Lee, at four and five years old, found the train exciting. One day Elizabeth heard him upstairs yelling at the top of his voice. She dashed up to see what was the matter. He was jumping up and down at the window yelling, "See choochoo! See choochoo!" Often we would walk down to the corner with him when the train came through, to give him a closer look. Now that railroad track has been converted into a beautiful paved bike trail—full of traffic.

Alas, those trains are no more. I could board a Pulman in Yellow Springs at 10 p.m. and wake up in Chicago, returning the next night. A whole day in the city with a good night's sleep at both ends.

Art wasn't happy in school in Yellow Springs, so we asked if he would like to go away to school. He thought he would, so we gave him some choices. He picked Oakwood Friends School because it was near a river and there was a riding stable nearby. The river proved to be out of bounds and the riding stable too expensive However, he did tolerably well there and would have returned the following year except for a mixup at their end. So he went to high school in Yellow Springs.

For two summers he went off to High School work camps conducted by the American Friends Service Committee, and each time came home inspired, only to lose steam after a few weeks.

It was during his last years of high school that he became involved with the Antioch Area Theatre. At first he helped around the stage and was given bit parts. These he handled well, and they gave him more important parts. In the lead part of Clarence in *Life with Father*, his performance was brilliant, and the show had a long run. In plays by Shakespeare, O'Neill, Moliere and others, he had important parts which he performed well.

It was characteristic of him that whatever part he might have, he lived that part the entire time the play was running. When he was playing Clarence he greeted Elizabeth each morning with lines from the play.

"Good morning, Mother."

"Good morning, Clarence."

"Did you sleep well, Mother?"

In Moliere's comedy *A Physician in Spite of Himself,* Art, still a teenager, was cast in the role of a gruff old man. He carried the part well, but all the time that play was running he went about with a scowl on his face and a limp.

After a few successes, Art quit studying and proclaimed that he didn't need to. He was going to be an actor. This came to the ears of Meredith Dallas and Arthur Lithgow, leaders of the Area Theatre. "But Art," one of them said, "don't you realize that all the staff of the Area Theater have at least a Master's degree? The future is in the university theater, not in being a ham actor!" This hit Art squarely between the eyes. He studied furiously and pulled up his grades.

Another valuable teenage experience which Art had was a job in the Bookplate shop. We were publishing the *Yellow Springs News* at that time, and once a week the linotype metal had to be melted, cleansed and cast into *pigs* for re-use. Also, stereotype plates had to be cast and then trimmed down on a power saw. It was a hot and somewhat dangerous job and illegal for anyone under eighteen. Since Art was my son I figured we could get by with it, and we hired him for the job. I think it meant a lot to him in the process of growing up.

After Art graduated from high school, I arranged a job for him in a logging camp run by cousins of ours on Prince Rupert Island, off the coast of Alaska. These cousins were descendants of Squire Morgan, my grandfather's brother.

Art hitchhiked to Vancouver, where he took passage on a small, north-bound seaplane. Heavily overloaded, it started across the harbor, heading for a stone breakwater. The engines roared and the plane went faster and faster—straight for that stone wall! There seemed no chance of its being air-borne in time. Art was scared stiff. Then, at the last moment, the plane hopped over the wall onto the open sea and continued speeding up for the takeoff.

Prince Rupert Island was apparently close to the epicenter of the violent earthquake of 1949. On that Sunday Art was walking in the woods near the camp when a rumbling began and the earth started to move in waves. Having the earth no longer solid was terrifying, and Art started to run. Then a dead tree came crashing down in his path and he stopped. The timekeeper's wife appeared at a second story window and screamed. The men came pouring out of the bunkhouse—a building on stilts—and vaulted over the railing of the narrow walkway. Big oil tanks broke loose from their bases and rolled into the ocean. A good time was had by all.

Art's stay in the logging camp ended when I called him to come home and run a press in the Bookplate Company, which he did for the better part of a year before enrolling at Miami University.

During that time the rest of us had an adventure closer to home. Elizabeth, Jenny, Beni, and I, with five-year-old Lee as a passenger, took off for Canada on a long-range bicycle trip.

We camped in parks and, with permission, in farmers' pastures. On one occasion we sent the two girls to a farmhouse to buy some eggs. The farm family gave them the eggs but wouldn't take any money. On another occasion the girls went on an errand to a supermarket that was about to open for the day. The driver of a bakery truck, making a delivery to the store, gave the girls a couple of pies. Elizabeth and I thought maybe we were missing an opportunity—we should be sending our children out to beg!

During the first week, Lee was a passenger on my bike. I had a long nar-row seat bolted to the bar and he sat on that, gripping the ropes of the blanket roll which I lashed in front of the handle bars. Sometimes he would rest his head on the blanket roll and go to sleep. When we stopped we would have to wake him up before he would let go of the ropes.

At Lake Erie we parted, and I took a train back to Yellow Springs to return to the shop. Lee transferred to a buddy seat on the back of Elizabeth's bike, and the four of them went on into Canada for several more weeks of travel. At one point Jenny lost the family purse and they wired me for money. You couldn't wire collect for money, so we had a code. "Please ship —— vellums." ("Vellums" meant dollars.) This worked fine but it took a couple of days for the cash to reach them and they got pretty hungry. They managed to find a few empty bottles which they turned in for the deposit, and that helped some. Our little crew arrived home in due time, tanned, tough, and happy.

Lee, our youngest, really hit the jackpot in teenage experience. While he was in high school the idea emerged of making a trip around the world between high school and college. This was possible because he was graduating at seventeen. At eighteen, if he were not in college, he would have had to register for the draft. As it was, the law gave him a year of freedom.

During his last years of high school, Lee worked at the Bookplate Company after school every day, setting type—and saved money for the trip. In addition he inherited a small sum from his grandmother, and I agreed to deposit $15 a week in his account while he was gone. He set forth carrying a letter of credit on the Chase Manhattan Bank, through which he could draw on his account anywhere in the world. I gave our bank an undated note which they could activate should he have an emergency and need to draw beyond his regular balance. By such measures we were able, despite modest family resources, to put Lee "into orbit."

As it turned out, Lee's itinerary and the nature of his travels were greatly influenced by a number of family connections and previous events.

Taking off early in the summer of 1960, Lee went first to England, where he got a job with the Scott-Bader Commonwealth, England's pioneer worker-owned firm. This came about through a curious set of circumstances. Ernest Bader, the founder of the Commonwealth, had visited America. He came to Yellow Springs to see the Bookplate Company because of its attempts to develop worker participation in management and ownership. Later, back in England, he read an article in the English *Peace News* about a peace demonstration in Ohio. With the article was a picture of a group of demonstrators, along with their names. Among them was Lee Morgan. Bader wrote, asking if this was a relative of mine. I replied that he was my son, that he would be coming to England soon, and asked if the Commonwealth might have a temporary job for him, which they did.

After a period on that job, Lee hitchhiked about Europe and then flew to Kenya, where he was received by Tom Mboya, a charismatic young leader of that country. A couple of years before, Tom's younger brother, Alphonce Okuku, had lived with us while he was in high school.

Arriving in Kenya, Lee was greeted as Tom Mboya's American brother. For ten weeks Lee lived and travelled with Tom, in the midst of the intense independence ferment. Then for ten more weeks he lived with Tom's parents in the Luo Tribe on Rusinga Island in Lake Victoria, another rare experience. At seventeen Lee was at a perfect age for this sort of adventure—big enough to take care of himself, but young enough to be taken freely into people's hearts and homes and to need no excuse for travelling.

Following his African sojourn Lee went to Asia. At the Bangkok Airport he was met by the Dutch doctor who headed the World Health Organization in that part of the world. This, too, reflected a previous event. In my office, some months before, I had received a letter of thanks from UNICEF because the Bookplate Company had paid for an ad in the *Yellow Springs News,* urging contributions to UNICEF. I immediately wrote back asking if they knew of some temporary job in Asia that might be filled by an energetic teenage boy. Sure enough, this took Lee to Bangkok.

What happened there was remarkable. The Dutch doctor had sent a team of Thai doctors and nurses into the field to inspect villages and innoculate children. In typical western fashion he had given them quotas, and he expected reports. In characteristic Thai fashion, the reports showed all quotas filled exactly 100%. Obviously, they were more interested in pleasing the doctor than in providing information, and he was frustrated.

So when he got his hands on this American boy he took him home, sized him up, explained the situation to him, and gave him some days of intensive training. Then he put Lee in charge of a team inspecting rural health centers, with orders to bring back meaningful reports. The team worked well with Lee, and the doctor was pleased with his reports.

Enroute through Asia he spent time in India, Pakistan, Ceylon, and Thailand. In India he worked at Mitraniketan, an innovative community project. The founder of the project, K. Viswanathan, had come to America some years before and had fallen in with Dad, who encouraged him to return to his village and try to build up the quality of life there. For a time, Viswan, as we called him, had worked in the Bookplate Company. When Lee arrived at Mitraniketan, Viswan gladly put him to work.

Lee had been interested in Antioch but had not applied because he felt his high school grades were not good enough, so much of his energies having gone into extra-curricular projects. While he was in India, I happened to mention this to my cousin, Eric Curtis, who was the Admissions Director at Earlham College. Eric contradicted this idea, saying that Lee's travel experience would make him an appetizing candidate.

I managed to get Lee on the phone all the way in south India. Quickly he travelled to a distant city where Scholastic Achievement Tests were being given. By the time he got home he had been accepted at Antioch. By that time, too, he was a happy and confident young adult.

Lee entered Antioch with enthusiasm and, at the end of his first academic quarter, elected to travel as a salesman for the Bookplate Company. I scheduled him to call on our dealers all the way to the west coast, then up the coast and back again. He had taken a lot of slides during his travels, and, in addition to his business calls, I booked him in churches and service clubs along the way to give illustrated talks about his trips. One reviewer commented, "His descriptions of what he saw and heard and felt are spontaneous and entertaining. At the same time, he often shakes loose the fixed pictures of African and Asian peoples that we Americans are likely to carry around in our heads."

It turned out that Lee's return to Antioch was not the end of his involvement with Mitraneketan. Three years later an Antioch student came into my office. He was about to leave for Mitraniketan to serve as a volunteer worker there. He had learned that Mitraniketan had lately acquired a printshop, and he asked if I would give him a few pointers on printing, so that he could be useful there. A few pointers on printing? I just sat there and looked sad—at least, I felt sad.

Then he went to the *Yellow Springs News* and repeated his request to my friend, Ken Champney. Ken, too, just sat there and looked sad. Shortly after, I said to Dad, "If you're going to send someone to India to help with printing, you'd better send Lee." So Lee got clearance from his draft board, took two years off from college, and headed out for India.

There were four printers and four apprentices working in the Mitraniketan printshop. A few days before Lee arrived they all quit except one apprentice. Lee walked into a deserted shop full of strange equipment and type in three languages. The shop had no electricity, no running water, and no glass windows. But he got it all running, and trained a crew, headed by Viswan's younger brother Sahadu. Not only that, he organized a local credit union to shut out the Indian loan sharks.

At Antioch, Lee had been dating a schoolmate, Vicki Neff. Dad was strong for Vicki, and when Lee went to India for two years Dad was "afraid we might lose her." So he arranged, during Lee's second year there, for Vicki to go also. A highly competent person, Vicki was shortly put in charge of the school at Mitraniketan. Things worked out as Dad had hoped; after college Lee and Vicki were married.

A family bike camping trip in 1948. Lee and Ernest up front; then Benetta, Jenny, and Elizabeth. Wiggy barely shows behind.

18

MY RELIGIOUS LIFE

To make sense of my diverse and seemingly inconsistent adult career, my readers need to know something of my perception of self and of reality—in a word, of my religious life and of my values and motivation. In this chapter I undertake to briefly set them forth.

Each evening, when I was a little boy I recited at bedtime:

> *Now I lay me down to sleep*
> *I pray the Lord my soul to keep.*
> *If I should die before I wake*
> *I pray The Lord my soul to take.*

When I was about six I graduated from that to The Lord's Prayer. When I was seven or eight I started puzzling and asking questions. One day my grandmother told me that God could see everything I did. I was a literal-minded kid.

"Can He see right through everything?" I asked.

"Yes."

"But if He sees right through everything, He can't see anything and might as well be blind." A sense of humor isn't necessary for being a Christian, but it sure helps. My grandmother was amused rather than annoyed by my juvenile logic.

Walking in the woods once, at age ten, I came onto a large caterillar to whose back had been attached the eggs of a predatory insect. The eggs were hatching and the larvae were burrowing into the body of the caterpillar.

Undergoing a slow and agonizing death the poor creature had gripped a twig with its rear feet and was thrashing helplessly back and forth.

A kind and loving god would not treat his creatures that way, I thought. I could no longer accept the concept of God as a conscious and caring personality.

As a boy, I won a prize for regular attendance at the Unitarian Sunday School, but the most important religious influence I experienced was in the lives and habits of my family. They had a strong spirit of love and caring, of nonviolence, and of respect for personality. The importance of wealth and power were played down, and social justice and human wellbeing were played up.

In time I got acquainted with the teachings of Jesus. They supported the habits and values which I had experienced within the family. (Very likely they were at the root of those habits.) "That's the way things ought to be," I thought.

As years passed I came to perceive my life as a thread in the fabric of humanity, helping to give it strength and color. I perceived the fabric as giving value and meaning to my life. Thus, my life and how I lived it became very important.

Later I came across a statement by Albert Einstein which expressed this concept in still broader terms:

> A human being is part of the whole, called by us the "universe," a part limited in time and space. He experiences himself, his thoughts and feelings as something separated from the rest . . . a kind of optical illusion of his consciousness. This delusion is a kind of prison for us, restricting us to our personal desires and to affection for a few persons nearest to us. Our task must be to free ourselves from this prison to widen our circle of compassion to embrace all living creatures and the whole of nature in its beauty. Nobody is able to achieve this completely, but striving for such achievement is in itself a part of the liberation and a foundation for inner security.

This perception of the relation of self to reality places little dependence on conventional theology, and I soon abandoned any reliance on supernaturalism, or on myths either, except for their symbolic value.

I continued to use the term "God" from time to time as synonymous with nature, and sometimes as a symbol for the totality of the universe, or as a symbol of virtue and wisdom, as in "doing the will of God." But I am careful now where I use it. As Walter Kahoe once remarked, "It takes two to tell the truth; one to tell it and one to hear it." Thus I need to be careful in using the term, either with my orthodox friends or my nontheist friends, lest I be misunderstood.

After Elizabeth and I were married, we deliberated what religious affiliation to seek, or whether to seek any. What we wanted was an association that would help us deepen the quality of our lives, clarify our ideals and values, and strengthen our human commitment. That was a big order, and we finally decided on two affiliations which seemed to supplement each other: the Society of Friends and the American Humanist Association, which was closely related to the Unitarian environment of my childhood.

We did not come to these organizations through any conscious process of "convincement," but because they seemed to fit in with the perceptions and ideals which we had already formed.

Among the different branches of the Friends, we preferred the nonpastoral type, in which there is no paid ministry (that function being shared by the congregation). The nearest nonpastoral Meeting was at Green Plain, a few miles from Yellow Springs. It was a small rural Meeting made up primarily of farmers. The Meeting House was in a pleasant wooded setting, out in the country.

We attended for a time and were warmly received, but when we applied for membership there was some doubt as to whether this controversial young couple from Yellow Springs would be good for the Meeting. As the discussion was reported to us later, one wise old Quaker told a story about a little boy whose mother said he shouldn't play with a certain boy who might not be good for him. "But Mother," the boy replied. "Think how good I am for him." That did the trick, and the Meeting accepted us. Later, under the care of that rural Meeting, a new Meeting was established in Yellow Springs, and we transferred our membership there.

We were not disappointed in the Quakers. Their habits of simplicity, their profound respect for personality, their active commitment to social justice and their meditative approach to life found expression in love and non-violence and vigorous participation in social causes. We felt right at home.

Years later I taught the Sunday School Class for the young teenagers in the Yellow Springs Meeting. Taught isn't quite the right word; actually I led them in a variety of activities.

One thing we did was to buttonhole some of the adult members of the Meeting one by one and get them to tell the stories of their lives. Another project we carried on was the writing and publishing of a monthly newsletter for the Meeting. We also put together, with typed copy and paste-up, one issue of a wall newspaper, *The Early Times*, which purported to be published in Egypt following the birth of Jesus. The kids wrote the articles for it. Sometimes we would do a money-making project to help some worthy cause. One problem we had was that kids from the Methodist and Presbyterian Sunday Schools wanted to get in on it, and I couldn't handle so many.

Our most ambitious project was the production of an imaginary radio program for Christmas, which we recorded on magnetic wire (this was in

1954 before tapes were available.) I took the theme of a story by Alfred Hassler, "The Carol That Never Was Sung," reversed the sequence and fleshed it out. The plot: Jesus has just been born and the Heavenly Hosts are assembling for a mighty concert in celebration of the event. A Carol, represented as a person, is hurrying on her way to be sung. But along the way she encounters someone in trouble, stops to help them, and so arrives too late.

The same thing happens each year, right on down through history. The Carol always stops in response to some new injustice. Each day I wrote another episode and after school the kids would come in and record the lines. I found myself writing the lines to fit the personalities of the individual kids, as well as to tell the story. Between the episodes of the Carol's adventures we recorded Christmas Carols.

After the Carol fails to show up in time for nearly 2,000 years, the Choir Director gets exasperated and sends her to the Throne Room, where she confronts *The Voice*. She promises to be on time next year but *The Voice* says no, "Next year, my dear, you will do as you have always done, next year and for many years to come, for you are the Carol that will never be heard until all men sing together in a mighty chorus that covers the earth. Only in the hearts of men who have seen the vision of brotherhood can you honor the Child with your harmony."

"Then shall I never be sung? Must I be silent forever?"

"Not so. Your day will come. Men flee from the vision in fear and greed, but with their fear is shame, and through their greed shines love. One day that love will lead them into the rich habitation that awaits them. Then, at last, all men will join in singing the sweetest Carol of all—the song of universal brotherhood." The recording made a rich dramatic sequence and we played it at a Christmas Party of the Friends Meeting.

Elizabeth was a delegate to the World Meeting of Friends in 1936, and became a charter member of the Friends World Committee for Consultation. This was the international body established by the Friends at that time to maintain contact between their sections in various parts of the world. She took part in calling the first Friends Conference on Race Relations.

A valuable technique, which I learned from the Quakers, was to tap the resources of my subconscious. Confronted by a problem, I would reflect on it deeply, in the evening, reviewing relevant information and ideas. I would then go to sleep with the problem on my mind. Toward morning I would awaken with the wheels turning and a solution taking shape. A couple of times the solutions took the form of dreams. I used the process frequently, and still do, finding it highly productive. More orthodox religionists might interpret this as "listening to the voice of God." That's all right with me, though I don't formulate it that way.

The other wing of our philosophical life was the American Humanist Association. The major contribution of this movement is that it affirms the ethical and social values of Christianity and other great religions. It asserts that these values have strength and merit in and of themselves and need not depend on supernatural authority. One of the tragedies of our times is that all too often persons who can no longer accept the supernatural tend to abandon or water down the social and ethical values too. Humanism supports these values as being universal to human life. Rather than being regarded as an enemy of orthodox Christianity, Humanism should be recognized as a valuable ally. The most vocal opponents of Humanism have an almost totally inverted concept of it.

For a considerable period I was registered as a *Humanist Counselor,* the closest Humanist equivalent to a minister, and for several years I also served as Chairman of the Resolutions Committee of the Association. In this capacity it was my responsibility to formulate positions on various issues, for discussion and adoption by the organization. In editing and writing resolutions I changed the conventional style, dropping the "whereas" and "be it therefore." Instead I tried to state the issue directly and clearly and with as few trimmings as possible. This format was readily accepted by the membership.

At one time the Association developed a document called "The Humanist Manifesto." It was a ringing affirmation of basic human values and a challenge to pursue those values. It was signed by the leading Humanists of the country. I didn't sign it, though I agreed with what it said. My reason for not signing was that it centered solely on humankind and made no reference to the fellow creatures with whom we share the earth.

My involvement with Humanism got me into some interesting situations in later years when I was traveling as a Bookplate Company salesman. I had once debated a clergyman at East Tennessee State University on the subject, "Does Contemporary Man Need Traditional Christianity?" The central theme of my talk was that the moral and ethical values of Christianity are important, but that it is a mistake to make them dependent on an archaic theology. Such dependency, I said, would tend to undermine and weaken them. It was a friendly debate and at the close my "opponent" turned to me with a grin. "You won't like this," he said, "but God has blessed you."

The text of my talk appeared later as an article in the *Humanist* magazine. Calling on a Christian Bookstore as a Bookplate Company salesman, I noticed on the counter a copy of *Moody Monthly* magazine, with the cover showing a full color picture of the word *humanism,* constructed of sand, being washed away by the ocean. Looking inside I found the same picture, followed by an article attacking Humanism. Imagine my astonishment when I found myself quoted at length at the beginning of the article. Those quotes had been selected from my article in the *Humanist.* Only such parts had been taken as were critical of orthodox theology. The portions of my article which affirmed the ideals and values of Christianity had been omitted.

I was afraid the bookseller, who was one of my regular customers, might have read that article. Fortunately he hadn't, nor apparently had any other Christian booksellers whom I ran across.

A happier incident occurred at about that time when I was calling on another Christian bookstore on behalf of the Bookplate Company. When we finished our business the woman in charge asked how long I had been a Christian. I responded with a thumbnail sketch of my religious philosophy. She and her assistant liked what I had to say, but were concerned by the lack of reference to God and Christ. While this was going on, a young woman customer had joined us. At the conclusion of my remarks she asked if she might pray for me. I said certainly, so we bowed our heads and had a prayer meeting in which she prayed beautifully.

After that they raised the question of Heaven and Hell, so I told them a story from Tolstoy. A selfish woman, having died and gone to Hell, requested a transfer. She was asked if she had ever done a kind act in her life. After some reflection she said yes, she had once given a carrot to a starving woman. "We'll fetch that carrot," they said. The carrot was fetched and the woman was told to hang onto it. They started to lift and, wonder of wonders, the carrot held and the woman was being lifted out.

Then another suffering sinner hung onto her foot, and he too was being lifted out. A third sinner got hold of his foot, and then another, and so on. The woman looked down at the long string of sinners, and up at the skinny little carrot. Giving a kick, she said, "Let go. This is my carrot." Instantly the carrot broke, and they all fell back.

This story pleased my listeners, though it treated Hell as a symbol rather than as a literal place. I left those people without having theological agreement but with a happy sense of fellowship.

Joseph Campbell, an inspired student of mythology, has asserted—rather convincingly—that all human cultures have myths by which they live. Confronted with this idea, I wondered if it was possible that I too had myths by which I lived.

I thought long and deeply on this matter and believe I do have such myths and can identify them. Actually, the term "myth" isn't quite the word I want. I'm referring to such things as a positive concept of human character and the dream of a society of universal well-being. These concepts I inherited from my father and from the various religious and social movements to which I have related in the course of my life.

I believe in what the Quakers call "that of God in every person"—the potential of humankind to practice love and kindness toward one another and toward the natural world in which they live. I believe that sharing can replace exploitation and that we can develop habits and values and institutions which will permanently enhance human life and preserve nature and the earth.

I see my own life as an instrument for bringing this about and I reach out in fellowship to persons of all cultures and religions whose ideals encompass these aims. In a word, I am a Utopian.

I do not for a moment underestimate the magnitude of this challenge or of the odds against us. We are faced with disastrous atmospheric changes, spreading deserts, dying oceans, diminishing rain forests, and vanishing species. The human population is exploding. Nations arm against nations. Our own government defies international law whenever it suits its convenience. Greed and exploitation dominate our economic life with a rising tide of wealth and poverty. Communism has failed and Capitalism is on the skids.

Against this forbidding background, where do I stand?

There are three options:

The first is business as usual: Look out for Number One; pursue wealth, possessions, and power; let the world take care of itself.

The second is to accept reality, give up on humanity, and take refuge in cynicism and despair, as expressed in the following fragment from James Thomson's *The City of Dreadful Night*:

> As if a being, god or fiend, could reign,
> At once so wicked, foolish and insane
> As to create man when he might refrain.

"After all," one might say, "I'll probably be dead and gone before things really go to pot."

The third option, basically religious, is the one I try to live by. It is like the first option in that I seek to function as a solvent person, socially and economically, in existing society. In and along with that process, however, I try to face the problems of the world with my eyes wide open, but without despair, and with the will to pursue creative solutions to those problems as opportunity offers and as my strength and vision permit.

It is my central myth that the paradigm of growth and greed, which threatens to destroy civilization and devastate the planet, will give way to a new paradigm in which we are moved to quiet our egos, control our numbers, and simplify our lifestyles. A paradigm in which cooperation replaces rivalry, in which caring and sharing replace aggrandizement and in which each person feels themselves to be a responsible part of society and nature.

It is this myth to which I hold in the face of the probable self-destruction of civilization. I am not alone in this. The same myth is inherent (though commonly played down) in most of the world's religions.

Self-styled realists may disparage this dream as utopian—which it is. To them I can only say, "I'm sorry for you. I challenge you to take off your blinders and look at the world as it really is. Then consider the options."

I turn once more to Einstein, who put it succinctly when he said that we shall require "a substantially different way of thinking" if civilization is to survive.

These are emblems of three great religions. Ernest welcomes fellowship with them and shares their moral and ethical concerns but he isn't formally affiliated.

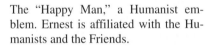

The "Happy Man," a Humanist emblem. Ernest is affiliated with the Humanists and the Friends.

19

INTO THE POLITICAL ARENA

*A complement to my religious life was my political life which
began in my teens and came to a crescendo in my career as a
Socialist leader in the 1930s and '40s. This chapter recounts
some of the experiences of those years, and the excitement and
challenge which I and my colleagues felt.*

The July 6, 1905, *St. Cloud Daily Times* carried the news of my birth (on
the front page!). Also on the front page, more prominently displayed, was
the news that the crew of the Russian battleship Potemkin had revolted,
taken over the ship and declared Russia a republic. Commenting on this
event, and on my birth, my father remarked, "I have no doubt our man
Ernest will see a free Russia, restricted only by the limitations of Russian
character."

Was I born under a revolutionary star? That depends on how you look at
it. As a boy I was deeply imbued with the ideals and values of Christianity
and of America. I said my prayers every night, saluted the flag and sang all
the right songs. But I discovered early on that the values and ideals which
I cherished were too often ignored or violated in our society. I was even
more distressed to find them frequently used as a screen to cover greed,
exploitation, and social injustice.

I remember, as a boy, becoming aware of wealth and poverty. I saw pain
and anger on the face of a black man when he was refused service because of
his color. I experienced hostility. I saw drunkenness. I resented that the
women in my family, strong, educated persons, were not allowed to vote. It
struck me that the world needed a lot of changes.

When I was about fifteen I walked down the street in Dayton, looking at
the houses and wondering which were above "the line," and which were

below it. By "the line" I meant the level of economic prosperity they would enjoy if income were distributed equally. Was it right, I wondered, for a family to live above that line?.

I rejoiced when the Czar was finally overthrown and Alexander Kerensky, a Democratic Socialist, established a provisional government in Russia. I lamented when his government in turn was overthrown by the Bolsheviks with the connivance of Germany.

The Bolshevik seizure of power in Russia in 1917 was to have been the signal for workers everywhere to seize their governments, redistribute the land, take over the factories and put an end once and for all to human injustice—poverty, exploitation, imperialism, and war. The call went out from Moscow to the Socialist parties of the world to rise.

The Socialist parties at that time were well-nigh universal, especially in the West, and were relatively strong. They were, however, predominantly democratic and nonviolent in character. Whereas they might condone violent revolution against a tyrannical government, they were in the main committed to peaceful change in democratic nations.

The Russian call for revolution split the Socialist parties wide open. Militant minorities all over the world split off to form Communist parties, taking their signals from Moscow. In addition, thousands of Socialists, discouraged by the internecine strife, left the movement altogether, especially in the United States.

Despite this setback, Eugene Debs polled over a million votes as a Socialist presidential candidate in 1920. At the time he was serving a term in a Federal Penitentiary for having spoken out against the war. It was joked that if he were elected they would have to put bars on the White House. (He was later pardoned by Warren Harding.)

There occurred, at about that time, the infamous "Palmer Raids" conducted by an agency of the Federal Government, in which Socialist Party offices were smashed and party members severely harassed.

In 1920, at age fifteen, I was strong for Herbert Hoover. He was an able man of personal integrity, who strongly supported international cooperation and opposed militarism. Had he become president in 1920 it might have made an important difference in history. While conservative in economics, he was progressive in other ways. When he finally did become president in 1929 he was just in time to take the rap for the Great Depression. He was partly to blame because he cut back on the military and moved to balance the budget. Under the free enterprise system, as presently structured, you can't do that without wrecking the economy.

Actually, this isn't strictly true. A substantial expansion of private debt and/or vigorous growth of industrial investment can serve the same purpose. One or more of these factors is necessary to offset the maldistribution of

income in our society. If continued indefinitely, however, such developments will lead to economic and ecological disaster.

In 1924, at age 19, I took a more active interest in the presidential campaign, and supported Robert Lafollette and his Progressive Party. In that year
the Socialist Party set aside its own campaign and cast its lot with the Pro-
gressives. The presidential campaign garnered something like five million
votes. The Socialists were delighted, feeling that a viable third party movement was under way but Lafollette, thinking in more conventional political
terms, took the election as a defeat, and disbanded the Progressive Party.
With their own political apparatus suspended, the Socialists were left high
and dry. It was at this point that Norman Thomas emerged into leadership
and began to rebuild the shattered movement.

The election of 1928 was the first in which I was old enough to vote. I
walked into the booth expecting to vote for Hoover as the more progressive
of the two old-party candidates. At the last moment I reflected, "Hoover is
going to win by a landslide anyhow. Why not vote for Thomas?"

After Elizabeth and I were married we considered not only what religious affiliation to seek but also what political alignment might best fit in with
our values and social ideals. The Socialist Party of Gene Debs and Norman
Thomas was our choice.

Our decision to cast our lot with the Socialist Party was influenced in
large part by two people. One of these was a cousin of Lucy's, Caroline Urie,
a charming and highly educated woman from a prestigious Quaker family,
who settled in Yellow Springs.

Caroline had lived in Italy after World War I and had been active with the
Socialists there. She told of seeing factories taken over by the workers in the
social upheaval following the war, and run very efficiently. Mussolini put a
stop to that, and also ran Caroline out of the country. Ordinarily he killed
prominent opponents by forcing them to drink castor oil so that they died in
convulsions. Caroline's American citizenship protected her from that fate,
but he found other ways to get such people out of the country. Returning
home from a shopping errand one day, she found her house surrounded by
soldiers and could not get in. She left for America with just the clothes on her
back.

Caroline's passion for social justice found a variety of expressions. She
learned that persons in Yellow Springs who needed money but were unable
to borrow from the bank were paying 36% interest to loan sharks. In response to that she called a meeting at her house one evening to form a Credit
Union. There were eight of us there, and we each put in five dollars capital.
With this forty dollars we started making loans to needy people at 12%. We
made a twenty-five dollar loan very cautiously in those days, but the Credit
Union thrived and grew.

For a long time it had its headquarters in the Bookplate Company office, where our treasurer handled the accounts. Then, one day, we discovered that most of the traffic through our front door (we were on the main street then) was headed for the Credit Union. This was too much. So they bought the building across the street and moved out. Today that Credit Union counts its assets in millions, and the loan sharks have long since disappeared.

It was ironic that Caroline, a pacifist, was married to a surgeon in the U.S. Navy. In consideration for his feelings she soft-pedalled her pacifist sentiments until after his death. Then she decided to take a stand. She would be a tax refuser.

In preparation for this she placed all her property in a Non-Revocable Trust for her daughter. Caroline, however, would receive the income from the trust during her lifetime. I agreed to serve as a trustee, to manage the trust and remit the income to Caroline.

I made one suggestion to her which I felt would strengthen her moral position, namely that she contribute to the American Friends Service Committee the percentage of her tax which she calculated would be used for war, then remit the balance of her tax to the Internal Revenue Service, along with a receipt from the Service Committee. This she did, accompanying her tax payment with a letter explaining what she was doing and saying that now her tax was paid in full.

The IRS, of course, would not hold still for this. They sent two men to talk with her. I vividly recall one of those visits, the elderly lady, bright and alert, crippled up with arthritis, sitting in her bed with wisps of white hair projecting from under her lace nightcap, and the slightly embarrassed IRS men asking her questions.

Caroline carefully explained her position. "But Mrs. Urie," one of the men said, "we can't let each person decide these things for himself." Caroline came right back at him. "You hung men at Nuremberg for violating their consciences. Do you expect me to violate my conscience and pay for that murderous hardware?" Clearly, the IRS men were no match for this sharp old lady. Furthermore, her action repeatedly made the press wires. She never did pay those taxes!

So the IRS tried to come after me, as trustee. At one point they threatened to attach Elizabeth's and my bank account. We didn't think they could legally do this, but they might well tie up our account, so we transferred the account to a bank in a different town. For some reason, they never followed through on this threat.

Caroline had a long record as a Socialist, and it was she who suggested that we organize a branch of the Party in our county.

The other person who encouraged us, and who pitched in to help, was Bishop Paul Jones, the College pastor at Antioch. Paul was an Episcopal Bishop who had been removed from his bishopric for his antiwar position.

The church's loss was Antioch's gain. A quiet, friendly man, with a keen mind and a strong sense of justice, he too had been a long-time Socialist.

So the Greene County Socialist Party was launched in our living room, and its regular meetings were held in the front office of the Bookplate Company. A Socialist Party Headquarters sign, complete with the official Arm & Torch, was neatly drawn on one of the windows. Someone once threw a rock at it but missed and broke the adjacent pane.

Our first task was to recruit a nucleus of like-minded people. Then we would reach out through the area. Aside from an inactive branch in Dayton there was no other Socialist Party organization in the southern part of Ohio. So we formed The Miami Valley Socialist League with me as Executive Secretary and proceeded to reach out.

Elizabeth and I visited neighboring towns to find people who had been Socialists before. This was not as difficult as you might think, as such people tend to become known in their communities. We gradually built up a network.

One startling discovery was that in some towns there were several people who claimed to have cast the only Socialist vote there in previous years. Apparently it was the practice of some election boards to report only one or two Socialist votes and throw out the rest. We found a parallel situation in our own county, where the board of elections informed our local precinct officials that they "could count the Socialist votes if they wished, but they didn't have to." In time we started nominating slates of candidates. I ran for the Legislature, for Congress, and finally for Governor of Ohio.

The precinct officials in Yellow Springs cooperated well, but in the county seat the officials would not permit our legally authorized watchers to witness the counting of the votes. It is easy to understand why Norman Thomas was credited with only a fraction of the number of votes which the polls predicted he would receive.

Our most noteworthy campaign was Elizabeth's run for Congressman-at-Large in 1940. We contrived a street platform with folding legs, which we loaded on our farm trailer along with a lot of camping gear. Taking a crew of young people with her, Elizabeth stumped the southern half of the state. They would set up the platform in a public square, hook up the amplifier, light the gasoline flare, and stage a meeting/performance.

They performed in town after town. Elizabeth was a brilliant concert singer and would sing labor and socialist songs accompanying herself on her accordion. A young man in the group, Ben Hudson, would stage a magic show interspersed with political commentary. Then three young men would stage a dramatic skit with a political message. They drew good crowds and collected many signatures.

In the city of Springfield they were refused a permit, so Elizabeth went into the City Hall, unslung her accordion, and let go with a rousing Socialist song that brought the city government momentarily to a halt. They quickly gave her a permit.

They were also refused a permit in Columbus. This time an old ordinance was cited which banned street shows on the grounds that they might frighten the horses. Columbus hadn't seen a horse in years.

At one point Elizabeth was indicted by the County Grand Jury for having petitions notarized that had been circulated by someone else—a practice routinely followed by local Republicans and Democrats. But the Yellow Springs community rose up in indignation and the indictment was dropped.

Our political campaigns had a buoyant quality about them. We would throw ourselves into the struggle, then, on election night, we would sleep soundly. The next morning we would review the returns. "Hey. We increased our vote by 25%." Then we were ready to start the next campaign. Norman Thomas, a repeated visitor at our house, once quipped that Yellow Springs should be called Red Springs, since we had the highest percentage of Socialist votes in the state.

During our early years in the Socialist Party we took considerable inspiration from what was happening in Russia. A brave new world was being built. Social justice seemed on the march, that nation was being restored in a humane manner. I studied up on Russia, wrote articles about it and gave talks, sometimes under Communist Party auspices.

But we were not attracted to the Communist Party itself. The monolithic structure, the uncritical acceptance of ideas and policies from above, the willingness to subordinate the means to the ends—those things were not for us.

I remember an occasion when a Communist Party representative came to the Convention of the Socialist Party of Ohio, and asked to address the Convention. There was opposition from some of the delegates, but I argued vigorously to let him speak, which he did.

Imagine my chagrin, a while later, when I picked up a copy of the Communist *Daily Worker* and read the report of the Socialist Convention written by this man. Whereas we had given him a friendly reception, his article grossly misrepresented the meeting. And I was the one responsible for letting him in. Phooey!

But there was worse to follow in Russia itself. Stalin had proved to be totally ruthless. In order to cement his control he was, among other things, systematically killing off almost the entire first generation of revolutionary leadership. One by one his secret police would arrest these men, force them to make a false confession of treason (apparently as a price for being allowed to die) and then kill them. He would destroy them morally before killing them physically.

Knowing Stalin's paranoia, Hitler's secret police rigged evidence purporting to show that Russia's leading generals were conspiring against the

Soviet Union. Obligingly, Stalin obtained "confessions" from these generals and had them killed. This crippled Russia's military leadership, expedited the German invasion and aggravated Russian casualties.

As knowledge of Stalin's actions leaked out, thousands of people throughout the world left the Communist Party and persons like myself, who were sympathetic to the Communist ideals of equality and brotherhood were deeply shocked. I no longer gave talks about Russia but, on the contrary, published an article in November of 1937 entitled *The Bankruptcy of Bolshevism.*

During and following World War II the Democratic Socialist movement continued, but at a greatly reduced level. A merger was concluded between the Socialist Party and the more conservative Social Democratic Federation, which had split off from it in 1936. But this merger was followed, in the 1960s, by a new split: one group, the Democratic Socialists of America, preferred to work through the Democratic Party, while the Socialist Party of the U.S.A. continued to stress direct political action.

Socialists and Communists alike, along with thousands of sympathizers and completely uninvolved people came under vicious attack during the heyday of anti-Communist hysteria which occurred in the early '50s. It was incredible. There was a Communist hiding under every bed and crouching behind every garbage can. Senator Joseph McCarthy sparked that craze, and for a time made political hay with it.

Ultimately, of course, McCarthy was censured by the U.S. Senate and later died from too much drinking. In the meantime, however, America went through a period of witch-hunting and red-baiting such as it had never seen before. Thousands of non-Communists were pilloried as "reds" and many lost their jobs. Yellow Springs was not immune.

A friend of mine who worked at the Wright-Patterson Airforce Base was dismissed from his job because he had once held a position at a college which was later taken over by the Communist Party. It ruined his career and broke his heart.

I had a neighbor across the street, Louis Katz by name, who also worked at the Base. Louis rented a room to an Antioch professor who went away for a time, leaving his books in the room. Among the books was one about Red China. Louis brought this book to me and asked me to keep it for him. If it were found in his house, he said, it might cost him his job.

It was well known that at the Bookplate Company I employed all sorts of suspicious characters: Japanese-Americans, Jewish refugees, blacks, Socialists, and conscientious objectors. Then there was my own involvement in a variety of progressive causes. I viewed my business as a social and political instrument as well as a livelihood. Small wonder that the FBI beat a path to my door.

This was one of the tactics in those days: to get a man fired from his job, the authorities would cast suspicion on him by making inquiries of his employer concerning his loyalty and integrity. My people didn't have to worry about that. When the investigators came I would greet them cheerfully, sit them down and answer their questions. They usually wished also to probe my views. I would promptly oblige with a thoughtful lecture on economics.

Once a man came into my office claiming to be a radical and stating flatly that the only way to change the world for the better was through armed struggle. He was obviously from the FBI, so I gave him a harangue on non-violence and the importance of abiding by the law.

Then there was the House un-American Activities Committee, which investigated so many citizens. The Committee had an office in Cincinnati and I wrote them, saying that as a longtime Socialist I would be glad to have someone come and interview me. This created a bit of a sensation, I was told, because they weren't accustomed to getting invitations from Socialists.

The man came to my office. To put me at ease he remarked, "I've come to make a complaint. The last box of bookplates I bought had a couple of defective copies." Then we got down to business. I told him that some politicians in our county, both Republicans and Democrats, had used red-baiting as a tactic to try to discredit critics who sought to expose their shady activities. I went on to quote chapter and verse, with names and cases.

He seemed interested, but wary. I think he wondered if I was putting on an act. He asked leading questions, such as, "Was John Romer a Communist?"

"I don't know," I said. "What John was saying some years ago was not inconsistent with his being a Communist, but what he has been saying in the last few years is totally inconsistent with it."

"That's right," said the man. "He left the Party in 1948." From then on he seemed to recognize that I was on the level.

We had some crooked politicians in our county who tried to use red-baiting as a tactic to discredit their critics. The little community of Yellow Springs became a vortex of political controversy but never bowed its head to McCarthyite witch-hunting. It was looked at askance for miles around and was the object of a powerful reactionary crusade to "clean it up." The ensuing struggle, and my own part in it, are recounted in detail in my chapter on the *Yellow Springs News* which, along with Antioch college, came under determined attack by the forces of McCarthyism.

The irrational fear and hatred of Communism that emerged in America after World War II arose from a perceived threat to our freedoms and even more from the threat to power and privilege. The image of Russian Communism as an "Evil Empire" threatening to take over the world was conjured up to provide our country with an enemy. Without such an enemy our military establishment and its industrial allies would have found it difficult to maintain their stranglehold on the political and economic life of the country.

Looking back, our years of Socialist struggle might be seen as a failure. The media and the money were on the other side. "Dimes against millions" was one of our slogans. We lost all the elections except for a few local offices. But our efforts had another dimension. This was neatly expressed in an editorial which appeared in the Cleveland *Plain Dealer* at the time of our 1936 National Convention. "Watch the Socialist convention closely," it said, "because some of the planks you see in the Socialist Platform this year will be in the Democratic and Republican platforms two years from now."

Social Security, Workmen's Compensation, Unemployment Insurance, the use of public works to relieve unemployment—all these things, and more, originated in the Socialist Platform and were popularized by Socialist Campaigns before they were taken up by the old parties. Most of Roosevelt's program for ending the Depression came from the Socialist Platform. So, our work proved to be overwhelmingly worthwhile. Knowing what I do now, I'd do the same thing over again.

In another sense, however, we *did* fail. Exploitation and military rivalries continue. The inner contradictions of our free enterprise system remain unresolved, with the Depression not cured but merely postponed by war and inflation.

I think we did well. I wish we had done better. The job of restructuring American economic life remains before us. Remembering the important contributions which the Socialist Party made to American political and economic wellbeing in the 30s, I feel that the lack of a strong Socialist movement at this time impoverishes the political and economic thinking of the country.

Norman Thomas, Socialist candidate for President. Ernest ran for Governor of Ohio on the same ticket.

20

I HOLD PUBLIC OFFICE

*I had no idea, when I filed for School Board in Yellow Springs,
what a tumultuous episode that would be in my life.*

In 1941 I decided to run for School Board. I felt that some progressive leadership would be helpful to replace Henry Federighi, an Antioch professor who was retiring from the Board. I campaigned vigorously. Every week for nine weeks I had an article in the paper about education. After these had appeared I summarized them in a form of syllogism which I contrived. This I printed and used as a campaign document. It follows:

THOUGHTS ABOUT OUR SCHOOLS
(A summary of Nine Articles)

I
*The world needs farmers who like farming,
 And printers who like printing.
Do our schools produce such farmers and printers?
No, nearly all the graduates want to wear white collars;
They will not find happiness, or do their best work.*

II
*Did you ever try to mix concrete without cement?
Try it some time.
Education without character is about as useful.
Character development is like cement.
It should permeate all education.*

III

Good citizenship is a habit.
Most habits are formed in childhood.
How shall we educate for citizenship?
By cultivating habits in the children;
By putting them at useful civic work.

IV

Religion is not confined to prayers and sermons;
It can be a way of living.
We can learn to seek truth within as well as without,
And make life finer—
And a great deal happier.

V

We all want our children to thrive and develop.
That is why we have schools.
But the schools aren't automatic;
They need the interest of many people.
Let's make our interest active.

VI

We go to school 12 years, 6 hours a day,
But we live 70 years, 24 hours a day.
Beyond their 6 hours, the schools should help
With Youth Council work
And adult education.

VII

Our children face a changing world.
Will they be ready for it?
The schools must train them well.
To think clearly about the world;
And to act courageously.

VIII

Our town can't buy fine teachers.
We must win them.
When teaching means fellowship and joy
Fine teachers stay
And discipline develops.

IX

Two rival "blocs" of men and women
Don't make a school board.

Five people of good will, working openly,
Can develop the schools
To serve the WHOLE community.

Every afternoon I went campaigning house to house, accompanied by my five-year-old Jenny. A perky little sprite with curly red hair, she would go up the walk ahead of me and soberly hand my campaign document to the person who came to the door. They would smile at her—and then at me. If I talked too long she would pull at my leg to get me moving.

This type of campaigning was particularly effective at remote farm houses, where the wife, who was usually in the house alone, would normally be a bit uneasy at the approach of a strange man. But with a charming little girl—no problem. We visited every house in the school district, except those of my opponents.

I was elected by a landslide, with the most votes cast for any candidate for any office.

One of the continuing Board members, W. A. Hammond, took a dim view of my election. He had referred to me as "that irresponsible and contemptible liar, Ernest Morgan," and to my father as "that bigoted but befuddled eccentric" whose office was "appropriately trimmed in red." In a last ditch effort, Hammond called a public meeting in the High School auditorium to expose Antioch College and me as subversive.

The date for the meeting arrived and the auditorium filled. I took a seat down front, ready for action. For a while we just sat there. Then Mr. Hammond got up and said he was resigning from the School Board. He felt the schools were very important, and he had wanted to help them, but he had been misunderstood. (This was true, in part, as I learned later.) As to the exposures he had planned to make, he had some documents in his hand which he would share with anyone who wished to come to his house. Then he sat down, and again we all waited.

Presently, Clark Meredith, the Chairman of the Board, came forward to explain that he had expected to chair the meeting. However, when Mr. Hammond came, sensed that the assembling crowd was against him, and decided to resign, he, Clark, was unwilling to chair the meeting for that purpose. Then Clark sat down and once more we waited.

Then I came forward and said I was sorry Mr. Hammond felt as he did, and added a few kind words about him. In the middle of my remarks he got up from the front of the room and walked out.

I finished my remarks and sat down. Then someone else stood up and said a few words, and sat down. Then I got up and asked if anyone else had anything to say. Someone did. Then another, and I found myself recognizing the speakers in turn. Then someone in the balcony, a friend of Mr. Hammond, called out, "Who made you chairman?"

"The point is well taken," I replied. "I'll entertain nominations for chairman."

Lowell Fess, an excellent parliamentarian, was quickly elected. As he took the chair he made a humorous gesture which seemed to ease the tension in the auditorium. Then the meeting organized itself and went to work.

Parliamentary procedure as a democratic tool is almost a folkway in American life. Here were several hundred miscellaneous people who had been brought together and left up in the air, so to speak, and they organized themselves immediately. A secretary was chosen, and a committee was formed to visit Mr. Hammond to see those papers which he claimed had incriminating evidence. The committee was selected with care, to represent all segments of the community. A time was chosen for another meeting at which the committee would report back. The whole process gave me a good feeling about our town and our country. The committee did see Mr. Hammond and reported back that they had found nothing substantive.

With Mr. Hammond gone from the School Board, there were four of us left: Clark Meredith, the Chairman, two women, and myself. By unanimous agreement we replaced Mr. Hammond with one of the defeated candidates who was a friend of his. Stresses ensued and the board became divided, the women forming one block, the two men another. This left me in the middle, always casting the deciding vote.

At this point the community was split wide open over the choice of the Supervising Principal. As the only uncommitted Board member, I was lobbied furiously by both sides. I was even denounced as a dictator because I had "been making all the decisions." Finally I voted with the two women and shortly after the other two men resigned.

Now the three of us had to recruit two new members. I suggested the next runner-up in the election, a black woman. She was intelligent and personable. When things didn't go the way she wanted, she would exclaim dramatically, "Truth crushed to earth will rise again!" My colleagues objected to putting her on the Board. It would look bad, they said, for them to be packing the board with women.

"Very well," I said. "I'll settle for a black man." But they wouldn't buy that either. They suggested that we fill the first vacancy with a white man and consider the matter of a black person when there were four of us. I refused to go along with that.

"We'd be glad to serve with a colored person," they said, "but the first colored person to come on the Board should do so by popular election." We had a stalemate. Finally I suggested that they formulate their position as a Board policy, which I could vote against. Once I had gone on record as opposing the policy, I could help choose a white person. They said, "OK, you draft the wording. It's like poison, but we'll vote for it."

So the resolution was passed, with me voting against it, and then we chose a white member. When we prepared to fill the last vacancy the new member spoke up. "How about a black person?" he said. "Damn," I thought, "I've already burnt the bridge." I was no longer outnumbered, but I had forced the matter into a policy which then had to be followed.

My years on the School Board were marked by turbulence—a teachers' strike, parents' protests, internal controversy. Despite all this, our relations were amiable. There was disagreement, of course, but no recrimination between the Board members.

World War II was on, and one of the Board members once casually suggested having military drill in the high school. Instantly my four colleagues swung around and looked at me. Perhaps my face spoke for me. Anyhow, nothing more was said and the matter was dropped.

The war issue came more seriously to the fore when we were seeking a new principal for the grade school. Our Supervising Principal brought in a young man, Gaston Scott, whom he recommended as outstanding. However, Scott was a conscientious objector to war and the Supervising Principal needed the Board's approval before hiring him. His political position would have no bearing on his work. The Chairman of the County Draft Board, my old friend Father Kelly, said, "He's no use to us. We'll defer him to you if you want him."

The School Board was reluctant. I was hardly in a position to carry the ball by myself, but one of my colleagues, Dick Odiorne, who was not a pacifist, spoke with eloquence. "If our American ideals mean anything," he began, and then he unfolded an impressive case for hiring the man.

"If all the citizens could hear you, Dick, we'd have clear sailing," said George Donley, the Chairman. "But they can't, and I don't think they'd approve." Dick made another appeal, but it was no use. The vote was three to two against Scott.

Then I put forward a candidate, Rita Chatterjee, a talented Scotch woman who was the wife of M. N. Chatterjee, a distinguished Hindu professor at Antioch. She came with superlative credentials and I had known her, too, as head of the Antioch School when my two daughters were there. "Her Scotch brogue would confuse the children," objected one of my colleagues. (Sheer nonsense.)

The real rub, however, was her husband. As an Indian, was he loyal to the Allied cause at a time when India was seeking independence? The ethnic issue was never raised, though it may have been a factor. At any event, we turned away the second outstanding candidate, finally settling for one who, though competent, was not in the same league.

Toward the end of my term on the Board, a remarkable chain of events occurred which had important repercussions. The High School was on the edge of town and a black man who lived nearby was hunting rabbits on the school grounds. I was on the Buildings and Grounds Committee and took a dim view of anyone shooting around the school. The incident had been re-ported to me by Abe Shafer, who delivered the *Yellow Springs News,* and I asked him to report it to the Police.

The hunter, Thurl Hickman, was arrested and fined, and the fine was sus-pended. His wife called me up, furious. "I thought you were a friend of the colored people," she said, "but now I see you're just a big hypocrite like all the rest."

"I'll come out and see you," I said.

That evening I sat in their living room and chatted. "If Jesus Christ him-self were shooting rabbits on the school grounds I'd turn him in," I ex-plained. Then we went on to more pleasant topics, and I left them in good spirits. Thurl was a good singer and he began to drop by our house now and then and sing while Elizabeth accompanied him on the piano.

On one of those occasions I talked to him about the School Board. I wanted to see a black person on the Board, I said, and had my eye on Bill Perry, who was highly regarded in the community. I wasn't sure how to con-vince him to run. I wondered who would be the right person to talk to him. Thurl reflected a moment. Then he suggested his brother-in-law, Lew Ad-ams. Lew and Bill were close and Lew could probably persuade him. It worked, and Bill announced his candidacy.

That done, I got into the act and prepared a campaign document for Bill. It dealt directly with the fact that Bill was black and said that the presence of an able, responsible black person on the Board would be valuable in the dif-ficult days ahead. It went on to say that black people should be encouraged to hold public office not because they "deserved" to hold office, but because they should be encouraged to carry their share of civic responsibility.

I took the draft of this statement to the local businessmen and they all signed it. Then I printed it over their signatures and we covered the town with it. It proved irresistible, and Bill Perry won in a landslide.

I ran for reelection myself and was roundly defeated. My opponents pointed to the fact that I had supported Gaston Scott, a conscientious objec-tor, for Grade School Principal. Dick Odiorne, who went to bat for Scott, was also defeated for reelection. I was also the person on the Board most accessi-ble to the public by virtue of the location of my home and office, so I was often the one who confronted 'agitated parents. Perhaps even more decisive, the black vote also went against me. True, I had voted against the resolution which held that the first black person to come on the Board should do so by popular election. But my opponents pointed out that I was the one who had drafted that resolution.

My father, however, was irked by my defeat. That was the only time I remember his saying anything unkind about Yellow Springs. In his disap-pointment, he called it a "narrow little town." But I had no regrets. I had cast the deciding vote on some very important decisions and I helped elect an excellent black man to the Board.

On a totally unrelated matter, I recall an occasion when I was on a picket line—I forget what for—and was approached by a man who gave me a harangue against abortion. I responded, "You are right, but you don't go far enough. The unfertilized ovum also is human. It has a right to be fertilized and born. Menstruation should be outlawed and every woman of child-bearing age should be pregnant or nursing at all times!"

"Don't be silly!" said the man, and walked away.

School Board Meeting.

This is the 300-foot greenhouse in which the Moraine Park School was conducted, and in which Ernest went to school for several years.

21

THE *YELLOW SPRINGS NEWS*

A small town weekly newspaper relates intimately to people's lives. Edited with understanding and imagination, it can be a creative force in the community. The publishing of the Yellow Springs News *was a meaningful and challenging episode in my career, which took place at a difficult time in the history of our country.*

When Dad reorganized Antioch College he also envisioned the enlivenment of the Yellow Springs Community, economically, socially, and culturally. It is not surprising, therefore, that the college bought the *Yellow Springs News* and made it the nucleus of the Antioch Press, the printing and publishing department of the college. The previous publisher, JN Wolford, was given a job in the Press and Antioch students were hired to edit the newspaper. (One of whom was Christine Frederiksen, who I married half a century later, after Elizabeth's death.)

The plan didn't work well. The student editors, though capable and energetic, were inexperienced and didn't know the community. The cost of printing the paper was too high and it ran a steady deficit. Finally, the Antioch Press returned the *News* to its former publisher.

JN Wolford, the publisher, had no first name. Just the letters JN—no periods. He had published the *News* for many years. Not a bad paper, but not outstanding either. I knew JN well and started contributing articles, sometimes on local issues and sometimes on national or international topics. In time these grew into a regular weekly column. Sometimes these contributions took the form of verse; "Bumptious Ballads" I called them.

Wolford was a Republican and I was a Socialist, but that didn't seem to bother him. Only once did he ask me to ease off, and that was when he felt my article might hurt someone's family. He received complaints about my articles from some of his readers, but he brushed them off. I once expressed concern about an angry subscriber who had canceled and JN remarked, "That's all right. He'll buy the paper on the newsstand." I think my articles stimulated readership, and JN appreciated that.

In 1941 an Antioch alumnus, Roland "Skip" Faust, offered to buy the *News,* but Wolford had a strong personal feeling about the paper and didn't want to sell to a relative stranger. So Skip decided to launch a competing paper.

Wolford, now well along in years, did not relish a battle, so, almost overnight, he sold the paper to my brother-in-law, Landrum Bolling, who had been doing a column for the *News.* By that time Skip was only a week away from his first issue. Taking Landrum with me, I hunted him up.

"Skip," I said, "I want you to meet the new publisher of the *Yellow Springs News.*"

Skip sat down heavily and said,"I know when I'm licked."

Landrum, a veteran journalist, put out a fine paper. But he had illness in his family which took much of his time so he gave up the *News.* Then Elizabeth and I bought the paper. We did this without consulting the Bookplate Company staff. This was a breach of trust on our part, since the *News* would cut into the Bookplate Company earnings which, in turn, were divided with the staff. But they took it in a good spirit.

Two editorials from our first issue on February 5th, 1942, tell the story. The first one, below, tells who was doing the work.

HOW ME AND BETSY KILLED THE BEAR

There is a story about a mountaineer and his wife whose cabin was entered one night by a large bear. The mountaineer scrambled up into the loft and pulled the ladder up after him. The wife grabbed an axe and fought the bear. While wife and bear struggled below, the mountaineer shouted from the rafters, "Go it, Betsy, go it B'ar." The next day he bragged to all the neighbors "how me and Betsy killed the b'ar."

So it was with us. We realized that Landrum might decide to turn the News *over to us, perhaps in June or August. But a rush of circumstances has thrown the job suddenly in our laps. The Bookplate Business cannot spare me, even part time, just now, and committee work on the School Board looms up large.*

So it is up to "Betsy." A busy housewife with three small children and a hundred baby chicks, but no newspaper experience, would not calmly tackle a lively eight-page community newspaper—not if she were sensible. But my wife is not sensible. (She would never have married me if she had been.) She has jumped right in. Dorothy Mattison and Leah Wolford trained her almost overnight and now she's going strong. My Mother, with her usual energy, has assumed much of the home responsibility. I sit in the rafters and give advice and encouragement. And that is how we manage the News!

—Ernest Morgan

The other editorial, written in an almost syllogistic form of verse which I liked to use, stated our aims and policies with respect to the paper.

WE BELIEVE
(A Statement of Aims)

I

We believe that the NEWS *belongs to the community.*
Its ownership is a public trust.
"Freedom of the press" means freedom,
Not just for the editors,
But for all who wish to speak.

II

Yellow Springs is a mixed and growing community;
Farmers, Negroes, tradesmen, teachers—-
Here they live and vote and rear their children.
They need to know each other,
And understand each other's problems.

III

In the community of Yellow Springs
Are many "little communities"
Which should understand and appreciate each other,
As this understanding grows,
Community life becomes stronger and finer.

IV

Many new people are moving to town.
The NEWS *should help make them feel at home.*
If we don't make them at home fast enough
We'll cease to be a real community
And will become a "residential suburb."

V

We believe that a community needs eyes and a voice.
That's what a newspaper should be.
The columns of the NEWS *should be open to all,*
To keep public issues public,
And to avoid gossip.

VI

Democracy demands that the paper be nonpartisan;
No party or clique should have the inside track.
When the editors write something partisan
It should be a "letter to the editor,"
And not an editorial.

VII

We believe that the editor who is on the school board
Must not take advantage of his position.
When he writes opinions about school affairs
He should do it as a "letter to the editor,"
Not as an editorial.

VIII

We realize the editors can't please everybody,
But they should know what people think.
They invite and appreciate criticism.
They will listen to it thoughtfully
And without getting sore.

IX

If you like the way they run the NEWS,
Then help them do it.
If you don't like the way they run it,
Then take a hand in it yourself;
IT'S YOUR PAPER, TOO.
                                        —*The Editors*

To handle production, Elizabeth hired a young printer, Donald Menn, who did a good job for us. He later married Leah Wolford, one of JN's daughters. After a short while we moved the *News* equipment into the Bookplate shop, and there it stayed until 1949.

Elizabeth continued as editor for six months. She did a good job and enjoyed it, but it took a heavy toll on our family life. With three young children she was needed at home. So she gave it up and was followed by a succession of other editors. I edited it now and then myself.

Publishing a small-town weekly was a unique adventure, intimately involved with the life of the community in all its dimensions. Much of the time we sailed peacefully along, reporting on visiting relatives and weddings, meetings of the village Council and School Board, plus church and club activities. Along the way we dealt with problems and issues. Now and then we struck sparks.

One of these times occurred during a political campaign. A local man proposed to develop a section of real estate on the edge of town. The Village Government said it could not provide sewer service to that area, as the lines would have to be blasted through rock—a costly process. So this man, along with a friend, ran for the Board of Trustees of Public Affairs, planning to put the sewer line through at public expense.

I wrote an editorial, pointing out his scheme. He called me up. "Ernest," he said, "if you don't retract that statement we're going to have trouble—and I mean hand-to-hand trouble—the next time we meet, even if it's in church."

So I went to see him at his place on the edge of town and sat in his office —not without a few chills—for almost an hour. We had a long and animated conversation, in the course of which he paid me an unintentional compliment. "Ernest" he said, "people don't read your damn paper because they like it. They just want to see what your next move is going to be."

Fortunately, the hand-to-hand trouble didn't materialize and he and his colleague lost the election by a wide margin.

I have already told how we brought in a young Japanese-American printer, Frank Kakoi, to help with the *News*. There were immediate repercussions. Some of our subscribers were served by mail, others by carrier. The man who did the carrying was an elderly fellow named Abe Shafer. Abe called me up and informed me that he wasn't going to carry the *News* any more, "on account of that fellow you brought in from California."

"Abe," I said. "Didn't your folks come from Germany?" It was a random shot, but it proved to be on target.

"That's different," said Abe.

"Very well," I said, "bring in your list of subscribers."

"No," said Abe, "that list belongs to me."

"Look Abe," I said, "next Thursday afternoon when their papers don't come, everybody is going to be cussing Abe Shafer." So he brought in the list.

"Abe," I said to him, "you can quit, but I don't want you quitting on those grounds." He softened a bit and said that he was really too busy to keep the route. He then suggested a couple of high school boys who took it on. One of them was Ken Champney who, years later became the publisher of the *News*.

Abe Shafer's son became a good friend of Frank's, and after the first plunge the community as a whole took kindly to the Japanese-Americans, some of whom settled there permanently and contributed their full share of business and civic leadership.

Another ethnic incident at the *News* involved a young black woman. This girl went away to college and lost any trace of an ethnic style of speech. She subsequently married, returned to Yellow Springs with her husband, and began working at the Bookplate Company.

The time came when I needed a new society editor for the paper. I looked over the organization to see if there were some woman in it who might be promoted to the job. The outstanding choice seemed to be this young woman, Louise Riddock, so I offered her the position. Black society editors weren't very common in those days, and she wondered if people would stand for it.

"Here's how we'll work it," I said. "The people in Yellow Springs don't know you by your married name, and they can't tell your race on the phone. You're plenty literate and articulate. I'll give you a list of the folks we call each week. You can phone them, introduce yourself and have a little chat. By the time they find out who Louise Riddock is, they will already like you, and it will be too late for them to change their minds." The strategy worked, and Louise did a good job as society editor.

During the seven years we published the *News* I learned the fascinating lore of the country weekly. I wrote for the paper, and sometimes made up the pages on the big stone slab. Now and then I fed the old drum press. It was a Babcock, a huge machine, a relic of the 19th Century, which clanked and rumbled as it ran. It had a little platform on the side where the operator stood as he flipped the sheets one by one against the guides. Most printing machines have a sprightly rhythm; this one was funereal. I knew a song which exactly fit this rhythm. Sometimes I sang it while I fed the press:

> *Did you ev - er think*
> *As the hearse - - rolls by*
> *That it won't - - be long*
> *Before you - - and I*
> *Will be roll - - ing by*
> *In a big - - black hack*
> *And we won't - - be thinking*
> *Of com - - ing back.*

(The remaining stanzas are worse.)

After two or three short-time editors, we hired Earl Hamilton, a retired Swedenborgian minister. A quiet little man, he was scholarly and systematic and put out a good, though not distinguished, paper. Normally a mild-mannered man, he would now and then, in the privacy of his office, relieve his feelings by roaring "Damn!" He was with us a long time.

After the war a young man, Kieth Howard, just out of Civilian Public Service, came to see Dad. He wanted to do something worthwhile with his life and was responding to an ad for a person to write a syndicated column on community. Kieth had worked as an ad man on a city daily, but didn't have the background needed to write that column. Dad was impressed with him, however, and sent him down to see me.

I found him to be a vigorous person, and a kindred spirit. He'd make a fine editor. But there was Mr. Hamilton, still two or three years away from Social Security. So I made a deal with Dad to hire Mr. Hamilton, and our company would pay a share of his salary until he qualified for Social Security.

When Kieth moved into the editorship a new era began, not only for the *Yellow Springs News* but to some extent for the town as well. Kieth's news coverage was perceptive, his editorials relevant and he built up the circulation and advertising. In spite of this, the paper still required subsidy by the Bookplate Company.

We didn't mind that, as long as we had the money. But after the war the Company sales slumped badly and we were hard put to survive. It became necessary to sell the *News*. We offered it to Kieth, but he was not in a position to buy it.

Although we had built up the paper considerably, we were willing to sell it to Kieth for the $4500 we had paid for it. For anyone else it would have been $8,000, and at that price we found no takers. Finally Kieth got a partner, Lee Bullen, a congenial young man who was a printer, and they bought the paper.

Lee was a good printer but he was not what is known in the trade as a "swifty." The paper took so much time that he hardly saw his family, and his half of the earnings were not enough to live on. Kieth was in better shape because his wife, Margaret, taught school and helped support the family. Finally, Lee left to work for a city paper.

This would have been disastrous for Kieth but for another development. Ken Champney, the son of my old insurgent schoolmate, Horace Champney, had been attending Penn College in Iowa, which was headed by a social activist Quaker, Cecil Hinshaw. A conservative element got control of the board and dismissed Hinshaw. Many students quit, including Ken, who then applied at Antioch, where he was turned down. He then offered to help with the *News* if Lee Bullen would teach him printing. He proved a quick learner and a swift printer. By the time Lee left, Ken was able to handle production; furthermore he was congenial with Kieth. Ken, by the way, had been one of the two boys who had taken over News distribution from Abe Shafer.

But this arrangement carried with it potential disaster. Ken had some of his father's insurgent qualities. He was not only a draft refuser, he refused even to register for the draft. He was not evasive about it, but wrote the Draft Board, explaining his convictions and telling them where to find him when they were ready to arrest him. This put Kieth in a precarious position.

One day Ken came into my office. With him was a quiet little girl named Peggy with glasses and pigtails, who looked like a high school sophomore. Ken explained that he and Peggy were getting married, and that she would handle *News* production while he was in prison. My heart sank. Was Ken crazy? That job could kill a strong man; Peggy wouldn't have a chance.

But she went to work learning the trade. I remember her standing on a box to operate the paper cutter. In due time Ken was picked up and taken to the Ashland Penitentiary, and Peggy was on her own. With the help of another friend, Joe Letson, she carried on. Meeting Kieth on the street not long after that, I asked how things were going. Kieth grinned. "I never had so little problem with production." With Ken in prison, Peggy became the new partner.

However, Kieth still had another problem. As long as the *News* was under the wing of the Bookplate Company, the conservative element hesitated to attack it, but as soon as Kieth was on his own they went for him.

The McCarthyites looked upon Yellow Springs as a hotbed of subversion. An organization was formed—The Miami Township Civic Improvement Association—to combat the "left wing tendencies" of the community. Their first move was to try to buy the *Yellow Springs News*. Mistakenly judging Peggy to be the softest point to approach, they made her an offer for the paper. Kieth had paid us $4500 for it not long before; the Association offered $20,000. Peggy and Kieth promptly turned this down.

The people in the Civic Action Association found this hard to understand. "With $20,000 he could have bought a county seat paper," said one. "They just aren't normal," said another. Lucky for Yellow Springs they weren't.

Failing to buy the *News*,, the Civic Action Association took another tack. They formed the Greene County Publishing Company and bought the neighboring Cedarville and Jamestown papers, including the printing plant at Cedarville. Then, with a printshop at their disposal, they launched the *Yellow Springs American* to compete with the *News*. The battle was on. By that time Ken was back from prison and the *News* team was at full strength.

The *American* went right down the McCarthy line, swinging wildly. Kieth, a veteran newspaper man, edited the *News* with dignity and restraint and the community supported the *News*. Some *News* backers, wishing to read what the *American* had to say, but not wishing to support it, had a little trick. They would buy copies in the drugstore, read them, and then slip them quietly back on the newsstand. This way the drugstore got all the money.

In the midst of this struggle the *News* suddenly blossomed out with lots of pictures. Meeting Kieth one day I said, "Kieth, how can you afford all those cuts you're using now?"

Kieth laughed. "The *News* is just a well-managed newspaper, that's all."

"Come off it, Kieth," I said. "I know what cuts cost."

Kieth paused. "I'll tell you," he said. "But you mustn't pass it on. The publisher of the Fairborn paper, which came out against us a while back, is friendly now. They have a cut-making machine which they let me use once a week."

The *American* had a hard time and lasted for about ten months. The public turned against it and the advertisers began to drop off. The paper championed free enterprise, but its business manager was a bit too free in his enterprises. He privately cut himself in for a $10,000 slice on one of their deals, and then ducked out when the going got rough. Finally, in indignation over the editorial policy, the bank pulled out its ad. That was the signal for the end. It was at about that time that a member of the staff of the *American* said to me, "You'll have to admit that we've made a darn good paper of the *Yellow Springs News*."

The other Civic Action Association papers continued for a while. Sometimes, when they had a special message involving Yellow Springs they would print it in their Cedarville paper and distribute free copies in Yellow Springs. One such message was a violent attack on scientist Linus Pauling, when he was being entertained at Antioch. A banquet was held at the college in Pauling's honor and Clyde Adams, who headed Antioch's Chemistry Department, was seated beside him.

Kieth was covering this banquet for the *News* and observed the seating arrangement. Knowing that Adams was a leader in the Civic Action Association he quickly snapped a picture of the guest of honor with Adams seated at his right hand. This he printed in the *News,*, along with the story of Pauling's visit.

Finally the Greene County Publishing Company went bankrupt and lost the other papers, and the Miami Township Civic Action Association gave up the struggle as a bad job.

Then a new champion picked up the torch. Lowell Fess, formerly our mayor but at that time our state senator, reportedly went to see Joe McCarthy, who said to him, "Give 'em Hell."

A veteran of World War I, Fess went to meetings of the American Legion and persuaded them at both the District and State levels to adopt resolutions condemning Antioch and Yellow Springs as subversive, and calling for a Congressional investigation.

Then he wrote two long and vitriolic letters to President Douglas McGregor of Antioch College, calling for a "cleanup" of the college and repeating his demand for an investigation. In one of these letters he said:

I will not rest until every vestige of Communism, Marxism, pinkos, leftists, socialists, radicals, etc., is eliminated from the Village of Yellow Springs and the Antioch Community.

He went on to say what a fine village Yellow Springs had been until the crackpots came and ruined it. The *Yellow Springs News* gave freely of its space, and printed his letters in full.

I rose up in wrath and came back at him with a hot reply, which I took to the paper. Soon I had a call from Kieth. He was at the home of Mayor Paul Kintzel, and he asked me to come there, which I did. He and Paul sat on me. "Simmer down, Ernest," they said. "Go home and write a calm reply to Fess." Thus chastened, and having gotten the venom out of my system with the first letter (which was discarded), I wrote the following, addressed to Fess himself, and sent a copy to the *News*.

> *Dear Red:*
>
> *You're right. Yellow Springs was a mighty nice little village, back in the old days, with beautiful trees and friendly people. Us kids swam naked at Grinnell's Mill without fear of embarrassment. That was back in '21. You had been here 15 years.*
>
> *There were about three bathtubs in town, no water or sewer systems, few sidewalks, no paved streets and only two streets where a car couldn't sink to the hubs in wet weather. The college was down to two-or-three dozen students and a $15,000 budget. The two small industries were fading out. Most young people, including you, moved away as soon as they could.*
>
> *Then came the "crackpots." Instead of going away, people began coming here again, "even from foreign countries," just as you said.*
>
> *Today, our village of shady streets and friendly people has become a famous center of science, art, and industry. The Antioch budget is now $1,500,000, and the educational ideas tested and proved there influence the lives of millions. Great research projects probe the mysteries of photosynthesis and child development, while industries over the nation seek help here with special problems. Important books, pamphlets, and articles flow from Yellow Springs in a steady stream.*
>
> *More than a dozen small thriving industries, every one of them home-owned, do a total of about $10,000,000 annual business and make jobs for nearly 1,000 people. Every plane and tank and motor vehicle that fought for America in World War II carried a device invented and partly built here. This same device, which makes automatic washers possible, will be found also in fifty million cars and trucks, which, by the way, are shod with tires made in Yellow Springs molds. Electronic devices designed and built here test America's aircraft and do many other jobs. Specially developed farm seeds help improve farming. Important parts for diesel locomotives and other machines are cast. Industrial products designed here roll off the assembly lines of great factories.*
>
> *Paintings, etchings, and photographs from our town grace countless homes and art galleries; our bronze statuary is unveiled in public parks and buildings; our drama is enjoyed by*

thousands; our stained glass windows lend atmosphere in many churches; and our bookplates (excuse the ad) are found in thousands of libraries and millions of private volumes. Our Community Council is studied and copied by other towns.

In this creative ferment, conservatives, liberals, and radicals have dreamed and built in freedom and friendliness, each doing his own job in his own way, and respecting the other fellow. You, Red, are ashamed and disgusted with our community. I am very proud of it.

—*Ernest Morgan*

After that the sky seemed to fall on Fess. The community turned against him. The *News* ran a full-page ad, signed by all the local businesses: "WE ARE PROUD OF YELLOW SPRINGS." Even some of the local Republicans repudiated him. In the ensuing election he failed, for the first time, to carry the town—it went almost two-to-one against him. He did win in the district, but he was low man on the ticket. We made red-baiting so unprofitable for him that no one has tried it in Yellow Springs since.

Prior to the McCarthy era the college community had a rather condescending attitude toward the *News* and its publishers. But that changed completely, and ever since that time the *News* people have "stood tall" in the community.

During the years the Bookplate Company published the *News* it never won any awards. Under the management of Kieth and the Champneys, however, it covered itself with glory, being judged first among country weeklies in America in General Excellence. It also won awards for Community Service, Editorial Excellence, and News Coverage.

The *News* partners regarded the paper as a social trust, not as private property to be bought and sold. They arranged, among themselves, that when one of them retired, he or she would not claim their full pro-rata share of ownership. (That would make it costly for successors.)

That policy paid off. Kieth and Eleanor are long retired, but succeeding generations of editors have carried on the tradition. Yellow Springs is extremely fortunate in having a printing and publishing team with the philosophy, skill, and commitment of these people.

I've always felt that, of all the activities that Elizabeth and I carried on in Yellow Springs over a period of half a century, by far our greatest contribution to the community was putting the *Yellow Springs News* in the hands of Kieth Howard and his associates and successors.

JN Wolford, from whom the company bought the *News*. Here he is running the paper through the folder.

Kieth Howard, who was hired as editor and later bought the paper. Here he is putting the paper together.

22

A WORM'S-EYE VIEW OF
THE CIVIL RIGHTS STRUGGLE

The South had no monopoly on the civil rights struggle! This chapter tells, in a nutshell, the story of the dramatic struggle for civil rights in my home town of Yellow Springs. It tells also the background of this struggle and of the part that I and my family played in it.

Once, when I was about four years old, I was walking down the sidewalk in St. Cloud, Minnesota, with my Aunt Jessie when we met a black man. I had never seen a black person before, and I was scared. Taking refuge behind Jessie, I peered around at the man. "I don't hurt little children," he said, "I just eat them." Who would have thought that, later in life, I would become active in the civil rights movement.

In the early 1920s, civil rights had not yet emerged as an active issue. In Yellow Springs they even slipped back a little. This is what happened.

A black shoemaker, James Johnson, had a little shop on the main street. In front of it hung a sign shaped like a boot, with the words, TRY ME ON—JAS. JOHNSON. From this he got the nickname, Jazz. He hobbled about on artificial legs. Purportedly he lost his original legs on a railroad track while drunk. He was a rather course fellow, with a loud laugh, and the college students enjoyed bantering with him.

There was a restaurant across the street called Moxies, and Jazz frequently hobbled over there to linger on one of the stools and chat with the customers. The proprietor, T. W. Mock, was concerned that this might hurt business, especially with the college community. He solved the problem by putting a sign in his window which read, WE CATER TO THE CAUCASIAN RACE.

Jazz sputtered angrily, and stayed away. The college students looked upon it as a joke. Antioch at that point did not yet have the concern for social justice that would later become one of its hallmarks. The practice of excluding black people quickly spread to the other restaurants and continued until we put a stop to it more than twenty-five years later.

In the 1930s the economic struggle largely transcended the issue of civil rights. Often blacks and whites found themselves together in this struggle, as in the unemployed organizations and in the Southern Tenant Farmers Union. The issue was muted through the war years, too, though concern for it was building.

In the early 1920s, a local man, Dick Denison, sold his auto garage and started showing movies in the old Opera House. These were the first "talking pictures" which carried the sound on disc records. These movies were fun to watch, because the action and sound were always a little out of step.

Later, as modern sound films came into use, Dick built a theater on the main street and went into the movie business in a serious way. It was a small, attractive place which I had helped name "The Little Theater." But there was one thing I didn't like about it: black people had to sit in a special roped-off section in the back.

In my column for the *Yellow Springs News*, I needled Dick now and then about that rope. But there came a day when Elizabeth and I took over the *News*. Dick was an important advertiser; what to do?

It took a few tries, but I got him to come over and talk to me about it. His position was clear. "If your attitude is going to be the same as it has been," he said, "I don't want my ad in your paper!"

I gave that a little thought. "I'll tell you what," I said. "Any time I'm going to print something critical of your theater I'll let you know in advance, so you can take your ad out." He said he thought that was fair, and then he tried to clarify his position. "In a place where you meet the public, like in your office, for example, you can't afford to . . ."

At that instant, as if on cue, in walked Nina Hamilton, a pretty, intelligent black high school girl. She hung up her coat and went to work in the office, as she did each day after school. The expression on Dick's face was priceless.

The rope in the theater finally did come down. This is how it happened. A group of college students, some white and some black, bought tickets and entered the theater. The blacks seated themselves politely behind the rope and the whites scattered through the theater. When all were seated and the show was about to commence a solitary black youth came in, and took a seat in the very front.

Dick walked to the front and touched the boy on the shoulder, beckoning him to move. The youth pretended not to understand, and he took a long time to catch on that he was being told to move. Then he stood up, and he and Dick looked toward the back of the theater. While he had been distracted, the black students had come out from behind the rope and were now scattered throughout the theater, seated on both sides of the aisle. Between them and the aisle, in every case, were white students. Dick walked back and took down the rope, and it never went up again.

Several times during the 1940s a small group of white people met in Yellow Springs to consider what might be done to combat color discrimination, but each time, no blacks showed up. Critics would point their fingers at us and say, "Can't you see? The black people are perfectly content. Why do you trouble makers try to stir things up?" Obviously, we couldn't get very far under those conditions.

When World War II was over, the young black veterans came home. No longer intimidated, they stood tall and looked the world in the eye. When we called an interracial meeting, they came out. With them came Bill Perry, the middle-aged black man who had recently been elected to the School Board in a landslide. (It was I who had persuaded Bill to run for the Board.)

Now we had a strong social base. Our first goal was to open up the two restaurants. Persuasion failed, so we planned legal action. Our strategy was to have a white family enter each restaurant and get served. They would be followed by black customers, who would presumably be refused service. Then more white families would come in and get served. This would give us court evidence.

Accordingly, one evening a group assembled at the Bookplate Shop. The Glen Cafe was located across the street and the Old Trail Tavern just two doors down the street. Elizabeth and I and five-year-old Lee were assigned to enter the Tavern, while another family entered the Glen Cafe. The situation was tense. The restaurant people obviously knew what was happening. There were signals back and forth between the restaurants, and then both places locked their doors. So our family was locked inside, quietly eating, while most of the excitement was on the outside.

After a while everybody went home. I was still in the office when our editor, Kieth Howard, walked in. His nose was bloody and his clothing torn. Frank and Ray Dewine, who ran the Glen Cafe, had attacked him on the street. Tough and wiry, Kieth had wrenched himself loose from their grip, managing in the process to roll one of the big men into the gutter.

A few days later we held a meeting in our living room to plan the next step. About forty people were present, black and white. In the middle of the meeting a rock the size of a man's fist crashed through a window, sprinkling broken glass in Dave Sallume's hair and landing at the feet of my daughter, Jenny, who was sitting on the rug.

For a moment the emotional shock was paralyzing. I wondered fleetingly if the water heater in the basement had blown up. Then I heard a woman say, in alarm, "I'm not coming to any more of these meetings!" That triggered me, and I jumped to my feet and delivered a fiery harangue.

Elizabeth wasn't at that meeting. She was a block away, making music with our friend Leontine Price. She got home just as the last people were leaving. We were sweeping up broken glass, and the rock was lying on the floor. "So that's what it was!" she exclaimed. She said that in the middle of the music she suddenly stopped, with a strong feeling that something was wrong at home. The only thing she could think of was fire, and the siren didn't go, so she dismissed the idea.

The next morning I told our kids to keep their ears open at school. "Whoever threw that rock is going to talk, and the kids are likely to get wind of it." Sure enough, they came home that afternoon with verbatim quotations that left little doubt about the identity of the offender. He was a young war veteran from a Catholic family, so I went to see my friend Father Kelly, and talked the matter over with him. He, in turn, called in the young man.

One evening not long after that I was intercepted by this chap and a couple of his friends as I approached the side door of the Bookplate Company. He protested my having put the priest on him. Another grievance he had was my involvement on behalf of the Jews. "The Jews have all the money!" he said.

That was a perfect opening. "Do you really think so?" I asked. "John D. Rockefeller, J. P. Morgan, the DuPonts, Andrew Mellon—they control great wealth, but none of them are Jews. Can you name any wealthy Jews?" They couldn't.

"I can name some," I said. "There's Samuel Fels, of Fels-Naptha Soap, who supports the Fels Institute here in Yellow Springs, devoted to research in child development. That is for the benefit of all children, not just Jewish children. And there is Rosenwald, of Sears Roebuck, one of the most generous philanthropists in America. Really," I said, "Jews are like the rest of us, good, bad, and indifferent." The young men seemed impressed by this little speech. We talked a bit further and they left in a good spirit.

Not long after that the bartender at the Tavern reported he had been riding his motorbike when he was forced into the ditch by five black men in a yellow Jeep. They had stood over him, he said, as he lay in the ditch, and threatened him. This galvanized the local American Legion. The young veterans roared up and down the streets with their cars and motorcycles, and congregated in and around the Tavern.

I heard later that the blacks all retired to their homes and that some of them got out their guns, turned out their lights, and sat by their windows, ready for the worst.

It was evening then, and I went down to the Tavern to see the bartender. He was sitting by himself in a booth, so I joined him. We spoke briefly and I said to him, referring to his mishap, "All decent people deplore that sort of thing."

"You're not decent!" he snarled. "You're the ringleader!"

No use talking further, so I got up to leave. Quickly he left his seat and came to the center of the room where he confronted me with clenched fists. At that point my rock-throwing friend and one of his companions grasped the man's arms. There was a moment of silence. Then he went back to his seat and I left.

I went to the *News* office next door and got on the phone, trying to get some trace of that yellow Jeep. The *News* office was in a big bay window, in full view of the street. A crowd was milling around outside. In the midst of my efforts there was an incoming call. It was Marge Swann who, with her husband Bob, was a lifelong activist. "How are things going down there?" she asked. I told her it was pretty tense, and she offered to find some help.

There was a liberal servicemen's organization in town, The Miami Township Veteran's Association—mostly college men. Marge started phoning them. In a short while, one by one, they began to appear, each wearing some item of military regalia. They mingled with the crowd and some came in the door to chat with me for a few minutes. I felt much better, but I never did get track of that yellow Jeep.

Under all the pressure it wasn't long before the restaurants integrated, and soon it was hard to realize that all that nonsense had actually happened.

Although the American Legion did not look very good in this instance, they redeemed themselves later on. The Village Manager wanted to integrate the Volunteer Fire Department but was afraid that some of the white members would quit, leaving the crew shorthanded. The Legion came forward and volunteered men to replace any firefighters who left during that time.

The last and most dramatic episode of the Civil Rights struggle in Yellow Springs involved three generations of our family. The three barber shops in town were the last places to hold out against integration. One of these, run by a black barber, came across early in the game but the two white barbers held out.

In April, 1963, the Antioch Committee for Racial Equality (ACRE) attempted to integrate Gegner's Barber Shop. (Our son, Lee, was one of the organizers.) Gegner insisted he didn't know how to cut the hair of black people—and he wasn't about to learn!

When the other students showed reluctance to take action, Lee reportedly told them that if they didn't he would resort to his old man and mobilize town support. The prospect of being bypassed in favor of a middle-aged businessman seemed to stimulate them.

Legal action had previously been started but was at a standstill. As a first move, ACRE trained teams of pickets and sit-ins and sent them into action. They were disciplined and neatly groomed—no beards or long hair.

Gegner resisted vigorously and the contest quickly built up. Jim McKee, the black police chief, and other local officials were caught in the middle, sympathetic to the integration effort but determined to keep order. Successive sit-in teams were arrested.

At one point a crowd of integration supporters sang freedom songs outside the shop, and were joined by an opposition crowd singing "God Bless America." Thereupon the integrationists shifted to "America the Beautiful," while the sheriff proceeded to haul them away.

Dudley Dawson, Antioch's Dean, expressed approval of social action by students but set up specific guidelines, requiring the signing of documents and the obtaining of parental permission by students under twenty-one.

The *Yellow Springs News*, not surprisingly, gave active support. The *Dayton Daily News* offered moderate support, but Dayton radio station WHIO castigated the college and the students. The situation made the news wires and was picked up by *The New York Times*, *The Washington Post,* and many other papers throughout the country.

Gegner won the first round in the courts, and the case was promptly appealed. A county injunction was declared, limiting pickets to four at a time. Students picketed during the week and townspeople on Saturdays. I was one of the Saturday pickets, frequently accompanied by other corporate executives.

With Gegner's initial victory in the courts, two factions emerged on the campus. There were those—including Lee—who preferred to operate within the rules of the injunction, and a more militant group who proposed to buck the law. Finally they agreed on a plan to stage a giant protest march. They applied for a permit to march down Xenia Avenue, but this was refused. Then they decided to march, two abreast, down the sidewalk on the west side of the street.

Complications arose. Gangs from out of town threatened to come and break up the march. The Ohio Civil Rights Commission urged the students to call it off. So did the college administration. Lee and two of his cohorts were called in to confront President Dixon, Dean Dawson, and Police Chief McKee, and again were urged to cancel the march. Lee was the official spokesman for the organization. He pointed out to the authorities that they had called in the more moderate leaders and that if these leaders tried to call off the march, the more militant element would take charge.

At the appointed hour some 500 people—students and townspeople—gathered in the college parking lot. Again, no beards or long hair. With Arthur Morgan, now 85 years old, in the lead along with Walter Anderson, Antioch's distinguished black professor of music, the procession headed downtown. Student "marshals" were spaced at intervals. I was in it too, of course.

An out-of-town crowd was there, all right, but so were the police, the

Arthur Morgan and Mayor James Lawson leading a march in Yellow Springs following the assassination of Martin Luther King, Jr.

sheriff and his deputies, and the Highway Patrol. The spectators were confined to the east side of the street while the marchers went down the west side. The officers in their cars patrolled slowly up and down the street to keep the groups apart.

Downtown, in front of the bank, some of the opposition managed to get across the street and into the path of the march, but, confronted by the venerable leaders, they just stood there and glared, and the marching column went around them. At the end the marchers assembled in an open area, where Dad addressed them and Walter Anderson led them in song.

The event got good newspaper, radio, and television coverage and the town and college authorities were pleased with the way it had gone. Legal picketing was resumed (four pickets at a time) and all sides waited for a court decision on the appeal.

But this tranquility was short-lived. A delegation of students from Wilberforce University, a nearby black school, came into town to defy the injunction. "We've waited a hundred years and we aren't going to wait any longer," they said. They were joined by the militant element from Antioch, and headed for the barber shop, where they began mass picketing.

At this point Chief McKee was set aside and a contingent of Springfield police was brought in, complete with clubs and helmets. A large group of Antioch students came downtown to watch. The pickets refused to disperse, and sat down with their arms locked together. More than a hundred were arrested. Then the police sprayed them with a fire hose and followed this with tear gas.

Apparently the police had neglected to check the wind direction and the gas blew back on them, effectively routing everybody. The gas and water made a sticky mess. The whole affair was more than the spectators from Antioch could stand, so as soon as the gas cleared they started to advance, to join the pickets. The police, likewise returning, formed a solid front and, holding their clubs rigid, advanced toward the students, who then drew back.

But when the police started to draw back, the students moved forward again. There remained, however, a narrow no man's land between the swaying lines. At this point Horace Champney, and his crippled wife, Beulah, walked in between the groups, urging the students to disperse. "We've made our point," he said. This defused the situation and brought the demonstration to an end. Again Yellow Springs got nationwide publicity, including a picture story in Life Magazine.

The emotional impact on Gegner must have been severe. Shortly after that he sold his barber shop. That ended discrimination in "places of public accommodation" in Yellow Springs.

With the barber shop struggle past, a Human Relations Commission was set up and Dad was called to chair it. He illustrated his opening remarks by telling this story:

Once, when he was a boy, he mixed a batch of gunpowder. Then he called his mother to come watch him set it off. She got to the window just in time to see the gunpowder blow up in his face. He rolled over on the ground and she rushed out and took him in her arms to comfort him.

His eyes had snapped shut and weren't damaged, but his face was peppered with little black specks, embedded in the skin. Each evening after that, for a long time, his mother took his head in her lap and picked out two or three of those specks with a needle. He protested vigorously that he'd rather wear those specks for the rest of his life than have them picked out, but she persisted.

Dad commented that when his mother took him in her arms, that expressed the *emotion* of love, and when she patiently picked out the specks, that was the *reason* of love. Similarly, he said, our integration struggles represented the emotion of the movement. Now, he said, we had come to the slow, patient removal of minor irritants and the building of goodwill—the reason part.

And that is what Yellow Springs has done. Today the blacks are first class citizens and contribute their full share of skill and leadership in the community. There is an unpleasant incident now and then, but the dominant social pattern is one of friendly equality. But it didn't come easy!

There has been a gradual influx of middle class black families until, today, there is not a block in Yellow Springs that doesn't have a black family living in it or facing on it. The percentage of blacks has not increased, but their income level has. In the last census the average income of black families was higher than that of white families.

Ernest is shown here at the Antioch Bookplate Company with employee Naomi Adams. Naomi later married the young man who became police chief in Yellow Springs and served for twenty years. Naomi herself became personnel director for the Yellow Springs Instrument company, which had 400 employees.

Ernest with African colleague Alphonce Okuku, wife Christine, and daughter Jenifer.

23

A QUAKER TEAM IN GAZA

One of the great challenges and adventures of my life was my involvement, in 1950, in the administration of relief for 200,000 Palestinian Refugees in the Gaza Strip. In this chapter I tell of the events leading to my involvement, the background of the situation there, the brilliant performance of the Quaker team, and of my own work with UNICEF.

One afternoon in November, 1949, while I was away from the office, something happened which, had I been there, would probably have turned out very differently. A call came through from Bronson Clark of the American Friends Service Committee asking if I would go to the Gaza Strip to help administer Arab Relief there. Had he reached me I would have said that I couldn't possibly get away.

Bronson had once worked for me and knew our family pretty well. Missing me at the office he shrewdly called Elizabeth at home and laid out the situation in detail. She immediately responded, "Ernest would love that!"

Then she hurried down to the office and got the executives together and asked if they could keep things going without me for a few months. They talked it over and decided they could. By the time I got home it was settled. I was going to Gaza.

First there were two trips to Philadelphia. They went over me with a fine-tooth comb: interviews, a physical examination, and a whole battery of personality and psychological tests. Some of their recruits, it seems, had been cracking under the strain, so they hired a psychologist to screen the candidates. She eliminated quite a few.

One of the tests included questions clearly intended to detect paranoia. I spoke to the psychologist about this. "If some of my answers suggest paranoia," I said, "it's because I've been through a sharp civil rights struggle lately and actually do have enemies. I'm not really paranoid."

"I'll bear that in mind," she said.

The tests over, the psychologist said, "You'll do all right at Gaza." Then she added, "But I certainly wouldn't hire you for a salesman."

With interviews and examinations past, the next trip was for training. For this I went to Pendle Hill, a Friends Center near Philadelphia where, with several other recruits, I expected to be briefed on administrative policies, Middle East History and Arab culture. We did indeed get into these things but, more importantly, we were briefed on how to function as a democratic team under stress.

I left in mid-December. The timing was perfect, with the Christmas rush past in the bookplate business. Two of us took off from the New York International Airport on *The Flying Dutchman*, bound for Egypt, via Amsterdam and Tunis.

About half-way across the Atlantic, one of our engines quit. It was the one just outside my window, and I watched puffs of smoke come out of the engine housing and the propeller come to a fitful stop. This didn't worry me, as the descriptive literature at my seat said the plane could maintain altitude with three motors. However, we had to put down at Crestwick, Scotland, for repairs, so we missed our connection in Amsterdam. After a couple of days stopover in Holland, I got passage on a plane carrying freight to Tunisia and Egypt.

The plane flew just above the clouds, which formed a vast, billowy ocean. To our left the snow-covered Alps jutted up through the clouds, forming a shore to this ocean. Soon we were crossing the Mediterranean and could see in the distance a column of smoke rising from Mt. Aetna, which had just opened a new fissure.

There were two other passengers on that plane—a man and his wife—and we shared a compartment. The man asked me how I liked Amsterdam.

"Very much," I said, "except for those godawful Coca-Cola signs. I wish that slop had never been invented."

"Just a minute," said my friend. "If you were in a place where the drinking water wasn't safe, you'd be mighty glad to see a Coca-Cola sign." This man, it turned out, was Coca-Cola distributor for Europe and the Middle East.

Coming in for a landing at Tunis, we looked down into small houses with four walls and no roofs, obviously inhabited, but with few belongings. Poverty like I'd never seen. At Tunis we were put up for the night at a hotel. I wanted to go out and look around the town.

"Oh no," I was told. "Don't do that. You might not be here when we're ready to leave in the morning." A tough town, apparently.

Then on across the Sahara. From the air, parts of it looked as if it had once been occupied by water. Then came those colossal monuments to egotism, the pyramids, incredibly large even from the sky. At Alexandria the customs inspectors glanced at the Quaker emblem on my luggage and waved me through with a smile. Then into a taxi and off to Cairo. Going from the peaceful security of the air to the frenzied confusion of Cairo traffic was quite a shock.

The Quaker office in Cairo was run by Kelly and Betty Peckham, Antioch alumni, who had costarred with Elizabeth years before in Gilbert & Sullivan's *Gondoliers*. Betty showed me around a bit. When we came to a military checkpoint she would stick her head out of the window and snap, "Quaker," almost as if to say, "Get out of the way. Can't you see we're royalty?" The soldiers would smile and step aside. We proceeded across the Sinai desert by car, to Gaza.

At this point, before plunging into the Gaza adventure, let me briefly recount the background of the situation that brought me there.

In most of Europe, for centuries, so-called Christians villified and persecuted other religions. Only the Jewish religion managed to hang on, often under severe pressure. This persecution reached a high pitch in Russia around the turn of the century, when the infamous pogroms took place, driving Jews from the country.

It was in reaction to these pogroms that the idea of a national home for the Jews was born. This movement was given impetus following World War I, when the British Government, in recognition of the services rendered by the Jewish people to the Allied cause, agreed, in the Balfour Declaration, to designate Palestine as a "Jewish Home." This declaration specified, however, that nothing must be done which "would prejudice the interests of the Arabs." An intermittent flow of Jewish immigrants followed.

Also, following World War I, the Versailles Treaty was signed, a venomous document, harshly enforced, designed to promote the cause of British and French imperialism. The German people, humiliated and punished, became vulnerable to the appeal of Hitler and his anti-Semitism. We know what followed: World War II and the murder of six million Jews.

Prior to World War II, Zionism—the concept of a Jewish state—had only scattered support among Jewish people throughout the world.

Fifteen years later, with the war and the Holocaust behind us, Zionism had become a powerful world movement. It was at this time that a resolution was introduced by the United States in the U.N. General Assembly, calling for the partitioning of Palestine into Jewish and Arab zones. The U.S., with a strong Jewish constituency, pushed hard for this resolution.

Britain, which had been governing Palestine under a mandate from the League of Nations, opposed the plan. So also did the Arab states, who promised to fight if the plan were carried out. It was likewise opposed by many Third World countries, to whom the colonization of an undeveloped country smacked of imperialism and even of racism. The American delegation at the U.N. worked actively for the measure, but lacked a few votes of being able to put it across.

Seeing the resolution about to fail, the Soviet Bloc cast their seven votes in support of it, tipping the scales in its favor. While the Soviets had been firmly anti-Zionist, they saw, in the creation of a Jewish state under U.S. sponsorship, an opportunity to push the Arab states into a more favorable relationship with the Soviet Union. After all, the Middle East is almost in Russia's back yard. So the Resolution passed.

Immediately the British withdrew, first turning the police stations (military strong points) over to the Arabs. The State of Israel was declared and at once recognized by the United States. As promised, the Arab states invaded to prevent partition. Haganah, the Jewish militia, was mobilized and the war was on.

The U.S., in confusion, declared an arms embargo on both sides. Israel, short of weapons, was supplied by the Soviet Bloc, through Czechoslovakia. The survival of Israel was important to the Soviets because of the leverage it gave them on the Arab countries. As soon as Israel gained the upper hand and was clearly there to stay, Russia switched sides and became pro-Arab.

Jewish survivors in Europe, seeking new homes after the war, were discouraged by the Zionists from emigrating to America or to other countries that might be willing to receive them. They were urged to settle in Israel.

To make room for them, some 900,000 Palestinians were driven from their homes. As a result of the expulsion of the Palestinians thousands of Jews living in Arab countries, especially Yemen, found themselves under attack by their neighbors and had to flee to Israel. Between the Palestinians who had to flee from Israel and the Middle Eastern Jews who had to flee into Israel, three new refugees were created for every European Jew who found a home there. This compounded the disaster.

At the time I went to Palestine, my sympathies were totally with the Jews, on whose behalf I had long been active. Under the impact of new experience and knowledge, my sympathy did not diminish as far as the Jews were concerned, but broadened to include the Palestinians and all people who are oppressed or exploited. I came to recognize violence, oppression, and cruelty not as Russian, or German, or Jewish, or Arab faults, but as essentially an historical process. One injustice leads to another and so on unless, as the American Friends Service Committee slogan goes, we can "give history a new turn."

The real enemies are poverty and hunger, likewise religious and cultural intolerance, personal greed, narrow nationalism, and the imperialistic urge of nations to extend their political and economic power to ever wider areas. Unless and until these evils are effectively addressed, no enduring progress will be made.

Be all that as it may, I finally arrived at Gaza.

Gaza! Straight out of the Old Testament. People walking around in biblical costumes. Houses with flat roofs. Walled courtyards. A few ruins here and there—left from World War I. Time might have been standing still.

It was almost Christmas—a good time to be in the Holy Land. The Quakers had planned a carol sing in a large hall, and there was a big turn-out of Christian Arabs. Song sheets were passed out and hearty voices filled the hall. But there had been a diplomatic error—inexcusable, I thought. The song "The First Noel" had been included. The crowd sang lustily.

> *Noel, Noel*
> *Noel, Noel.*
> *Born is the king of . . .*

At that point every voice stopped, and you could have heard a pin drop.

The Quaker team was operating under UNWRA, an agency of the United Nations which kept a mixed Armistice Commission as observers in the Gaza Strip and managed an air strip at which only U.N. planes landed. Security was in the hands of the Egyptian military, which meant, in effect, that we were under martial law. In addition to the fifty-two people in our group, there were a number of hired doctors, and last, but not least, we had some 1400 Palestinian employees, including some fine, able people. We were systematically training this group to take over our administrative responsibilities.

The team was composed entirely of volunteers. However, the AFSC had difficulty in finding volunteer doctors, so all but the head doctor were hired— mainly from Europe and the Middle East. The nurses, however, were volunteers and therefore full-fledged members of the team. Thus, at our various health centers, the doctors were, organizationally, under the direction of the nurses, though the nurses took their medical instructions from the doctors.

This led to some curious situations. At the Rafah Medical Center we had a tough Italian doctor and a modest young American nurse. When three o'clock came and there were still patients to be seen, the nurse told the doctor to stay and see them, but he ignored her and went home. So…after that when three o'clock came and there were still patients waiting, the nurse drove away in the Jeep so the doctor couldn't leave. As the saying goes, there's more than one way to kill a cat.

The Quaker team had its headquarters and living arrangements in the town of Gaza. It was headed by another pair of Antioch alumni, Paul and Jean Johnson. Antioch cast a long shadow in that part of the world.

This "Quaker" team included some Quakers of course, but there were also Methodists, Presbyterians, Unitarians, Catholics, Moslems and the unchurched. All had been briefed in Quaker procedures. The ethnic and national mix was worldwide. Sometimes, on Sunday, we would hold a meeting for worship on the roof of one of the houses, as was done in biblical days. Such meetings were unprogrammed, with the attenders speaking as they felt moved, and in terms of their various philosophies—Quakers, Catholics, Moslems and the rest. These gatherings were rich in diversity and warm in fellowship.

One could hardly imagine a more clean-living, wholesome bunch of young people. (At forty-four I was one of the few middle-aged members of the team.) There was friendly give-and-take and rarely any profanity. Men and women lived in the same houses without rules or chaperons, and apparently without needing any. It was a pleasure to mix with such a mature and disciplined, yet lighthearted group of young folks. I wish that more of the world might be that way.

Being part of this team was, in a way, a realization of an old dream of mine. We were all there because we cared. Not one of us was being paid. There was fellowship with buoyancy and enthusiasm and mutual support. Of course, we had problems, and disagreements, too. Once a week we had a general meeting at which we discussed these things. Our Palestinian assistants took part in these meetings. In Quaker fashion, each meeting opened with a period of silence. Quietly coordinating the work and making personnel decisions was Paul Johnson. His wife, Jean, was registrar. It was her job to record and keep track of the 200,000 refugees for whom we were responsible.

The Quaker team lived well. We slept in warm beds, in comfortable, but unheated, houses. We took our meals in a common dining room, and after supper we sang together with enthusiasm. The Service Committee had wisely planned things so that our highly cosmopolitan group functioned as a happy and cohesive community.

Before I went to Gaza I was admonished firmly: "You will find thousands of people cold and hungry and suffering. Your heart will go out to them and you'll want to give them your coat, and deny yourself. But you mustn't. You must live well and take care of yourself, for they will be depending on you. If you become ill, their suffering will be compounded." Not until I was immersed in the work did I realize how important that advice was.

Every night at ten the portable generator at the mobile U.N. radio station was turned off and our lights went out. I would be sitting in bed, with my little Hermes portable on my lap, typing a letter home. One night the letter *f* came off of my typewriter. This was serious. How could I go on writing? I tried substituting *ph* but this looked a bit phishy.

The next day I took the Hermes downtown to get that letter soldered back. First I went to a little radio shop. They said they couldn't do it. A couple of bystanders overheard the conversation. They went outside, where a friendly crowd quickly gathered. There was a brief animated discussion—in

Arabic, of course —and then they shepherded me down the street to a jewelry shop.

Again no luck; the jeweler soldered only silver. By this time the crowd was larger and the discussion even more animated. I was seized and conducted to a tinner's shop, some distance away. Behind the work table was a big man with a large mustache, wearing an Arab headdress and long gown. On the wall hung a row of huge soldering irons. I had an impulse to clutch my little typewriter and run, but of course I couldn't do that.

The man viewed my typewriter from all angles. Then he slipped a piece of paper into place to prevent solder from dripping into the mechanism. Selecting the smallest of his huge irons he deftly soldered that tiny letter back. The crowd was pleased—and so was I.

My experience with that crowd typified the relationship of our team with the people there. They appreciated that we were unpaid volunteers who had come to help them. This was in contrast, I was told, to the areas administered by the Red Cross, where administrators were paid comfortable salaries to administer lean relief.

But were we really unpaid? That depends on how you look at it. We received food, lodging, health-care, and postage, plus one pound Egyptian ($3.85) "squander money" each week. Business arrangements had been set up for each volunteer in such a way that he/she would be no better or worse off financially at the end of the service than at the beginning. Furthermore, no amount of money could have bought such a challenging and interesting adventure.

My first assignment on the Gaza Strip was to take charge of UNICEF Milk Distribution at the town of Rafah, at the southern end of the Strip. This center provided milk each day for several thousand children. Powdered milk was delivered in drums, by the ton.

When the first truck load of milk came after my arrival, I shed my jacket and was about to pitch in and help unload it, but my laborers intervened. "No, no," they said. "We work; you manage."

A crew of about fifteen men mixed the milk and served it to the families each day. At first I wasn't popular with these men. My predecessor had been a nice young woman who had taken a personal interest in the wives and children of the men. The balding, middle-aged businessman who had taken her place was not a welcome substitute. However, she hadn't been quite on top of the job. That's why I was there.

Each day a long line of people formed outside the building, carrying their containers. Sometimes, when I arrived in the morning, the people would already be there, waiting. That was a sure sign that a sandstorm was coming. I finally had a new door cut through the end of the building, and reorganized the space, so we could get the queue inside the building and away from the driving sand.

My Arab assistant, Mohammed Abdul Jawad, was an intelligent, thoughtful man. We worked together as a team, and things went well. We saw eye-to-eye on most social issues. For instance, Jawad agreed that women should be the equals of men. "Just give us ten more years," he said. His heart was in the right place—but his decimal point was not.

Before I had been at Rafah very long, I was asked to supervise an additional milk center in a nearby camp. With Jawad largely running the Rafah center, I was able to do this.

In addition to supplying milk to families, we also supplied single portions to children who came to the center. Our system was to rub each child's thumb on a stamp pad so we could tell if they were trying to sneak back for a second helping. Actually, we could generally tell by a child's face. An impish look plus a freshly scrubbed thumb was a giveaway.

As part of my education, Virginia Chapman, who had overall charge of the Milk Program, took me to see another milk center in action. It was run by an Armenian man. He had arranged the room symmetrically, with the mixing tubs in a row along either side of the room. Behind each tub stood a man in a white coat holding a mixing whip made of wire loops. At one end of the room were two more rows of men, also in white coats, each holding a bucket. The director, very poised and straight, stood in the center of the end of the room.

For a few moments this tableau was motionless. Then the director, as with an orchestra, raised his arms and gave the signal. In perfect unison the men with the buckets ran down the room, pouring water into the tubs while the men with beaters started mixing. All the while the director was beating time to keep the rhythm perfect. A lively milk-mixing ballet, but extremely inefficient. Virginia changed all that, and soon had them doing the job simply and directly, getting the milk ready in half the time.

We had a program also for dispensing cod-liver oil—much less popular than the milk program. The kids would line up in front of a box where two men were seated with a basin of cod-liver oil, a bowl of disinfectant, and a box of raisins. Each child was served a spoonful of oil, then the spoon was swished in the disinfectant and ready to serve the next child. Each child was given a raisin which had to be eaten right there. The raisin was to make sure the child didn't slip away and spit out the oil.

Near the Rafah Milk Center was a boys' school, conducted in a huge tent. The headmaster came to see me and asked to have the milk for his boys distributed at the school. I agreed and we started lugging some equipment over there. Then I noticed that the end base for a table was being carried by a boy who wasn't big enough for the load, so I took it from him.

Two of my men, carrying a ten-gallon can of milk between them, saw me pick up the heavy base. They stopped and one of them took the big can on his back so the other could relieve me of the base. I looked around and spied the man staggering under the huge can, ran to him, got the can off his back, and took one handle. The headmaster observed this little comedy. Previously he had been very sober—almost hostile. Now he smiled, walked over to me and squeezed my arm approvingly—right on my typhoid inoculation.

The refugee schools in the Gaza Strip were a remarkable achievement. When the Quaker team moved into the Strip they found some 70,000 refugee children there, with no schools at all. They asked the U.N. agency for money for schools, but there was none available.

The Quakers then proposed selling the empty food containers and using the money for schools. There was no objection, so they instructed the work-men to open the containers carefully and save them. These were then shipped to Cairo and sold, yielding a revenue of about $3,000 a month.

With this money they started a school system, under the leadership of two Egyptian educators who were members of the Quaker team. From among the refugees they recruited four hundred and thirty trained teachers. These teachers were asked to serve as volunteers, for the benefit of their people. However, each teacher was to receive a token monthly stipend, 2¾ pounds to 4½ pounds, depending on their roles. With that double appeal —service, plus a stipend—they found the needed teachers. Soon they had a school system going; 50,000 children in school on a budget of $3,000 a month.

The Church of England contributed money for the purchase of Korans to be used in the schools, which I thought was Christianity at its finest.

Not content with setting up the school system, the Quaker team stretched the "Empty Container Fund" still further. At each of the camps they set up washing rooms where women could do their laundry. They also established a series of carpentry shops, in which a master carpenter had a group of apprentices who made furniture from empty crates.

Even more impressive was the weaving project. Most of the refugees had come with little more than the clothing on their backs, and this was wearing out. The U.N. Agency proposed sending 100,000 meters of cloth for making clothing. The Quakers suggested that instead of sending cloth, they send enough thread to weave it and the difference in cash Then they could have the weaving done on-site. Many of the refugees in Gaza were from Majdal, which had been a weaving center.

The thread was sent, and the weavers were put to work. It didn't go too well at first. A man would contract to produce cloth for thirty-four piasters per meter. He would subcontract to someone else to do it for twenty-four piasters. This person in turn would let the work out to someone else for seventeen piasters, and this fellow would sit in the coffee house while his wife and daughters did the work. Exploitation was rife and quality was poor.

So the Quakers took a fresh grip on it. The owner of the loom got a specific amount. Likewise the person who ran the loom. The quality had to be just so, or no money. Things straightened out.

There had been only abut fifteen hand looms in Gaza to start with. More appeared as if by magic. Hardware and critical parts were smuggled in. Most of the wooden parts were built. Instead of putting legs on the looms they dug a hole in the ground and mounted the loom over the hole. At the time I left there were about 1200 hand looms running in the Gaza Strip, and they were exporting cloth for other U.N. needs as well.

Like other members of the team, I found time to pursue projects outside of my official responsibilities. My pet project was a plan to publish a news bulletin for the refugees, to keep the people informed of developments. These thousands of people had no source of information except word of mouth. This project met with some opposition, though Paul Johnson, our Head of Mission, encouraged it and my Arab friends supported it vigorously. We had bulletin boards made in the carpentry shops to put in the various centers and issued the first two numbers of a mimeographed Gaza Newsletter.

I was able to carry on peripheral activities of this sort because my duties with the UNICEF Milk Program were relatively light. When, however, I was transferred to a more demanding role I didn't have the time or energy to keep the news bulletin going, and it had not yet developed enough momentum to carry on without my leadership.

Finally the day came when I left the Milk Program. My Arab assistants had things well in hand and the two centers for which I was responsible were running smoothly, and it was decided that my energies were needed elsewhere. The men at the Rafah Milk Center put on a farewell party for me. By way of elegance, blankets were spread over the tables. Refreshments were served and two Bedouin Gypsies were hired as entertainers. (These were authentic Gypsies who had adopted the Arabic language and Bedouin life style but retained many traits from Gypsy culture.)

These men sang, and accompanied themselves on their instruments. One instrument was a pottery drum. The other was a spike fiddle. I had never seen anything like it before. The sound box consisted of a wooden frame with a skin stretched over it. It had one horsehair string which rested on a bridge. The neck had metal frets. The most striking feature was an iron spike which took the place of a chin rest. The proper way to play this instrument was to sit cross legged, jab the spike into the sand, and bow it like a cello.

The men produced lively music with these instruments and at the end I asked the fiddler if he would sell me his instrument. I offered him one pound Egyptian—a whole week's squander money. I said I'd take it as soon as he had time to make himself a new one. He said he'd make me a new one. I told him that I wanted one that came from the life of the people. So, lest I might change my mind, he said I could have it right away. We made the deal and I took the fiddle.

As we climbed into the truck to return to Gaza, Jawad glanced at the fiddle. "Here, let me see that," he exclaimed, taking it from me. Immediately he jumped out of the truck and collared the Gypsy, getting from him the bridge and the resin, which the man had quietly abducted.

I enjoyed my contacts with Arab life, though there was plenty of culture shock. I was once invited to an official feast, held in a huge tent. I sat on the ground at one end, along with the Governor and the major sheiks and mukhtars (village headmen). We were served generously on large platters from which we ate with our bare hands, several men eating from each platter. When we had eaten all we wanted, these platters were set before the lesser sheiks and mukhtars. What was left when they were through was taken to the kitchen for the women and children to finish up.

My main impression of Arab culture, however, was that it dramatically illustrated one of my father's sociological principals—that the small community is the seedbed in which desirable social traits are developed and preserved—the very foundation of civilization.

I observed three distinct cultures: the Bedouins or nomads, the fellahin or farmers, who live in small villages, and the town people or city dwellers.

The Bedouins move about a lot and are frequently among strangers. They are strong on some virtues, such as hospitality, but tend to be a shifty lot. One of our team members visited a Bedouin Sheik in his tent. When my friend came out, lo and behold, all four wheels of his Jeep were gone and it was sitting there on the sand. The Sheik was outraged. This was a breech of hospitality. To steal from the guest of the Sheik was like stealing from the Sheik himself! He demanded that the wheels (which had been concealed in the sand) must be dug up and returned at once.

The Bedouin women wore veils of heavy black cloth to shield their faces from the lustful gaze of strangers. They would wrap the veils around their faces, with just their eyes showing. If both hands were occupied they would grip the edge of the veil in their teeth as a gesture of modesty.

The urban situation was somewhat comparable. In Cairo I was wearing a penlight in the outside breast pocket of my coat. My friend said, "Don't do that. Someone will brush against you on the street, and it will be gone." There were honest city dwellers but a lot of devious ones. The homes had high walls around the yards, with strong metal gates. Windows were commonly high up on the walls, and had metal bars in them. The town women, too, covered their faces, not with heavy cloth but with black gauze, which let them see out without their faces being clearly visible. In Egypt I saw extremes of wealth—rich landlords living in mansions and poor families living in corn shocks.

The third Arab culture, the fellahin, was in total contrast. Living in small villages where everyone knew each other, they were characteristically honest and the women wore no veils. My crew of fellahin was completely trustworthy. Once, at my Food Center, a sum of money, inadvertently left lying around for several hours, was viewed by all the men, but not a piaster was taken.

The three Arabic cultures had the same language, the same religion, the same ethnic background. It would be hard to imagine a more eloquent testimonial to the importance of the small community in human society.

Arab mother and child, with milk jug.

24

MY EXPANDED ROLE AT GAZA

From the relatively easy job of Director of a couple of UNICEF Milk Centers, I plunged into the much bigger job of Camp Leader, responsible for food and shelter for 25,000, living in two tent cities. In the midst of that responsibility one of my tent camps was struck by a near-hurricane, creating a new emergency. This chapter tells that story, plus the story of my journey home.

After a couple months running the milk centers, I was suddenly transferred from the UNICEF milk program to food distribution, as Camp Leader for the combined camps of El Bureij and Nuseirat. Apparently I was being used as a troubleshooter and sent into the hot spots. Part of my job in each situation was to get things running smoothly and work myself out of a job, turning my responsibilities over to my Arab assistants. I had done this in the milk centers, and now I was functioning as a Camp Leader.

The young Englishwoman who had been Camp Leader for Bureij and Nuseirat was not experienced in administration and had committed some organizational blunders—also some social blunders. I visited the food center for a day before taking over, and I didn't need to know Arabic to see that her assistant was cutting the ground out from under her at every step. The stock clerk, whom she had dismissed, was threatening to blackmail her on the grounds of her alleged fondness for the chief clerk. A continuous riot was going on outside in connection with tent distribution, and crowds kept trying to break in one of the doors. In the midst of this confusion new ration cards were being issued, and two lines of people were receiving rations. It was a complicated and tumultuous scene.

The incident which finally cooked the young woman's goose happened when a riot broke out in the Food Center during ration distribution. The Center staff rallied and pushed the rioters out. In the commotion a woman got pushed out who had come to get rations for her family. Her ration card had already been punched, but she had not yet received the food.

She came back in to get the food, but the Arab assistant said no, her card had been punched. With a two-week ration period ahead, and no food, the woman was desperate. She cried and wrung her hands and pleaded, but to no avail. Then the young Camp Leader came on the scene, checked the matter out, and was convinced that the woman had not gotten her rations. She ordered her assistant to give the woman her rations.

"But what about my face?" he said.

"Her rations are more important than your face," she replied.

This was the right thing to do, but the wrong way of going about it. An experienced administrator would have had the woman come back later. Then, privately, she would have talked with her assistant, explained matters to him, so that he could give the rations without being overruled.

The food center was housed in a Quonset hut, about ninety feet long and thirty-five feet wide, set in a small area of ground surrounded by barbed wire—mostly in tangled masses. Connected to the Quonset were two little mud masonry buildings, one housing our office, the other a carpentry shop. In the background was the Mediterranean Sea, looking very close but actually a mile distant.

We issued a two weeks supply of rations at a time, and this distribution went on for about seven days out of the fourteen. Each family had a number and the people came in sequence, in a long queue through a narrow barbed wire passage leading to a door at the side of the Quonset. Once inside, the people's cards were punched and the queue divided into two lines going in opposite directions, one toward the front of the building, the other toward the back, past duplicate lines of barrels, tables and bins. At the two ends of the building they walked out with their rations. A typical distribution included beans, flour, sugar, cooking oil and kerosene. When in full swing, we served about a thousand portions per hour of all five items, and passed out the monthly UNICEF milk cards, all correctly filled out. We distributed about 150,000 pounds of flour alone each work week—about four days.

This is how we managed to do it so quickly: A man stood in the flour bin in his bare feet, up to his knees in flour, scooping it up in measures which he set on the edge of the bin. Another man scraped the measures level with a board and dumped the flour into the "customer's" sack. Two more men opened bags of flour and dumped them into the bin. Sometimes the sacks got torn and spilled flour onto the floor where it was promptly swept up and tossed into the bins.

The refugees sometimes accused our laborers of giving some people more than their share, especially of flour. To reduce this possibility I rotated the laborers in the line from time to time. Once a young man was sent from kerosene distribution to stand in the flour bin. His feet were covered with kerosene and sand, and there was no soap and water, nor were there rags. I saw the young man struggling unhappily to get his feet clean on an onion sack.

Distributing food was a spectacular operation. Even more spectacular was the unloading of shipments as they came in. On Wednesday mornings a fleet of huge army trucks—former British mobile army kitchens—arrived loaded with supplies. They would drive up beside the building where a line of laborers received the two-hundred-pound bags on their backs and staggered into the Quonset to stack the bags in huge piles.

It was grueling work, so I had my men cut a big door through one end of the Quonset, to let the trucks in. After that the trucks drove inside and unloaded directly onto the piles. The men were delighted. In their enthusiasm they landscaped the Food Center, planting flowers and building paths. Word got out to the other Food Centers and the workmen there demanded, and got, doors on their Quonsets, too.

Things went smoothly at the Center. The ration lines moved efficiently, staff morale was good and the days were livened by incidents—none of them serious. But that was just the lull before the storm—a storm in more ways than one. We had a near-hurricane which blew down hundreds of tents. Driving to work I saw masonry walls which had been blown down. The storm was followed by a cold rain and then—unheard of in Gaza—snow.

Hundreds of tents went down, some of them torn to pieces. The occupants crowded into the already packed tents of neighbors and moved into school buildings and every other bit of shelter they could find. Those whose tents remained standing I found huddled together on the ground in a pitiful effort to keep warm in what clothing and blankets they had. In tent after tent the rain had driven through the fabric and soaked the bedding and the ground. Everywhere there was suffering and the people were frantic. All the police stations and food centers were the scenes of large riots. Hardest hit was the El Bureij Camp, for which I was responsible. I immediately assembled a crew of clerks and laborers and went there. We divided the camp into six zones and I assigned two men to inspect the tents in each zone. They were to classify the damaged tents by the degree of damage suffered: severe, medium, and slight.

While that was going on I got an issue of good tents from Quaker headquarters—all they had left—and had them hauled to a storeroom at Bureij.

The next day, at the height of the misery, I started distributing tents. I sat in a small sheet-iron office with my clerk/interpreters, Kolak and Halabi. Beside me was Hafiz, a smallish young fellow in a checked red and white Arab headdress who was my inspector of tents. When I had any doubt about the condition of a tent I sent him to look at it and report back. Two of my laborers stood at the door to keep out the surging crowd. In the warehouse next door I had a crew of men handling the tents. Police, from the police station next door, tried to help my doormen, but they carried sticks. Door struggles kept turning into fights. I would shout, "No sticks! No sticks!" and rush to the door to break up a melee. So we excused the policemen and got along better with just our doormen.

There was a great crowd of people outside pushing against the door. Referring to our list of neediest cases, I would tell Shaweesh, one of our doormen, to call out the name of the person to receive a tent. Shaweesh was a big fellow with a powerful voice who could make himself heard above the noise of the crowd.

Immediately, out in the crowd, a man would start struggling to get through, and finally reach the door, where our two doormen would pull him in. Every time we opened the door it was a major struggle to get it shut again, even with two sturdy laborers doing their best. Section by section we got the people in and assigned tents to them, negotiating with each family to get the most people possible into each tent and stretch our pitiful supply as far as we could.

Each time a tent was assigned to a family we gave the man a memo which he took to the tent warehouse next door, where my crew gave him the designated tent. Then they took his ration card, which would be returned to him when he brought us his old tent.

In the midst of this activity, the Egyptian officer in charge of the police at El Bureij, Lt. Sa'ad Radi, came in. He told me that he had a whole truckload of tents to give me. This seemed like a great windfall, but it wasn't quite as good as it looked. After the storm, Lt. Sa'ad had become alarmed at the suffering and the riots. He said it looked like a "revolution." He rushed to the Quaker headquarters, begging for tents. The only ones they had left by then were some old ones considered unfit for use, which they had been unwilling to distribute. Lt. Sa'ad said he'd take them anyhow.

Arriving in the midst of all the rioting and confusion he didn't know what to do. Observing that tent distribution was going forward in an orderly way, he gave them to me. I soon learned where they came from, and what condition they were in. It then took some persuasion to get headquarters to let me use them.

My scheme was to cut up the worst of these tents and use them as flies. A fly is a square piece of canvas stretched over the top of a tent, making otherwise leaky tents serviceable. Some of the damaged tents were suitable for making flies and some could be used satisfactorily with flies over them. They proved a great resource.

I had a fine crew with good morale, energetic and resourceful. It was augmented by a couple of Arab tentmakers who showed up—deaf mutes. I was impressed by how well my men were able to communicate with these fellows. We had a good operation going which gave promise of getting everybody under canvas.

Tent distribution was not the worst of our problems, however. On the second day after the storm, a delegation of determined, unfriendly men got in to see me and said they wanted to talk about rations. I told them I was busy with tents and couldn't talk about rations just then. Soon after, a woman managed to get in, pleading that her family couldn't live on their rations. I just looked sad—at least, I felt sad—and she left. Unfortunately, she had a point. The refugee rations of 1650 calories per day came to about 60 percent of what Americans normally consume.

A little later there was a big commotion at the door, and my doormen were overpowered. A crowd quickly filled the room, everyone shouting at the same time. I stood up behind my desk, shaking my head and gesturing with my hands. *"Mish aref Arabic,"* I kept saying. ("I don't understand Arabic.") Finally the men in the front of the room turned around and pushed out the men in the back of the room. The shouting subsided and my assistants began interpreting.

There were two complaints about rations. First, Lt. Sa'ad had gone to the Nuseirat food center with a set of scales and had weighed some of the rations. He reported that the refugees were being short-measured. Rations were decided upon by weight, but we were using bulk measure, and the two methods didn't always jibe. This was something I knew nothing about. (Later the centers changed over to measurement by weight.)

The second complaint was worse. Food distribution at El Bureij had recently been discontinued, and the people there were now being served at Nuseirat. The mechanics of the shift were such that some families who had been receiving their rations early in the two-week ration period found themselves shifted to near the end. Thus they might suddenly find themselves having to stretch two weeks rations to last for three weeks or more. Clumsy management, it seemed to me, but I hadn't known anything about it. It was clear, however, that we wouldn't be able to do any more tent distribution that day, so I decided to go back to Gaza. I didn't have a vehicle at that moment, so I started walking over to the health center to see if I could catch a ride with Clarissa Geiger, the nurse there.

I set out across the big central square, which was filled with people, my assistants walking with me, urging me to take refuge in the police station next door. Presently, over the heads of the crowd, I saw a group of several hundred boys, of all ages, coming into the square. They were being herded along by some men walking beside the group. Then I noticed that the men around me were pulling me forward, to get me into the path of this group. At about this time the boys saw me and began shouting and gesturing. I pushed past the men who were pulling at me and waved at the boys, smiling. To my pleasure the boys shouted again and waved back.

Clearly, though, it looked as if I'd never make it to the health center, so I took my friends' advice and made my way back to the police station, which was next door to the office I had been using. The police were standing around outside with their rifles. They didn't try to control the riot, but neither did the crowd press in on them. We went inside, and I phoned Gaza to see if someone could come and pick me up. Then I spoke to one of my men.

"Do you know that woman who complained about her rations, and do you know where she lives," I asked.

"Yes," he replied.

"Then go back to the office. On top of the file cabinet you will find a shredded wheat box with my lunch in it. Take this to the woman and tell her I'm sorry I can't increase her rations but as a token I'm sending her my lunch."

Then I asked Shaweesh, the man with the big voice, to go outside and give a message to the people. He was to tell them that I did not know about their complaints before, but that I would go to Gaza and try to find out what was going on. Then I would come back and finish distributing tents.

Shaweesh stepped to the door and gave a loud shout and a sweeping gesture. The crowd quieted and he began to speak. He talked a lot longer than seemed necessary. Kamal Halabi, one of my clerks, interpreted back to me what Shaweesh was saying. It wasn't exactly what I had told him. He was making me sound mighty good.

Shortly a Jeep arrived from Gaza to pick me up. It was driven by Bernie Klausner, our supply director. He was Swiss, and the person largely responsible for developing the weaving project. Simultaneous with Bernie's arrival, Col. Bureini of the Egyptian Army arrived, accompanied by a couple of his officers. He was commander of Egyptian forces in the Gaza Strip, and responsible for security there. He had come in response to the riot.

So, instead of going directly to Gaza, Bernie and I went next door with Col. Bureini to talk about rations. Bernie did the talking, arguing with the Colonel, while I stood to one side chatting with one of the officers, who spoke English. Quickly a big crowd gathered outside, peering in through the windows. Presently we got ready to leave and walked outside.

We had only gone a few steps when two men grabbed me and dragged me into the crowd. In the midst of the crowd I turned to the two men, smiled and pushed one of them in the chest. To my surprise, they smiled back, and let me go. Then I looked around for Bernie and the Egyptians. The crowd had been throwing rocks at them, and they had retreated back into the office. Finally, one of the Colonel's officers drove up with Bernie's Jeep and we were able to leave for Gaza.

The next day I went to The Food Center at Nuseirat and again found myself in a hot spot. A group of refugees were protesting short rations, rioting and refusing to accept their food. I checked the measures and made some adjustments but they weren't satisfied and demanded that the food be weighed—which we were not equipped to do. Finally my Arab assistant set off for Gaza with some of the muhktars to take the matter up at headquarters. The upshot was that the people were told to take their rations on our terms, or the Egyptian Military would move into the situation. They bowed to this and took their rations. We kept the center open extra time in order to take care of them all. For us to turn to the military for a solution I considered a defeat for our Quaker principles. With more imagination I think it might have been handled otherwise.

One cheering bit of news. My clerk, Halabi, who lived at Bureij, was at Nuseirat that day. He told me that in the time I had been working on tents there I had apparently won the people's hearts. The finishing touch came when the woman to whom I sent my lunch went through the crowd waving the shredded wheat box and saying, "Why have you behaved so shamefully to that kind man? See, he has given me his lunch and gone himself hungry to Gaza."

Hafiz, my young tent inspector, said to Halabi, "How can I face Mr. Morgan again after what has happened today? I think I'll get my people together and find the culprits who caused the trouble, and quarrel with them." Halabi assured Hafiz that I would not approve of that. He also told me that the men who dragged me into the crowd did so to keep me from being hit by the rocks that were going to be thrown at Bernie.

I wish I could have run for Congress from that district.

The following day I went back to El Bureij to work on tents again. I could hardly believe my eyes. Instead of a shouting, surging crowd, there were two long lines of people waiting quietly. I had Shaweesh thank them for that but explain that we were working from lists—the neediest cases first—and that people would be called in turn. No need to stand in line.

A lean and hostile fellow who had previously been inciting the crowd to riot came to see me, all smiles this time, and apologized through an interpreter, assuring me that the trouble would not happen again.

My tent crew went into high gear that morning, and we put a lot of canvas to good use. At noon we paused for lunch. I had not planned to stop for lunch but Kolak brought us some food—pretty hot, but appreciated. No knives and forks of course; we ate with our fingers.

Halabi, Hafiz, and I found a secluded spot, sat down to the meal and chatted. I was concerned that I had been putting Hafiz on the spot, since his word could determine who got a tent and who didn't.

"Why doesn't somebody kill Hafiz?" I asked Halabi.

Halabi smiled. "No one is going to lightly tamper with Hafiz. He comes from a village of famous fighters who resisted the Jews for a long time. Also, Hafiz comes from a large family." There is an Arab saying: "A man with no family backing has no backbone."

During lunch Hafiz said to Halabi, "Mr. Morgan has two sons in America. We will be his two sons here." It was during this same luncheon visit that I said to Halabi, "How do you see the future?" Halabi's reply was, "There is no future—only darkness."

We were about to resume our tent work when Lt. Sa'ad came in. I must come with him, he said, to inspect the El Bureij Widows' Camp. So I went with him. A driver brought a truck, and Sa'ad took the wheel. (Driving had a connotation of dignity and power there.) We drove to the Widows' Camp and got out. Alas. The widows had obviously been primed for my coming. They gave me the bum's rush, wailing, and grabbing at me from all sides. Happily, my two Arab sons had anticipated something like this, and had quietly gotten into the back of the truck. They quickly came forward and pushed the women back.

Lt. Sa'ad's goal was to get a food center opened again at El Bureij. He had prompted some of the rioting and was now trying other tactics. On the way back from the Widows' Camp we paused and got out at a public place where a crowd was gathered. Sa'ad drew out of the crowd an alert old man who looked to be in his seventies.

"This old man," said Lt. Sa'ad, "is a hundred and forty years old."

I made an appropriate gesture of respect. "I am honored to meet such an old man."

Then Sa'ad got down to business. "How can such an old man walk all the way to Nuseirat for his rations?"

"Surely," I said, "such an old man must have many relatives."

At this point Halabi moved into the act. "You're too old to want another wife," he said to the man. The crowd laughed.

The old man grinned and said he'd like to have two new wives. The crowd laughed again. Lt. Sa'ad had lost the initiative.

Back to the tents again—and a new complication. The tents where the TB patients were housed had gone down in the storm, and the patients had been moved into some old barracks that were being used for a school, and the doctor wanted to keep them there. This closed the school. There were other barracks, occupied by refugee families, that the school people wanted to get. The families strenuously resisted moving into tents. As Camp Leader, this was my problem. After much wheeling and dealing and negotiating we finally worked it out, and everyone seemed satisfied.

The Quakers had almost life and death power over these people. If a family refused to cooperate we could simply stop their rations. Then they would come to terms. This expedient was repeatedly used to get cooperation in difficult situations, although I never used it myself.

At last it was time to go home. The Quaker team was winding down, and our Arab assistants were taking over. They were capable and willing, but most of them lacked experience. "Stand by us awhile," they had said. "We're new at this. The British never gave us much responsibility." But they were doing OK.

There was considerable soul-searching on the Quaker Team. We had come to Gaza to help the refugees for a little while, until they could go home. The General Assembly of the U.N. had passed a resolution that they be allowed to go home. We were not willing to be a party to the injustice of keeping the refugees in these camps indefinitely. This concern, alas, was tragically borne out in the years that followed. The refugees are still there today—more than forty years later.

Looking back on my Gaza episode I have mixed feelings. For me it was a wonderful experience—one of the finest and most challenging of my life. My work was a mixed bag of successes and failures. I did well both in the Milk Program and as a Camp Leader, but I sometimes jumped the traces and made difficulties for the team. The Refugee Newsletter which I started petered out after two issues.

The really sad part was leaving the refugees in the same situation I found them in. I was going back to a comfortable home, a creative business, and a stimulating community. They were staying behind, crowded into drafty tents, living on 1650 calories a day—and without hope.

Some were able to emigrate to more favorable life situations, but for everyone who emigrated, two babies were born. The Gaza Strip has one of the highest birthrates in the world. That is a classic pattern—privation and despair raise the birthrate. As one Palestinian said to me, "Our people have nothing to do but manufacture babies." By 1994, the population of the Gaza Strip had grown from 200,000 to over 800,000.

Immediately on leaving Gaza I went for a few days to Cairo, where I stayed at Quaker headquarters with Kelly and Betty Peckham. On my way back from Egypt I paused at Gaza for a day, and was shocked to learn that Clarissa Geiger, the Quaker nurse in charge of the Health Center serving Nuseirat and El Bureij, had died suddenly of meningitis. Clarissa and I were the only team members in that entire complex of 25,000 people. She belonged to a large family, all of whom were active in international service work. One brother, Elwood, was in charge of the motor pool in the Gaza operation. Another brother, Calhoun, later worked with Elizabeth and me at the Arthur Morgan School.

Leaving Gaza I flew by U.N. plane via Jerusalem to Haifa, in Israel, where I spent a few days in the nearby town of Acre (Akko), at the Friends Center run by Norman and Elizabeth Moody. As an expression of neutrality the Quakers were carrying on a service project there.

I had never seen anything like Acre before. It was surrounded on three sides by ocean, with formidable reefs. On the fourth side was a huge moat, commanded by cannon emplacements set in deep chambers in a vast masonry wall. Napoleon laid siege to Acre once, but finally gave up.

The high spots of my time in Israel were my visits to Kibbutzim. To me, the most interesting was Ein Hame Fratz, on Haifa Bay. This had originated many years before with a troop of Polish Boy Scouts who dreamed of settling in Palestine. When they grew up, they married and moved in a group to Haifa, where they lived communally as a working kibbutz. They studied farming and saved their money. When they were ready, they bought land and carried out their dream of having a farming kibbutz. I was impressed by the spirit and quality of life of the people there.

They were impressive, too, in the imagination and creativity of their farming practices. Against the advice of the agricultural experts, they bought a big salt swamp at the base of Haifa Bay, and drained it. It wouldn't raise fruit but would produce grain, so they started a dairy. A hundred and twenty-five acres of the land however were so salty that it wouldn't even produce grain. This area they diked off into ponds for raising carp. They would drain a section, plow in manure from the dairy, flood it, then seed it with small water creatures which multiply rapidly. Then they would introduce carp from their own hatchery. The carp grew quickly and the entire cycle was repeated twice a year, producing good food—and their most important revenue.

On March 16, I took passage, along with a Gaza colleague, Brooke Anderson, on the Fillippo Grimani, an Italian liner of the Adriatica Line. It was a small, slow boat, which had been sunk during the war and later raised and restored. The voyage to Marseilles took us eight days. We paused at the Island of Cyprus, in Greece, and at Naples, and went ashore at all these places and visited historic sites.

It was a memorable voyage. Let me give you an excerpt from my letter home, of March 19:

> *This has been a wonderful day. I have, in the course of my life, wound through mountains by car, by train and with a pack horse, but I never expected to do it in an ocean liner. There are no valleys here, just great rugged mountains with ocean in between. Mount Parnassus was only the beginning and for hours we wound in and out between the peaks, with many beautiful views of snow-covered ranges. Across the water, in the hazy distance, we could dimly make out other mountains, in a gigantic fairyland.*
>
> *It is easy to think of this mysterious mountain seascape as peopled with Greek gods. Each principal island and famous peak seems to have its own story in Greek mythology. Truly, it would take a lot of gods, of extraordinary vigor, to occupy such country and I think the Greeks were quite reasonable to invent them.*

The ancient Hebrews, on the other hand, were desert nomads who faced quite a different world. There is room for only one god in the desert, and a stern, relentless god at that. Perhaps both theologies were influenced by the countries in which they developed. Perhaps the culture of Greece flowered most when her religion matched her landscape.

The significance of Greece looms larger here. It was the synthesis of Greek and Hebrew which gave rise to Jesus' moral stature. It was Greek philosophy, plus Hebrew and Christian, on which Mohammed built his system. And it was the Roman conquest of Greece, followed by the cultural conquest of Rome by Greece, that spread Greek ideas and culture throughout the west. And it was Islamic culture which preserved much of Greek culture through the dark ages of Europe, and reintroduced that culture to the west to inspire the Renaissance. What an impact this little country has had.

Israel was fascinating, Greece inspiring, but the most important aspect of that voyage was the opportunity to become acquainted, in depth, with Israeli citizens, particularly veterans of the Arab-Israeli war. They confirmed what the Arabs had told me but what I had been reluctant to accept.

Said one Israeli veteran, "We had to drive out the Arabs like you drove out the Indians." He seemed to feel that I would understand. Alas, I did. Then he added, "I'm afraid there will be another war. I hope it won't be soon."

"Why do you say that?" I asked.

"Because we are going to need more land," he replied.

On one occasion I mentioned the massacre, by a Jewish terrorist organization, of the Arab village of Dier Yassin. In response one of the Israelis quoted a friend of his who had taken part in the massacre. "Dier Yassin was a tragedy," I was told, "but it was necessary. The Arab farmers didn't want to fight and they didn't want to run, so we had to do something to get them started because we needed their land." That massacre was a key factor in the flight of 900,000 Palestinians from their homes.

I could report other and similar stories. Palestine was deliberately colonized by Jewish settlers, and most of the inhabitants driven out. America has never heard the Arab side of the story. Reports by the American Friends Service Committee, given to the press, were largely unpublished. Dorothy Thompson, whose syndicated column appeared in many papers, told me that whenever she presented the Arab side of the story in her column most of the papers didn't use it that week.

Be all that as it may, I have no desire to point my finger at the Jews. We are all guilty together: the so-called Christians who persecuted the Jews and other minorities for centuries, the dignified men at Versailles who went calmly about the evil business of empire, the German people who, crushed in the mud and kicked in the face, responded to Hitler's promise of dignity, the American corporations (who now wish to be nameless) who contributed generously to Hitler's campaign fund. And then, of course, there were the Jewish pogroms in Czarist Russia and the ghastly Holocaust in Germany.

The Jews would have been superhuman if they had not given rise to Zionist nationalism and produced some terrorist gangs. Don't forget also the old Jewish ethic that cries out against injustice on behalf of the Arabs as well as the Jews. In 1986, Elie Wiesel, a survivor of the Nazi Concentration Camps, was awarded the Nobel Peace Prize for his activity in drawing world attention to human cruelty and injustice, as represented by the Nazi treatment of the Jews. In his acceptance speech Wiesel said he spoke for all victims of injustice, and he specifically included the Palestinians. This, to me represented the finest Jewish ideals. Wiesel is not alone among the Jews in this. There is a vigorous peace movement in Israel. And if Israel has pursued intransigent policies and nationalist expansion, it has done so with a blank check from America.

I witnessed the suffering of the Palestinians and their helpless rage against the injustice they suffered and continue to suffer. I predicted in 1950 that any Arab leader advocating reconciliation with Israel would be signing his own death warrant. My worst fears have been realized; witness King Abdullah of Jordan, Prime Minister Sadat of Egypt, and Dr. Sartawi, the distinguished Palestinian brain surgeon who served on the Board of the PLO and dared urge rapprochement. Little known is the fact that when Sartawi found himself under pressure on the PLO Board and tried to resign, Arafat refused his resignation, saying that he was needed.

History is a continuous process. No one should be surprised that Palestinians, helpless in the face of power and injustice, should turn to terrorism, shooting Israeli athletes and blowing up airliners. The invasion of Lebanon was carried out with American weapons and the full knowledge of the U.S. State Department. Small wonder, in the ensuing melee, that American Marines are bombed and American hostages are seized. Bear in mind, too, that official counter-terrorism has wrought vastly more suffering than the original terrorism. Now we see the rise of militant Islamic Fundamentalism in the Islamic Jihad (Holy War) and in Hamas.

How can we break this weary round of hatred and death? Secret arms deals, tougher policies and more severe penalties won't deter suicide fighters. Only the patient pursuit of social justice offers any real hope, not only for the fading of terrorism, but also, I am convinced, for the long-term survival of Israel.

For Israel there must be peace and safety. For the Palestinians there must be statehood and security, and an end to Israeli expansionism. For Lebanon there must be a new, democratic government in which there can be at least an approach to harmony between the diverse religious and cultural elements that make up that troubled country.

How can these things come about? The Israel/PLO rapprochement is an important first step. This faces the opposition of nationalist diehards on both sides. Joint constructive action and encouragement by the West, especially by America is vital. The road ahead is long and difficult.

An important step would be the conversion of Israel/Palestine into a single state in which Jews and Arabs would be equal citizens. An additional and highly relistic approach would be to follow the procedure which was so successful in Europe after World War II—the launching of a Community of Nations.

World War II was the culmination of centuries of hatred and conflict. It killed 45 million people and caused vast devastation. Yet, aided by the Marshall Plan, the European Community brought the enemy nations together in a peaceful anf mutually supportive relationship,

This can be done in the Middle East if we put our minds to it, and would vastly benefit the entire Middle East.

Scene at UNICEF Milk Center.

An old Bedouin with his camel. This beast can carry 600 pounds of freight, travel ten days without food or water, pull a plow, and eat cactus!

25

A CREATIVE TRANSITION

Unexpectedly my Gaza interlude turned out to be a midlife watershed in my career. New roles emerged and new horizons started to appear, both for me and for Elizabeth. This chapter chronicles the changes which began at that time.

Home again from the Middle East and once more in the bosom of my family. What a joy! Things to do, places to go, news to catch up on, stories to tell.

Not so at the office. Personally, my colleagues were glad to see me; organizationally I was a ghost from the past, come back to haunt them. In five short months they had settled happily into their expanded roles. What was going to happen now that I was back? Dave Sallume even suggested that I set up my office at home.

For twenty-four years I had scheduled production, handled procurement, managed personnel, and conducted most other management functions. But I didn't grab back the reins. Instead, I sort of tiptoed in and looked around. Things were going smoothly—better, in fact, than when I had been there trying to run everything myself. Where did I fit in? What important jobs needed doing that weren't being done?

To begin with I took a motor trip to the west coast with Elizabeth, our two teenage daughters and six-year-old Lee. (Art was away at a logging camp at the time.) We camped along the way, visited relatives we had never met before, and enjoyed seeing the country.

Home again, relaxed and collected, I knew what I wanted to do. I expanded my title to "President, in Charge of Sales and Product Development," Those two areas were the ones in greatest need of attention. Sales, especially, were in trouble. The Rome Creations organization, which handled our dealer sales during the war years, had folded and our sales were down.

That was the beginning of a new era in the business. Instead of haphazard sales promotion I classified our thousands of dealers by type, volume, and kind of display. Then I planned mailings pinpointed to the needs and interests of each. Sixty separate mailings a year. And I installed equipment to carry this out.

A nice thing about my change of roles was that, while I was doing an essential job and one requiring skill, it was not consuming and I had a new sense of freedom. When the Christmas rush came on I was no longer in the middle of the tumult, but quietly designing next year's promotion. For me, no more frenzied filling of orders followed by the usual post-Christmas illness.

Clearly, my sojourn in the Middle East turned out to have been good for the Antioch Bookplate Company—and for me.

To be a good sales manager I needed experience on the road: Accordingly I took a territory and travelled it regularly. Having learned to be a company rep myself, I recruited Antioch students to travel for the company during the work portions of their Antioch College work/study program. I trained each one personally, not only in our line but in how to look out for the interests of our dealers.

These student reps had an important advantage over experienced salesmen. They were more teachable and able to take a fresh view of their work and their travels. The dealers became not just customers, but colleagues, and the calls became enjoyable human contacts.

Travelling, too, could be stimulating and enjoyable: the open road, the trees and sky, the city streets. To open one's eyes to the interest and charm of the familiar—rather than being bored by it—that was something I could teach the students. The old professionals, alas, were trapped in loneliness and boredom. Small wonder that alcoholism is almost an occupational disease of travelling salesmen. It is one of the tragedies of work, of marriage—indeed, of life itself—that we allow ourselves to become bored with the familiar.

Among the students I employed were exchange students from Europe and Asia. I always sent notices to the dealers ahead of the reps, telling something about them, so they were received with interest. These young men, despite their necessarily frequent turnover, did well for our company, for the dealers, and for themselves.

A novel innovation, which I tried later, was to recruit Antioch College alumni. The responding alumni consisted of middle-aged housewives who were able to cover small territories on a part-time basis. They were excellent.

With the two girls away at school and Lee starting in the grades, Elizabeth revived her dream of becoming a school music teacher. But she needed additional college credits and our finances were tight. The nearest public college was Central State College, a black school located at Wilberforce, seven miles away. Dr. Wesley, the president of Central State, was a friend of ours, so we asked how he would feel about having white students. He was all for it, so Elizabeth enrolled and "integrated" the place. She was joined there shortly by a young Socialist friend of ours, Niilo Koponen, who became the second white student at the college. Elizabeth made the fourteen-mile round trip each day by bicycle.

The college scheduled a production of Shakespeare's *Merchant of Venice* and Elizabeth was drafted to play the lead role of Portia. Carrying a full college load plus keeping house and commuting on a bicycle made this difficult, but, being white, she couldn't refuse.

Most of the cast had no dramatic experience and from time to time some of them would get temperamental and quit. Then rehearsals would have to start all over. They rehearsed that play all winter and finally scheduled it for commencement. On the day of the performance the leading man got drunk, but they managed to sober him up by curtain time and a triumphant performance was given.

The college had to send Elizabeth's report card to someone so, to my amusement, they mailed it to me. Assuming a parental manner, I perused it carefully.

"All A's. Very good, Elizabeth. Very good."

"Gimme that," she snorted, and snatched the card.

With one year of college to go, Elizabeth transferred to Miami University, at Oxford, Ohio, some seventy miles away. She had a special reason for making the change. Her mother had died some years before and her father, who had an apartment in our home, was at loose ends. Intelligent and well educated, he nevertheless had few friends and interests and followed Elizabeth about the house. She wanted to see him settled in a good resident home, and her going away for a year was intended to accomplish this. Sure enough, he soon was happily located in a Congregational Home in Illinois which seemed to meet his needs well.

Lee went with his mother to Oxford, where they occupied a comfortable mobile home. Lee was in fifth grade there and was lucky in getting a fine teacher. I joined them on weekends.

That was a lonely year for me but I was busy as usual and didn't mind too much. I still remember the valentine I found for Elizabeth that year. It started off:

> *If I were Johann Sebastian Bach*
> *I'd see what tocattas I had in stock*

Then it went on to describe all the wonderful music I would make for her.

This seemed to hit the spot, so I bought the card and added a stanza of my own:

> *But since I'm only your lonesome spouse*
> *Rattling around in an empty house*
> *Without command over reed or string*
> *There's little music that I can bring,*
> *Except one song that is strong and true—*
> *The love that sings in my heart for you.*

The year finally came to an end and Elizabeth resumed her life in Yellow Springs. She soon found a job as music teacher in the Clifton Village School, some three miles from where we lived.

She was unprepared for what she found. Her parents had kept her home as a child on the dubious grounds that her health was delicate. They had tutored her lightly and, when she reached the appropriate age, enrolled her in the eighth grade. Primary school had been outside her experience, and as a teacher she was shocked by it. "If they were trying to stamp out creativity, responsibility and imagination they couldn't do it better!" she exclaimed. However, she swung into the job, and her teaching was well received.

There were crises, of course. One of these came from a local minister. Along with their music instruction, Elizabeth had the kids doing singing games. This minister objected, saying dancing was wicked. Elizabeth went to see him. He asked if she believed in divine revelation. She said that as a Quaker she believed in universal revelation. He said the Devil starts with little things. She replied that God, too, starts with little things. There was no meeting of minds. The School Board not only backed Elizabeth but got the minister fired from his pulpit, and he wound up as a clerk in a shoe store.

The next crisis was very different. The McCarthy hysteria was at its height. I got into a public exchange with our state senator, Lowell Fess. From this the people of Clifton suddenly learned that their nice Mrs. Morgan, whom they appreciated so much, was a *Socialist!* The School Board was dismayed.

The time came for the annual teaching contracts to be renewed. Elizabeth's contract didn't come. Finally the chairman of the Board came to see her and they had a long conversation. He asked if Socialists were the same as Communists. They got that straightened out. Then he wanted to know if Elizabeth believed in mixed marriages. She said she believed in marriage. He nodded.

Then came the most remarkable question of all. Did our friend Maynard Finley, who directed the Presbyterian Choir, have a shortwave radio hidden in the church, which he used to communicate with Moscow? The basis of that rumor was almost as incredible as the rumor itself. Some electronic equipment had been stolen from the U.S. Air Force Base eight miles away and hidden—of all places—in the organ loft of the Yellow Springs Presbyterian Church. It had been found there and Maynard Finley, who worked at the Base had taken the responsibility for returning it. With that matter cleared up the chairman reported back to the Board, and Elizabeth's contract was renewed, along with a pledge of support if anyone should raise objections.

From then on things went smoothly for Elizabeth at the Clifton School until it was closed through consolidation. Elizabeth was offered a job in the consolidated school, but declined. She told me then that she wasn't going to teach again in a public school if she could help it. At that point we started dreaming of a new school, patterned somewhat after Arthur and Lucy's early dreams for Jacob's Pillow.

While these things were going on, parallel events were taking place which were destined to have an even greater impact on our lives. Back in the mid-1930's Dad had been approached by Henry Regnery, a textile manufacturer in Chicago, who had accumulated a considerable amount of money and wanted to do something socially worthwhile with it.

Never short of ideas, my father proposed that an experimental community be established, in which imaginative people would come together with the deliberate intention of creating meaningful community life. This would be what has since become known as an "intentional community."

My brother Griscom, then unattached and footloose, was sent to scout for a location. There must be a large piece of land available at a reasonable price. The climate must be good. The location must not be too far from urban centers. The social climate must be reasonably friendly. After six months of searching Gris came up with a 1200 acre site in the mountains of Western North Carolina in the South Toe River valley between the Black Mountains and the Blue Ridge. Dad and Regnery liked it, and it was purchased. They formed a corporation, Celo Community, Inc., to hold the land. Together with Clarence Pickett, Secretary of the American Friends Service Committee, they formed a three-man board. That was in 1937.

A lively, innovative group, from diverse social and religious backgrounds, came together at Celo. Soon the community was self-governing and converted itself into a type of land trust, one of the first in America. A land trust is an innovative form of land tenure, designed to avoid exploitation and abuse of the land. At Celo, the corporation holds legal title to the land, and the members buy "holdings," which carry most of the privileges of ownership but involve a modest degree of social control. A holding may be sold only to the community or to another member, and the holder must get community permission before building houses, roads, or power lines or cutting a tree over six inches in diameter. These restrictions are not onerous, and they help minimize destructive land use.

At the time Elizabeth and I were absorbed with our own family, business, and political activities in Ohio and were barely aware of what was going on at Celo. However, in 1948, a couple in Celo Community, Doug and Ruby Moody, set up at their homestead an unusual summer camp for young children. It was a "Farm-Home Camp" where the kids helped with the chores as well as taking part in a regular camp program. It was a unique project: lively, noncompetitive, and with a minimum of regimentation. On the recommendation of friends, we sent Lee there in 1953.

He was a fidgety youngster, active and high strung; I hoped they could stand him. Soon we had letters from Doug about how great Lee was, and what good leadership he gave to the other kids. Good PR, I thought. But when Lee got home he was so happy, calm, and well-motivated that we hardly knew him. So every year after that he spent the summer at Camp Celo until he was too old for it.

My parents, years before, had bought an old log cabin in the Black Mountains above Celo. They had expected to spend their vacations there and fixed it up with gravity water and planted lots of berry bushes. But they never actually spent much time there. When we took Lee to Camp Celo we stayed in that cabin, and were delighted with it. Soon we were vacationing there—and my folks gave it to us.

So between having a boy in Camp Celo and a beautiful vacation home, we unwittingly started putting down roots. An incident occurred in the summer of 1955 that stimulated our interest in the community. An old friend, Martin Langeveld, from Holland, came to visit us with his daughter. It occurred to us that Celo Community people might enjoy meeting this distinguished man, so we invited them up to the cabin. They came in force, bringing all their children with them.

"Oh dear," thought Elizabeth. "We'll have no peace with that gang of kids around." But the kids played happily without adult supervision. The older ones kept an eye on the younger ones. No quarrels broke out and no children came running to their parents. Elizabeth, especially, was struck by this. There must be something special in a social milieu to make this possible. Perhaps it was because all the families took an interest in all the kids, and the kids in turn enjoyed a sense of security and belonging. Anyhow, it looked good.

Again, that December we came down to the cabin and that is where we were at Christmas time in 1954 when we learned that Doug and Ruby were leaving Celo to join The Society of Brothers (Bruderhof) at Rifton, New York. Camp Celo was going to be shut down. We were distressed. Lee had grown past the camp age, but a rare institution like that must not be allowed to die.

We approached various Celo people about carrying it on but none were willing. The most likely prospects were Bob and Dot Barrus, a young couple who seemed well qualified, but they, too, backed off. The day before we were to return to Yellow Springs, Elizabeth suddenly turned to me and asked, "What about us?" So we went back to the Barruses. and proposed that we take on the camp as partners. Almost at once they agreed.

Right away we began planning our strategy. I would arrange the finances and go to Rifton to negotiate with the Moodys. Then I would handle recruitment. Bob would supervise the program. Dot would take care of the accounts and the domestic end. Elizabeth would handle music and drama. We were off to the races—and one step deeper in Celo.

There was one detail that troubled Elizabeth and me. It was my desire to include black children in my recruiting efforts. The Civil Rights struggle was heating up and Camp Celo was in the South. Up north, with my own business, I had nothing to worry about. But jobs were scarce at Celo, and Bob, with a young family to support, worked as teacher in a public school system which was making a last ditch stand against integration. Elizabeth and I agreed that it was not for us to raise the issue. But we didn't need to. Early in our conference with the Barruses, Dot spoke up. "We must make it clear that all children are welcome, regardless of color, nationality or religion." Elizabeth and I glanced at each other happily.

The day approached for the opening of camp. I arranged to take my annual monthly vacation during the first session. We hooked up our old farm trailer and prepared to load. I told Elizabeth to set out in the yard everything she wanted to take, so I could look at it all at once and plan how to load it. We brought out our family refrigerator, since the Barrus's refrigerator would not be enough by itself. We brought out our canoe, and a big tent with its poles, and a trunk full of dry goods, and tools and utensils and other equipment. One might have thought we were having a yard sale.

I mounted a top carrier on the car, piled it high, covered it with a tarp and lashed the load down. Then I filled the back seat, leaving just enough space on the floor for our dog Wiggie to curl up. I filled the car trunk and the trailer, then built a deck above the trailer to carry the canoe and lashed the canoe full of luggage. Elizabeth came out and viewed this monstrosity.

"Good heavens!" she exclaimed. "We can't drive all the way to North Carolina with that load."

"It's only the stuff you put out in the yard."

"Yes, but why didn't you *say* something?"

"We'll get there OK," I assured her. And so we did—in 14 hours—though we made one stop enroute for a quick welding job.

At camp there was a rush of activity, pitching tents and getting everything ready. Soon the kids arrived. There was rarely a dull moment and the staff had to be on their toes. I enjoyed it.

One of my jobs was to serve as a tent counsellor, sharing a tent with five boys. The first morning the boys wanted to jump out of bed at daylight and I had to keep them quiet until the sound of Elizabeth's recorder gave the appropriate signal. The second morning was a different story. Following a day of strenuous activity nobody wanted to get up. The music came but no one stirred. I beseeched and argued—to no avail. So, selecting the largest of the boys I approached him slowly, making threatening and dramatic sounds and gestures as I went. Alas, he was in a sleeping bag so I had to pull him out by the neck— slowly. He entered into the spirit of the thing beautifully, emitting sounds of anguish and terror. Together we put on a good act. Then I looked around. The other boys were up and standing by their beds.

Another one of my jobs was supervising the carpentry shop. We had some nice work benches, a pile of scrap lumber and lots of tools. The kids mostly wanted to make guns, boats, and bird houses.

The goat stall was next to the carpentry shop and one day the mother goat gave birth during shop time. Having had experience with goats, I knocked off from shop to assist the mother who, as it happened, needed help. The children assembled to watch, and seemed fascinated.

One of the camp chores which I supervised was the cleaning of the toilets. This job, I told the boy, was not a bum chore but a skilled operation. I used a little mirror to check under the rim and we did a careful job. The following week this boy asked for the toilet cleaning job again, and when he got home he took his mother to the bathroom to show her how to clean a toilet properly.

During our first summer or so at Camp Celo we were puzzled by the number of cars that drove by the camp on weekends. We were on a dead end gravel road, with only a couple of houses beyond us. Finally we realized what it was. These people were driving by to look at the black and white children playing together. Always, when they passed, the occupants of the cars were looking intently at the groups of children. Eventually the the novelty must have worn off, and these sightseers quit coming.

An excellent mountain woman was employed as cook at the camp, along with her teenage daughter who served as dishwasher. They had never associated with blacks and weren't too sure about it at first. They were, however, intelligent and outgoing people and soon became staunch supporters of equality.

In time the daughter graduated from high school and entered Berea College. At the time she arrived, a white girl from Georgia was refusing to room with a black girl from Chicago. Our friend was asked if she would accept a black roommate, and she did, cheerfully. That Thanksgiving Elizabeth and I had dinner with the girl's parents, in the course of which her mother remarked, "I'm so proud of Mary Ellen, rooming with that nice nigger girl."

Happily, running an integrated camp did not cost Bob his job. On the contrary, the local schools were eventually integrated without significant trouble. In fact, to the best of my knowledge, our county was the first one in the South to integrate its public schools.

For three happy and successful summers we shared with Bob and Dot in the operation of Camp Celo. By that time they had it well in hand and we turned our interest in the camp over to them. They continued to run the camp for thirty-five years. When they retired, Bob and Dot placed the camp in the hands of two of their children and their spouses, giving Camp Celo the prospect of another thirty-five years of creative life. I take great satisfaction in that development.

A remarkable personality whose path crossed ours repeatedly, in positive ways during that period, was Clarence Jordan. Clarence was a Southern Baptist minister and Bible scholar. Determined to practice Christianity at the grassroots level, he decided to start a cooperative farm community which would include both black and white families. In preparation for this, he enrolled in the University of Georgia and studied agriculture. In due time he graduated and raised the necessary capital to establish the farm, which he called Koinonia.

During the first years things went well—until the Supreme Court decision of 1954 which outlawed segregation in public educational institutions. As a maneuver to avoid integration, the University of Georgia adopted a policy whereby no one could be admitted to the University without the recommendation of a graduate of that institution. Early in 1956, Clarence was asked to assist two black students who wanted to enroll in the Georgia State College of Business. He agreed to sign their applications but was disqualified from doing so because he had graduated from a different school in the university system.

The press mistakenly reported that he had signed. Then Hell broke loose and Koinonia Farm, big and defenseless, became the target for pent-up public wrath. Threatening phone calls, cut fences, windows shot through, buildings set afire, garbage dumped on the land, their roadside stand dynamited, and insurance policies canceled—life at Koinonia became very difficult. Then followed a tight boycott in which the only things that Koinonia could buy in the nearby town of Americus were postage stamps.

Under siege, Koinonia stood firm. Unable to sell their products locally, they developed a national mail order market for pecans and pecan candy. Unable to borrow locally, they borrowed nationally from private individuals in $25 units. Unable to buy insurance commercially, they appealed to their friends to insure them in small units. Elizabeth and I took a share of that.

At Camp Celo, in the Moodys' last season, a young man from Koinonia, John Eustice, served on the staff. Knowing that the Moodys were leaving, he launched a similar camp at Koinonia, serving a slightly older age group. I received a copy of his camp brochure, followed by a letter from him, apologizing for starting the camp and explaining that he didn't know that we were continuing Camp Celo. Immediately I sent in Lee's registration for Camp Koinonia. Lee, as it happened, was the first white child to be enrolled.

Camp Koinonia had ample enrollment and the first season was a success. Before the second season, however, Koinonia Farm was coming under siege and the local authorities determined to close the camp. First they found some minor sanitary violation, but that was quickly remedied. Then they raised other complaints. One I remember was that "the children might see baby pigs being born," and that would be immoral. Clarence responded that he had read all the latest developments in hog raising and had found no way to get baby pigs except by birth. He added that the process of birth could not be called immoral without calling God immoral. But the legal hassle put the Koinonia camp sharply in doubt. Learning of this, I phoned our friend Myles Horton at the Highlander Folk School in Tennessee and proposed moving Camp Koinonia to "higher ground." Myles didn't hesitate a moment, and the camp was moved.

The siege of Koinonia continued. In late summer of 1957, as Camp Celo was being closed for the season, we had a visit from Bob Swann, a friend from our Antioch days. He had just come from Koinonia and reported that their office manager had developed a heart condition and had left. This added inner confusion to outer terror.

Elizabeth was a skilled secretary, so she phoned Clarence and volunteered her services. He accepted immediately, and she loaded her typewriter and dictating machine into the car and headed for Georgia. Clarence greeted her warmly, and started dictating at once.

She continued there for several months and had some exciting experiences. One of these she didn't tell me about—I read about it in the Catholic Worker. Jenny and I were living in the family apartment in Yellow Springs. She was a student at Antioch and I was working in the Bookplate Company. We received the Catholic Worker, a newspaper founded by Dorothy Day.

Dorothy had paid a visit to Koinonia Farm and reported this visit in some detail in her column in the newspaper. It was the custom at Koinonia at that time for the women to do the nighttime guard duty so that the men, who had to work in the fields all day, could sleep. In her column, Dorothy told how she and Elizabeth (she didn't say Elizabeth who) were on guard duty in a station wagon by the front gate when a car drove by and started shooting at them. Dorothy dove for the floor boards, while Elizabeth just sat there, counting the bullets as they struck the station wagon. I read this report to Jenny. "You tell Mother," she said, "that it's a small world, and honesty is the best policy."

Elizabeth and I communicated right along by wire recorder, mailing the recordings back and forth. That was before the days of tape recorders. One of Elizabeth's recordings gave a vivid account of a frightening experience. A hundred-car cavalcade of Ku Klux Klansmen drove to Koinonia and planted flares at either end of their column. Then their leaders came into the farm where they were met by a group of Koinonia people. They wanted to *buy* the farm. Clarence Jordan was away at the time, but his colleagues knew what to do. They were polite, but firmly declined. The Klan left.

Koinonia had stood up to the Klan and gotten away with it. This gave heart to the black people and helped them overcome their fear of the Klan. Shortly after, when the Klan held a big demonstration in Americus, the blacks did not take refuge in their homes as expected but turned out in force to watch the show. That dampened the atmosphere of the affair.

Elizabeth told the story well and her recording was a priceless document. I listened to it repeatedly, and shared it with my friends. Then I did one of the stupidest things I have ever done—I used that spool to send a message to Elizabeth.

During this time, Lee was attending Scattergood school. Both of his sisters had done well there despite its tight regimentation and tough discipline. Lee had the advantage of older and wiser parents, who gave him more freedom, however, and Scattergood brought out the worst in him. He apparently set out to break all the rules the place had. Finally he was kicked out. Then, by cordial invitation from Clarence Jordan, who had known him as a Koinonia Camper, he joined Elizabeth at Koinonia.

The kids from Koinonia attended the public schools, which put them in a delicate situation, but Lee made friends. Once, when they showed a Civil War movie, he found himself cheering at the wrong times and had to be reminded where he was. By the time he returned to Yellow Springs at the end of the school year he was talking with a strong Georgia accent.

When Elizabeth moved from Yellow Springs to Koinonia, I accepted it because I recognized her need for periodic change—but I didn't like it. Now, with Lee expelled from Scattergood we had a strong reason for resuming family life in Yellow Springs—which we did for three more years. I was indeed grateful for Lee's expulsion. He adjusted happily to Yellow Springs, and it was during this three years that, with our help, he laid the basis for his trip around the world.

It was during those last three years in Yellow Springs that we were joined by Alphonce Okuku, the younger brother of the famous Kenya leader, Tom Mboya. He was a member of our family for eighteen months while he went to high school with Lee. A tall, handsome boy, vigorous and articulate, he and Lee were inseparable companions.

One episode that the two boys shared is especially worth telling. The Yellow Springs High School, during the time Lee and Alphonce were there, had a "Junior Council on World Affairs," one of the series of such councils in Dayton area high schools. Lee and Alphonce were active in this organization; so when the regional organization held a "Mock General Assembly" of the United Nations Lee went as Ambassador from Ceylon, and Alphonce as the Ambassador from India.

Alphonce was elected President of the Assembly but was "assassinated" by one of the delegates. He played along with the comedy, pretending to die.

Subsequently, a regional banquet was held, at which awards were given for the best performance of various activities by local councils. Lee and Alphonce came home jubilant that night. Yellow Springs, the only "Class B" high school in a group composed otherwise of large "Class A" high schools, had won *all* the awards.*

---

*Thirty-odd years later, in June, 1992, Alphonce's son, Tom Mboya Okuku, graduated from Antioch College. Two months later, Alphonce was killed in a motor accident in Kenya.

Mr. and Mrs. Alphonce Okuku.

26

THE ARTHUR MORGAN SCHOOL

This school which, in our later years, was to become the chief focus of our lives, reflects a remarkable combination of factors. One was Elizabeth's intense creativity and, possibly corollary to that, her urgent need for change every few years; also her remarkable educational background, both as a child and through the Antioch experience. Another factor was the heritage of four great educational pioneers. Then, too, there was the Morgan dream of Jacob's Pillow, and the support of three Morgan institutions—two at Celo and the Antioch Company. This chapter reviews the launching of the school and how it functioned in the early years.

Recruiting for Camp Celo had been a lot of work but it kept getting easier—almost too easy. Finally, the time came when I phoned Bob Barrus in February to enter a couple of reservations for campers.

"Sorry," said Bob. "Camp is full."

"I don't think you need any more recruiting help from me," I replied.

Bob and Dot had the operation well in hand. Their equipment was good; they were able to recruit excellent counselors, the finances were in order, the program was excellent and—very important—the camp's reputation was good, and it was spreading.

At this point Elizabeth and I revived the old Jacob's Pillow dream of a new kind of school and decided to start it at Celo. Our first step was to turn our share of Camp Celo over to Bob and Dot. They, in turn, generously offered free camp scholarships for each of our grandchildren.

By way of preparing for the school we projected a summer work camp for the junior high school age. The land and buildings adjacent to Camp Celo had been evacuated by their occupants at the same time that the Moodys had gone to the Bruderhof. This was a plausible site for the school.

We raised the issue with Celo Community, and the members were receptive. In fact, they agreed to lease fifty acres of land to the projected school for a dollar a year. There were four structures on the land: an unfinished basement in which a family had lived, a privy, a large, leaky chicken barn, and a small masonry brooder house.

Now, with land and a few crude buildings at our disposal, we hit another problem. With a modest salary and two daughters in college we didn't have much money to put into the school. And for what we did put in we desperately needed tax exemption. But at that point the school existed only in our imaginations and the Internal Revenue Service wasn't likely to honor that. Happily there was in Celo Community a broadly chartered nonprofit corporation which governed the Celo Health Center. The charter had been drawn up by my father and it was called the Celo Health Education Corporation. We asked if they would accept our school as one of their activities—provided we didn't ask them for money. This would provide us simultaneously with tax shelter—and a sympathetic Board of Directors. After some deliberation they accepted.

It was a member of this board, Gorman Mattison, a fellow Antiochian of my vintage, who suggested that we call it the Arthur Morgan School. That, he said, would give it definition and would help rally support. We took his advice, and never regretted it.

As a starter for putting the buildings and grounds into shape, Elizabeth used her summer's counselling fee from Camp Celo to buy aluminum roofing, which she put on the barn. Each morning before camp got going she would go over to the barn for an hour and nail on some more roofing. Then, in 1958, we took the next major step—we opened Celo Work Camp.

The purpose of the work camp was twofold. First of all, we didn't have much money, and there was a lot of work to be done: fixing the roads and buildings, digging ditches, painting, clearing brush.

But we also had a secret reason—we wanted to see if young teenagers liked to work. A.S. Neill, in *Summerhill,* said he never knew kids to work without being driven to it. But work was to be a central feature of our projected school. After reading what Neill had to say, we wanted to find out if our ideas were practical or not.

The Work Camp went great guns. The first summer we started with four kids: a niece, a nephew, and two of their friends. That went fine. The next summer we went to twelve for two thirty-day sessions, again with good results. After that we set the limit at twenty.

Elizabeth was overall Camp Director. I was Work Director. I carried in my pocket a sheaf of cards on which I noted down jobs, large and small, which needed doing. I circulated among the work teams, checking them out and telling them what to do when their jobs were finished. I tried to put together congenial teams and fit them realistically to the jobs. Sometimes I would designate one of the kids as a leader. We worked hard all morning. In the afternoons we swam, hiked and played games. At night we sang, danced and had more games.

One unusual work-camp project was installing a local telephone system. This was urgently needed because the local phone company was accepting no new customers until construction was finished on the new highway. I bought, for forty dollars, twenty old crank phones from an exchange that was modernizing, and I collected a lot of old wire from the dump at Oak Ridge. Using locust poles from our woods, our work camp team constructed three miles of line in Celo Community and had twelve crank phones operating. (Years later, when commercial phones were again available, our system was gradually abandoned.)

The kids loved the camp. They worked hard and played hard. The group morale was wonderful. But there was a problem we hadn't expected. As a four-week session drew to a close, some of the kids couldn't face it. For that experience to end seemed almost like death, and we had behavior problems. Our solution was to wear them out. All-night hikes were helpful. One night we had a contest to see who could do the Hora (a strenuous Israeli dance) the longest. That night everybody was in bed by eleven.

In later years, after the school was started, we tried to keep the work camp going in the summers but, following nine strenuous months of directing a boarding school, Elizabeth needed a respite. We did, however, conduct a couple of good camp sessions attended by entire families.

Early on we asked the Barruses if they would care to join us in the school. They had been interested, but backed off. The project was indeed tenuous. No money, no significant experience, no buildings to speak of, no organizational backing except for tax shelter from the Celo Health Education Corporation.

Then something happened which changed the picture. Bob lost his job in the public school. He had taken up teaching after coming to Celo some eight years before and it had gone well—so well, in fact, that he was sure it was his calling. But enrollment at the school had been declining and he was the last one hired—so he had to go. His dismissal later proved to be in violation of the law—but it was a godsend for the Arthur Morgan School!

With the job gone, Bob and Dot changed their minds about working with us. We were still two years away from opening the school. Could we speed it up? they asked. We really couldn't. So Bob got a job in a well-financed and well-equipped private school in Asheville, and the Barrus family spent the school months there.

Elizabeth was uneasy about that. After two years in a substantial, well-equipped school, would Bob want to join our shaky project, out there in the mud? But it had just the opposite effect. His experience in a conventional and civilized environment made him more appreciative of the environment and philosophy of the projected Arthur Morgan School, and he could hardly wait for it to open. When it did open, he was our main teacher.

When Lee finished high school and took off on his year's pilgrimage around the world, Elizabeth shifted her permanent base to Celo. During the four years of work camp she lived year round in an unfinished basement, which was to become part of the school. There she had her piano (sitting on four bricks), her books and music. The only telephone within a couple of miles was at the Barrus house a quarter of a mile away. The Barrus family was in Asheville during the school year so I got some old wire and ran a line to Elizabeth's abode, then put the telephone on a plug and installed jacks at the Barrus house and Elizabeth's place. Thus the phone could be shifted back and forth as desired. At one point the old wire I used developed a short circuit and knocked out all the phones in the valley. The phone company came to check the Barrus' phone and found that it had been "stolen." They traced the wires through the woods and recovered the phone.

One might wonder what was happening to our family life, with Elizabeth running a school in North Carolina and me still running the business in Ohio. As I have mentioned before, Elizabeth needed a change about every seven years. During her last years in Yellow Springs she suffered from arthritis, which cleared up when she moved to Celo. I recognized her need for change and tried not to drag my feet, but underneath it disturbed me. I became aware of this through two incidents. I had occasion to drive to another town to attend a meeting—and arrived there the wrong week. Not long after I made the same flub again.

I wondered what was happening to me. I had never done that sort of thing before. Finally I realized that it was an unconscious protest against Elizabeth's going away—a form of self-destructive behavior intended to suggest that I couldn't get along without her. As soon as I had that figured out there was no more trouble.

From 1958 to 1970, Elizabeth was based at Celo and I at Yellow Springs. I wrote every day and phoned once a week. I was also able to get away to Celo a lot. My company work at that stage mostly involved designing, planning and selling, but not much supervision. Hence I could concentrate it by working sixty or seventy hours a week and thus spend almost half my time with Elizabeth. Now and then, during the early years of the school, she would find herself under too much stress and would call me up. Then I'd drop everything and go down to give her some emotional support.

In 1962 the Arthur Morgan School was off to a running start, with a lot of enthusiasm. It never quite achieved the same level of excitement as the short-term work camps, but it did very well.

The school drew its inspiration from several sources. One was Pestalozzi, the Swiss educator who initiated the practice of experiential education in a community setting. Another was Maria Montessori. A third influence was Gruntvig, who initiated the Danish Folk Schools. Still another was Arthur Morgan who did more, perhaps, than any other American to develop and implement the educational philosophy first enunciated by Pestalozzi. Inspiration was derived also from Gandhi's program of "Basic Education." (Actually, this was based on some of Arthur Morgan's writings.}

AMS, as we call it, is a coeducational boarding school for students in grades 7-9. The school is a working/learning/caring community in which students share with the staff in decision-making and in the daily responsibilities of life. The students live in family groups in the homes of teachers.

A full academic program is carried out but, more importantly, a sense of caring is actively cultivated whereby students are encouraged to affirm one another as individuals instead of competing and "putting down" one another, as happens all too often in modern education.

For a time AMS was strong on folk dancing and sent a dance team to the annual Mountain Youth Jamboree at Asheville, where a lot of teams competed in a program lasting several days. For two years in a row the AMS team won first place in its class. The third year Elizabeth wouldn't let our team compete.

"Dancing is for joy," she said, "not to beat somebody." She had seen kids leave the auditorium crying because their teams had lost. Happily there was an "audition" of teams, and the AMS dancers were accepted as an exhibition team.

I watched their performance from the balcony. Our kids danced beautifully, smiling and happy, in contrast to the competing teams who danced with tension—almost grimly—as if their lives depended on it.

One of our best dancers was a black girl. Her partner was a white boy with very light hair. This created a sensation in the audience. People were exclaiming to one another about the "albino Negro."

AMS also had a coed soccer team in those years. We didn't have much talent to choose from. We played larger schools and there was considerable rejoicing when our team lost by only a small margin. Sometimes, when we played another school, we would scramble the teams. This may not have made for sophisticated soccer but it certainly resulted in a sense of fellowship.

At the school I was more of an observer than a participant. I enjoyed attending the all-school meetings, where ideas and problems were discussed. Again and again problems would come up which Elizabeth would simply toss back to the kids for discussion and solutions. I would feel frustrated. Why didn't she take a grip on the problem herself, I would think, instead of keeping the kids floundering around at it? But she knew what she was doing.

At one of the all-school meetings the students were testing out just how far their democratic privileges might reach. Said one, "Could we vote to abolish classes?"

"That's an interesting idea," said Elizabeth. "Let's discuss it."

A lively discussion followed and the students quickly decided that it would be a serious mistake to abolish classes. "How could we go on to other schools after AMS?"

I recall one occasion when Isabel Ballew, the fine mountain woman who served as our dietitian and supervised the cooking, came into the pantry and found a screwdriver jabbed through the lid of a jar of peanut butter. She complained strongly about this at the next meeting, and the matter was discussed at some length. Bob Barrus, for the next assignment to his English class, told the students to write papers telling why they thought someone would jab a screwdriver into a jar of peanut butter.

The papers were interesting. Some would have done credit to a trained psychologist. Some would not. At the next meeting the papers were read, and the matter discussed again. The morning classes were canceled to let the discussion continue. At the end the question was raised, should the pantry be locked? The consensus was to not lock it. The students felt that the matter had been well discussed and that they had learned a lot. That obscure and almost ridiculous incident had been built up to a valuable experience in understanding and personal growth. Also, there was no more trouble in the pantry.

Equally entertaining was an occasion at an all-school meeting when the students voted to abolish assigned seating in the dining room. With a bunch of lively teenagers, noise in the dining room tends to be a recurrent problem. In an effort to solve this problem the staff had arranged assigned seating for the kids, with at least one staff member at each table.

The kids didn't like it, and brought the matter up at the meeting. Ordinarily, decisions were reached by consensus, but in this case a motion was made and seconded by students to abolish assigned seating. The students all voted for it, the staff against it. There were more students than staff, so the motion carried. How, I wondered, is the staff going to squirm out of this situation?

Bob Barrus came to the fore.

"Now that we've passed that motion," he said, "it brings us back to the original problem which assigned seating was intended to solve—noise in the dining room. I suggest that we adopt a perspective—not a rule, but a perspective—of leaving at least one place at each table for a staff member. Otherwise the students can sit wherever they wish." Then he made a motion to that effect.

The motion was discussed briefly and passed with the unanimous support of the students. The problem had been solved within the framework of democratic procedures.

A problem we had to deal with in the early days was the lack of buildings. It's hard to run a school—especially a boarding school—with no buildings.

We arranged housing by renting empty houses from Celo Community. The same exodus which pulled the Moody family out of Camp Celo had taken out four other families. The community was, temporarily, reduced to an almost caretaker status, and houses were available. The chicken barn provided space for kitchen, dining room, classes, meetings and dances—not all at the same time, of course.

In the long-run this wouldn't work, so very soon we began to plan a new building. I argued that it should be of "rubble masonry," which consists of stones laid in a form, with concrete stuffed in between them. My friends wouldn't hear of this—until I came up with a copy of Helen and Scott Nearing's book, *Living the Good Life,* which included a convincing chapter devoted to rubble masonry.

The Hopkins Foundation gave us $5,000. The American Friends Service Committee agreed to hold a high school work-camp to put up the building, and Paul Hoover, who had just graduated from Antioch in physics, came to supervise the job. A friend gave us an old cement mixer which we drove from the motor of our garden tractor.

Our river was full of rocks which our campers would scrub free of algae and load into the school Jeep. These rocks were placed in wooden forms and fresh concrete was packed in between them. As soon as the concrete hardened the forms were raised for the next layer. The walls rose steadily and our forty by sixty foot building emerged—a beautiful structure.

By the end of the work camp the walls were up, but that was all. Then we hired the nineteen-year-old son of a local builder to supervise the AMS students in carrying the work forward. He rigged a crude hoist and our kids swarmed on the rope, hauling the heavy rafters into place. The sight of those rafters waving in the air scared Elizabeth, and she couldn't bear to watch. But the framing all went safely into place.

At the end of the job, with snow predicted, Celo Community turned out for the final push and we got the roof on—just in time. That sturdy, handsome building has served us well ever since. We named it Hopkins. Another fine building was later constructed by staff and students under the leadership of staff members Mark Buchanan and Randy Raskin, which accommodates classes, dances, and dramatic performances. It was named Green Cay, in honor of the Winsberg family.

A wonderful new building was completed and put into service in 1995, housing kitchen, dining room, offices and assembly room. It is named, of all things, "Elizabeth's Shed."

Reflecting on these buildings I am reminded of Gandhi's admonition: "A school should be built by the children—and should never be finished."

Another great step forward was the purchase of an adjacent fifty-acre property, a rugged tract, from a neighbor who was moving away. The mountain people often have a special feeling about their land and are willing to sell only to someone they know and care about. Our friend could probably have gotten more for his property on the open market. Gradually, over the years, we built houses on this tract for the use of our staff and students. Here again, staff and student labor and summer work camps were called into action. It is remarkable what can be accomplished with small money and large enthusiasm and dedication.

One reason Elizabeth liked building a school in the wilderness was that it would be close to nature. An equally important reason, in her mind, was that, with the kids doing a major part of the work, the care and maintenance would be distinctly rough and ready, and it would be well to stay somewhat remote from civilization.

But with all due allowance for the beautiful setting in a mountain wilderness, surrounded by Celo Community and National Forest, one might ask if this didn't take the kids away from modern life and thus lose an important element of education.

To this we have two answers. One is that social concerns are close to the life of the school. The *Rural Southern Voice for Peace* (RSVP) newsletter was launched by AMS staff members and was originally published under the wing of the school. It involves socially concerned people from a wide area in the south and most particularly, of course, people in Celo Community. AMS students help in mailing out the newsletter.

The second is that, in their classes, the students confront social and political issues. From an educational standpoint they are far from isolated.

Equally important are the field trips, which take the students away from the usual routine. Once a year the school closes for three weeks while staff and students, in small groups, go off on field trips. These vary from year to year and cover a wide range of activities.

Show business has been an important part of these trips. One year there was a song and dance team which toured the South. Another year a troupe performed the play *Peace Child,* all the way from Washington, D.C., to Florida. Another year a group of six girls wrote their own drama, *Sisters: A Drama of Our Lives,* which consisted of a series of charming skits based on their own lives and concerns. This was a great success which kept its audiences laughing and crying for an hour-and-a-half.

Some trips are essentially recreational, but often incorporate service projects along the way. I led one such trip myself. Eight students, one staff member, and myself loaded into my Travelall with five borrowed canoes on the roof and headed for the Everglades.

First we paused for a few days at Koinonia Farm, where we did volunteer labor. Then, at the Everglades, we had another service project, clearing logs and brush from an old canal. Then on to Flamingo and, finally, Cape Sable on the Gulf. Plenty of adventure, excitement and hard paddling; too long to tell about here, but all a happy part of the AMS experience.

There were no two years alike at AMS. Talented young staff came from all over the country—and from foreign countries—for a year or so of experience at the school. One brilliant Antioch co-op, Charles French, who had come for a single quarter, became so wrapped up in it that he asked Antioch to let him stay for another quarter. When he asked for a third quarter, they said no, so he dropped out of college in order to spend the rest of the year there. "I'm learning more here than I would there," he said. He made an important contribution to the school that crucial first year.

Dad always held that a school should have businesses connected with it. Gandhi went so far as to say that a school should be self-supporting. Arthur Morgan and Gandhi were two of our guiding stars, so it is not surprising that AMS got into business.

The first business was Celo Press, which did printing for memorial societies and which published my book, *Dealing Creatively with Death: A Manual of Death Education and Simple Burial*. We printed it in small sections (signatures) on the little press in the school printshop. It took a lot of work to assemble these sections into complete books. One night, when a new edition had just been printed, the kids sneaked out of their houses, gathered at the school, and assembled the entire edition. Imagine our surprise when we found it in the morning, all neatly collated.

Our next business was Celo Labs. Dad had long commented that many generic drugs had been given fancy trade names and sold at fancy prices, and that someone could perform a real service by merchandising generic drugs under their generic names at reasonable prices. Harry Abrahamson, a chemist with a background in the Cooperative Movement, had established at Celo a project in which he did just that. He called it Celo Laboratories and in it he tested generic drugs and packaged these drugs, and vitamins, for distribution to co-op stores. In response to popular demand he started also filling retail orders by mail.

There came a day when Harry and his wife, Julia, were drafted by the American Friends Service Committee to head up a community project in India. The wholesale portion of Celo Labs was taken over by the Co-op Wholesale in Albert Lea, Minnesota, and the retail part by the Arthur Morgan School. To run the project we hired Tom Lee, a former colleague of Harry's. We assigned a ninth-grade girl to help out; she went to the office each day, outside of class hours.

Suddenly Tom died of a heart attack. The next morning Elizabeth and another staff member and the ninth-grade girl, went to the Celo Labs office to see what might be done about the business. To the astonishment of Elizabeth and her colleague, they found that the girl knew the business—how to handle shipments, control the inventory, keep the records. Soon we hired a new manager, Herb Smith, and assigned the girl to break him in.

The impact on the girl was remarkable. She was an attractive and intelligent person but had been very shy and unsure of herself and rather tense. Suddenly she discovered that she was somebody, and almost overnight emerged as a poised and confident young woman. I have often wished that Tom Lee might have seen her and realized the contribution he had made. Later we transferred Celo Labs to the Greenbelt Cooperative, near Washington, D.C.—but that is another story.

A similar story relates to a young AMS alumna who returned for a visit after she had gone on to tenth grade in a more conventional school.

"How did you find the transition?" I asked.

"Very difficult," she replied.

"In what subjects?"

"Academics? No problem. The difficult part was going from a place where people care about each other to a place where no one cares about anyone but him or herself."

Perhaps the most urgent need of young people today, both at home and at school, is the cultivation of healthy self-esteem. The cultivation of such esteem is essentially a social process whereby people reach out to one another with encouragement and sharing. Only in this way can we hope to arrest the rising tide of cynicism, drugs and suicide which seems to afflict modern youth.

It is not just the wellbeing of the young people which is at stake but the future of modern society itself, which urgently needs to outgrow the exploitation, violence and greed which we see all about us. The Arthur Morgan School, in its small way, is accepting the challenge of changing that. I hope the philosophy and methods of AMS will spread.

But, returning to Celo Labs and Celo Press—wholly unexpected benefit came from these projects, in terms of leadership. After Elizabeth retired from the AMS directorship we drafted Herb Smith from Celo Labs to fill her shoes— which he did well for four years. Later on, Jim Lenhart moved from Celo Press to assume leadership of the school.

During the 1970s and '80s, AMS experienced a succession of directors. It is interesting to note that the three who were recruited from outside—all of them fine and able men—were the least successful; two of them didn't even complete a full year. Those, however, who were drawn from inside the organization—including from the school enterprises—all gave successful leadership. Through all its changes, the school has shown a powerful inner thrust of its own, which seems to be transmitted from one generation of leadership to the next.

In recent years the school has given up having "directors" and, after the manner of Friends, now has "clerks." Likewise it considers itself a staff-run school, though legal authority still rests with the board. This arrangement has both strengths and limitations, which I won't go into here.

Elizabeth's retirement from the directorship of AMS was a sad and difficult process. In 1969, after directing AMS for seven years (her usual cycle), she offered her resignation to the board. They refused it, saying, "No one but you can possibly do it." So she kept on, but during her eighth year she developed cancer. I had missed the boat in not supporting her in her resignation.

In July, 1970, when I reached my sixty-fifth birthday and Lee took over the Bookplate Company management, I joined Elizabeth full-time at Celo. She wanted to build a house there, but I had been reluctant. We would have to mortgage our house in Yellow Springs and, because of the structure of Celo Community, we might not be able to get our money out of the new one should we decide to move.

After Elizabeth's first round of surgery I had a change of heart and resolved to build the house, come what may. The house was completed quickly, and the year between her two bouts of cancer was one of the best of her life. At first she kept away from the school to avoid cramping Herb Smith, who succeeded her, but he quickly drew her back into action and declared that, far from being cramped by her, he found her very supportive. This, I think, reflected the democratic spirit in which she had run the place.

The high point of that year was her production of Gilbert & Sullivan's operetta, *The Mikado*. Barely enough kids came out for it to cover the lead parts, but they were fortunately divided correctly between boys and girls. Most of them had never sung before. Lacking scenery they used a simple backdrop contrived from government surplus parachutes. Elizabeth played the music on a piano. She didn't invite the community to attend, as she didn't expect much of a performance. But people got wind of it and turned out in force. The kids threw themselves into the show and really sang. It was a smashing success.

Elizabeth's fight with cancer and her eventual death in 1971 is related in detail in a later chapter.

After her death I pulled myself together to face the financial realities of the situation. I had no salary and no savings. I was in debt, my Yellow Springs property was mortgaged. The school not only needed buildings but was in debt and needed subsidy to meet its regular budget. My efforts at fundraising produced very little. The Bookplate Company, in process of transition between two different kinds of printing and two generations of management, was having a hard time and paying only a token dividend. Then, to punctuate the situation, the Pension Fund of the International Typographical Union, into which I had paid for thirty-five years, went dry. I had my Social Security—and that was it.

An old saying that Elizabeth liked to quote was, "There's more than one way to kill a cat if you really want the hide." I arranged for AMS to act as representative of the Antioch Bookplate Company in the Southeastern states. By making the school the rep we avoided income tax. I did the work and AMS reimbursed me for my expenses. Soon I was bringing in upwards of $25,000 a year (in 1970s dollars)—travelling half time. The debts melted away, houses went up, and an endowment began. I often thought of the American Friends Service Committee psychologist who said she would never hire me as a salesman.

The remarkable story of my travels is told in the next chapter.

Beautiful "rubble masonry" building at the Arthur Morgan School, built by a teenage work camp.

27

A KNIGHT OF THE ROAD

Late in my life circumstances conspired to offer a tough new challenge. The Arthur Morgan School was bankrupt, and I had to bail it out. This turned out to be a great adventure. The following chapter tells the story.

Would I be able to bail out the school with the commissions earned by selling bookplates, bookmarks, and calendars? A long shot, but I couldn't let the Arthur Morgan School die. So I hit the road.

What kind of a salesman was I? That all depends on how you look at it. In one respect I was a lousy salesman. As soon as I got into a store I found myself identifying with the store instead of with my company.

I carried with me, for each dealer, an inventory chart, color-coded, showing what they had bought of each item and when, and what they had on hand each time I had called. As a printer I had learned to count and estimate quantities at high speed, so these records didn't require much time.

Items that were slow I took back. If a larger display fixture was justified I assembled one on the spot, using components which I carried with me. The dealers loved it, and after two or three of my calls gave me carte blanche to send whatever I thought they needed. I was a member of their staff—not a salesman.

I recall when I first took over Florida. The dealers there didn't know me yet, and I was swimming upstream all the way. Then I crossed back into Georgia where my roots were established. In the first bookstore I entered the woman in charge stretched out her arms in a gesture of welcome and exclaimed, "Oh, how I need thee!"

Good fellowship was one of the rewards of my travelling and Lee commented that my travels seemed to be an important part of my social life.

Important too, was my ability to look at old familiar sights as if they were fresh and new. I loved the curving highways, the rivers and mountains and prairies. Likewise, the bustling cities.

My travels were frequently punctuated by interesting experiences. Whereas in 1926 I had stayed in Tourist Homes, in later decades they were hard to find and I stayed in inexpensive downtown hotels. Later, these also went out of business—to my sorrow.

Once I drove into Kinston, North Carolina, and went to the cheap hotel, only to find it closed. So I betook myself to a hostelry at the edge of town —one of those chain outfits—and inquired their prices. Astronomical! I went to a phone booth and looked in the Yellow Pages to see if, by any chance, there might be a Tourist Home. Amazingly, there was one, so I called them up. Yes, they had rooms, so I headed that way. I did a bit of wandering before I found the place. In the course of this wandering I drove down a dark, unpaved street, full of potholes and lined with dismal, unpainted shacks. At the end of the block I read the name of the street: GOLDEN PROSPERITY.

Soon I found the Tourist Home. It was a large bungalow, rather nice looking. I came into the hall and then into a large room with a bar, where a black woman was presiding. I said I'd like a room—if they didn't object to white people. She ignored the last part of my remark and brought a key, and I paid her. The rooms, she said, were out behind the house. She suggested that I might like to leave my valuables at the desk. I said no, they'd be all right.

As I came into the hall again a young woman appeared from another room. "Would you like some company?"

"No," I said, "I just want to sleep."

Then I drove my car, over a low pile of rubbish, back to the indicated room. There was a long, low building consisting of small rooms, each opening onto the same long porch. I unloaded my luggage and walked back to the office for something. On my return I was met by a young couple. The man's arm was on the girl's shoulder.

"Would you like a woman?" he said. "She's very nice."

"No, thank you," I said. "I'm a bit old for that." My response may not have been strictly accurate but at least it got me off the hook gracefully.

The lock on the door didn't work, so I wedged the back of the chair under the knob. I tried to open the window at the rear but it was stuck. That didn't matter, though, as the glass was broken out of it anyhow. I turned in and went to sleep but after an hour or so was awakened by voices on the other side of a thin partition.

It turned out that I was next to a washroom and a series of couples were coming into it. They talked a lot. I didn't pay attention to the words but was interested in the voices. The men's voices were loud and strident, the women's low and decisive.

The washroom quieted and I went to sleep once more, only to be awakened later by unearthly screams under my window. Two cats were fighting there. Morning finally came and I left. I was glad to have had the experience but not anxious to repeat it.

The cheap hotels I stayed in, for the most part, were clean and comfortable but now and then I'd hit a rough spot. One of these was a hotel in Alabama in which the walls were thin and transmitted sound readily. The adjacent room was occupied by a couple—a man with a hoarse, rasping voice and a prostitute with a baby voice.

Their conversation sounded like a soap opera and it was quite a while before I realized that it was real people—not a radio—that I was listening to. Then I found it somewhat disturbing.

Another experience of a totally different kind during that period was more alarming. I was driving through the hills on a winding highway and fell sound asleep. But my eyes were open and I was steering the car.

How long this went on I don't know but after awhile my car was shaken by the turbulence of a passing semi and I awoke with a start. Hey! Where am I? What's going on here?

After that I was more careful. When I felt the least bit sleepy I would stop and nap—or munch something. Munching keeps me awake, so I always carry a big bag of popcorn or pretzels on long trips.

After a while I introduced a new dimension in my travels—living in my vehicle. On the roof of my old International Travelall I built a forty cubic foot top carrier in which I carried display equipment—and returned merchandise. This carrier had side doors which I swung open at night to form eaves over the car windows, in which I installed movable screens.

In the back I installed a bunk for sleeping—half way to the roof to leave space underneath for luggage. I built a little table which hooked over the back of the front seat. At this table I ate, bathed, and did my office work. I installed an electrical device for converting 12 volt battery current into 110 volt AC which was very convenient.

I was happier in this rig than I had been in hotels.

At first I camped mostly in truck stops but later I shifted to filling stations where I was given permission by the managers. Urban camping has its hazards. Not surprisingly I had encounters with prowlers and with the police. In anticipation of this I carried with me a single weapon—a three-celled flashlight. I got the idea for this from Clarence Jordan, of Koinonia Farm. When the farm was under siege during the integration crisis, with its fences being cut, its windows shot through, and its buildings set afire, the only weapons its members used were these big flashlights. "Light," said Clarence, "is a powerful weapon."

My first experience along this line came when I was parked behind a filling station near one of the Tidewater towns. My top carrier doors were open, to serve as eaves over my windows. In the middle of the night I was awakened by two men rummaging in my top carrier. I could sleep through all kinds of noise, but if someone touched the car I woke up in a hurry. Quietly I drew back the curtain and shot a beam of light at the men. They yelled and ran.

A very different incident occurred in a little town on the coastal plains of North Carolina. I drove into a filling station at night and got some gas. Then I asked the attendant, a friendly black man, if I might park beside the station for the night.

He said yes, I might park there, but he wouldn't advise it, as the neighborhood was pretty rough—especially the joint across the street. I thanked him and pulled around beside the station, where I settled down for the evening.

I was sitting at the little table which hooked over the back of the front seat, doing my office work for the day, when a black man approached the window, demanding money.

"I don't have too much money," I said, "or I wouldn't be here."

"But I'm hungry."

"Do you like graham crackers?" No, he didn't like graham crackers.

"Do you like bananas?" Yes, he liked bananas. I gave him one and he ate it.

"Did you ever make banana sandwiches?" he asked me.

"No. It sounds good. How do you do it?"

"You slice the bananas the long way and put them between slices of bread with a little mayonnaise." I thanked him, and said I'd try it. Then he left.

Later in the evening, on his way from the rough joint, he waved to me, and I waved back.

Banana sandwiches, by the way, are best with brown bread.

On one of my early trips to Gatlinburg, Tennessee, I couldn't find a good place to park, so I drove to the nearby town of Pigeon Forge—another tourist center, where I paid for the privilege of parking in a commercial campground. There I crawled into my bunk without bothering to lock the doors.

At about midnight I was awakened by the opening of one of the front doors. I had a curtain over the back of the front seat, so I couldn't see what was happening.

"I beg your pardon!" I exclaimed. "I beg your pardon?"

A weary voice responded, "Yass—I know."

"You just want to sit down and rest?"

"Thass right," was the inebriate reply.

"All right. Just push the stuff over on the seat, and make yourself comfortable."

There was a period of silence during which I dozed. Then I heard my visitor fumbling with one of the windows.

"Don't try to close the windows. They've got screens in them."

Again there was a period of silence. Then more fumbling.

"Somebody else is going to have to operate this thing. I can't," said my visitor.

"Look," I said, "if you can't be quiet you'd better hop out and run along ."

"O-kay," was the reply. The door opened and closed and the man was gone. I never did see him.

Sleeping beside a filling station in Charleston, West Virginia, I was awakened during the night by three young men talking just outside my rear window. That window had a large screen in it held in place by a flexible magnetic rim. Inside the screen, of course, was a curtain. The young men were having a lively conversation just a few feet from my head.

Mainly, one of them was bragging to the other two about his sexual exploits and his shady deals. Never having associated much with that kind of person I found it interesting. I was tempted to offer an opinion of the young fellow's behavior—but thought better of it.

Arriving one night at Hendersonville, North Carolina, I pulled in beside my favorite filling station, which had closed for the night, and went to bed.

What I didn't know was that the station had changed hands. When the new owner, a woman, came to work in the morning and saw my rig there she called the police. Soon two squad cars swung into the parking area and the officers got out and approached my car.

I was sitting at my table beside the back window, doing my daily paper work. I pretended not to see the officers until they were right at the window. Then I looked up and greeted them. They asked what I was doing there. Then we chatted a bit.

I remarked that I had parked there once or twice a year for years and that in a few minutes, as soon as I finished my office work, I would be on my way.

Finally one of the officers remarked, "It's illegal to park here overnight —but it's all right as long as you don't get caught." Then they left. As soon as I finished my paper work I drove around to the pumps, got some gasoline, and made my peace with the new owner.

As I did with the Arabs—I tried never to show anger or fear. Then, too, it helps a lot to be elderly just as—for a teen-ager—it helps to be young.

It seemed logical that, by the laws of chance, I would sooner or later have an accident, and it finally happened. Driving west on four-lane I-85 near Burlington, North Carolina, the driver in a car to the left of me suddenly swung into my lane without looking. I saw him coming an instant before he struck and thought to myself, "Well, here it comes."

We were crossing a bridge at the time and the impact of the crash swung my car sharply to the right, heading me for the concrete railing. "I hope it holds" was my only thought.

It held, and the front end of my car was crunched for a time between the vehicle on the left and the bridge on the right. Happily, some time before, I had gotten a couple of steel bars welded into my front bumper to strengthen it. This may well have saved my car but it tore up the other one as it ground past me. We came to rest just beyond the bridge and got out of our cars. My station wagon and its accessories weighed over three tons, so I was scarcely shaken up. The other driver, too, was uninjured, but he started to collapse, and I helped him sit down.

Soon the wreckers arrived and hauled in our vehicles. I asked the driver to stash my vehicle in a shady place, which he did. Then I phoned the insurance company and set the wheels in motion for the restoration of my car. After that I tidied up the contents, which were in a mess from the wreck, and settled down to live there for a while. Within a day the car was moved across the road to a body shop and work was begun. The insurance man located a used front end that fit my car. It was bright blue, which contrasted pleasantly with the cream color of the rest of the car.

The restoration was a big job requiring several days. Fortunately, there was a place close by where I could rent a car to continue my business calls. In the evenings the body shop would push my vehicle outdoors so I could sleep in it. In less than a week I was back at the wheel, though as I went from town to town I inquired at all the junk yards for a few remaining parts that the car still needed. Back home again, I had the frame of the car straightened a little, and it was good as new.

Once I pulled into a state park and camped for the night. Suddenly, at about one p.m., I was awakened by a siren and a blue flasher a few feet behind my car. Approaching my car, the officer barked, "Come out!" as though I were a desperado.

I climbed out and stood there in my pajamas, holding my big three-celled flashlight. In the glare of his headlights I didn't need a flashlight, but I held it in my hand as a symbol of nonsubservience.

"Don't you know this is a state park, and it's illegal to camp here?" said the officer.

"The map shows it as a camping area," I said.

"The map's wrong."

"Well, what do you want me to do?"

The officer softened a bit. "I can't turn you out on the road at this hour of night. Would you like me to lead you to a camping area?"

"I'd appreciate that."

So I got behind the wheel in my pajamas and followed the patrolman for several miles to a camping area, where he signed me in without charge. There I slept for the rest of the night.

I enjoyed a cheerful relationship with the stores and buyers, and was usually welcomed wherever I went. One day I walked into a bookstore in central Tennessee where they knew me well, and the clerks gave a little cheer. This was overheard by another rep who was in the office talking with the manager. "I like that!" he exclaimed indignantly. "When I came in, they just said 'Oh no!'"

However, my calls didn't always go smoothly. Visiting a Waldenbooks store in Alabama I noticed their bookplate stock piled on the floor.

"I thought you had a rack?" I said.

"We decided not to use it."

"Where is it?" (I always picked up unwanted racks, as they were expensive.)

"We threw it away."

"You threw it away?" I exclaimed.

This offended the manager who promptly asked that Antioch reps not call at her store any more. Later, alas, she became district supervisor, in charge of a lot of stores. Fortunately, she mellowed with time.

At another Waldenbooks, in Tampa, Florida, I called in the evening when the manager was out. They hadn't been serviced in a long time and their stock was in bad shape. I sorted it over and made a pile of the stuff to be returned. The manager of that store turned out to be a tough old biddy, a retired Women's Army Corps captain. When she came in the next morning and found that an obstreperous salesman had been meddling with her inventory she blew her stack, calling the Waldenbooks headquarters in Connecticut to lodge a complaint.

Then, when I came in, she gave me Hell. When she stopped for breath I said, "Look! I've sorted out the slow moving stuff that needs to go back. If you want to keep that garbage you're welcome to it."

After that the woman simmered down and did business properly. However, her earlier call to headquarters resulted in their sending a warning to their southern stores to watch out for an officious Antioch rep. But I could never tell that it hurt me. There came a day, years later, when Antioch reps were the only ones permitted to service the Waldenbooks stores.

Another outfit that gave me a hard time was a big Christian bookstore. It was one of the very few such stores in my territory that didn't handle the Antioch line. Furthermore, they had two big floor racks of our leading competitor's merchandise. I visited them every trip, but the manager always threw me out. Then one trip I came in and found that the manager had died At long last I got our line into the store. Once in, I knew it would soon dominate. I wrote the office that night, "If you can't sell 'em, outlive 'em."

Another time I got into trouble with a Christian bookseller, but it was over a piece my father had written fifty years before, and which I had reprinted in my newsletter. It was titled "The One True Faith as a Cause of

War." It pointed out that religious differences had led to many wars through-out the centuries, and urged that we exercise humility in the way we hold our convictions, and that we show respect for other people's convictions.

This bookseller KNEW that he had the one true faith. He was aware that the commissions on what I sold were going to support the Arthur Morgan School, named for the very man who wrote that article. Hence, he said, he couldn't buy from me any more.

Far from resenting this, I found a certain justice in it. Some of my writings, years earlier, had embarrassed my father. It was entertainingly appropriate that one of his writings should rise up posthumously to embarrass me.

Camping as a sales rep had a lot of ramifications. For one thing, it saved nearly a thousand dollars a month which went directly to the Arthur Morgan School. My travels were supporting a valuable institution and, in the process, helping to carry on Elizabeth's work. Furthermore, I was enjoying myself and was contributing to the health and growth of my old company. What more could I ask?

Other ramifications had to do with my lifestyle. In former times, when I stayed in hotels, I wore a business suit and washed my nylon shirt every night. In my Travelall I had facilities for bathing but not for washing clothes. So I dressed differently. I wore tee shirts in summer and turtlenecks in winter.

Once in a big department store, I was waiting to see the buyer, along with another rep. This man was dressed in a three-piece suit, his pants sharply pressed, his shoes shined and his hair neatly brushed. Quite a contrast to the balding old man in slacks and a turtleneck. He looked me up and down—rather rudely I thought. Presently the buyer came out of her office. "Oh, Mr. Morgan!" she exclaimed. "I'm so glad to see you." Again the man looked me up and down.

Urban camping changed more than just my clothing habits. It also changed my eating habits. In restaurants I had dined on conventional fare, but in the car it was a different story. First of all I had a special drink which I carried in powder form and mixed with water for each meal. I called it my "High Octane Drink." It consisted of two parts powdered milk, one part natural-flavor malted milk, and one part toasted carob powder. It had a good flavor and tasted sweet without the addition of sugar, and it had a healthy mix of starch and protein.

For solid food I had cheese, bananas, wholewheat graham crackers, and raisins, with the occasional addition of sprouted seeds for salad. This diet proved unwholesome in one respect, however—too much dairy, which apparently led to arthritis in my fingers. So I switched from powdered cow's milk to soy milk, and from cheese to peanut butter, and the arthritis cleared up. I ate the same diet three times a day—it was certainly inexpensive and I enjoyed it. The peanut butter I bought in thirty-pound drums. I'm still using those plastic containers for waste baskets.

To keep food and water cool I used a wet towel. It took me about twenty minutes to prepare a meal, eat it and clean up.

I bathed each morning, using two small wash bowls, with a quart of water and two wash cloths. One cloth was clean, the other soapy. In the course of bathing the water would be gradually transferred from one basin to the other. I found it neat, comfortable and efficient. In cold weather I would eat breakfast while the car was warming up, then I would bathe in the warm car. An aluminum canteen, with a piece of rock wool over it, was held against the engine manifold by a flat spring, and provided warm water for bathing.

Current from my 110-volt converter operated a tape recorder and also a hot pad under my feet on cold nights. All the major amenities of home were there, plus the challenge of travel and work. My life on the road was a happy and exciting one, and in a few years I had paid off my personal mortgage and the school debts, got some buildings up and an endowment started. And I was the fellow the psychologist wouldn't hire as a salesman!

My sales were going well, but clearly I was getting older, and my family felt that my travels were crowding things a bit. They persuaded me to reduce my territory a state or two at a time, but my sales kept growing. Finally my territory was reduced to a narrow strip of North Carolina and Tennessee, about two-hundred miles—and then eliminated entirely. My faithful Travelall, with 288,000 miles on it, was sold to a friend for five hundred dollars.

At the end of my travels a celebration was held at the Arthur Morgan School. Staff member Mary Dart wrote and sang this parody of the "Little Buttercup" song from Gilbert & Sullivan's *Pinafore*:

LITTLE BOOKPLATE REP

I'm called little bookplate rep
Dear little bookplate rep
Though I could never tell why
But still I'm called bookplate rep
Poor little bookplate rep
Sweet little bookplate rep, I.

I've calendars witty in colors so pretty
With March, July, August and May.
I've bookmarks, come pick 'em,
And bookplates with stickum,
Oh won't you come buy some today?

When I want something yummy
To fill up my tummy
And my energy's starting to sink

I use carob exalted, and milk—soy and malted,
To mix up my high octane drink.

So buy of your bookplate rep
Dear little bookplate rep
Dealers should never be shy
So buy of your bookplate rep
Poor little bookplate rep
Come, of your bookplate rep, buy.

When I see the sun setting
And tired I'm getting
A friendly gas station I'll find.
It's cheaper by far if I sleep in the car
So I ask, "Can I park 'round behind?"

When snoopers come snooping
And troopers come trooping
And thieves creep around in the night.
I haven't a rifle or any such trifle
For a weapon I just use my light.

So buy of your bookplate rep
Dear little bookplate rep
Dealers should never be shy
So buy of your bookplate rep
Poor little bookplate rep
Come, of your bookplate rep, buy.

This is the International Travelall which Ernest drove for 200,000 miles to bail out the school.

28

DEALING CREATIVELY WITH DEATH

It has been wisely said that until we accept the reality of death we are not really living. My own experiences with death had a profound and creative impact on my life and especially on my relationship with others and with nature. In this chapter I tell of my pilgrimage and try to share the values which emerged.

When my mother died I was too young to know what was happening but, as I explained in the first chapter, her death paradoxically served to illuminate my life and was a factor in giving me an almost idyllic childhood.

The second death which had an impact on my life was my Aunt Jessie's when I was about sixteen. This time, of course, I was old enough to know what was going on. My father and I were with Jessie when she died, and I served as one of the pallbearers at her funeral.

Jessie had been my foster mother and we had remained very close, even after my father remarried when I was six. She and my grandmother shared an apartment in Yellow Springs, and I spent a lot of time there. Jessie and I enjoyed hiking together, and I remarked to her once, "You're my best girl now, but one of these days you're going to have to take a back seat!" She laughed. "That will be fine," she said.

I was bereft by Jessie's death, and overcome with a feeling of helplessness. There was nothing I could do for her now. After some reflection I realized that there was, indeed, something I could do for her—I could carry on her life! Not necessarily her habits or ideas, with which I didn't always agree, but rather the quality of her life, which was dedicated to human service. When I realized this, not only did my grief go away but my life became more challenging and meaningful.

It was almost twenty years before I again became concerned with the subject of death, and this time it was the beginning of a new type of creative work which was to continue for the rest of my life. Ironically, I had not the slightest intention of becoming involved—it just happened.

My father had always taken a dim view of conventional funerals. He felt they were ostentatious and extravagant and did not serve the social and emotional needs of the survivors as well as they should. Accordingly, in 1948, he organized a committee of the Yellow Springs Friends Meeting to see what might be done to develop new practices within our meeting. For five years this committee corresponded with people all over the country but was not able to get much help. At the same time they studied the Ohio laws and explored various alternatives.

They found that most of the members of the Meeting opted for cremation or medical school donation rather than for burial. Accordingly they made connections with a crematory that was willing to accept cases without going through a funeral director. Then, invoking a clause in the Ohio code which said that "nothing in the law shall be interpreted as preventing a religious organization from caring for its own dead." they proceeded to eliminate funeral directors entirely from their plans.

The committee printed appropriate forms and built plywood funeral boxes. I still remember when they planned those boxes—Dad simply fetched a yardstick and measured himself! They visited each hospital and board of health in the three nearby cities to explain the legality of the practical arrangements which the committee projected. Families signing up with the committee were instructed to carefully clear their plans in advance with other branches of their families, to avoid misunderstandings.

Finally, when everything was in order and ready to function, my father resigned from the committee to devote his attention to other things. Then the Meeting appointed me chairman in his place. I had taken no part in the activities, and in fact had not been interested. At the same time, I had no intention of ducking out on my share of responsibility in the Meeting. After all, I reasoned, I'm a grown man and can probably handle a dead body as well as the next fellow!

During the five years that the committee was doing its basic work, no one had died. Then, as soon as I became chairman, members started dying! The plans had been well laid and things went smoothly. Furthermore, what I had anticipated to be a disagreeable chore turned out to be a meaningful privilege.

I well remember the first death that occurred in our Meeting. The Committee quietly came forward with comfort and assistance. It brought in meals, helped with child care, took charge of the body, handled the paper work and planned a memorial service. Visiting relatives were given hospitality. The whole thing was handled beautifully. The modest cost of cremation was the only expense.

Following this first experience, the two local funeral directors became alarmed and sent for the state official responsible for regulating the funeral industry. The three men met with our Committee. We stressed the importance of the spiritual aspect of the occasion. They sat there and nodded. We cited the law. The men went quietly away and we never heard from them again.

Then a new development occurred, introducing a fresh and challenging dimension. The Dayton Unitarian Church, in which I had grown up, called a meeting to consider organizing a memorial society in Dayton. I decided to attend that meeting and tell the people about our Burial Committee and how it worked.

Entering the church for the meeting, I met the new minister there, who didn't know me. Feeling a bit devilish I remarked, "I'm from the Funeral Directors Association. I just came along to see that you didn't do anything rash." The young man seemed a bit taken aback, but was promptly reassured by a mutual friend, who introduced us.

In the course of the meeting I gave a brief account of how the Yellow Springs Friends Burial Committee worked. Mildred Jensen Loomis was at that meeting. Mildred was well-known as a one-time disciple of Ralph Borsodi, the famous decentralist, and for many years was head of the School of Living which promoted the values of simplicity. At that time she was publishing *The Interpreter* (now the *Green Revolution*). Unobserved by me, she made careful notes on my talk, and these she used as the basis for an article in her newspaper.

The first I knew of this was when the inquiries started to pour in that said: "Tell us more about your burial committee and how it works!"

"Gosh," I thought, "I can't answer all this mail. I'll just mimeograph a few sheets to send out."

Then it occurred to me that, whereas a burial committee was suitable to a cohesive rural group, for an urban situation a memorial society, which involves cooperation with funeral directors, was probably a more realistic approach to funeral reform. I decided to include information about memorial societies—even a listing of them.

Then another event transpired. Lucy, my stepmother, wished to bequeath her body to a medical school. She was a biologist and a thrifty old Quaker. "I don't want my body wasted," she said, and asked me to visit a medical school and see if I could make arrangements.

Accordingly, I dropped in on Dr. Graves (sic), Dean of the Department of Anatomy of the Ohio State University Medical School in Columbus. He was almost too eager. "This is a wonderful idea! There is a great shortage of anatomical material. Maybe the idea will spread!"

I had stumbled onto another need and decided to include information about body bequeathal—including a directory of medical schools, with detailed information about each.

To make a long story short, my few mimeographed sheets grew into a sixty-four-page book, *A Manual of Simple Burial.*

As to the Dayton Unitarians, they did indeed organize a memorial society. In the course of this effort they received a letter from a local funeral director: "What you are doing is strictly illegal." By mistake the funeral director's secretary enclosed a memo he had received from his lawyer: "Tell them anything that sounds good."

In the course of my involvement with matters relating to death, a new complication had arisen. Elizabeth and I were preparing to launch the Arthur Morgan School, and Elizabeth had said to me, "Are we agreed that from here on out the school will be the central focus of our activities and that we won't let ourselves get distracted in other directions?"

I had agreed to this, but here I was, up to my neck in funeral reform. So, I had to find some excuse. "The book will make money for the Arthur Morgan School." And so it did. To publish the book we set up Celo Press as a department of the school. In the ensuing thirty-four years it sold nearly 300,000 copies. One edition followed another and I realized that before we could have effective funeral reform we needed death education. Hence the scope of my work gradually broadened to include the social, emotional, and philosophical aspects of death. The thirteenth edition, expanded to 192 pages, appeared under the title *Dealing Creatively with Death: A Manual of Death Education and Simple Burial.*

I also had personal reasons for this interest, although at the time I was only dimly aware of them. Even in middle-age I had not been able to accept the fact that in the normal course of nature my father would die before I did. This simply couldn't happen! It would be the end of the world. Obviously, I hadn't quite grown up. I urgently needed to come to terms with death as a necessary part of life. My work as chairman of the Burial Committee and my increasing role in the field of funeral reform helped me to mature.

I had still another motive in pursuing activities in this field. One night I was on a TV show along with a spokesman for the funeral industry. In the course of our exchange he exclaimed that the movement for simplicity in funeral practices was "a Communist plot to undermine the American way of life!" This statement missed the mark—but not very far. For me the funeral reform movement is indeed a plot—though not a Communist one—to undermine what is phony, ostentatious and exploitative in American life. At no time are persons more open to reflection on their ideals and values—and to the refinement of these ideals and values—than at the time of a death in the family. This is another reason why the ceremonies and other practices associated with death are important in life.

Again, as so often happened in my life, circumstances beyond my control came into play to shape my ideas and activities. In 1963 the Cooperative League of the USA called an international meeting of memorial societies to form a federation of these societies, embracing Canada and the United States. Because of my little book I was called to give a keynote talk at that meeting. Apparently I had become some sort of an authority.

I soon found myself serving on the board of the Continental Association of Funeral and Memorial Societies and editing its news bulletin. Likewise, I provided material for the appendix to Jessica Mitford's bombshell book, *The American Way of Death.* (What was once the Continental Association is now called the Funeral & Memorial Societies of America.)

In 1965 I had the opportunity to benefit first-hand from the work that my father had begun at the Yellow Springs Friends Meeting. It was a beautiful Sunday morning. I was in Ohio, on the phone with Elizabeth in North Carolina. Suddenly an operator broke in with an emergency call from Detroit. Our younger daughter, Benetta, age twenty-nine, had been killed in a motor accident.

First, I called back to Elizabeth and broke the news to her. That was the hardest part. We set up plans for her to fly to Ohio. Then I phoned one of our friends, who was a member of the Friends Meeting, asking him to get the word to the other Meeting members. At 11:00 a.m. I went to Meeting. Not much was said, but I could feel the love and support. I still remember the words of a thoughtful young man who spoke. "Until we have learned to accept death we are not really living."

Later, I met Elizabeth at the airport and brought her home. As if by magic, meals appeared, chores were done, and errands run. Old friends came to see us. Hospitality was arranged for relatives from out of town. A memorial meeting was quietly arranged. We seemed to be carried along on a gentle wave of love. We never learned who coordinated things—probably several people helped. Arrangements for immediate cremation were made through a call to the Detroit Memorial Society, which was helpful also in arranging a memorial service in Detroit.

Of course, the death which affected me most profoundly, as it did many others, was Elizabeth's. Early in 1969, she suffered from what she took to be "intestinal flu." Alas, it turned out to be a total blockage of the lower intestine by cancer. She was rushed to the hospital, and I authorized emergency surgery.

Elizabeth was well-known and loved by the mountain people and word quickly got about when she was taken to the hospital. A group of them gathered there, in the waiting room, to hold her in their thoughts and pray for her through the night.

Our close friend, Dorothy Barrus, had phoned me in Ohio when Elizabeth was taken to the hospital and I authorized the surgery needed to save her life. Then Lee drove me to the hospital at Spruce Pine, over four hundred miles, in seven hours.

Elizabeth showed a strong spirit and put up a brave fight. Family and friends rallied to her support in every possible way. The little hospital at Spruce Pine was magnificent, the nurses giving Elizabeth warm personal encouragement at all times. The management there waived their usual rules about visiting hours and let me virtually move into the place to keep Elizabeth company and help with her care. When she was out of immediate danger I brought her home and nursed her there, and in time she moved happily back into activity at the school, as music teacher and librarian, taking great satisfaction in the work.

In 1971, alas, the cancer recurred. There was further surgery, followed by chemotherapy. Again I virtually moved into the hospital and again Elizabeth put up a brave struggle. I recall one evening when the doctor dropped by to see her.

"Doctor," she said, "there is a little girl at school to whom I promised the lead in next year's operetta. She needs it so badly. I've just got to have another year!"

The doctor left the room with tears in his eyes and put her back on chemotherapy for one more try. Actually, he held out no significant hope of recovery.

I had never heard of hospice, but I decided to bring Elizabeth home where I could take care of her myself and where she would be surrounded by loving friends. Our daughter, Jenifer, who was living in Chicago at that time and serving as Executive Secretary of the Continental Association of Funeral and Memorial Societies, resigned her job to come to Celo and help me take care of Elizabeth. Her governing board, however, declined her resignation and told her to take the job with her. Each day a packet of mail was shipped to her at Celo so that she could continue to function as executive head of the organization. She hired a competent secretary to help and was free to devote a fair amount of time each day to Elizabeth's care.

Through reading, correspondence, and telephone calls I searched doggedly for some way to save her life. I bought a juicer and prepared special "green drinks" which were said to have remarkable curative powers. I did intensive meditation, hoping to effect some change in that way.

I obtained the various medicines that the doctor specified, and Jenny and I learned how to give shots for the relief of pain. We kept a regular hospital chart and consulted with the doctor each day.

The bright side of the picture was that she enjoyed a steady stream of visitors, including her students, who came to talk with her. Some friends sang for her, some brought little presents, some embraced her. I read her favorite poetry to her. We played records of her favorite music. It was a warmly human situation. One of Tagore's songs, which she used to sing, she asked me to read to her shortly before she died. It goes:

> *On the day when death shall knock at thy door,*
> *what wilt thou offer him?*
> *Oh, I will set before my guest the full vessel of*
> *my life—I will never let him go with empty hands.*
> *All the sweet vintage of my autumn days and summer nights,*
> *all the earnings and gleanings of my busy life*
> *will I place before him at the close of my days*
> *when death will knock at my door.*

When I finished she remarked that her vessel was full.

She accepted the prospect of death calmly—almost cheerfully. "The trouble is," she said, "that I love life too much." She remarked to me how much it helped that her family was able to accept her death.

She expressed concern that her death might upset the students. Accordingly, I prepared a brief talk in which I referred to her impending death and gave a thoughtful discussion of life and death. I went over this with her, and when we had it done to our satisfaction I gave the talk to the students, who seemed to respond well.

In time, as Elizabeth's condition deteriorated, she was stricken with severe nausea which exhausted her body fluids. To compensate for this I arranged with a friend of ours, a registered nurse, to come twice a week to replace the body fluids intravenously. She would start the IV and I would monitor it and remove the needle at the appropriate time.

After a while Elizabeth asked to have the IV discontinued. This, she assumed, would be the end. At that point I did what should have occurred to me sooner—I phoned the doctor to learn if there might be some medicine that could relieve the nausea. There was, and the immediate crisis passed.

But Elizabeth's condition continued to worsen. Clearly, we were losing the battle, but I was determined that her suffering be minimized and that her last days be filled with love and fellowship. The doctor had supplied me with morphine and a hypodermic, and had instructed me on the permissible dosage and frequency. At any time of the day or night she could call for relief —and get it in thirty seconds. Her mind remained clear and our friends continued to visit.

At last a massive intestinal hemorrhage took place, and she quietly died. I was swept by grief and by thankfulness that her ordeal was over.

A death certificate was needed, of course, so I called a doctor friend who came immediately. I explained that Elizabeth had suffered a hemorrhage, and the doctor appropriately recorded this on the death certificate.

My next move was to call a member of the Burial Committee of Celo

Friends Meeting. A burial box was brought to our house and I helped lift Elizabeth's body into it. A crew of students and community members was promptly recruited to dig a grave at the Friends Burial Ground, after which we loaded the box into the back of my old Travelall, in which Elizabeth and I had travelled so many miles together. I drove it myself to the burying ground, where we placed the box beside the grave. Our friends had gathered there. Then one of my grandchildren placed on the box a canister containing the ashes of our daughter Benetta who had been killed some five years before. After that, with the help of a son, grandson, nephew, and a couple of close friends, I lowered the box into the ground. Then I recited one of Elizabeth's favorite poems, by Lew Sarett:

> Deep wet moss and cool blue shadows
> Beneath a bending fir,
> And the purple solitude of mountains,
> When only the dark owls stir—
> Oh, there will come a day, a twilight
> When I shall sink to rest
> In deep wet moss and cool blue shadows
> Upon a mountain's breast,
> And yield a body torn with passions
> And bruised with earthly scars
> To the cool oblivion of evening,
> Of solitude and stars.

That poem, by the way, was later engraved on stone and placed at the entrance of the burial ground.

Reading this account, my grandson comments, "I remember that day vividly. As Grandma Elizabeth was buried it rained a warm shower. We were all standing in the rain. Then, as we started to walk down the hill, the clouds parted, the sun came out, and the birds sang. It was painfully beautiful—a forcible reminder that life continues with its own energy and force."

The next day, at the school, we had a memorial meeting at which we celebrated Elizabeth's life. A poem which Elizabeth wanted me to recite at her memorial meeting, but which I forgot, is by Ralph Chapman:

> Mourn not the dead that in the cool earth lie,
> Dust unto dust,
> The calm sweet earth that mothers all who die,
> As all men must;
> But rather mourn the apathetic throng,
> The cowed and meek,
> Who see the world's great anguish and its wrong
> And dare not speak.

What I did do was to talk for an hour and twenty minutes, telling of Elizabeth's life. This did me a world of good. Men, in our culture, are denied ready access to tears, but they can find helpful emotional release in talking. We held a second memorial meeting, a little later, in Yellow Springs, where she and I had spent most of our adult lives. There I spoke for only forty minutes! I was getting better.

The burial and memorial arrangements in connection with Elizabeth's death were beautifully handled, and yet my only expenses were $23 for plywood and $2 for a filing fee. There is no connection between the amount of money spent on a funeral and the degree to which it meets the social and emotional needs of the survivors.

While I was able to respond to the immediate challenge of Elizabeth's death, I knew that unless special measures were taken I would become ill once my life returned to normal. So, as quickly as possible, I set forth on a business trip, which would involve me in a tight schedule, associating closely with people. My health soon stabilized. I well remember my return from that trip. It was dusk and as I drove down the mountain road I thought sadly, "Elizabeth won't be there." The house was dark and I felt lonely. I phoned the school, which was nearby. "How about holding an all-school meeting at my house tonight?" I asked. A few minutes later, students and staff arrived, filling the big music room, and a warm sense of fellowship came over me.

Happy involvement with friends and ongoing projects soon restored to me a sense of wellbeing. It seemed I had handled my bereavement well, and I had, but Elizabeth kept appearing in my dreams. She wasn't dead after all— she had merely been away. It seemed so real that the happiness of her return would linger after I awoke.

One aspect of bereavement that I had not anticipated was the loss of identity. With Elizabeth gone I was no longer me! For forty years we had shared a broad spectrum of life. Together we had hiked forest trails, canoed lakes and rivers, climbed mountains. Together we had homesteaded, raised a family, built a business, carried on political campaigns, organized concerts, published a newspaper, founded a school. I did not have a separate identity. Clearly, I still had a long way to go. This was not painful, nor did it interfere with my activities, but it was very strange, and several years were required to get over it and develop a new identity.

Some seven years after her death I found myself attracted to a young woman who embodied some of Elizabeth's qualities. Because of the age difference I had no idea of marrying her, but the attraction continued. I finally realized that I was, in effect, projecting my wife onto her—trying in this way to bring back Elizabeth. With time and effort I was able to realize this and let go of my wife. My attraction to the young woman then subsided to a cordial friendship. I was helped in this by being able to talk freely about it with my daughter.

My stepmother, Lucy, had attitudes and concepts relating to death which were remarkable—as was her own death.

Once, early on, when we were discussing the case of a man who was being kept alive when all prospects of a happy and useful life were past, she exclaimed, "If you let that happen to me, I'll come back and haunt you." In later years her attitude toward death was modified somewhat by a leaning toward spiritualism—the idea that individual life continues on a nonmaterial plane.

An interesting expression of this occurred when she had a seance with the famous medium, Arthur Ford. In the course of this session Ford made reference to "guardian angels" and Lucy asked if she had one, and if so whether she might speak with this angel. Ford said yes, she did, whereupon a voice, purporting to be that of a woman, was heard. Lucy asked the name of the guardian angel and was told, "I was named for a star."

Lucy was quick to recognize her guardian angel as my mother, Urania, who went on to thank Lucy for the care she had given to her husband and little boy. For the rest of her days Lucy cherished the concept that Urania was, indeed, her guardian angel.

My father, skeptical of such phenomena, commented to me that there was nothing in the interview which Ford could not have derived from reading my father's write-up in *Who's Who in America*.

In 1972, at age 93, Lucy found herself in a nursing home, almost blind and deaf, and unable to speak coherently, yet she had taken no steps to end her life. Dad went to visit her every afternoon, and fed her supper. There were warm bonds of affection between them, and this continued to give meaning to her life. In time, as her condition deteriorated, she decided she had gone far enough. Her only recourse at this point was to refuse food— which she did. The nursing home, in response, proceeded to force-feed her, a brutal process. Dad protested vigorously, "Offer her food; give her every consideration, but *don't* force her." The nursing home ignored him and continued the force-feeding.

Thereupon Dad produced a copy of an article Lucy had written years before entitled "On Drinking the Hemlock," in which she argued that a responsible person should have the option of terminating their own life if it was coming to an end and circumstances had become unbearable. Still they ignored the old man.

At about this point I had occasion to drop in at the nursing home on my way from Celo to Yellow Springs. Dad was there and, while I was visiting, the attendant came in and force-fed Lucy—a brutal process. That evening, my brother and father and I got on the phone with the doctor and said,

"Either get the feeding stopped, or get her out of there!" Accordingly, the doctor threatened legal action, and the nursing home stopped the practice.

A few days later, Lucy died in peace. The supervisor at the nursing home called a funeral director. Simultaneously, I called my brother to fetch a box from the Burial Committee of the Yellow Springs Friends Meeting. When my brother and I walked into the nursing home with this box, to claim Lucy's body, we met the funeral director and his helper in the lobby, bent on the same errand. An unusual confrontation. The lady in charge was flabbergasted and said she had never heard of such a thing. "They know what they're doing," said the funeral director, and graciously bowed himself out.

Lucy had opted for leaving her body to a medical school. We took her body home in a station wagon and the next morning my daughter-in-law Vicki and I took the body to the medical school in Columbus. There we lifted it out of the box, which we took back for future use.

The very day we took Lucy's body to the Medical School, her senior granddaughter, Becky Bolling, was being married at Earlham College, in Richmond, Indiana. We all went. The event turned out to be a joint celebration of Lucy Morgan's life and her granddaughter's marriage. My father spoke of the "almost unbearable joy" he felt at this sense of continuity. The following evening we held a memorial gathering in Yellow Springs and that, too, was an inspiring occasion.

In due time, Lucy's ashes were returned from the medical school to Vicki Morgan, who was serving as chairperson of the Burial Committee of the Friends Meeting. On the edge of the Antioch campus was a magnificent eighty-ton boulder which had been designated to serve as a monument to Dad and Lucy. After the return of Lucy's ashes, the family gathered at the monument for a little ceremony, in the course of which the ashes were buried at the base of the boulder.

Some time later, Vicki received another set of ashes from the medical school, also purporting to be Lucy's. She was somewhat taken aback, and asked me what to do. I told her to put them in the closet.

In November of 1975, my father died at the age of ninety-seven. During his last weeks I wrote to him every day, reminiscing about our times together and discussing projects and ideas and developments that I knew would interest him. When his death took place, I was on the way to Yellow Springs. As with Lucy, I helped lift his body into a box, and took it to the medical school. They would have paid for the transportation, but this was something which I could do for Dad and Lucy myself, and I was unwilling to relinquish the privilege to a professional.

While naturally saddened by my father's death, it was not a traumatic occasion for me. Happily, I had matured through the years by virtue of my activities in the field of funeral reform and death education, and, by then, could accept not only his death, but my own as well.

After Dad's ashes were sent from the medical school, a two-day convocation was held at Antioch to celebrate his life. It was a big occasion, attended by people from all over the country. In the course of that event, a ceremony was held at the base of the Morgan Boulder, to inter the ashes. The interment was presided over by Don Harrington, Minister Emeritus of the Community Church of New York, who had attended Antioch during Dad's administration and was a long-time friend of the Morgan family.

Before the ceremony, I got out the canister of Lucy's "duplicate" ashes and placed them in a small carton beside the canister of Arthur's ashes. Then I sealed the carton and brought it out for the ceremony. At the appropriate moment his two senior great-grandchildren placed it in the hole and buried it.

No one but Lee and Vicki and me knew that there were two sets of ashes in that box. Lee remarked to me that this was the only way he could think of to get "Granther" to sleep with another woman!

If Lucy was right about a personal life after death, and if she was an invisible witness to the event I have just described, I am sure that she thoroughly enjoyed both the incongruity of the situation, and Lee's remark.

But there is a more symbolic interpretation of that incident. Dad and Lucy were intensely committed to humanity and to nature. Their careers were an active expression of this. They were constantly reaching out to people and taking them into their lives. For the ashes of an unknown fellow human (like the Unknown Soldier!) to be interred with theirs seemed eminently fitting.

Ed Wilson greeting Ernest in 1976 beside the big boulder, where Arthur's and Lucy' ashes have just ben interred.

29

OLD AGE

Another important transition in my life took place when, at age sixty-five, I retired as President of the Antioch Bookplate Company, turning the leadership over to my son Lee. My "retirement" proved as strenuous and diverse in activities, and as exciting, as had my previous career.

In 1983, twelve years after Elizabeth's death, at age seventy-seven, I married again, very happily. My bride was Christine Frederiksen Wise, a woman of my own age whom I had known when we were students at Antioch half a century before, and who, like me, had been widowed. We shared the same ideals and values. The marriage was a new one, not the reincarnation of an old one (though I find no fault with such reincarnations).

In contemplating this marriage, the problem of death gave me serious pause. Did I really want to become vulnerable to death once more? During my marriage with Elizabeth there was always the shadow of a fear that I might die first, thus deserting her. With her death, this shadow was gone and I no longer feared death. Did I really want to give hostage to life again? Finally I and my new love made peace with death and agreed to a marriage which would be temporary—until one of us died. We deliberately accepted death and grief as part of life and were happy.

It is interesting to note, in passing, that Christine took the initiative in our relationship. I had argued, since college days, that women should have equal social initiative with men. When a charming and congenial woman exercised such initiative, I was delighted!

At our age, however, there was no such thing as a "simple wedding." We got married all over the place. We wanted to be married under the care of the Yellow Springs Friends Meeting and to have the ceremony performed by an old friend, Ralph Templin. But Ralph was going away, so there wasn't time to arrange that. Accordingly, we took our marriage license and went to Ralph's home, where he conducted a formal ceremony with his wife as a witness.

Shortly thereafter we had another marriage ceremony at the Friends Meeting House. The place was packed, and we repeated our vows there. Following that ceremony we had a reception at the Antioch Inn, with a couple of hundred people in attendance.

Then we went to Christine's old home in Appleton, Wisconsin. We didn't actually repeat our vows there, but we were given a wedding feast and another big reception.

Then we went to our new home at Celo. Again there was a gala reception in the school assembly room, at which the community turned out in force and we sliced up a gorgeous wedding cake. Never do anything halfway, I always say.

We lived for a time in my house at Celo. Then Christine sold hers in Wisconsin and used the money to build an attractive new home for us near the Arthur Morgan School, with a beautiful view of the mountains and generous office and workshop space for me. The house belongs to the school, with us to have the use of it during our lifetimes.

Things didn't slow down for me after retirement, as I had expected. I continued into the 1980s on the board of the Continental Association of Funeral and Memorial Societies, and hosted an important meeting at Celo.

At the same time, I was drafted to chair the board of the Antioch Publishing (formerly Antioch Bookplate) Company. The business had grown more complicated, and often I didn't understand what was going on—but I kept the meetings moving and got them over by five o'clock.

I also served for years as secretary of the board of the Celo Health Education Corporation, which governs the school and the Celo Health Center. Later I switched to become Secretary of the board of Celo Community, Inc., and Corresponding Secretary of the Community. This latter role I continue to this day.

Because Celo Community is the oldest and one of the most successful land-trust communities in America, it has lots of families wanting to join—far more than it can accommodate. So I get much mail. My job is to be cordial, helpful—and discouraging.

In addition, I was invited to serve on the board of Community Service, Inc., which had been founded by my father. On the fiftieth anniversary of the founding I was asked to write a biography of my father. *Arthur Morgan Remembered* was published by Community Service in 1991.

Every few years my book, *Dealing Creatively with Death*, requires revision—a big job.

I hadn't looked forward to all these ramifications, but I find them highly worthwhile.

Once, years ago, I asked Lucy if I had shown any vocational tendencies when I was a boy. She said she couldn't think of any, "unless it might be that of junk collector."

She was right on target. In addition to a substantial layout of hand and power tools, I collected junk. Early on I bought, from Government Surplus, a cabinet with 84 little drawers in it. In these drawers I gradually accumulated nuts, bolts & washers, screws, mending plates, assorted cements and tapes, electrical components, and so on ad infinitum. In one drawer I put a card file, listing alphabetically what was in the other drawers. After a while, eighty-four drawers weren't enough, so I made fifty small uniform boxes of Masonite, which I put on shelves and included in the index.

Not long ago a friend of mine asked if I had a spare electrical plug. No problem; I gave him one.

A few days later he needed a piece of aluminum sheet metal to make a cover for an item of camping equipment. It took me about thirty seconds to produce the desired piece. Not long after that he brought in a small machine that had a spring missing. After glancing at the card file I pulled out a little drawer full of old springs. One of them just fit. Still later he mentioned that he had lost the key to his bicycle padlock. Again glancing at the card file, I pulled out a small box filled with old keys. One of them fit the padlock. I really scored in that ball game!

An unusual item of equipment in my workshop is a basin of sand. When I have a broken item that needs cementing, I place it in the sand at exactly the correct angle so that the broken piece will balance on it. Then I apply the appropriate kind of cement and set the fragment in place to dry. I use this mainly for ceramic repairs but occasionally also for plastic, wood, and metal.

Making and fixing things has been a satisfying part of my life.

Back in the '80s a member of the Arthur Morgan School staff, Herb Walters, got steamed up over the issue of world peace and launched a new publication, *The Rural Southern Voice for Peace (RSVP)*. I couldn't resist taking a hand in that, so I recruited from the subscribers a network of people who were willing to write letters to the editors of their local papers every couple of months. I would draft eight or ten letters on various issues of peace and social justice and mail them out to the 140 people in our network.

That part was easy. The tough part was to organize the letter writers in such a way that two people didn't send the same letter to the same editor! We had some close calls but I don't think we ever actually fumbled. We reached a large number of readers but it took a lot of my time. I suspended that project to write this autobiography and to edit the thirteenth edition of *Dealing Creatively with Death*.

We had started Celo Press back in 1962, as a Department of the Arthur Morgan School, to publish my Manual. At first we farmed out the printing. After awhile we developed a modern printshop, and printed it ourselves. By that time the book had become *A Manual of Death Education and Simple Burial*. The shop did other printing, too.

I arranged to have two excellent young men trained as printers. They did a good job and worked well together. I figured we had it made. If one of them left, we'd still have the other. Alas, they both left to start their own businesses.

So the school decided to sell the printing equipment, but keep the publishing business. Managers were hired to run that. Able young people but too ambitious. They attempted to build up a regular publishing business with a lot of titles. Whereas my little *Manual* had made money, Celo Press now ran a deficit. So the Endowment Committee decided to close out Celo Press.

By that time my *Manual* had grown into a full fledged book and was about to appear in its twelfth edition. So it was picked up by Zinn Communications, a firm run by Bill Zinn and his son David, who had attended the Arthur Morgan School twenty years before.

But Celo Press left a residue. The letterpress equipment was left, and I added to it. We called it Celo Printing. The Antioch Bookplate Company, going into a new technology, gave us their old type material—a priceless collection—and other outdated equipment. The *Yellow Springs News* did likewise. We wound up with almost a printing museum. On the door I put a sign: WELCOME TO THE NINETEENTH CENTURY.

Actually, there is a lot of printing for which this equipment is competitive. I'm something of an antique myself, and enjoy working part-time in this museum—where I turn out occasional printing. Most of this is done for the Arthur Morgan School and the Rural Southern Voice for Peace. What is to be done with the printshop when I'm gone is an open question. I have some ideas about it, yet to be developed.

My driver's license expired when I was eighty-five and I applied for a renewal. I had undergone cataract surgery not long before, in both eyes. My right eye was fairly good, but the left had scar tissue on the retina, which reduced my vision. I flunked the eye test.

I needed to drive a good deal, especially to and from the airport, seventy miles away. So I consulted my ophthalmologist. He said the left eye still had good peripheral vision and that I was competent to drive. On his testimony my license was renewed.

The doctor's judgment was confirmed a few month's later. I had to drive home one night, seventeen miles, on winding mountain roads in a blinding snowstorm. I did it without difficulty.

My license expired again when I was ninety—and I got it renewed again —again with the help of the eye-doctor. With seventy-five years of driving experience behind me, this wasn't too difficult. We'll see what happens at ninety-five.

The Arthur Morgan School recently asked me to write a short biography of Elizabeth, as she was the principal founder of the school. I did this with pleasure, and it has now been printed.

Christine's book *Alabaster Village,* based on her letters home from Transylvania sixty years ago, has been skillfully edited by Anne Welsh and has been published.

Still another book is Elizabeth's *Socialist and Labor Songbook,* which she collected and edited nearly half a century ago. A wonderful collection, complete with music. I had been sitting on that for years but finally, with considerable effort and expense, found an excellent publisher.

A major event in our family was a severe stroke which Christine had late in March of 1994. Totally disabled, she spent a week in the hospital, then nine weeks in a nursing home where I spent five hours with her each day —and got some nurse's training in the process. Then I brought her home and gave her twenty-four-hour nursing care for fifteen months. I didn't feel this as a burden, and we were happy together, but my health gradually deteriorated and I lost weight.

Then our doctor sent me to the hospital for an examination, in the course of which the nurse accidentally punched a hole in my colon. So I underwent major surgery and was in the hospital for a week.

As luck would have it a friend, Lydia Wexler, had come in to sit with Christine during my examination. An experienced nurse, she stayed on and took charge, continuing after my return.

Finally, in May, 1996, Christine died. Her two daughters had come to be with her. As my parents did, and as I am planning to do, she left her body to a medical school.

On the urging of my daughter, Jenny, I arranged for Lydia and her young son to continue living with me, and found her an excellent manager.

In 1998 Lydia left, and my sister, Frances Bolling, age 84, came to stay with me for a time. The Arthur Morgan School brought our lunches during the school year, and Camp Celo brought them in the summer. We commonly had our suppers with my daughter Jenifer, who, by the way, has taken major responsibility for my health and general well-being.

Jenifer does my shopping, guides me to the doctors and dentists, and lays out a generous assortment of pills for me to take.

My life seems to have entered a curious new phase. I feel as if I had died and been reincarnated in my old haunts. An exciting new adventure. Familiar sights and sounds are fresh and exciting. Old friends are rediscovered.

I am wobbly and get about with a cane, and need at least two naps every day. I can no longer do many of the things I did in my former life. But my mind continues clear and I serve happily as Corresponding Secretary of Celo

Community. I produce a steady flow of letters and articles, and give an occasional talk.

Clearly, in old age my life has taken on fresh color, and I have no fear of death—which cannot be very far away.

Ernest and Christine, who had known each other in college sixty years before, were married happily in their late seventies. Ernest's second marriage and Christine's third.

IN CONCLUSION

In the course of a long life I have planted saplings and seen them grow into giant trees. I have seen generations come and go and have two great-great-grandchildren. I have witnessed the rise and fall of institutions and nations.

In writing this autobiography a feeling has come over me that I have been witnessing, not just a period of history, but also a moment of eternity. Thus I am enjoying the wonderful sights and sounds with which I am surrounded.

As I said before, Christine and I accepted death and grief as a normal and necessary part of life. We had our own special version of "living will," which goes beyond the standard form. In it, each of us says:

> *I want to have some control over my own death. In the event of* any *illness I want to know whether any given treatment is for recovery or life support, or whether it is for comfort. And I want to be free to accept or decline any specific treatment. In the event of my incapacity to make such decisions, because of unconsciousness or other condition, for more than twenty-four hours, that circumstance shall constitute a decision against treatment directed toward recovery or life support.*
>
> *When death does come, I want to go as gracefully and comfortably as possible, and not be held back by well-meaning medics and family.*

This document has been endorsed by our doctor and by our respective children. I should point out, however, that the twenty-four-hour clause is chiefly appropriate to old people, who are less likely to be revived than younger people.

What chiefly concerns me in the prospect of my own death are the responsibilities I leave behind me. A major problem in these late years is to anticipate the complications which will result from my death, and to provide for meeting them as well as possible.

I am happy to see the leadership of my company in good hands, and likewise the leadership of the Arthur Morgan School. My rather copious papers have been requested for the Morgan Archives in the Antioch College Library. But there are a lot of loose ends. Many of these are dealt with in a big looseleaf book in my office captioned *House in Order.* Still other loose ends remain unresolved, but I'm working on them.

While I am able to contemplate my own death with equanimity, I am deeply troubled by the state of the world, though I cling to the dream that human civilization can be saved, and the earth with it.

Once, when I was a little boy, a mouse got into a metal waste basket and couldn't get out. I watched as an adult dumped that mouse into a toilet and flushed the toilet. I still remember how desperately the little creature swam as the whirlpool sucked it down to a miserable death in the sewer. That is where I see civilization headed today.

Communism might have worked, if the necessary human qualities had existed in the leadership and in the society from which the movement emerged. Capitalism, likewise, might survive if the ideals and values and structures are sound. The Mondragon experiment, for example, demonstrates a form of capitalism in which the capital is owned by the workers themselves, not by a privileged few. As Edward Bellamy pointed out, where there is concentration of wealth, political democracy is little more than an empty shell. He might have added that production and consumption would get out of balance and the economy would collapse. My own company is now mostly employee-owned, and the percentage is growing.

The syndrome of greed and perpetual growth which characterizes our society at the present time can ultimately lead only to disaster. I dream of a society motivated by genuine human concern and characterized by a spirit of caring and sharing—a society in which our lifestyle, technology, and economic organization are geared to the well-being of our planet and the creatures who live on it— especially humankind.

I realize this dream may be "impractical" and that our civilization may well go down the sewer, as did that mouse, but I challenge my readers to share the dream and to pursue it.